INTERNATIONAL TERRORISM AGREEMENTS: DOCUMENTS AND COMMENTARY

DONALD J. MUSCH

Sixteenth Volume, Second Series
Terrorism: Documents of International & Local Control

OCEANA PUBLICATIONS, INC., DOBBS FERRY, NEW YORK

Information contained in this work has been obtained by Oceana Publications from sources believed to be reliable. However, neither the Publisher nor its authors guarantee the accuracy or completeness of any information published herein, and neither Oceana nor its authors shall be responsible for any errors, omissions or damages arising from the use of this information. This work is published with the understanding that Oceana and its authors are supplying information, but are not attempting to render legal or other professional services. If such services are required, the assistance of an appropriate professional should be sought.

You may order this or any Oceana publication by visiting Oceana's website at <http://www.oceanalaw.com>.

Library of Congress Control Number: 2004112356

Terrorism: Documents of International and Local Control, Second Series

ISSN 1064-9352

ISBN 0-379-21535-7

© 2004 by Oceana Publications, Inc.

All rights reserved. No part of this publication may be reproduced or transmitted in any way or by any means, electronic or mechanical, including photocopy, recording, xerography, or any information storage and retrieval system, without permission in writing from the publisher.

Manufactured in the United States of America on acid-free paper.

TABLE OF CONTENTS

INTERNATIONAL CONVENTIONS AND PROTOCOLS

Introduction. 3

Convention on Offences and Certain Other Acts Committed on Board Aircraft
    Commentary. 7
    Convention. 9

Convention for the Suppression of Unlawful Seizure of Aircraft
    Commentary 27
    Convention 29

Convention for the Suppression of Unlawful Acts Against the Safety of Civil Aviation
    Commentary 41
    Convention 43

Convention on the Prevention and Punishment of Crimes Against Internationally Protected Persons, Including Diplomatic Agents
    Commentary 61
    Convention 63

Convention on the Physical Protection of Nuclear Material
    Commentary 89
    Convention 91

International Convention Against the Taking of Hostages
    Commentary 119
    Convention 121

Protocol for the Suppression of Unlawful Acts of Violence at Airports Serving International Civil Aviation
    Commentary 141
    Protocol 143

Convention for the Suppression of Unlawful Acts Against the Safety of Maritime Navigation
    Commentary 153
    Convention 155

Protocol for the Suppression of Unlawful Acts Against the Safety of Fixed Platforms Located on the Continental Shelf
    Commentary 167
    Protocol 169

Convention on the Marking of Plastic Explosives for the Purpose of Detection
    Commentary 179
    Convention 181

International Convention for the Suppression of Terrorist Bombings
    Commentary 191
    Convention 193

International Convention for the Suppression of the Financing of Terrorism
    Commentary 213
    Convention 215

REGIONAL TERRORISM TREATIES AND CONVENTIONS

Commentary 265

OAS Convention to Prevent and Punish the Acts of Terrorism Taking the Form of Crimes Against Persons and Related Extortion That Are of International Significance 269

European Convention on the Suppression of Terrorism 275

South Asian Association (SAARC) Regional Convention on Suppression of Terrorism. 287

Arab Convention for the Suppression of Terrorism 293

Treaty on Cooperation Among the States Members of the Commonwealth of Independent States in Combating Terrorism 309

Convention of the Organisation of the Islamic Conference on
Combating International Terrorism 319

Inter-American Convention Against Terrorism 337

PROPOSED INTERNATIONAL AGREEMENTS

Draft International Convention for the Suppression of Acts of
Nuclear Terrorism 363

Draft Comprehensive Convention on International Terrorism 371

Working Document Submitted by India on the Draft
Comprehensive Convention on International Terrorism 383

APPENDICES

Status of International Conventions Pertaining to International
Terrorism 403

Significant Terrorist Incidents 1961-2003: A Brief Chronology 429

INTERNATIONAL CONVENTIONS AND PROTOCOLS

INTRODUCTION

A compilation of international agreements is nothing new. In fact, one can find several works with such documents on any given subject including some covering terrorism. And yet, an updated volume of those treaties and agreements which the international community has adopted to meet the growing threat of terrorism serves a real purpose—to bring into one location the voice of that international community on a topic of major concern.

Producing this work presented much the same dilemma as is faced by the international body of nations in defining "terrorism". They have been unable, or unwilling to resolve this critical issue. And the lack of a universal definition of terrorism is no small matter. Making such choices is difficult. Preparing a volume of the major international agreements on terrorism also requires selection, and this means certain documents which might meet one's requirement will not be included. In the end, this documentation includes twelve international conventions and protocols which cover terrorist acts involving aircraft, the maritime world, nuclear and plastic explosives, bombings, and the financing of terrorist activities. It also includes seven regional international agreements covering terrorism and two draft conventions being considered by the United Nations.

What has been omitted? As discussed in the American Bar Association's publication *International Terrorism: Legal Challenges and Responses*, there *are* other agreements which have some bearing on terrorism, including:

> "... the Universal Postal Union Convention ... July 10, 1964 ... Additional Protocol to the Constitution of the Universal Postal Union of July 10, 1964 ... Second Protocol to the Constitution of the Universal Postal Union of 10 July 1964 ... Third Additional Protocol to the Constitution of the Universal Postal Union of July 10, 1964 ... Fourth Additional Protocol to the Constitution of the Universal Postal Union of 10 July 1964 ... Fifth Additional Protocol to the Constitution of the Universal Postal Union of 10 July 1964 ... Universal

INTRODUCTION

> Postal Union Postal Parcels Agreement... Nov. 14, 1969... Agreement Concerning Postal Parcels... Sept. 14, 1994."

Also excluded is the Convention on the Law of the Sea. All these documents relate in some fashion to terrorism. But, in terms of specificity and in the eyes of most who address terrorism, these documents would not be included in a list of the fundamental agreements on the topic. In addition, at a very practical level, it is impossible to produce, in one volume, *all* international agreements which touch on the subject.

Much that seems new concerning terrorism is, in reality, very old. The very term *terrorism* can be traced back to the French Revolution (1789-1799) when, according to *The World Book Encyclopedia*, 2003:

> "... Some of the revolutionaries who seized power in France adopted a policy of violence against their enemies. The period of their rule became known as the Reign of Terror." (Vol. 9, at page 179).

And, if one investigates the use of the word hostage one can find a reference to the "Original Documents Relating to the Hostages of John, King of France, and the Treaty of Bretigny, in 1360" (1890 Edited, with historical notices by Sir G. F. Duckett).

But, rather than dwelling on the historical antecedents, it is enlightening to focus on what steps the modern world has taken, through the medium of international agreements, to fight against newly emerging and ever more potent terrorist acts. As can be seen from a review of these documents, the international response has, for the most part, been linked to specific acts of violence perpetrated by terrorists modulated by the give and take of international politics. In a sense, the community has continually played "catch up" with the expanding potential for terrorist activities amid the technological advances which make terrorist acts more and more lethal. As discussed by Claude Emanuelli in his note in *The American Journal of International Law* (Vol. 10 at page 503):

> "The international community has chosen to deal with unlawful interference with civil aviation from a repressive viewpoint and as an individual problem treated in response to events."

In spite of this criticism, Emanuelli adds that "Under the piecemeal approach, the response of the international community has been quite thorough."

To many, without being cynical, concluding international agreements has been of little import. For example, Brett D. Schaefer, writing for The Heritage Foundation in a web site article entitled "U.N. Treaties and Conferences Will Not Stop Terrorism" stated on January 17, 2002:

> "... That these accords have had no substantial impact is underscored by the striking fact that all seven of the state sponsors of terrorism identified by the United States Department of State are signatories or state parties to one or more of these 12 treaties or conventions" (which address terrorism and related activities).

INTRODUCTION

Yet, there is an indefinable positive return when a multiplicity of nations can agree to a document which, in a direct fashion, does try to cope with international terrorism. Japan's Ambassador to the United Nations on October 2nd, 2001 stated:

> "While our measures to combat terrorism must extend over a broad variety of areas, it is the solemn responsibility of the United Nations General Assembly to create a more effective international legal framework in order to bring to justice not only the perpetrators, organizers and sponsors of terrorism, but also those who aid, support or harbor terrorists . . ."

Ironically, the speech of Ambassador Satoh also pleaded for approval of two conventions which have yet to be concluded: The International Convention for the Suppression of Acts of Nuclear Terrorism and The Comprehensive Convention on International Terrorism.

Mention was made earlier that these agreements fail to adequately define terrorism. Another distinct drawback has been that agreements offer the country which apprehends any terrorist the option not to act. Hence, in the celebrated case of the Kurdish terrorist, Abdullah Ocalan, the apprehending state, Italy, refused to extradite him to Turkey for trial while Germany (which had an outstanding warrant for his arrest) decided not to ask for his extradition. Ocalan was ultimately spirited out of Italy, returned to Turkey, and sentenced to death for his terrorist activities.

In addition to articulating what is a normative framework covering terrorism, the agreements affect state practices, diplomatic interplay, and can weigh heavily on the conduct of both nations and individuals. Examples of conventions which strive to be totally relevant in the 21st Century environment for terrorists, would be the Convention for the Marking of Plastic Explosives and the Convention for the Suppression of the Financing of Terrorism. The former brings recognition to the need for scientific validation of the explosives used in terrorist acts; the latter recognizes the importance of eliminating terrorist funding to impede their activities.

Though it is no doubt accurate to state that the United States has been instrumental in negotiating and concluding most, if not all of the major international agreements fighting terrorism, this country has not always acted with alacrity to give its total assent to such conventions. For example, The International Convention Against the Taking of Hostages was opened for signature on December 19, 1979. Six years later it entered into force for the United States. Much the same was the experience with The Convention for the Suppression of Unlawful Acts Against the Safety of Maritime Navigation which was signed on March 10, 1988 and which entered into force for the United States on March 6, 1995.

Included in this work (at Appendix B) is a list of significant terrorist attacks produced by the Department of State. When one examines that list, and other information concerning terrorist attacks, it is very apparent that inter-

INTRODUCTION

national action has been stimulated by specific attacks, or by the realization that technology requires new vehicles to cope with terrorism.

Thus, there is no doubt the bombing of Pan Am 103 prompted the negotiation and conclusion of The Convention on the Marking of Plastic Explosives for the Purpose of Detection (1991); a spate of attacks and killings of diplomatic personnel prompted agreement on The Prevention and Punishment of Crimes Against Internationally Protected Persons, Including Diplomatic Agents (1973); the Achille Lauro hijacking and murder of a U.S. citizen accelerated production of The Convention for the Suppression of Unlawful Acts Against the Safety of Maritime Navigation, and there are ample other examples which link specific events to the passage of these agreements.

With difficulties such as basic definitions and time wasting processing one can ask what the future portends? Will the United Nations and the community produce newly drafted and clearly worded effective international agreements in the future? And, will it take such actions before terrorists embark on new and even more horrific attacks? Perhaps so, but as Brett D. Schaefer, writing for The Heritage Foundation, points out in his web site article "U.N. Treaties and Conferences Will Not Stop Terrorism" of January 17, 2002:

> "As evidenced by the September 11, 2001, terrorist attacks on the United States, these conventions and protocols are not sufficient in and of themselves to prevent terrorism and have value only as one component of a larger, comprehensive, and coordinated strategy to combat terrorism . . . "

CONVENTION ON OFFENCES AND CERTAIN OTHER ACTS COMMITTED ON BOARD AIRCRAFT

COMMENTARY

This Convention was negotiated under the auspices of the International Civil Aviation Organization in August and September of 1963, to come into force after ratification by twelve countries. It is routinely cited as the first in a series of conventions and protocols which comprise the international response to acts of terrorism. By granting authority to the aircraft commander, crew members, and passengers to disembark or deliver an offender upon landing, the Convention seeks to ensure that air travel will be safer.

A decided weakness of the Convention is that it offers the country which "accepts" the offenders an option to either prosecute the offenders in that country or to grant extradition to another State which has jurisdiction to try the offender. Unfortunately, the State holding the alleged offender can also choose to do nothing against the offender. This opened the door for offenders to ensure they have landed in a country which will be hospitable to either a cause or to a personality involved in the offence. In his Message transmitting the Convention to the United States Senate for advice and consent to ratification President Johnson stressed the "positive rule of international law . . . " established by the Convention by giving the State where an aircraft is registered the power to exercise jurisdiction over the offences which occur in flight.

CONVENTION ON OFFENCES AND CERTAIN OTHER ACTS COMMITTED ON BOARD AIRCRAFT

Signed at Tokyo 14 September 1963
Entered into force 4 December 1969*

BY THE PRESIDENT OF THE UNITED STATES OF AMERICA

A PROCLAMATION

WHEREAS the Convention on Offences and Certain Other Acts Committed on Board Aircraft was signed at Tokyo on September 14, 1963;

WHEREAS the text of the Convention, in the English, French and Spanish languages as certified by the Legal Bureau of the International Civil Aviation Organization, is word for word as follows:

CONVENTION ON OFFENCES AND CERTAIN OTHER ACTS COMMITTED ON BOARD AIRCRAFT

* * *

THE STATES PARTIES TO THIS CONVENTION HAVE AGREED AS FOLLOWS:

Chapter I—Scope of the Convention

Article 1

1. This Convention shall apply in respect of:

    a) offences against penal law;

---

* Treaties and International Agreements Online, CTIA 8069.000 (Oceana Publications, Inc. <www.oceanalaw.com>.

b) acts which, whether or not they are offences, may or do jeopardize the safety of the aircraft or of persons or property therein or which jeopardize good order and discipline on board.

2. Except as provided in Chapter III, this Convention shall apply in respect of offences committed or acts done by a person on board any aircraft registered in a Contracting State, while that aircraft is in flight or on the surface of the high seas or of any other area outside the territory of any State.

3. For the purposes of this Convention, an aircraft is considered to be in flight from the moment when power is applied for the purpose of take-off until the moment when the landing run ends.

4. This Convention shall not apply to aircraft used in military, customs or police services.

Article 2

Without prejudice to the provisions of Article 4 and except when the safety of the aircraft or of persons or property on board so requires, no provision of this Convention shall be interpreted as authorizing or requiring any action in respect of offences against penal laws of a political nature or those based on racial or religious discrimination.

Chapter II—Jurisdiction

Article 3

1. The State of registration of the aircraft is competent to exercise jurisdiction over offences and acts committed on board.

2. Each Contracting State shall take such measures as may be necessary to establish its jurisdiction as the State of registration over offences committed on board aircraft registered in such State.

3. This Convention does not exclude any criminal jurisdiction exercised in accordance with national law.

Article 4

A Contracting State which is not the State of registration may not interfere with an aircraft in flight in order to exercise its criminal jurisdiction over an offence committed on board except in the following cases:

a) the offence has effect on the territory of such State;

b) the offence has been committed by or against a national or permanent resident of such State;

c) the offence is against the security of such State;

d) the offence consists of a breach of any rules or regulations relating to the flight or manoeuvre of aircraft in force in such State;

e) the exercise of jurisdiction is necessary to ensure the observance of any obligation of such State under a multilateral international agreement.

Chapter III—Powers of the aircraft commander Article 5

1. The provisions of this Chapter shall not apply to offences and acts committed or about to be committed by a person on board an aircraft in flight in the airspace of the State of registration or over the high seas or any other area outside the territory of any State unless the last point of take-off or the next point of intended landing is situated in a State other than that of registration, or the aircraft subsequently flies in the airspace of a State other than that of registration with such person still on board.

2. Notwithstanding the provisions of Article 1, paragraph 3, an aircraft shall for the purposes of this Chapter, be considered to be in flight at any time from the moment when all its external doors are closed following embarkation until the moment when any such door is opened for disembarkation. In the case of a forced landing, the provisions of this Chapter shall continue to apply with respect to offences and acts committed on board until competent authorities of a State take over the responsibility for the aircraft and for the persons and property on board.

Article 6

1. The aircraft commander may, when he has reasonable grounds to believe that a person has committed, or is about to commit, on board the aircraft, an offence or act contemplated in Article 1, paragraph 1, impose upon such person reasonable measures including restraint which are necessary:

    a) to protect the safety of the air-craft, or of persons or property therein; or

    b) to maintain good order and discipline on board; or

    c) to enable him to deliver such person to competent authorities or to disembark him in accordance with the provisions of this Chapter.

2. The aircraft commander may require or authorize the assistance of other crew members and may request or authorize, but not require, the assistance of passengers to restrain any person whom he is entitled to restrain. Any crew member or passenger may also take reasonable preventive measures without such authorization when he has reasonable grounds to believe that such action is immediately necessary to protect the safety of the aircraft, or of persons or property therein.

Article 7

1. Measures of restraint imposed upon a person in accordance with Article 6 shall not be continued beyond any point at which the aircraft lands unless:

    a) such point is in the territory of a non-Contracting State and its authorities refuse to permit disembarkation of that person or those measures have been imposed in accordance with Article 6, paragraph 1 c) in order to enable his delivery to competent authorities;

b) the aircraft makes a forced landing and the aircraft commander is unable to deliver that person to competent authorities; or

c) that person agrees to onward carriage under restraint.

2. The aircraft commander shall as soon as practicable, and if possible before landing in the territory of a State with a person on board who has been placed under restraint in accordance with the provisions of Article 6, notify the authorities of such State of the fact that a person on board is under restraint and of the reasons for such restraint.

Article 8

1. The aircraft commander may, in so far as it is necessary for the purpose of subparagraph a) or b) of paragraph 1 of Article 6, disembark in the territory of any State in which the aircraft lands any person who he has reasonable grounds to believe has committed, or is about to commit, on board the aircraft an act contemplated in Article 1, paragraph 1 b).

2. The aircraft commander shall report to the authorities of the State in which he disembarks any person pursuant to this Article, the fact of, and the reasons for, such disembarkation.

Article 9

1. The aircraft commander may deliver to the competent authorities of any Contracting State in the territory of which the aircraft lands any person who he has reasonable grounds to believe has committed on board the aircraft an act which, in his opinion, is a serious offence according to the penal law of the State of registration of the aircraft.

2. The aircraft commander shall as soon as practicable and if possible before landing in the territory of a Contracting State with a person on board whom the aircraft commander intends to deliver in accordance with the preceding paragraph, notify the authorities of such State of his intention to deliver such person and the reasons therefor.

3. The aircraft commander shall furnish the authorities to whom any suspected offender is delivered in accordance with the provisions of this Article with evidence and information which, under the law of the State of registration of the aircraft, are lawfully in his possession.

Article 10

For actions taken in accordance with this Convention, neither the aircraft commander, any other member of the crew, any passenger, the owner or operator of the aircraft, nor the person on whose behalf the flight was performed shall be held responsible in any proceeding on account of the treatment undergone by the person against whom the actions were taken.

Chapter IV—Unlawful Seizure of Aircraft

Article 11

1. When a person on board has unlawfully committed by force or threat thereof an act of interference, seizure, or other wrongful exercise of control of an aircraft in flight or when such an act is about to be committed, Contracting States shall take all appropriate measures to restore control of the aircraft to its lawful commander or to preserve his control of the aircraft.

2. In the cases contemplated in the preceding paragraph, the Contracting State in which the aircraft lands shall permit its passengers and crew to continue their journey as soon as practicable, and shall return the aircraft and its cargo to the persons lawfully entitled to possession.

Chapter V—Powers and Duties of States

Article 12

Any Contracting State shall allow the commander of an aircraft registered in another Contracting State to disembark any person pursuant to Article 8, paragraph 1.

Article 13

1. Any Contracting State shall take delivery of any person whom the aircraft commander delivers pursuant to Article 9, paragraph 1.

2. Upon being satisfied that the circumstances so warrant, any Contracting State shall take custody or other measures to ensure the presence of any person suspected of an act contemplated in Article 11, paragraph 1 and of any person of whom it has taken delivery. The custody and other measures shall be as provided in the law of that State but may only be continued for such time as is reasonably necessary to enable any criminal or extradition proceedings to be instituted.

3. Any person in custody pursuant to the previous paragraph shall be assisted in communicating immediately with the nearest appropriate representative of the State of which he is a national.

4. Any Contracting State, to which a person is delivered pursuant to Article 9, paragraph 1, or in whose territory an aircraft lands following the commission of an act contemplated in Article 11, paragraph 1, shall immediately make a preliminary enquiry into the facts.

5. When a State, pursuant to this Article, has taken a person into custody, it shall immediately notify the State of registration of the aircraft and the State

of nationality of the detained person and, if it considers it advisable, any other interested State of the fact that such person is in custody and of the circumstances which warrant his detention. The State which makes the preliminary enquiry contemplated in paragraph 4 of this Article shall promptly report its findings to the said States and shall indicate whether it intends to exercise jurisdiction.

Article 14

1. When any person has been disembarked in accordance with Article 8, paragraph 1, or delivered in accordance with Article 9, paragraph 1, or has disembarked after committing an act contemplated in Article 11, paragraph 1, and when such person cannot or does not desire to continue his journey and the State of landing refuses to admit him, that State may, if the person in question is not a national or permanent resident of that State, return him to the territory of the State of which he is a national or permanent resident or to the territory of the State in which he began his journey by air.

2. Neither disembarkation, nor delivery, nor the taking of custody or other measures contemplated in Article 13, paragraph 2, nor return of the person concerned, shall be considered as admission to the territory of the Contracting State concerned for the purpose of its law relating to entry or admission of persons and nothing in this Convention shall affect the law of a Contracting State relating to the expulsion of persons from its territory.

Article 15

1. Without prejudice to Article 14, any person who has been disembarked in accordance with Article 8, paragraph 1, or delivered in accordance with Article 9, paragraph 1, or has disembarked after committing an act contemplated in Article 11, paragraph 1, and who desires to continue his journey shall be at liberty as soon as practicable to proceed to any destination of his choice unless his presence is required by the law of the State of landing for the purpose of extradition or criminal proceedings.

2. Without prejudice to its law as to entry and admission to, and extradition and expulsion from its territory, a Contracting State in whose territory a person has been disembarked in accordance with Article 8, paragraph 1, or delivered in accordance with Article 9, paragraph 1 or has disembarked and is suspected of having committed an act contemplated in Article 11, paragraph 1, shall accord to such person treatment which is no less favourable for his protection and security than that accorded to nationals of such Contracting State in like circumstances.

Chapter VI—Other Provisions

Article 16

1. Offences committed on aircraft registered in a Contracting State shall be treated, for the purpose of extradition, as if they had been committed not only in the place in which they have occurred but also in the territory of the State of registration of the aircraft.

2. Without prejudice to the provisions of the preceding paragraph, nothing in this Convention shall be deemed to create an obligation to grant extradition.

Article 17

In taking any measures for investigation or arrest or otherwise exercising jurisdiction in connection with any offence committed on board an aircraft the Contracting States shall pay due regard to the safety and other interests of air navigation and shall so act as to avoid unnecessary delay of the aircraft, passengers, crew or cargo.

Article 18

If Contracting States establish joint air transport operating organizations or international operating agencies, which operate aircraft not registered in any one State those States shall, according to the circumstances of the case, designate the State among them which, for the purposes of this Convention, shall be considered as the State of registration and shall give notice thereof to the International Civil Aviation Organization which shall communicate the notice to all States Parties to this Convention.

Chapter VII—Final Clauses

Article 19

Until the date on which this Convention comes into force in accordance with the provisions of Article 21, it shall remain open for signature on behalf of any State which at that date is a Member of the United Nations or of any of the Specialized Agencies.

Article 20

1. This Convention shall be subject to ratification by the signatory States in accordance with their constitutional procedures.

2. The instruments of ratification shall be deposited with the International Civil Aviation Organization.

Article 21

1. As soon as twelve of the signatory States have deposited their instruments of ratification of this Convention, it shall come into force between them on the ninetieth day after the date of the deposit of the twelfth instrument of ratification. It shall come into force for each State ratifying thereafter on the ninetieth day after the deposit of its instrument of ratification.

2. As soon as this Convention comes into force, it shall be registered with the Secretary-General of the United Nations by the International Civil Aviation Organization.

Article 22

1. This Convention shall, after it has come into force, be open for accession by any State Member of the United Nations or of any of the Specialized Agencies.

2. The accession of a State shall be effected by the deposit of an instrument of accession with the International Civil Aviation Organization and shall take effect on the ninetieth day after the date of such deposit.

Article 23

1. Any Contracting State may denounce this Convention by notification addressed to the International Civil Aviation Organization.

2. Denunciation shall take effect six months after the date of receipt by the International Civil Aviation Organization of the notification of denunciation.

Article 24

1. Any dispute between two or more Contracting States concerning the interpretation or application of this Convention which cannot be settled through negotiation, shall, at the request of one of them, be submitted to arbitration. If within six months from the date of the request for arbitration the Parties are unable to agree on the organization of the arbitration, any one of those Parties may refer the dispute to the International Court of Justice by request in conformity with the Statute of the Court.[1]

2. Each State may at the time of signature or ratification of this Convention or accession thereto, declare that it does not consider itself bound by the preceding paragraph. The other Contracting States shall not be bound by the preceding paragraph with respect to any Contracting State having made such a reservation.

3. Any Contracting State having made a reservation in accordance with the preceding paragraph may at any time withdraw this reservation by notification to the International Civil Aviation Organization.

---

1   TS 993; 59 Stat. 1055.

Article 25

Except as provided in Article 24 no reservation may be made to this Convention.

Article 26

The International Civil Aviation Organization shall give notice to all States Members of the United Nations or of any of the Specialized Agencies:

a) of any signature of this Convention and the date thereof;

b) of the deposit of any instrument of ratification or accession and the date thereof;

c) of the date on which this Convention comes into force in accordance with Article 21, paragraph 1;

d) of the receipt of any notification of denunciation and the date thereof; and

e) of the receipt of any declaration or notification made under Article 24 and the date thereof.

IN WITNESS WHEREOF the undersigned Plenipotentiaries, having been duly authorized, have signed this Convention.

DONE at Tokyo on the fourteenth day of September One Thousand Nine Hundred and Sixty-three in three authentic texts drawn up in the English, French and Spanish languages.

This Convention shall be deposited with the International Civil Aviation Organization with which, in accordance with Article 19, it shall remain open for signature and the said Organization shall send certified copies thereof to all States Members of the United Nations or of any Specialized Agency.

Certified to be a true and complete copy
Legal Bureau
ICAO OACI

AFGHANISTAN	CHILE
ARGENTINA	COLOMBIA
AUSTRALIA	CONGO (BRAZZAVILLE)
AUSTRIA	COSTA RICA
BELGIUM	CUBA
BOLIVIA	ECUADOR
BRAZIL	FEDERAL REPUBLIC OF GERMANY
BYELORUSSIAN SOVIET SOCIALIST REPUBLIC	FINLAND
CAMBODIA	FRANCE
CANADA	GREECE
CEYLON	GUATEMALA

OFFENCES COMMITTED ON BOARD AIRCRAFT

HOLY SEE	PORTUGAL
HUNGARIAN PEOPLE'S REPUBLIC	REPUBLIC OF CHINA
	REPUBLIC OF HAITI
INDIA	REPUBLIC OF KOREA
INDONESIA	REPUBLIC OF MALI
IRAQ	REPUBLIC OF THE UPPER VOLTA
ITALY	RUMANIAN PEOPLES REPUBLIC
IVORY COAST	SENEGAL
JAPAN	SPAIN
KUWAIT	SWEDEN
LAOS	SWITZERLAND
LIBERIA	UKRAINIAN SOVIET SOCIALIST REPUBLIC
MEXICO	
NETHERLANDS	UNION OF SOVIET SOCIALIST REPUBLICS
NICARAGUA	
NIGERIA	UNITED ARAB REPUBLIC
NORWAY	UNITED KINGDOM OF GREAT BRITAIN AND NORTHERN IRELAND
PAKISTAN	
PANAMA	UNITED STATES OF AMERICA
PERU	VENEZUELA
PHILIPPINES	YUGOSLAVIA
POLISH PEOPLES REPUBLIC	

WHEREAS the Senate of the United States of America by its resolution of May 13, 1969, two-thirds of the Senators present concurring therein, did advise and consent to the ratification of the Convention;

WHEREAS the Convention was duly ratified by the President of the United States of American on June 30, 1969, in pursuance of the advice and consent of the Senate;

WHEREAS it is provided in Article 21, paragraph 1, of the Convention that it shall come into force on the ninetieth day after the deposit of the twelfth instrument of ratification;

WHEREAS instruments of ratification were deposited with the International Civil Aviation Organization as follows: Portugal on November 25, 1964; the Philippines on November 26, 1965; the Republic of China on February 28, 1966; Denmark, Norway, and Sweden on January 17, 1967; Italy on October 18, 1968; the United Kingdom of Great Britain and Northern Ireland on November 29, 1968; Mexico on March 18, 1969; Upper Volta on June 6, 1969; Niger on June 27, 1969; and the United States of America on September 5, 1969;

AND WHEREAS, pursuant to the provisions of Article 21, paragraph 1, the Convention will come into force between the aforementioned States on December 4, 1969;

NOW, THEREFORE, be it known that I, Richard Nixon, President of the United States of America, do hereby proclaim and make public the Convention on Offences and Certain Other Acts Committed on Board Aircraft to the end that the same and every article and clause thereof shall be observed and fulfilled with good faith, on and after December 4, 1969, by the United States of America and by the citizens of the United States of America and all other persons subject to the jurisdiction thereof.

IN TESTIMONY WHEREOF, I have hereunto set my hand and caused the Seal of the United States of America to be affixed.

DONE at the city of Washington this first day of October in the year of our Lord one thousand nine hundred sixty-nine and of the Independence of the United States of America the one hundred ninety-fourth.

By the President:
RICHARD NIXON

Acting Secretary of State
ELLIOT L. RICHARDSON

States which are currently parties:

- Afghanistan
- Albania
- Algeria[1]
- Angola
- Antigua and Barbuda
- Argentina
- Armenia
- Australia
- Austria
- Azerbaijan[1]
- Bahamas[2]
- Bahrain[1,3]
- Bangladesh
- Barbados
- Belarus[1,4]
- Belgium
- Belize
- Benin
- Bhutan
- Bolivia
- Bosnia and Herzegovina[5]
- Botswana
- Brazil
- Brunei Darussalam
- Bulgaria[6]
- Burkina Faso
- Burundi
- Cambodia
- Cameroon
- Canada
- Cape Verde
- Central African Republic
- Chad
- Chile
- China[1,7,8,33]
- Colombia

OFFENCES COMMITTED ON BOARD AIRCRAFT

Comoros
Congo
Costa Rica
Côte d'Ivoire
Croatia[9]
Cuba[1]
Cyprus
Czech Republic[10]
Democratic People's Republic of Korea[1]
Democratic Republic of the Congo
Denmark
Djibouti
Dominican Republic
Ecuador
Egypt[1]
El Salvador
Equatorial Guinea
Estonia
Ethiopia[1]
Fiji[11]
Finland
France
Gabon
Gambia
Georgia
Germany[12]
Ghana
Greece
Grenada
Guatemala[1]
Guinea
Guyana
Haiti
Honduras[1]
Hungary[13]
Iceland
India[1]
Indonesia[1]
Iran(Islamic Republic of)
Iraq[14]
Ireland
Israel
Italy
Jamaica
Japan
Jordan
Kazakhstan
Kenya
Kuwait[15]
Kyrgyzstan
Lao People's Democratic Republic
Latvia
Lebanon
Lesotho
Liberia
Libyan Arab Jamahiriya
Liechtenstein
Lithuania
Luxembourg
Madagascar
Malawi[1]
Malaysia
Maldives
Mali
Malta
Marshall Islands
Mauritania
Mauritius
Mexico
Monaco
Mongolia
Morocco[16]
Mozambique[35]
Myanmar
Nauru
Nepal
Netherlands[17]
New Zealand
Nicaragua
Niger
Nigeria

OFFENCES COMMITTED ON BOARD AIRCRAFT

Norway
Oman[1, 18]
Pakistan
Palau
Panama
Papua New Guinea[1, 19]
Paraguay
Peru[1]
Philippines
Poland[20]
Portugal[31, 32]
Qatar
Republic of Korea
Republic of Moldova
Romania[1]
Russian Federation[1, 21]
Rwanda
Saint Lucia
Saint Vincent and the Grenadines
Samoa
Saudi Arabia
Senegal
Serbia and Montenegro[34]
Seychelles
Sierra Leone
Singapore
Slovakia[22]
Slovenia[23]
Solomon Islands[24]
South Africa[1]
Spain
Sri Lanka
Sudan
Suriname[25]
Swaziland
Sweden
Switzerland
Syrian Arab Republic[1]
Tajikistan
Thailand
The former Yugoslav Republic of Macedonia[26]
Togo
Tonga
Trinidad and Tobago
Tunisia[1]
Turkey
Turkmenistan
Uganda
Ukraine[1, 27]
United Arab Emirates[28]
United Kingdom[29, 30]
United Republic of Tanzania
United States
Uruguay
Uzbekistan
Vanuatu
Venezuela[1]
Viet Nam[1]
Yemen
Zambia
Zimbabwe

NOTES

[1] Reservation: Does not consider itself bound by Article 24, paragraph 1, of the Convention.

[2] On 12 June 1975, a declaration dated 15 May 1975 was deposited with the International Civil Aviation Organization by the Government of the Bahamas indicating that the Bahamas considers itself to be bound to the Tokyo Convention by virtue of the ratification of the United Kingdom and pursuant to customary international law. The Bahamas attained independence on 10 July 1973.

[3] Reservation: "The accession of the State of Bahrain to the Convention shall not be considered or interpreted as recognition of 'Israel' either generally or implicitly under the Convention".

[4] Declaration dated 17 December 1987 by the Byelorussian Soviet Socialist Republic (now the Republic of Belarus) that "the accession of the Byelorussian Soviet Socialist Republic to

OFFENCES COMMITTED ON BOARD AIRCRAFT

the Convention on Offences and Certain Other Acts Committed on Board Aircraft does not affect its rights and obligations under agreements in force on the suppression of acts of unlawful interference with civil aviation, to which it is a Party".

[5] An instrument of succession by the Government of the Republic of Bosnia and Herzegovina was deposited with the International Civil Aviation Organization on 7 March 1995, with effect from 6 March 1992.

[6] Declaration dated 21 August 1989 by the People's Republic of Bulgaria (now the Republic of Bulgaria) that "the accession of the People's Republic of Bulgaria to the Convention on Offences and Certain Other Acts Committed on Board Aircraft does not affect its rights and obligations under the multilateral and bilateral agreements on acts of unlawful interference against civil aviation, to which it is a Party".

[7] The instrument of accession contains the following statement: "The Chinese Government declares illegal and null and void the signature and ratification by the Chiang clique usurping the name of China in regard to the above-mentioned Convention".

[8] Notification issued by the Government of the People's Republic of China dated 5 June 1997:

"The Convention ... to which the Government of the People's Republic of China deposited its instrument of accession on 14 November 1978, will apply to the Hong Kong Special Administrative Region with effect from 1 July 1997. The Government of the People's Republic of China also makes the following declaration:

The reservation to Paragraph 1 of Article 24 of the Convention made by the Government of the People's Republic of China when it deposited its instrument of accession on 14 November 1978 will also apply to the Hong Kong Special Administrative Region.

The Government of the People's Republic of China will assume responsibility for the international rights and obligations arising from the application of the Convention to the Hong Kong Special Administrative Region."

[9] An instrument of succession by the Government of the Republic of Croatia was deposited with the International Civil Aviation Organization on 5 October 1993, with effect from 8 October 1991.

[10] By a Note dated 8 March 1993, received on 25 March 1993, the Government of the Czech Republic informed the International Civil Aviation Organization that, as a successor State created as a result of the dissolution of the Czech and Slovak Federal Republic, it considered itself bound by the Convention with effect from 1 January 1993.

[11] On 31 January 1972, a declaration dated 18 January 1972 was deposited with the International Civil Aviation Organization by the Government of Fiji indicating that Fiji succeeded, upon independence, to the rights and obligations of the United Kingdom in respect of this Convention. Fiji attained independence on 10 October 1970.

[12] The German Democratic Republic, which acceded to the Convention on 10 January 1989, acceded to the Federal Republic of Germany on 3 October 1990.

[13] On 12 December 1989, a declaration dated 16 October 1989 was deposited with the International Civil Aviation Organization by the Government of Hungary whereby that Government withdraws the reservation made at the time of accession on 3 December 1970 with regard to Article 24, paragraph 1, of the Convention. The declaration took effect on 12 December 1989.

[14] Accession by the Republic of Iraq to the Convention shall, however, in no way signify recognition of Israel or entry into any relations with it.

[15] It is understood that the accession to the Convention on Offences and Certain Other Acts Committed on Board Aircraft, done at Tokyo, 1963, does not mean in any way recognition of Israel by the State of Kuwait. Furthermore, no treaty relation will arise between the State of Kuwait and Israel.

[16] "In case of a dispute, all recourse must be made to the International Court of Justice on the basis of the unanimous consent of the parties concerned".

[17] Declaration: ". . . the Convention, with respect to the Kingdom of the Netherlands, shall not enter into force for Suriname and/or the Netherlands Antilles until the ninetieth day after the date on which the Government of the Kingdom of the Netherlands will have notified the International Civil Aviation Organization that in Suriname and/or in the Netherlands Antilles the necessary steps for giving effect to the provisions of the above-mentioned Convention have been taken".

> Note 1: On 4 June 1974, a declaration dated 10 May 1974 was deposited with the International Civil Aviation Organization by the Government of the Kingdom of the Netherlands stating that the necessary steps for giving effect to the provisions of the Convention have been taken in regard to making the Convention applicable to Suriname and the Netherlands Antilles. Accordingly, the Convention takes effect for Suriname and the Netherlands Antilles on 2 September 1974. (See also footnote 25)

> Note 2: By a Note dated 30 December 1985 the Government of the Kingdom of the Netherlands informed the International Civil Aviation Organization that as of 1 January 1986 the Convention is applicable to the Netherlands Antilles (without Aruba) and to Aruba.

[18] The accession by the Government of the Sultanate of Oman to the Convention does not mean or imply, and shall not be interpreted as, recognition of Israel generally or in the context of this Convention.

[19] On 15 December 1975, a declaration dated 6 November 1975 was deposited with the International Civil Aviation Organization by the Government of Papua New Guinea indicating that Papua New Guinea desired to be treated as a party in its own right to the Tokyo Convention, which had entered into force for Australia on 20 September 1970 and had applied to the Territory of Papua and Trust Territory of New Guinea. Papua New Guinea attained independence on 16 September 1975.

[20] On 18 June 1997, a declaration dated 30 April 1997 was deposited with the International Civil Aviation Organization by the Government of the Republic of Poland whereby that Government withdraws the reservation made at the time of accession on 19 March 1971 with regard to Article 24, paragraph 1, of the Convention. The declaration took effect on 18 June 1997.

[21] Declaration dated 4 December 1987 by the Union of Soviet Socialist Republics (now the Russian Federation) that "the accession of the Union of Soviet Socialist Republics to the Convention on Offences and Certain Other Acts Committed on Board Aircraft does not affect its rights and obligations under bilateral and multilateral agreements in force on the suppression of acts of unlawful interference with civil aviation, to which it is a Party".

[22] By a Note dated 16 February 1995, received on 20 March 1995, the Government of the Slovak Republic informed the International Civil Aviation Organization that, as a successor State, born from the dissolution of the Czech and Slovak Federal Republic, it considered itself bound by the Convention with effect from 1 January 1993.

[23] An instrument of succession by the Government of the Republic of Slovenia was deposited with the International Civil Aviation Organization on 18 December 1992, with effect from 25 June 1991.

[24] An instrument of succession by the Government of Solomon Islands was deposited with the International Civil Aviation Organization on 23 March 1982, with effect from 7 July 1978.

[25] The instrument of succession was deposited with the International Civil Aviation Organization on 10 September 1979. Prior to that date the provisions of the Convention applied to Suriname by virtue of a declaration dated 10 May 1974 by the Government of the Kingdom of the Netherlands. The Republic of Suriname attained independence on 25 November 1975. (See also footnote 16.)

[26] An instrument of succession by the Government of the former Yugoslav Republic of Macedonia was deposited with the International Civil Aviation Organization on 30 August 1994, with effect from 17 September 1991.

[27] Declaration dated 13 January 1988 by the Ukrainian Soviet Socialist Republic (now Ukraine) that "the accession of the Ukrainian Soviet Socialist Republic to the Convention on Offences and Certain Other Acts Committed on Board Aircraft does not affect its rights and obligations under bilateral and multilateral agreements in force on the suppression of acts of unlawful interference with civil aviation, to which it is a Party".

[28] Reservation: "In accepting the said Convention, the Government of the United Arab Emirates takes the view that its acceptance of the said Convention does not in any way imply its recognition of Israel, nor does it oblige to apply the provisions of the Convention in respect of the said Country".

[29] Declaration: ". . . the provisions of the Convention shall not apply in regard to Southern Rhodesia unless and until the Government of the United Kingdom informs the International Civil Aviation Organization that they are in a position to ensure that the obligations imposed by the Convention in respect of that territory can be fully implemented".

> Note: On 1 December 1982, a declaration dated 12 November 1982 was deposited with the International Civil Aviation Organization stating that the provisions of the Convention shall extend to Anguilla. Accordingly, the Convention takes effect for Anguilla on 1 December 1982.

[30] Statement issued by the Government of the United Kingdom of Great Britain and Northern Ireland, dated 18 June 1997:

> ". . . in accordance with the Joint Declaration of the Government of the United Kingdom of Great Britain and Northern Ireland and the Government of the People's Republic of China on the Question of Hong Kong, signed on 19 December 1984, the Government of the United Kingdom will restore Hong Kong to the People's Republic of China with effect from 1 July 1997. The Government of the United Kingdom will continue to have international responsibility for Hong Kong until that date. Therefore, from that date the Government of the United Kingdom will cease to be responsible for the international rights and obligations arising from the application of the Convention to Hong Kong."

[31] By a Note dated 6 July 1999 deposited with the International Civil Aviation Organization on 7 July 1999, the Government of Portugal informed the International Civil Aviation Organization that, by Presidential Decree No. 130 dated 15 April 1999 and published on 22 April 1999, Portugal extended application of the Tokyo Convention to the Territory of Macao. Accordingly, the Convention took effect for the Territory of Macao on 7 July 1999.

[32] By a Note dated 27 October 1999, the Government of Portugal advised the International Civil Aviation Organization as follows:

> "In accordance with the Joint Declaration of the Government of the Portuguese Republic and the Government of the People's Republic of China on the Question of Macao signed on 13 April 1987, the Portuguese Republic will continue to have international responsibility for Macao until 19 December 1999 and from that date onwards the People's Republic of China will resume the exercise of sovereignty over Macao with effect from 20 December 1999.
>
> From 20 December 1999 onwards the Portuguese Republic will cease to be responsible for the international rights and obligations arising from the application of the Convention to Macao."

[33] Notification issued by the Government of the People's Republic of China dated 6 December 1999:

> "The Convention . . . to which the Government of the People's Republic of China deposited the instrument of accession on 14 November 1978, will apply to the Macao Special

Administrative Region with effect from 20 December 1999. The Government of the People's Republic of China also wishes to make the following declaration:

The reservation made by the Government of the People's Republic of China to paragraph 1 of Article 24 of the Convention shall also apply to the Macao Special Administrative Region.

The Government of the People's Republic of China shall assume responsibility for the international rights and obligations arising from the application of the Convention to the Macao Special Administrative Region."

[34] On 4 February 2003, the name of the State of the Federal Republic of Yugoslavia was changed to Serbia and Montenegro.

By a Note dated 17 July 2001, deposited on 6 September 2001 with ICAO, the Government of the Federal Republic of Yugoslavia declared itself bound, as a successor State to the Socialist Federal Republic of Yugoslavia, by the provisions of, inter alia, this Convention, with effect from 27 April 1992, the date of State succession. (The former Socialist Federal Republic of Yugoslavia had signed the Convention on 14 September 1963 and ratified it on 12 February 1971).

[35] The instrument of accession by Mozambique contained the following declaration in accordance with article 24, paragraph 2 of the Convention: "The Republic of Mozambique does not consider itself bound by the provisions of Article 24, paragraph 1 of the Convention. In this connection, the Republic of Mozambique states that, in each individual case, the consent of all Parties to such a dispute is necessary for the submission of the dispute to arbitration or to the International Court of Justice."

CONVENTION FOR THE SUPPRESSION OF UNLAWFUL SEIZURE OF AIRCRAFT

COMMENTARY

This was the second major Convention to address terrorist acts involving aviation. It was produced through the diplomatic initiative of the International Civil Air Organization at a conference in The Hague in 1970. It was prompted by the increasing international concern over the threat of violence against civil aircraft. President Nixon, in his Message to the Senate seeking their advice and consent stated:

> "It is imperative that all countries accept the multilateral convention providing for the extradition or punishment of hijacking . . . "

The Convention provides for the detention of hijackers in response to a series of hijackings which took place subsequent to the Tokyo Convention, and it represents a distinct improvement over that Convention's coverage.

To cope with the question of safe havens for hijackers, the Convention states that each Contracting State "shall take such measures as may be necessary to establish its jurisdiction over the offence and any other act of violence against passengers or crew . . . " (a) in the State where the aircraft is registered, (b) where the aircraft lands, or (c) in the place of the permanent residence or principal place of business of the lessee of an aircraft. In essence, this Convention made hijacking an international crime.

CONVENTION FOR THE SUPPRESSION OF UNLAWFUL SEIZURE OF AIRCRAFT

Signed at The Hague on 16 December 1970
Entered into force 14 October 1971*

BY THE PRESIDENT OF THE UNITED STATES OF AMERICA

A PROCLAMATION

CONSIDERING THAT:

The Convention for the Suppression of Unlawful Seizure of Aircraft was signed at The Hague on December 16, 1970 in behalf of the United States of America and in behalf of a number of other States, the text of which Convention is annexed hereto;

The Senate of the United States of America, by its resolution of September 8, 1971, two-thirds of the Senators present concurring therein, gave its advice and consent to ratification of the Convention, and the Convention was ratified by the President of the United States of America on September 14, 1971;

It is provided in Article 13 of the Convention that the Convention shall enter into force thirty days following the date of the deposit of instruments of ratification by ten States signatory to the Convention which participated in The Hague Conference;

The Convention entered into force on October 14, 1971, instruments of ratification having been deposited by Japan on April 19, 1971, Bulgaria on May 19, 1971, Sweden on July 7, 1971, Costa Rica on July 9, 1971, Gabon on July 14, 1971, Hungary on August 13, 1971, Israel on August 16, 1971, Norway on August 23, 1971, Switzerland and the United States of America on September 14, 1971;

---

* Treaties and International Agreements Online, CTIA 8070.000 (Oceana Publications, Inc. <www.oceanalaw.com>.

NOW, THEREFORE, I, Richard Nixon, President of the United States of America, proclaim and make public the Convention to the end that it shall be observed and fulfilled with good faith on and after October 14, 1971 by the United States of America and by the citizens of the United States of America and all other persons subject to the jurisdiction thereof.

IN TESTIMONY WHEREOF, I have signed this proclamation and caused the Seal of the United States of America to be affixed.

DONE at the city of Washington this eighteenth day of October in the year of our Lord one thousand nine hundred seventy-one and of the Independence of the United States of America the one hundred ninety-sixth.

By the President:
RICHARD NIXON

Secretary of State
WILLIAM P ROGERS

Preamble

THE STATES PARTIES TO THIS CONVENTION

CONSIDERING that unlawful acts of seizure or exercise of control of aircraft in flight jeopardize the safety of persons and property, seriously affect the operation of air services, and undermine the confidence of the peoples of the world in the safety of civil aviation;

CONSIDERING that the occurrence of such acts is a matter of grave concern;

CONSIDERING that, for the purpose of deterring such acts, there is an urgent need to provide appropriate measures for punishment of offenders;

HAVE AGREED AS FOLLOWS:

Article 1

Any person who on board an aircraft in flight:

(a) unlawfully, by force or threat thereof, or by any other form of intimidation, seizes, or exercises control of, that aircraft, or attempts to perform any such act, or

(b) is an accomplice of a person who performs or attempts to perform any such act

commits an offence (hereinafter referred to as "the offence").

Article 2

Each Contracting State undertakes to make the offence punishable by severe penalties.

Article 3

1. For the purposes of this Convention, an aircraft is considered to be in flight at any time from the moment when all its external doors are closed following embarkation until the moment when any such door is opened for disembarkation. In the case of a forced landing, the flight shall be deemed to continue until the competent authorities take over the responsibility for the aircraft and for persons and property on board.

2. This Convention shall not apply to aircraft used in military, customs or police services.

3. This Convention shall apply only if the place of take-off or the place of actual landing of the aircraft on board which the offence is committed is situated outside the territory of the State of registration of that aircraft; it shall be immaterial whether the aircraft is engaged in an international or domestic flight.

4. In the cases mentioned in Article 5, this Convention shall not apply if the place of take-off and the place of actual landing of the aircraft on board which the offence is committed are situated within the territory of the same State where that State is one of those referred to in that Article.

5. Notwithstanding paragraphs 3 and 4 of this Article, Articles 6, 7, 8 and 10 shall apply whatever the place of take-off or the place of actual landing of the aircraft, if the offender or the alleged offender is found in the territory of a State other than the State of registration of that aircraft.

Article 4

1. Each Contracting State shall take such measures as may be necessary to establish its jurisdiction over the offence and any other act of violence against passengers or crew committed by the alleged offender in connection with the offence, in the following cases:

(a) when the offence is committed on board an aircraft registered in that State;

(b) when the aircraft on board which the offence is committed lands in its territory with the alleged offender still on board;

(c) when the offence is committed on board an aircraft leased without crew to a lessee who has his principal place of business or, if the lessee has no such place of business, his permanent residence, in that State.

2. Each Contracting State shall likewise take such measures as may be necessary to establish its jurisdiction over the offence in the case where the alleged offender is present in its territory and it does not extradite him pursuant to Article 8 to any of the State mentioned in paragraph 1 of this Article.

3. This Convention does not exclude any criminal jurisdiction exercised in accordance with national law.

Article 5

The Contracting States which establish joint air transport operating organizations or international operating agencies, which operate aircraft which are subject to joint or international registration shall, by appropriate means, designate for each aircraft the State among them which shall exercise the jurisdiction and have the attributes of the State of registration for the purpose of this Convention and shall give notice thereof to the International Civil Aviation Organization which shall communicate the notice to all States Parties to this Convention.

Article 6

1. Upon being satisfied that the circumstances so warrant, any Contracting State in the territory of which the offender or the alleged offender is present, shall take him into custody or take other measures to ensure his presence. The custody and other measures shall be as provided in the law of that State but may only be continued for such time as is necessary to enable any criminal or extradition proceedings to be instituted.

2. Such State shall immediately make a preliminary enquiry into the facts.

3. Any person in custody pursuant to paragraph 1 of this Article shall be assisted in communicating immediately with the nearest appropriate representative of the State of which he is a national.

4. When a State, pursuant to this Article, has taken a person into custody, it shall immediately notify the State of registration of the aircraft, the State mentioned in Article 4, paragraph 1(c), the State of nationality of the detained person and, if it considers it advisable, any other interested States of the fact that such person is in custody and of the circumstances which warrant his detention. The State which makes the preliminary enquiry contemplated in paragraph 2 of this Article shall promptly report its findings to the said States and shall indicate whether it intends to exercise jurisdiction.

Article 7

The Contracting State in the territory of which the alleged offender is found shall, if it does not extradite him, be obliged, without exception whatsoever and whether or not the offence was committed in its territory, to submit the case to its competent authorities for the purpose of prosecution. Those authorities shall take their decision in the same manner as in the case of any ordinary offence of a serious nature under the law of that State.

Article 8

1. The offence shall be deemed to be included as an extraditable offence in any extradition treaty existing between Contracting States. Contracting States undertake to include the offence as an extraditable offence in every extradition treaty to be concluded between them.

2. If a Contracting State which makes extradition conditional on the existence of a treaty receives a request for extradition from another Contracting State with which it has no extradition treaty, it may at its option consider this Convention as the legal basis for extradition in respect of the offence. Extradition shall be subject to the other conditions provided by the law of the requested State.

3. Contracting States which do not make extradition conditional on the existence of a treaty shall recognize the offence as an extraditable offence between themselves subject to the provided by the law to the requested State.

4. The offence shall be treated, for the purpose of extradition between Contracting States, as if it had been committed not only in the place in which it occurred but also in the territories of the States required to establish their jurisdiction in accordance with Article 4, paragraph 1.

Article 9

1. When any of the acts mentioned in Article 1(a) has occurred or is about to occur, Contracting States shall take all appropriate measures to restore control of the aircraft to its lawful commander or to preserve his control of the aircraft.

2. In the cases contemplated by the preceding paragraph, any Contracting State in which the aircraft or its passengers or crew are present shall facilitate the continuation of the journey of the passengers and crew as soon as practicable, and shall without delay return the aircraft and its cargo to the persons lawfully entitled to possession.

Article 10

1. Contracting States shall afford one another the greatest measure of assistance in connection with criminal proceedings brought in respect of the offence and other acts mentioned in Article 4. The law of the State requested shall apply in all cases.

2. The provisions of paragraph 1 of this Article shall not affect obligations under any other treaty, bilateral or multilateral, which governs or will govern, in whole or in part, mutual assistance in criminal matters.

Article 11

Each Contracting State shall in accordance with its national law report to the Council of the International Civil Aviation Organization as promptly as possible any relevant information in its possession concerning:

(a) the circumstances of the offence;

(b) the action taken pursuant to Article 9;

(c) the measures taken in relation to the offender or the alleged offender, and, in particular, the results of any extradition proceedings or other legal proceedings.

Article 12

1. Any dispute between two or more Contracting States concerning the interpretation or application of this Convention which cannot be settled through negotiation, shall, at the request of one of them, be submitted to arbitration. If within six months from the date of the request for arbitration the Parties are unable to agree on the organization of the arbitration, any one of those Parties may refer the dispute to the International Court of Justice by request in conformity with the Statute of the Court.[1]

2. Each State may at the time of signature or ratification of this Convention or accession thereto, declare that it does not consider itself bound by the preceding paragraph. The other Contracting States shall not be bound by the preceding paragraph with respect to any Contracting State having made such a reservation.

3. Any Contracting State having made a reservation in accordance with the preceding paragraph may at any time withdraw this reservation by notification to the Depositary Governments.

Article 13

1. This Convention shall be open for signature at The Hague on 16 December 1970, by States participating in the International Conference on Air Law held at The Hague from 1 to 16 December 1970 (hereinafter referred to as The Hague Conference). After 31 December 1970, the Convention shall be open to all States for signature in Moscow, London and Washington. Any State which does not sign this Convention before its entry into force in accordance with paragraph 3 of this Article may accede to it at any time.

2. This Convention shall be subject to ratification by the signatory States. Instruments of ratification and instruments of accession shall be deposited with the Governments of the Union of Soviet Socialist Republics, the United Kingdom of Great Britain and Northern Ireland, and the United States of America, which are hereby designated the Depositary Governments.

---

1   TS993; 59 Stat. 1055.

3. This Convention shall enter into force thirty days following the date of the deposit of instruments of ratification by ten States signatory to this Convention which participated in The Hague Conference.

4. For other States, this Convention shall enter into force on the date of entry into force of this Convention in accordance with paragraph 3 of this Article, or thirty days following the date of deposit of their instruments of ratification or accession, whichever is later.

5. The Depositary Governments shall promptly inform all signatory and acceding States of the date of each signature, the date of deposit of each instrument of ratification or accession, the date of entry into force of this Convention, and other notices.

6. As soon as this Convention comes into force, it shall be registered by the Depositary Governments pursuant to Article 102 of the Charter of the United Nations[2] and pursuant to Article 83 of the Convention on International Civil Aviation (Chicago, 1944).[3]

Article 14

1. Any Contracting State may denounce this Convention by written notification to the Depositary Governments.

2. Denunciation shall take effect six months following the date on which notification is received by the Depositary Governments.

IN WITNESS WHEREOF the undersigned Plenipotentiaries, being duly authorised thereto by their Governments, have signed this Convention.

DONE at The Hague, this sixteenth day of December, one thousand nine hundred and seventy, in three originals, each being drawn up in four authentic texts in the English, French, Russian and Spanish languages.

[Original signatories omitted]

---

2   TS993; 59 Stat. 1055.
3   TIAS 1591; 61 Stat. 1203.

UNLAWFUL SEIZURE OF AIRCRAFT

States which are currently parties:

Afghanistan
Albania
Algeria[1]
Angola
Antigua and Barbuda
Argentina[2]
Armenia
Australia
Austria
Azerbaijan
Bahamas
Bahrain[3]
Bangladesh
Barbados
Belarus[3]
Belgium
Belize
Benin
Bhutan
Bolivia
Bosnia and Herzegovina[4]
Botswana
Brazil[3]
Brunei Darussalam
Bulgaria[5]
Burkina Faso
Burundi
Cambodia
Cameroon
Canada
Cape Verde
Central African Republic
Chad
Chile
China[3,6,29]
Colombia
Comoros
Congo
Costa Rica

Côte d'Ivoire
Croatia[7]
Cuba[3]
Cyprus
Czech Republic[8]
Democratic People's Republic of Korea
Democratic Republic of the Congo
Denmark[9]
Djibouti
Dominican Republic
Ecuador
Egypt[3]
El Salvador
Equatorial Guinea
Estonia
Ethiopia
Fiji
Finland
France
Gabon
Gambia
Georgia
Germany[10]
Ghana
Greece
Grenada
Guatemala[3]
Guinea
Guinea-Bissau
Guyana
Haiti
Honduras
Hungary[11]
Iceland
India[3]
Indonesia[3]
Iran (Islamic Republic of)
Iraq

Ireland
Israel
Italy
Jamaica
Japan
Jordan
Kazakhstan
Kenya
Kuwait[12]
Kyrgyzstan
Lao People's Democratic Republic
Latvia
Lebanon
Lesotho
Liberia
Libyan Arab Jamahiriya[13]
Liechtenstein
Lithuania
Luxembourg
Madagascar
Malawi[3]
Malaysia
Maldives
Mali
Malta
Marshall Islands
Mauritania
Mauritius
Mexico
Monaco
Mongolia
Morocco[14]
Mozambique[3]
Myanmar
Nauru
Nepal
Netherlands[15]
New Zealand
Nicaragua
Niger
Nigeria

Norway
Oman[3,16]
Pakistan
Palau
Panama
Papua New Guinea[3]
Paraguay
Peru[3]
Philippines
Poland[3,28]
Portugal[25,26]
Qatar[3]
Republic of Korea[17]
Republic of Moldova
Romania[3]
Russian Federation[3]
Rwanda
Saint Lucia
Saint Vincent and the Grenadines
Samoa
Saudi Arabia[3,18]
Senegal
Serbia and Montenegro[27]
Seychelles
Sierra Leone
Singapore
Slovakia[19]
Slovenia[20]
South Africa[3]
Spain
Sri Lanka
Sudan
Suriname[21]
Swaziland
Sweden
Switzerland
Syrian Arab Republic[3]
Tajikistan
Thailand
The former Yugoslav Republic of
   Macedonia[22]

UNLAWFUL SEIZURE OF AIRCRAFT

Togo	United Republic of Tanzania
Tonga	United States
Trinidad and Tobago	Uruguay
Tunisia[3]	Uzbekistan
Turkey	Vanuatu
Turkmenistan	Venezuela
Uganda	Viet Nam[3]
Ukraine[3]	Yemen
United Arab Emirates[23]	Zambia
United Kingdom[24]	Zimbabwe

NOTES

1. Reservation: "The People's Democratic Republic of Algeria does not consider itself bound by the provisions of articles 24.1, 12.1 and 14.1 respectively of the Tokyo, The Hague and Montreal Conventions, which provide for the mandatory referral of any dispute to the International Court of Justice. The People's Democratic Republic of Algeria states that in each case the prior consent of all the parties concerned shall be required in order to refer a dispute to the International Court of Justice."

2. The instrument of ratification by Argentina contains a declaration which, in translation, reads: "The application of this Convention to territories the sovereignty of which may be disputed among two or more States, whether Parties to the Convention or not, may not be interpreted as alteration, renunciation or waiver of the position upheld by each up to the present time".

3. Reservation made with respect to paragraph 1 of Article 12 of the Convention.

4. An instrument of succession by the Government of Bosnia and Herzegovina to the Convention was deposited with the Government of the United States on 15 August 1994, with effect from 6 March 1992.

5. On 9 May 1994, a Note was deposited with the Government of the United States by the Government of Bulgaria whereby that Government withdraws the reservation made at the time of ratification with regard to paragraph 1 of Article 12 of the Convention. The withdrawal of the reservation took effect on 9 May 1994.

6. The instrument of accession by the Government of the People's Republic of China contains the following declaration: "The Chinese Government declares illegal and null and void the signature and ratification of the above-mentioned Convention by the Taiwan authorities in the name of China".

7. An instrument of succession by the Government of Croatia to the Convention was deposited with the Government of the United States on 8 June 1993.

8. An instrument of succession by the Government of the Czech Republic to the Convention was deposited with the Government of the Russian Federation on 14 November 1994, with effect from 1 January 1993.

9. Until later decision, the Convention will not be applied to the Faroe Islands or to Greenland.

Note: A notification was received by the Government of the United Kingdom from the Government of the Kingdom of Denmark whereby the latter withdraws, with effect from 1 June 1980, the reservation made at the time of ratification that this Convention should not apply to Greenland.

10. The German Democratic Republic, which ratified the Convention on 3 June 1971, acceded to the Federal Republic of Germany on 3 October 1990.

11. On 10 January 1990, instruments were deposited with the Government of the United Kingdom and the Government of the United States by the Government of Hungary whereby that Government withdraws the reservation made at the time of ratification with regard to paragraph 1 of Article 12 of the Convention. The withdrawal of the reservation took effect on 10 January 1990.

12. Ratification by Kuwait was accompanied by an Understanding stating that ratification of the Convention does not mean in any way recognition of Israel by the State of Kuwait. Furthermore, no treaty relations will arise between the State of Kuwait and Israel.

13. The instrument of accession deposited by the Libyan Arab Jamahiriya contains a disclaimer regarding recognition of Israel.

14. "In case of a dispute, all recourse must be made to the International Court of Justice on the basis of the unanimous consent of the parties concerned."

15. The Convention cannot enter into force for the Netherlands Antilles until thirty days after the date on which the Government of the Kingdom of the Netherlands shall have notified the depositary Governments that the necessary measures to give effect to the provisions of the Convention have been taken in the Netherlands Antilles.

Note 1: On 11 June 1974, a declaration was deposited with the Government of the United States by the Government of the Kingdom of the Netherlands stating that in the interim the measures required to implement the provisions of the Convention have been taken in the Netherlands Antilles and, consequently, the Convention will enter into force for the Netherlands Antilles on the thirtieth day after the date of deposit of this declaration.

Note 2: By a Note dated 9 January 1986 the Government of the Kingdom of the Netherlands informed the Government of the United States that as of 1 January 1986 the Convention is applicable to the Netherlands Antilles (without Aruba) and to Aruba.

16. Accession to the said Convention by the Government of the Sultanate of Oman does not mean or imply, and shall not be interpreted as recognition of Israel generally or in the context of this Convention.

17. The accession by the Government of the Republic of Korea to the present Convention does not, in any way, mean or imply the recognition of any territory or regime which has not been recognized by the Government of the Republic of Korea as a State or Government.

18. Approval by Saudi Arabia does not mean and could not be interpreted as recognition of Israel generally or in the context of this Convention.

19. Notification of succession by the Government of Slovakia to the Convention was deposited with the Government of the United States on 13 December 1995, with effect from 1 January 1993.

20. An instrument of succession by the Government of Slovenia to the Convention was deposited with the Government of the United Kingdom on 27 May 1992.

21. Notification of succession to the Convention was deposited with the Government of the United States on 27 October 1978, by virtue of the extension of the Convention to Suriname by the Kingdom of the Netherlands prior to independence. The Republic of Suriname attained independence on 25 November 1975.

22. Notification of succession by the Government of the former Yugoslav Republic of Macedonia to the Convention was deposited with the Government of the United States on 7 January 1998, with effect from 17 November 1991.

23. "In accepting the said Convention, the Government of the United Arab Emirates takes the view that its acceptance of the said Convention does not in any way imply its recognition of Israel, nor does it oblige to apply the provisions of the Convention in respect of the said Country."

24. The Convention is ratified "in respect of the United Kingdom of Great Britain and Northern Ireland and Territories under territorial sovereignty of the United Kingdom as well as the British Solomon Islands Protectorate".

25. By a Note dated 9 August 1999, the Government of the United Kingdom notified the International Civil Aviation Organization of the wish of the Government of Portugal to extend the Convention to the Territory of Macao, the extension taking effect on 19 July 1999.

26. By a Note dated 27 October 1999, the Government of Portugal advised the Government of the United Kingdom as follows:

> "In accordance with the Joint Declaration of the Government of the Portuguese Republic and the Government of the People's Republic of China on the Question of Macao signed on 13 April 1987, the Portuguese Republic will continue to have international responsibility for Macao until 19 December 1999 and from that date onwards the People's Republic of China will resume the exercise of sovereignty over Macao with effect from 20 December 1999.
>
> From 20 December 1999 onwards the Portuguese Republic will cease to be responsible for the international rights and obligations arising from the application of the Convention to Macao."

27. On 4 February 2003, the name of the State of the Federal Republic of Yugoslavia was changed to Serbia and Montenegro.

By a Note dated 17 July 2001, deposited on 23 July 2001 with the Government of the United Kingdom, the Government of the Federal Republic of Yugoslavia declared itself bound, as a successor State to the Socialist Federal Republic of Yugoslavia, by the provisions of, inter alia, this Convention, with effect from 27 April 1992, the date of State succession. (The former Socialist Federal Republic of Yugoslavia had signed the Convention on 16 December 1970 and ratified it on 2 October 1972.)

28. On 23 June 1997, Poland deposited with the Government of the United States a notification of withdrawal of the reservation made in accordance with Article 12, paragraph 1 (see note 3).

29. By a Note dated 29 November 1999, the Government of the People's Republic of China informed the Government of the United States as follows:

> "The Convention ... to which the Government of the People's Republic of China deposited an instrument of accession on 10 September 1980, will apply to the Macao Special Administrative Region with effect from 20 December 1999. The Government of the People's Republic of China also wishes to make the following declaration:
>
> The reservation made by the Government of the People's Republic of China to paragraph 1 of Article 12 of the Convention will also apply to the Macao Special Administrative Region.
>
> The Government of the People's Republic of China shall assume responsibility for the international rights and obligations arising from the application of the Convention to the Macao Special Administrative Region."

CONVENTION FOR THE SUPPRESSION OF UNLAWFUL ACTS AGAINST THE SAFETY OF CIVIL AVIATION

COMMENTARY

The Montreal Convention expanded further upon the coverage contained in the earlier Hague Convention by covering instances of aerial sabotage. Under Article I, an offence is committed, if one unlawfully and intentionally "performs an act of violence against a person on board an aircraft . . . destroys an aircraft in service or causes damage to such aircraft . . . places something on board an aircraft which might damage or destroy it . . . or acts in other fashions to endanger the safety of aircraft in flight, attempts to do so, or is an accomplice of such an attempt."

The punishment for committing offences under the Convention is left to each Contracting State (Article 3) and jurisdiction over the offences is established:

(a) when the offence is committed in the territory of that State;

(b) when the offence is committed against, or on board an aircraft registered, in that State;

(c) when the aircraft on board which the offence is committed lands in its territory with the alleged offender still on board;

(d) when the offence is committed against or on board an aircraft leased without crew to a lessee who has his principal place of business or, if the lessee has no such place of business, his permanent residence, in that State.

Libya, subsequent to the PanAm 103 bombing claimed that it had the right to try the Libyan suspects under this Convention. In the event, the United Nations chose to permit (at the urging of the United States) the offenders to be tried in the Scottish courts. Libya contended the suspects would not get a fair hearing in Scotland.

What the Convention does not cover are acts of violence committed before the aircraft is closed for departure, or where such acts occur within an airport.

CONVENTION FOR THE SUPPRESSION OF UNLAWFUL ACTS AGAINST THE SAFETY OF CIVIL AVIATION

Concluded at Montreal on 23 September 1971
Entered into force 26 January 1973*

BY THE PRESIDENT OF THE UNITED STATES OF AMERICA

A PROCLAMATION

CONSIDERING THAT:

The Convention for the Suppression of Unlawful Acts Against the Safety of Civil Aviation was signed at Montreal on September 23, 1971, a certified copy of which Convention in the English, French, Russian and Spanish languages, is hereto annexed;

The Senate of the United States of America by its resolution of October 3, 1972, two-thirds of the Senators present concurring therein, gave its advice and consent to ratification of the Convention, and the Convention was ratified by the President of the United States of America on November 1, 1972;

It is provided in Article 15 of the Convention that the Convention shall enter into force thirty days following the date of the deposit of instruments of ratification by ten States signatory to the Convention which participated in the Montreal Conference;

The date of entry into force of the Convention is January 26, 1973, instruments of ratification having been deposited by Trinidad and Tobago on February 9, 1972, South Africa on May 30, 1972, Canada on June 19, 1972, Israel on June 30, 1972, Chad on July 12, 1972, Brazil on July 24, 1972, Yugoslavia on October 2, 1972, Spain on October 30, 1972, the United States of America on November 1, 1972, Hungary on December 27, 1972;

---

* Treaties and International Agreements Online, CTIA 8071.000 (Oceana Publications, Inc. <www.oceanalaw.com>.

Now, THEREFORE, I, Richard Nixon, President of the United States of America, proclaim and make public the Convention to the end that it shall be observed and fulfilled with good faith on and after January 26, 1973 by the United States of America and by the citizens of the United States of America and all other persons subject to the jurisdiction thereof.

IN TESTIMONY WHEREOF, I have signed this proclamation and caused the Seal of the United States of America to be affixed.

DONE at the city of Washington this twenty-eighth day of February in the year of our Lord one thousand nine hundred seventy-three and of the Independence of the United States of America the one hundred ninety-seventh.

By the President:
RICHARD NIXON

Acting Secretary of State
KENNETH RUSH

THE STATES PARTIES TO THIS CONVENTION

CONSIDERING that unlawful acts against the safety of civil aviation jeopardize the safety of persons and property, seriously affect the operation of air services, and undermine the confidence of the peoples of the world in the safety of civil aviation;

CONSIDERING that, for the occurrence of such acts is a matter of grave concern;

CONSIDERING that, for the purpose of deterring such acts, there is an urgent need to provide appropriate measures for punishment of offenders;

HAVE AGREED as follows:

Article 1

1. Any person commits an offence if he unlawfully and intentionally:

    (a) performs an act of violence against a person on board an aircraft in flight if that act is likely to endanger the safety of that aircraft; or

    (b) destroys an aircraft in service or cause damage to such an aircraft which renders it incapable of flight or which is likely to endanger its safety in flight; or

    (c) places or causes to be placed on an aircraft in service, by any means whatsoever, a device or substance which is likely to destroy that aircraft, or to cause damage to it which renders it incapable of flight, or to cause damage to it which is likely to endanger its safety in flight; or

(d) destroys or damages air navigation facilities or interferes with their operation, if any such act is likely to endanger the safety of aircraft in flight; or

(e) communicates information which he knows to be false, thereby endangering the safety of an aircraft in flight.

2. Any person also commits an offence if he:

(a) attempts to commit any of the offences mentioned in paragraph 1 of this Article; or

(b) is an accomplice of a person who commits or attempts to commit any such offence

Article 2

For the purposes of this Convention:

(a) an aircraft is considered to be in flight at any time from the moment when all its external doors are closed following embarkation until the moment when any such door is opened for disembarkation; in the case of a forced landing, the flight shall be deemed to continue until the competent authorities take over the responsibility for the aircraft and for persons and property on board;

(b) an aircraft is considered to be in service from the beginning of the preflight preparation of the aircraft by ground personnel or by the crew for a specific flight until twenty-four hours after any landing; the period of service shall, in any event, extend for the entire period during which the aircraft is in flight as defined in paragraph (a) of this Article.

Article 3

Each Contracting State undertakes to make the offences mentioned in Article 1 punishable by severe penalties.

Article 4

1. This Convention shall not apply to aircraft used in military, customs or police services.

2. In the cases contemplated in subparagraphs (a), (b), (c) and (e) of paragraph 1 of Article 1, this Convention shall apply, irrespective of whether the aircraft is engaged in an international or domestic flight, only if:

(a) the place of take-off or landing, actual or intended, of the aircraft is situated outside the territory of the State of registration of that aircraft; or

(b) the offence is committed in the territory of a State other than the State of registration of the aircraft.

3. Notwithstanding paragraph 2 of this Article, in the cases contemplated in subparagraphs (a), (b), (c) and (e) of paragraph 1 of Article 1, this Convention shall also apply if the offender or the alleged offender is found in the territory of a State other than the State of registration of the aircraft.

4. With respect to the States mentioned in Article 9 and in the cases mentioned in subparagraphs (a), (b), (c) and (e) of paragraph 1 of Article 1, this Convention shall not apply if the places referred to in subparagraph (a) of paragraph 2 of this Article are situated within the territory of the same State where that State is one of those referred to in Article 9, unless the offence is committed or the offender or alleged offender is found in the territory of a State other than that State.

5. In the cases contemplated in subparagraph (d) of paragraph 1 of Article 1, this Convention shall apply only if the air navigation facilities are used in international air navigation.

6. The provisions of paragraphs 2, 3, 4 and 5 of this Article shall also apply in the cases contemplated in paragraph 2 of Article 1.

Article 5

1. Each Contracting State shall take such measures as may be necessary to establish its jurisdiction over the offences in the following cases:

(a) when the offence is committed in the territory of that State;

(b) when the offence is committed against or on board an aircraft registered in that State;

(c) when the aircraft on board which the offence is committed lands in its territory with the alleged offender still on board;

(d) when the offence is committed against or on board an aircraft leased without crew to a lessee who has his principal place of business or, if the lessee has no such place of business, his permanent residence, in that State.

2. Each Contracting State shall likewise take such measures as may be necessary to establish its jurisdiction over the offences mentioned in Article 1, paragraph 1 (a), (b) and (c), and in Article 1, paragraph 2, in so far as that paragraph relates to those offences, in the case where the alleged offender is present in its territory and it does not extradite him pursuant to Article 8 to any of the States mentioned in paragraph 1 of this Article.

3. This Convention does not exclude any criminal jurisdiction exercised in accordance with national law.

Article 6

1. Upon being satisfied that the circumstances so warrant, any Contracting State in the territory of which the offender or the alleged offender is pres-

ent, shall take him into custody or take other measures to ensure his presence. The custody and other measures shall be as provided in the law of that State but may only be continued for such time as is necessary to enable any criminal or extradition proceedings to be instituted.

2. Such State shall immediately make a preliminary enquiry into the facts.

3. Any person in custody pursuant to paragraph 1 of this Article shall be assisted in communicating immediately with the nearest appropriate representative of the State of which he is a national.

4. When a State, pursuant to this Article, has taken a person into custody, it shall immediately notify the States mentioned in Article 5, paragraph 1, the State of nationality of the detained person and, if it considers it advisable, any other interested States of the fact that such person is in custody and of the circumstances which warrant his detention. The State which makes the preliminary enquiry contemplated in paragraph 2 of this Article shall promptly report its findings to the said States and shall indicate whether it intends to exercise jurisdiction.

Article 7

The Contracting State in the territory of which the alleged offender is found shall, if it does not extradite him, be obliged, without exception whatsoever and whether or not the offence was committed in its territory, to submit the case to its competent authorities for the purpose of prosecution. Those authorities shall take their decision in the same manner as in the case of any ordinary offence of a serious nature under the law of that State.

Article 8

1. The offences shall be deemed to be included as extraditable offences in any extradition treaty existing between Contracting States. Contracting States undertake to include the offences as extraditable offences in every extradition treaty to be concluded between them.

2. If a Contracting State which makes extradition conditional on the existence of a treaty receives a request for extradition from another Contracting State with which it has no extradition treaty, it may at its option consider this Convention as the legal basis for extradition in respect of the offences. Extradition shall be subject to the other conditions provided by the law of the requested State.

3. Contracting States which do not make extradition conditional on the existence of a treaty shall recognize the offences as extraditable offences between themselves subject to the conditions provided by the law of the requested State.

4. Each of the offences shall be treated, for the purpose of extradition between Contracting States, as if it had been committed not only in the place in

which it occurred but also in the territories of the States required to establish their jurisdiction in accordance with Article 5, paragraph 1 (b), (c) and (d).

Article 9

The Contracting States which establish joint air transport operating organizations or international operating agencies, which operate aircraft which are subject to joint or international registration shall, by appropriate means, designate for each aircraft the State among them which shall exercise the jurisdiction and have the attributes of the State of registration for the purpose of this Convention and shall give notice thereof to the International Civil Aviation Organization which shall communicate the notice to all States Parties to this Convention.

Article 10

1. Contracting States shall, in accordance with international and national law, endeavour to take all practicable measures for the purpose of preventing the offences mentioned in Article 1.

2. When, due to the commission of one of the offences mentioned in Article 1, a flight has been delayed or interrupted, any Contracting State in whose territory the aircraft or passengers or crew are present shall facilitate the continuation of the journey of the passengers and crew as soon as practicable, and shall without delay return the aircraft and its cargo to the persons lawfully entitled to possession.

Article 11

1. Contracting States shall afford one another the greatest measure of assistance in connection with criminal proceedings brought in respect of the offences. The law of the State requested shall apply in all cases.

2. The provisions of paragraph 1 of this Article shall not affect obligations under any other treaty, bilateral or multilateral, which governs or will govern, in whole or in part, mutual assistance in criminal matters.

Article 12

Any Contracting State having reason to believe that one of the offences mentioned in Article 1 will be committed shall, in accordance with its national law, furnish any relevant information in its possession to those States which it believes would be the States mentioned in Article 5, paragraph 1.

Article 13

Each Contracting State shall in accordance with its national law report to the Council of the International Civil Aviation Organization as promptly as possible any relevant information in its possession concerning:

(a) the circumstances of the offence;

(b) the action taken pursuant to Article 10, paragraph 2;

(c) the measures taken in relation to the offender or the alleged offender and, in particular, the results of any extradition proceedings or other legal proceedings.

Article 14

1. Any dispute between two or more Contracting States concerning the interpretation or application of this Convention which cannot be settled through negotiation, shall, at the request of one of them, be submitted to arbitration. If within six months from the date of the request for arbitration the Parties are unable to agree on the organization of the arbitration, any one of those Parties may refer the dispute to the International Court of Justice by request in conformity with the Statute of the Court.

2. Each State may at the time of signature or ratification of this Convention or accession thereto, declare that it does not consider itself bound by the preceding paragraph. The other Contracting States shall not be bound by the preceding paragraph with respect to any Contracting State having made such a reservation.

3. Any Contracting State having made a reservation in accordance with the preceding paragraph may at any time withdraw this reservation by notification to the Depositary Governments.

Article 15

1. This Convention shall be open for signature at Montreal on 23 September 1971, by States participating in the International Conference on Air Law held at Montreal from 8 to 23 September 1971 (hereinafter referred to as the Montreal Conference). After 10 October 1971, the Convention shall be open to all States for signature in Moscow, London and Washington. Any State which does not sign this Convention before its entry into force in accordance with paragraph 3 of this Article may accede to it at any time.

2. This Convention shall be subject to ratification by the signatory States. Instruments of ratification and instruments of accession shall be deposited with the Governments of the Union of Soviet Socialist republics, the united Kingdom of Great Britain and Northern Ireland, and the United States of America, which are hereby designated by the Depository Governments.

3. This Convention shall enter into force thirty days following the date of the deposit of instruments of ratification by ten States signatory to this Convention which participated in the Montreal Conference. 4. For other States, this Convention shall enter into force on the date of entry into force of this Convention in accordance with paragraph 3 of this Article, or thirty

days following the date of deposit of their instruments of ratification or accession, whichever is later.

5. The Depository Governments shall promptly inform all signatory and acceding States of the date of each signature, the date of deposit of each instrument of ratification or accession, the date of entry into force of this Convention, and other notices.

6. As soon as this Convention comes into force, it shall be registered by the Depositary Governments pursuant to Article 102 of the Charter of the United Nations and pursuant to Article 83 of the Convention on International Civil Aviation (Chicago, 1944).

Article 16

1. Any Contracting State may denounce this Convention by written notification to the Depositary Governments.

2. Denunciation shall take effect six months following the date on which notification is received by the Depositary Governments.

In witness whereof the undersigned Plenipotentiaries, being duly authorized thereto by their Governments, have signed this Convention.

Done at Montreal, this twenty-third day of September, one thousand nine hundred and seventy-one, in three originals, each being drawn up in four authentic texts in the English, French, Russian and Spanish languages.

Certified to be a true and complete copy
Legal Bureau

Note by the Department of State

Signatures Affixed at Montreal and Washington to the United States Depositary Original of the Convention for the Suppression of Unlawful Acts against the Safety of Civil Aviation.[1]

ARGENTINE REPUBLIC, THE
  R. Temporini
  O.A. Ainchil
AUSTRALIA, THE COMMONWEALTH OF
  J. Plimsoll
  12 October 1972
AUSTRIA, THE REPUBLIC OF
  A Halusa
  13 November 1972

---

[1] Opened for signature at Montreal Sept. 23, 1971; after Oct. 10, 1971, open for signature at London, Moscow, and Washington. The undated signatures were affixed at Montreal; the dated signatures were affixed at Washington.

BARBADOS
  O H Jackman
BELGIUM, THE KINGDOM OF
  A X Pirson
BRAZIL, THE FEDERATIVE REPUBLIC OF
  E C Sanctos

Subject to reservation under Article 14 paragraph 2 and 1

BULGARIA, THE PEOPLE'S REPUBLIC OF
  L Geliazkov

with a reservation under p2, article 14

BYLORUSSIAN SOVIET SOCIALIST REPUBLIC
  V.I. Lukyanovich [Romanization]

"The Government of the Byelorussian Soviet Socialist Republic does not consider itself bound by the provisions of paragraph 1 of Article 14, which provides that disputes concerning the interpretation or application of the Convention shall be submitted to arbitration or to the International Court of Justice at the request of one of the Parties". [Translation]

CAMEROON, THE FEDERAL REPUBLIC OF
CANADA
  Andre Bissonette
CEYLON
CHAD, THE REPUBLIC OF
  A Aganaye
CHILE, THE REPUBLIC OF
CHINA, THE REPUBLIC OF
  S. M. Kao [Romanization]
COLOMBIA, THE REPUBLIC OF
CONGO, THE PEOPLE'S REPUBLIC OF THE
  F X Ollassa
COSTA RICO, THE REPUBLIC OF
  Georgiana Darlington
CZECHOSLOVAK SOCIALIST REPUBLIC
  B Vachata

With reservation under par. 2, Article 14

DENMARK, THE KINGDOM OF
  E Bartels
  October 17th 72
EGYPT, ARAB REPUBLIC OF
ETHIOPIA, THE EMPIRE OF
  G. Tuni
FINLAND, THE REPUBLIC OF
FRENCH REPUBLIC, THE
GABONESE REPUBLIC, THE
GERMANY, THE FEDERAL REPUBLIC OF
  H. Groepper

HUNGARIAN PEOPLE'S REPUBLIC
  Sandor, Istvan
INDIA, THE REPUBLIC OF
  L. K. Jha
  December 11 1972
INDONESIA, THE REPUBLIC OF
IRELAND
ISRAEL, THE STATE OF
  N. Ben-Yehuda [Romanization]
  E. Ben-Yakir [Romanization]
ITALIAN REPUBLIC, THE
  V Marabito
JAMAICA
  K. O. Rattray G. B. Morris
JAPAN
KENYA, THE REPUBLIC OF
KOREA, THE REPUBLIC OF
LEBANON, THE REPUBLIC OF
MALAGASY REPUBLIC, THE
MEXICAN STATES, THE UNITED
  J J de Olloqui
  January 25th 1973
NETHERLANDS, THE KINGDOM OF THE
  W Riphagen
  M R Mok
NEW ZEALAND
  G D L White
  September 26th 1972
NORWAY, THE KINGDOM OF
PHILIPPINES, THE REPUBLIC OF THE
  P Agcaoili
  L T Caday
  R. Carsi Cruz
POLISH PEOPLE'S REPUBLIC
  S Dabrowa
PORTUGAL, THE REPUBLIC OF
  J R Pinto-Soares
ROMANIA, SOCIALIST REPUBLIC OF
  G Ionita
  July 10, 1972

1. "The Socialist Republic of Romania states that does not consider herself bound by the provisions of Article 14, point 1, of the Convention for the Suppression of Unlawful Acts Against the Safety of Civil Aviation, done at Montreal on September 23, 1971, which stipulates that the differences concerning the interpretation or the putting into force of the present Convention, which have not been settled through negotiations, to be submitted to the International Court of Justice at the request of each of the parties involved. The position of the Socialist Republic of Romania is that such differences should be sub-

mitted to the International Court of Justice only with the consent of all the parties involved, for each single case."

SENEGAL, THE REPUBLIC OF
Y Diallo

SOUTH AFRICA, THE REPUBLIC OF
H E M I Botha

SPAIN

SWEDEN, THE KINGDOM OF

SWISS CONFEDERATION, THE
W. Guldimann

TANZANIA, THE UNITED REPUBLIC OF

TRINIDAD AND TOBAGO
Ellis Clarke
9th February, 1972

UGANDA, THE REPUBLIC OF

UKRAINIAN SOVIET SOCIALIST REPUBLIC
I. Iliuschenko [Romanization]

The Government of the Ukrainian Soviet Socialist Republic does not consider itself bound by the provisions of paragraph 1 of Article 14, which provides that disputes concerning the interpretation or application of the Convention shall be submitted to arbitration or to the International Court of Justice at the request of one of the Parties to the dispute. [Translation]

UNION OF SOVIET SOCIALIST REPUBLICS
N. Ossetrov [Romanization]

The Government of the Union of Soviet Socialist Republics does not consider itself bound by the provisions of paragraph 1 of Article 14, which provides that disputes concerning the interpretation or application of the Convention shall be submitted to arbitration or to the International Court of Justice at the request of one of the Parties to the dispute. [Translation]

UNITED KINGDOM OF GREAT BRITAIN AND NORTHERN IRELAND
Arnold Kean

UNITED STATES OF AMERICA
Charles Nelson Brower
Franklin Knight Willis
Robert Patrick Boyle

VENEZUELA, THE REPUBLIC OF
Ad referendum J. Mendez

YUGOSLAVIA, THE SOCIALIST FEDERAL REPUBLIC OF
T Curuvija

ZAMBIA, THE REPUBLIC OF

LUXEMBOURG, THE GRAND DUCHY OF
Jean Wagner

HAITI, THE REPUBLIC OF
R. Chalmers

PANAMA, REPUBLIC OF
J Antonio de la Ossa

THE SAFETY OF CIVIL AVIATION

GREECE, THE KINGDOM OF
  B Vitsaxis
  the 9th of February 1972

MONGOLIAN PEOPLE'S REPUBLIC
  M Dugersuren
  18 Feb. 1972

NIGER, THE REPUBLIC OF
  O G Youssoufou
  6th March 1972

JORDAN, THE HASHEMITE KINGDOM OF
  Z Mufti
  2 May, 1972

GUATEMALA, THE REPUBLIC OF
  J Asensio-Wunderlich
  May 9, 1972

DOMINICAN REPUBLIC
  S. Ortiz
  May 31, 1972

RWANDA, THE REPUBLIC OF
  Fidele Nkundabagenzi
  June 26, 1972

TURKEY, THE REPUBLIC OF
  Melih Esenbel
  July 5, 1972

LAOS, THE KINGDOM OF
  Pheng Norindr
  Nov 1st 1972

SINGAPORE, THE REPUBLIC OF
  E.S. Monteiro
  21. Nov 1972

CYPRUS, THE REPUBLIC OF
  Zenon Rossides
  28 Nov 1972

NICARAGUA, THE REPUBLIC OF
  Dr. Guillermo Sevilla-Sacasa

PARAGUAY, THE REPUBLIC OF
  Ad referendum Miguel Solano Lopez

THE SAFETY OF CIVIL AVIATION

States which are currently parties:

Afghanistan [1]
Albania
Algeria [2]
Angola
Antigua and Barbuda
Argentina
Armenia
Australia
Austria
Azerbaijan
Bahamas
Bahrain [1]
Bangladesh
Barbados
Belarus [1]
Belgium
Belize
Benin
Bhutan
Bolivia
Bosnia and Herzegovina [3]
Botswana
Brazil [1]
Brunei Darussalam
Bulgaria [4]
Burkina Faso
Burundi
Cambodia
Cameroon [5]
Canada
Cape Verde
Central African Republic
Chad
Chile
China [1, 6, 30]
Colombia
Comoros
Congo
Costa Rica
Côte d'Ivoire
Croatia [7]
Cuba [1]
Cyprus
Czech Republic [8]
Democratic People's Republic of Korea
Democratic Republic of the Congo
Denmark [9]
Djibouti
Dominican Republic
Ecuador
Egypt [1]
El Salvador
Equatorial Guinea
Estonia
Ethiopia [1]
Fiji
Finland
France [1]
Gabon
Gambia
Georgia
Germany [10]
Ghana
Greece
Grenada
Guatemala [1]
Guinea
Guinea-Bissau
Guyana
Haiti
Honduras
Hungary [11]
Iceland
India
Indonesia [1]
Iran (Islamic Republic of)

Ireland
Israel
Italy
Jamaica
Japan
Jordan
Kazakhstan
Kenya
Kuwait [12]
Kyrgyzstan
Lao People's Democratic Republic
Latvia
Lebanon
Lesotho
Liberia
Libyan Arab Jamahiriya
Liechtenstein
Lithuania
Luxembourg
Madagascar
Malawi [1]
Malaysia
Maldives
Mali
Malta
Marshall Islands
Mauritania
Mauritius
Mexico
Micronesia (Federated States of)
Monaco
Mongolia[1]
Morocco [13]
Mozambique[1]
Myanmar
Nauru
Nepal
Netherlands [14]
New Zealand
Nicaragua
Niger

Nigeria
Norway
Oman [1, 15]
Pakistan
Palau
Panama
Papua New Guinea [1]
Paraguay
Peru [1]
Philippines
Poland[1, 29]
Portugal[26, 27]
Qatar[1]
Republic of Korea[16]
Republic of Moldova
Romania[1]
Russian Federation[1]
Rwanda
Saint Lucia
Saint Vincent and the Grenadines
Samoa
Saudi Arabia [1, 17]
Senegal
Serbia and Montenegro[28]
Seychelles
Sierra Leone
Singapore
Slovakia[18]
Slovenia[19]
Solomon Islands[20]
South Africa[1]
Spain
Sri Lanka
Sudan
Suriname[21]
Swaziland
Sweden
Switzerland
Syrian Arab Republic [1]
Tajikistan
Thailand

The former Yugoslav Republic of Macedonia[22]
Togo
Tonga
Trinidad and Tobago
Tunisia[1]
Turkey
Turkmenistan
Uganda
Ukraine[1]
United Arab Emirates[23]
United Kingdom[24]
United Republic of Tanzania
United States
Uruguay
Uzbekistan
Vanuatu
Venezuela[25]
Viet Nam
Yemen
Zambia
Zimbabwe

NOTES

[1] Reservation made with respect to paragraph 1 of Article 14 of the Convention.

[2] Reservation: "The People's Democratic Republic of Algeria does not consider itself bound by the provisions of articles 24.1, 12.1 and 14.1 respectively of the Tokyo, The Hague and Montreal Conventions, which provide for the mandatory referral of any dispute to the International Court of Justice. The People's Democratic Republic of Algeria states that in each case the prior consent of all the parties concerned shall be required in order to refer a dispute to the International Court of Justice."

[3] Notification of succession by the Government of Bosnia and Herzegovina to the Convention was deposited with the Government of the United States on 15 August 1994, with effect from 6 March 1992.

[4] On 9 May 1994, a Note was deposited with the Government of the United States by the Government of Bulgaria whereby that Government withdraws the reservation made at the time of ratification with regard to paragraph 1 of Article 14 of the Convention. The withdrawal of the reservation took effect on 9 May 1994.

[5] "In accordance with the provisions of the Convention of 23 September 1971, for the Suppression of Unlawful Acts directed against the Security of Civil Aviation, the Government of the United Republic of Cameroon declares that in view of the fact that it does not have any relations with South Africa and Portugal, it has no obligation toward these two countries with regard to the implementation of the stipulations of the Convention."

[6] The instrument of accession by the Government of the People's Republic of China contains the following declaration: "The Chinese Government declares illegal and null and void the signature and ratification of the above-mentioned Convention by the Taiwan authorities in the name of China".

[7] An instrument of succession by the Government of Croatia to the Convention was deposited with the Government of the United States on 8 June 1993, with effect from 8 October 1991.

[8] An instrument of succession by the Government of the Czech Republic to the Convention was deposited with the Government of the Russian Federation on 14 November 1994, with effect from 1 January 1993.

[9] Until later decision, the Convention will not be applied to the Faroe Islands or to Greenland.

Note 1: A notification was received by the Government of the United Kingdom from the Government of the Kingdom of Denmark whereby the latter withdraws, with effect from 1 June 1980, the reservation made at the time of ratification that this Convention should not apply to Greenland.

THE SAFETY OF CIVIL AVIATION

Note 2: The Government of the United Kingdom subsequently received, on 21 September 1994, a notification from the Government of the Kingdom of Denmark whereby the latter withdraws, with effect from 1 October 1994, the reservation made at the time of ratification that this Convention should not apply to the Faroe Islands.

[10] The German Democratic Republic, which ratified the Convention on 9 June 1972, acceded to the Federal Republic of Germany on 3 October 1990.

[11] On 10 January 1990, instruments were deposited with the Government of the United Kingdom and the Government of the United States by the Government of Hungary whereby that Government withdraws the reservation made at the time of ratification with regard to paragraph 1 of Article 14 of the Convention. The withdrawal of the reservation took effect on 10 January 1990.

[12] It is understood that accession to the Convention for the Suppression of Unlawful Acts Against the Safety of Civil Aviation, done at Montreal, 1971, does not mean in any way recognition of Israel by the State of Kuwait. Furthermore, no treaty relation will arise between the State of Kuwait and Israel.

[13] "In case of a dispute, all recourse must be made to the International Court of Justice on the basis of the unanimous consent of the parties concerned".

[14] The Convention cannot enter into force for the Netherlands Antilles until thirty days after the date on which the Government of the Kingdom of the Netherlands shall have notified the depositary Governments that the necessary measures to give effect to the provisions of the Convention have been taken in the Netherlands Antilles.

Note 1: On 11 June 1974, a declaration was deposited with the Government of the United States by the Government of the Kingdom of the Netherlands stating that in the interim the measures required to implement the provisions of the Convention have been taken in the Netherlands Antilles and, consequently, the Convention will enter into force for the Netherlands Antilles on the thirtieth day after the date of deposit of this declaration.

Note 2: By a Note dated 9 January 1986 the Government of the Kingdom of the Netherlands informed the Government of the United States that as of 1 January 1986 the Convention is applicable to the Netherlands Antilles (without Aruba) and to Aruba.

[15] Accession to the said Convention by the Government of the Sultanate of Oman does not mean or imply, and shall not be interpreted as recognition of Israel generally or in the context of this Convention.

[16] The accession by the Government of the Republic of Korea to the present Convention does not in any way mean or imply the recognition of any territory or regime which has not been recognized by the Government of the Republic of Korea as a State or Government.

[17] Approval by Saudi Arabia does not mean and could not be interpreted as recognition of Israel generally or in the context of this Convention.

[18] An instrument of succession by the Government of Slovakia to the Convention was deposited with the Government of the United States on 6 March 1995, with effect from 1 January 1993.

[19] An instrument of succession by the Government of Slovenia to the Convention was deposited with the Government of the United Kingdom on 27 May 1992.

[20] An instrument of succession by the Government of Solomon Islands to the Convention was deposited with the Government of the United Kingdom on 13 April 1982. Solomon Islands attained independence on 7 July 1978.

[21] Notification of succession to the Convention was deposited with the Government of the United States on 27 October 1978, by virtue of the extension of the Convention to Suriname by the Kingdom of the Netherlands prior to independence. The Republic of Suriname attained independence on 25 November 1975.

[22] An instrument of succession by the Government of the former Yugoslav Republic of Macedonia to the Convention was deposited with the Government of the United States on 4 January 1995.

[23] "In accepting the said Convention, the Government of the United Arab Emirates takes the view that its acceptance of the said Convention does not in any way imply its recognition of Israel, nor does it oblige to apply the provisions of the Convention in respect of the said Country."

[24] The Convention is ratified "in respect of the United Kingdom of Great Britain and Northern Ireland and Territories under territorial sovereignty of the United Kingdom as well as the British Solomon Islands Protectorate".

Note: By a Note dated 20 November 1990, the Government of the United Kingdom declared that Anguilla has been included under the ratification of the Convention by that Government with effect from 7 November 1990.

[25] The instrument of ratification by the Government of Venezuela contains the following reservation regarding Articles 4, 7 and 8 of the Convention:

"Venezuela will take into consideration clearly political motives and the circumstances under which offences described in Article 1 of this Convention are committed, in refusing to extradite or prosecute an offender, unless financial extortion or injury to the crew, passengers, or other persons has occurred".

The Government of the United Kingdom of Great Britain and Northern Ireland made the following declaration in a Note dated 6 August 1985 to the Department of State of the Government of the United States:

"The Government of the United Kingdom of Great Britain and Northern Ireland do not regard as valid the reservation made by the Government of the Republic of Venezuela insofar as it purports to limit the obligation under Article 7 of the Convention to submit the case against an offender to the competent authorities of the State for the purpose of prosecution".

With reference to the above declaration by the Government of the United Kingdom of Great Britain and Northern Ireland, the Government of Venezuela, in a Note dated 21 November 1985, informed the Department of State of the Government of the United States of the following:

"The reserve made by the Government of Venezuela to Articles 4, 7 and 8 of the Convention is based on the fact that the principle of asylum is contemplated in Article 116 of the Constitution of the Republic of Venezuela. Article 116 reads: 'The Republic grants asylum to any person subject to persecution or which finds itself in danger, for political reasons, within the conditions and requirements established by the laws and norms of international law.'

It is for this reason that the Government of Venezuela considers that in order to protect this right, which would be diminished by the application without limits of the said articles, it was necessary to request the formulation of the declaration contemplated in Art. 2 of the Law approving the Convention for the Suppression of Unlawful Acts Against the Security (sic) of Civil Aviation".

The Government of Italy made the following declaration in a Note dated 21 November 1985 to the Department of State of the Government of the United States:

"The Government of Italy does not consider as valid the reservation formulated by the Government of the Republic of Venezuela due to the fact that it may be considered as aiming to limit the obligation under Article 7 of the Convention to submit the case against an offender to the competent authorities of the State for the purpose of prosecution".

[26] By a Note dated 9 August 1999, the Government of the United Kingdom notified the International Civil Aviation Organization of the wish of the Government of Portugal to extend the Convention to the Territory of Macao, the extension taking effect on 19 July 1999.

[27] By a Note dated 27 October 1999, the Government of Portugal advised the Government of the United Kingdom as follows:

> "In accordance with the Joint Declaration of the Government of the Portuguese Republic and the Government of the People's Republic of China on the Question of Macao signed on 13 April 1987, the Portuguese Republic will continue to have international responsibility for Macao until 19 December 1999 and from that date onwards the People's Republic of China will resume the exercise of sovereignty over Macao with effect from 20 December 1999.
>
> From 20 December 1999 onwards the Portuguese Republic will cease to be responsible for the international rights and obligations arising from the application of the Convention to Macao."

[28] On 4 February 2003, the name of the State of the Federal Republic of Yugoslavia was changed to Serbia and Montenegro.

By a Note dated 17 July 2001, deposited on 23 July 2001 with the Government of the United Kingdom, the Government of the Federal Republic of Yugoslavia declared itself bound, as a successor State to the Socialist Federal Republic of Yugoslavia, by the provisions of, *inter alia*, this Convention, with effect from 27 April 1992, the date of State succession. (The former Socialist Federal Republic of Yugoslavia had signed the Convention on 23 September 1971 and ratified it on 2 October 1972.)

[29] On 23 June 1997, Poland deposited with the Government of the United States a notification of withdrawal of the reservation made in accordance with Article 14, paragraph 1 (see note 1).

[30] By a Note dated 29 November 1999, the Government of the People's Republic of China informed the Government of the United States as follows:

> "The Convention ... to which the Government of the People's Republic of China deposited an instrument of accession on 10 September 1980, will apply to the Macao Special Administrative Region with effect from 20 December 1999. The Government of the People's Republic of China also wishes to make the following declaration:
>
> The reservation made by the Government of the People's Republic of China to paragraph 1 of Article 14 of the Convention will also apply to the Macao Special Administrative Region.
>
> The Government of the People's Republic of China shall assume responsibility for the international rights and obligations arising from the application of the Convention to the Macao Special Administrative Region."

CONVENTION ON THE PREVENTION AND PUNISHMENT OF CRIMES AGAINST INTERNATIONALLY PROTECTED PERSONS, INCLUDING DIPLOMATIC AGENTS

COMMENTARY

Terrorists clearly recognized the impact which could be gained from the holding, injuring, and killing of diplomatic personnel. During 1977 alone, terrorists killed diplomatic representatives from the United States in Mexico and in the Sudan. That practice continued with such widely publicized acts as the assassination of the Italian Prime Minister and the killing of the U.S. Ambassador to Cyprus and another in Afghanistan.

As pointed out by President Ford when he sought Senate Advice and Consent for the Convention:

> "... We have witnessed in recent years an unprecedented increase in acts of violence directed against diplomatic agents and other internationally protected persons ..."

and he went on to point out that this Convention is meant to create the legal mechanism whereby offenders will be prosecuted or extradited. The Convention still suffers from the weakness of its predecessors in that States are required to submit the case involving the offender "to its competent authorities for the purpose of prosecution ... " but there is no certainty that such proceedings would result in appropriate punishment of the offender.

The full text of the President's Message sending this Convention to the Senate follows:

> "*To the Senate of the United States:*
>
> With a view to receiving the advice and consent of the Senate to ratification, I transmit herewith a copy of the Convention on the Prevention and Punishment of Crimes against Internationally Protected Persons, including Diplomatic Agents, adopted by the United Nations General Assembly on December 14, 1973, and signed in behalf of the United States of America on

CRIMES AGAINST INTERNATIONALLY PROTECTED PERSONS

December 28, 1973. The report of the Department of State with respect to the Convention is also transmitted for the information of the Senate.

The effective conduct of international relations depends in large part on the ability of diplomatic agents to travel and live freely and securely while representing the interests of their respective countries. We have witnessed in recent years an unprecedented increase in acts of violence directed against diplomatic agents and other internationally protected persons. This development has demonstrated the urgent need to take affirmative action to minimize the threats which can be directed against diplomatic agents. Although the legal obligation to protect these persons was never questioned, the mechanism for international cooperation to ensure that perpetrators of serious attacks against them are brought to justice, no matter where they may flee, was lacking.

The Convention is designed to rectify this serious situation by creating a legal mechanism whereby persons alleged to have committed serious crimes against diplomats will be prosecuted or extradited. It also sets out a framework for international cooperation in the prevention and punishment of such crimes.

This Convention is vitally important to assure continued safe and orderly conduct of the diplomatic process. I hope that all States will become Parties to this Convention. I recommend, therefore, that the Senate give early and favorable consideration to this Convention.

Gerald R. Ford

The White House
November 13, 1974"

CONVENTION ON THE PREVENTION AND PUNISHMENT OF CRIMES AGAINST INTERNATIONALLY PROTECTED PERSONS, INCLUDING DIPLOMATIC AGENTS

Adopted by the United Nations on 14 December 1973
Entered into force 20 February 1977*

BY THE PRESIDENT OF THE UNITED STATES OF AMERICA

A PROCLAMATION

CONSIDERING THAT:

The Convention on the Prevention and Punishment of Crimes against Internationally Protected Persons, including Diplomatic Agents, was adopted by the United Nations General Assembly on December 14, 1973, and was signed on behalf of the United States of America on December 28, 1973, a certified copy of which Convention, in the English, French, Chinese, Russian and Spanish languages, is hereto annexed;

The Senate of the United States of America by its resolution of October 28, 1975, two-thirds of the Senators present concurring therein, gave its advice and consent to ratification of the Convention; On October 8, 1976, the President of the United States of America ratified the Convention, in pursuance of the advice and consent of the Senate;

The United States of America deposited its instrument of ratification on October 26, 1976, in accordance with the provisions of Article 15 of the Convention;

Pursuant to the provisions of Article 17 of the Convention, the Convention entered into force for the United States of America on February 20, 1977;

---

* Treaties and International Agreements Online, CTIA 8464.000 (Oceana Publications, Inc. <www.oceanalaw.com>.

Now, therefore, I, Jimmy Carter, President of the United States of America, proclaim and make public the Convention, to the end that it shall be observed and fulfilled with good faith on and after February 20, 1977, by the United States of America and by the citizens of the United States of America and all other persons subject to the jurisdiction thereof.

In testimony whereof, I have signed this proclamation and caused the Seal of the United States of America to be affixed.

Done at the city of Washington this eighteenth day of March in the year of our Lord one thousand nine hundred seventy-seven and of the Independence of the United States of America the two hundred first.

By the President:
JIMMY CARTER

Secretary of State
CYRUS VANCE

THE STATES PARTIES TO THIS CONVENTION,

Having in mind the purposes and principles of the Charter of the United Nations[1] concerning the maintenance of international peace and the promotion of friendly relations and co-operation among States,

Considering that crimes against diplomatic agents and other internationally protected persons jeopardizing the safety of these persons create a serious threat to the maintenance of normal international relations which are necessary for co-operation among States,

Believing that the commission of such crimes is a matter of grave concern to the international community,

Convinced that there is an urgent need to adopt appropriate and effective measures for the prevention and punishment of such crimes,

HAVE AGREED AS FOLLOWS:

Article 1

For the purposes of this Convention:

1. "internationally protected person" means:

> (a) a Head of State, including any member of a collegial body performing the functions of a Head of State under the constitution of the State concerned, a Head of Government or a Minister for Foreign Affairs, when-

---

1   1 TS 993; 59 Stat. 1031.

ever any such person is in a foreign State, as well as members of his family who accompany him;

(b) any representative or official of a State or any official or other agent of an international organization of an intergovernmental character who, at the time when and in the place where a crime against him, his official premises, his private accommodation or his means of transport is committed, is entitled pursuant to international law to special protection from any attack on his person, freedom or dignity, as well as members of his family forming part of his household;

2. "alleged offender" means a person as to whom there is sufficient evidence to determine prima facie that he has committed or participated in one or more of the crimes set forth in article 2.

Article 2

1. The intentional commission of:

   (a) a murder, kidnapping or other attack upon the person or liberty of an internationally protected person likely to endanger his person or liberty;

   (c) a threat to commit any such attack;

   (d) an attempt to commit any such attack; and

   (e) an act constituting participation as an accomplice in any such attack

shall be made by each State Party a crime under its internal law.

2. Each State Party shall make these crimes punishable by appropriate penalties which take into account their grave nature.

3. Paragraphs 1 and 2 of this article in no way derogate from the obligations of States Parties under international law to take all appropriate measures to prevent other attacks on the person, freedom or dignity of an internationally protected person.

Article 3

1. Each State Party shall take such measures as may be necessary to establish its jurisdiction over the crimes set forth in article 2 in the following cases:

   (a) when the crime is committed in the territory of that State or on board a ship or aircraft registered in that State;

   (b) when the alleged offender is a national of that State;

   (c) when the crime is committed against an internationally protected person as defined in article 1 who enjoys his status as such by virtue of functions which he exercises on behalf of that State.

2. Each State Party shall likewise take such measures as may be necessary to establish its jurisdiction over these crimes in cases where the alleged offender is present in its territory and it does not extradite him pursuant to article 8 to any of the States mentioned in paragraph 1 of this article.

3. This Convention does not exclude any criminal jurisdiction exercised in accordance with internal law.

Article 4

States Parties shall co-operate in the prevention of the crimes set forth in article 2, particularly by:

(a) taking all practicable measures to prevent preparations in their respective territories for the commission of those crimes within or outside their territories;

(b) exchanging information and co-ordinating the taking of administrative and other measures as appropriate to prevent the commission of those crimes.

Article 5

1. The State Party in which any of the crimes set forth in article 2 has been committed shall, if it has reason to believe that an alleged offender has fled from its territory, communicate to all other States concerned, directly or through the Secretary-General of the United Nations, all the pertinent facts regarding the crime committed and all available information regarding the identity of the alleged offender.

2. Whenever any of the crimes set forth in article 2 has been committed against an internationally protected person, any State Party which has information concerning the victim and the circumstances of the crime shall endeavour to transmit it, under the conditions provided for in its internal law, fully and promptly to the State Party on whose behalf he was exercising his functions.

Article 6

1. Upon being satisfied that the circumstances so warrant, the State Party in whose territory the alleged offender is present shall take the appropriate measures under its internal law so as to ensure his presence for the purpose of prosecution or extradition. Such measures shall be notified without delay directly or through the Secretary-General of the United Nations to:

(a) the State where the crime was committed;

(b) the State or States of which the alleged offender is a national or, if he is a stateless person, in whose territory he permanently resides;

(c) the State or States of which the internationally protected person concerned is a national or on whose behalf he was exercising his functions;

(d) all other States concerned; and

(e) the international organization of which the internationally protected person concerned is an official or an agent.

2. Any person regarding whom the measures referred to in paragraph 1 of this article are being taken shall be entitled:

(a) to communicate without delay with the nearest appropriate representative of the State of which he is a national or which is otherwise entitled to protect his rights or, if he is a stateless person, which he requests and which is willing to protect his rights; and

(b) to be visited by a representative of that State.

Article 7

The State Party in whose territory the alleged offender is present shall, if it does not extradite him, submit, without exception whatsoever and without undue delay, the case to its competent authorities for the purpose of prosecution, through proceedings in accordance with the laws of that State.

Article 8

1. To the extent that the crimes set forth in article 2 are not listed as extraditable offences in any extradition treaty existing between States Parties, they shall be deemed to be included as such therein. States Parties undertake to include those crimes as extraditable offences in every future extradition treaty to be concluded between them.

2. If a State Party which makes extradition conditional on the existence of a treaty receives a request for extradition from another State Party with which it has no extradition treaty, it may, if it decides to extradite, consider this Convention as the legal basis for extradition in respect of those crimes. Extradition shall be subject to the procedural provisions and the other conditions of the law of the requested State.

3. States Parties which do not make extradition conditional on the existence of a treaty shall recognize those crimes as extraditable offences between themselves subject to the procedural provisions and the other conditions of the law of the requested State.

4. Each of the crimes shall be treated, for the purpose of extradition between States Parties, as if it had been committed not only in the place in which it occurred but also in the territories of the States required to establish their jurisdiction in accordance with paragraph 1 of article 3.

Article 9

Any person regarding whom proceedings are being carried out in connexion with any of the crimes set forth in article 2 shall be guaranteed fair treatment at all stages of the proceedings.

Article 10

1. States Parties shall afford one another the greatest measure of assistance in connexion with criminal proceedings brought in respect of the crimes set forth in article 2, including the supply of all evidence at their disposal necessary for the proceedings.

2. The provisions of paragraph 1 of this article shall not affect obligations concerning mutual judicial assistance embodied in any other treaty.

Article 11

The State Party where an alleged offender is prosecuted shall communicate the final outcome of the proceedings to the Secretary-General of the United Nations, who shall transmit the information to the other States Parties.

Article 12

The provisions of this Convention shall not affect the application of the Treaties on Asylum, in force at the date of the adoption of this Convention, as between the States which are parties to those Treaties; but a State Party to this Convention may not invoke those Treaties with respect to another State Party to this Convention which is not a party to those Treaties.

Article 13

1. Any dispute between two or more States Parties concerning the interpretation or application of this Convention which is not settled by negotiation shall, at the request of one of them, be submitted to arbitration. If within six months from the date of the request for arbitration the parties are unable to agree on the organization of the arbitration, any one of those parties may refer the dispute to the International Court of Justice by request in conformity with the Statute of the Court.[2]

2. Each State Party may at the time of signature or ratification of this Convention or accession thereto declare that it does not consider itself bound by paragraph 1 of this article. The other States Parties shall not be bound by paragraph 1 of this article with respect to any State Party which has made such a reservation.

---

2   TS 993; 59 Stat. 1055.

3. Any State Party which has made a reservation in accordance with paragraph 2 of this article may at any time withdraw that reservation by notification to the Secretary-General of the United Nations.

Article 14

This Convention shall be open for signature by all States, until 31 December 1974 at United Nations Headquarters in New York.

Article 15

This Convention is subject to ratification. The instruments of ratification shall be deposited with the Secretary-General of the United Nations.

Article 16

This Convention shall remain open for accession by any State. The instruments of accession shall be deposited with the Secretary-General of the United Nations.

Article 17

1. This Convention shall enter into force on the thirtieth day following the date of deposit of the twenty-second instrument of ratification or accession with the Secretary-General of the United Nations.

2. For each State ratifying or acceding to the Convention after the deposit of the twenty-second instrument of ratification or accession, the Convention shall enter into force on the thirtieth day after deposit by such State of its instrument of ratification or accession.

Article 18

1. Any State Party may denounce this Convention by written notification to the Secretary-General of the United Nations.

2. Denunciation shall take effect six months following the date on which notification is received by the Secretary-General of the United Nations.

Article 19

The Secretary-General of the United Nations shall inform all States, *inter alia*:

(a) of signature to this Convention, of the deposit of instruments of ratification or accession in accordance with articles 14, 15 and 16 and of notifications made under article 18.

(b) of the date on which this Convention will enter into force in accordance with article 17.

CRIMES AGAINST INTERNATIONALLY PROTECTED PERSONS

Article 20

The original of this Convention, of which the Chinese, English, French, Russian and Spanish texts are equally authentic, shall be deposited with the Secretary-General of the United Nations, who shall send certified copies thereof to all States.

IN WITNESS WHEREOF the undersigned, being duly authorized thereto by their respective Governments, have signed this Convention, opened for signature at New York on 14 December 1973.

FOR AFGHANISTAN:
FOR ALBANIA:
FOR ALGERIA:
FOR ARGENTINA:
FOR AUSTRALIA:
FOR AUSTRIA:
FOR THE BAHAMAS:
FOR BAHRAIN:
FOR BANGLADESH:
FOR BARBADOS:
FOR BELGIUM:
FOR BHUTAN:
FOR BOLIVIA:
FOR BOTSWANA:
FOR BRAZIL:
FOR BULGARIA:
  [In translation reads: "With reservation as per art. 13, no.1"]
FOR BURMA:
FOR BURUNDI:
FOR THE BYELORUSSIAN SOVIET SOCIALIST REPUBLIC:
  [In translation reads: "With reservation as per art. 13, no. 1."]
FOR CAMEROON:
FOR CANADA:
FOR THE CENTRAL AFRICAN REPUBLIC:
FOR CHAD:
FOR CHILE:
FOR CHINA:
FOR COLUMBIA:
FOR THE CONGO:
FOR COSTA RICA:
FOR CUBA:
FOR CYPRUS:
FOR CZECHOSLOVAKIA:
FOR DAHOMEY:
FOR THE DEMOCRATIC PEOPLE'S REPUBLIC OF KOREA:
FOR THE DEMOCRATIC REPUBLIC OF VIET-NAM:
FOR DEMOCRATIC YEMEN:
FOR DENMARK:
FOR THE DOMINICAN REPUBLIC:
FOR ECUADOR:
FOR EGYPT:
FOR EL SALVADOR:
FOR EQUATORIAL GUINEA:
FOR ETHIOPIA:
FOR FIJI:
FOR FINLAND:
FOR FRANCE:
FOR GABON:
FOR GAMBIA:
FOR THE GERMAN DEMOCRATIC REPUBLIC:
FOR GERMANY, FEDERAL REPUBLIC OF:
FOR GHANA:
FOR GREECE:
FOR GUATEMALA:
FOR GUINEA:
FOR GUINEA-BISSAU:

CRIMES AGAINST INTERNATIONALLY PROTECTED PERSONS

FOR GUYANA:
FOR HAITI:
FOR THE HOLY SEE:
FOR HONDURAS:
FOR HUNGARY:
FOR ICELAND:
FOR INDIA:
FOR INDONESIA:
FOR IRAN:
FOR IRAQ:
FOR IRELAND:
FOR ISRAEL:
FOR ITALY:
FOR THE IVORY COAST:
FOR JAMAICA:
FOR JAPAN:
FOR JORDAN:
FOR KENYA:
FOR THE KHMER REPUBLIC:
FOR KUWAIT:
FOR LAOS:
FOR LEBANON:
FOR LESOTHO:
FOR LIBERIA:
FOR THE LIBYAN ARAB REPUBLIC:
FOR LIECHTENSTEIN:
FOR LUXEMBOURG:
FOR MADAGASCAR:
FOR MALAWI:
FOR MALAYSIA:
FOR THE MALDIVES:
FOR MALI:
FOR MALTA:
FOR MAURITANIA:
FOR MAURITIUS:
FOR MEXICO:
FOR MONACO:
FOR MONGOLIA:
FOR MOROCCO:
FOR NAURU:

FOR NEPAL:
FOR THE NETHERLANDS:
FOR NEW ZEALAND:
FOR NICARAGUA:
FOR THE NIGER:
FOR NIGERIA:
FOR NORWAY:
FOR OMAN:
FOR PAKISTAN:
FOR PANAMA:
FOR PARAGUAY:
FOR PERU:
FOR THE PHILIPPINES:
FOR POLAND:
FOR PORTUGAL:
FOR QATAR:
FOR THE REPUBLIC OF KOREA:
FOR THE REPUBLIC OF VIET-NAM:
FOR ROMANIA:
FOR RWANDA:
FOR SAN MARINO:
FOR SAUDI ARABIA:
FOR SENEGAL:
FOR SIERRA LEONE:
FOR SINGAPORE:
FOR SOMALIA:
FOR SOUTH AFRICA:
FOR SPAIN:
FOR SWEDEN:
FOR SWITZERLAND:
FOR THE SYRIAN ARAB REPUBLIC:
FOR SRI LANKA:
FOR THE SUDAN:
FOR SWAZILAND:
FOR THAILAND:
FOR TOGO:
FOR TONGA:
FOR TRINIDAD AND TOBAGO:
FOR TUNISIA:

CRIMES AGAINST INTERNATIONALLY PROTECTED PERSONS

FOR TURKEY:

[In translation reads: "With the following reservation: 'A dispute shall be submitted to the International Court of Justice only with the agreement of all parties to the dispute'."]

FOR TURKEY:

FOR UGANDA:

FOR THE UKRAINIAN SOVIET SOCIALIST REPUBLIC:

[In translation reads: "With reservation as per art. 13, no. 1."]

FOR THE UNION OF SOVIET SOCIALIST REPUBLICS:

[In translation reads: "With reservation as per art. 13, no. 1 of the convention."]

FOR THE UNITED ARAB EMIRATES:

FOR THE UNITED KINGDOM OF GREAT BRITAIN AND NORTHERN IRELAND:

FOR THE UNITED REPUBLIC OF TANZANIA:

FOR THE UNITED STATES OF AMERICA:

FOR THE UPPER VOLTA:

FOR URUGUAY:

FOR VENEZUELA:

FOR WESTERN SAMOA:

FOR YEMEN:

FOR YUGOSLAVIA:

FOR ZAIRE:

FOR ZAMBIA:

I hereby certify that the foregoing text is a true copy of the Convention on the prevention and punishment of crimes against internationally protected persons, including diplomatic agents, adopted on 14 December 1973 by resolution 3166 (XXVIII) of the General Assembly of the United Nations, the original of which is deposited with the Secretary-General of the United Nations.

For the Secretary-General:

The Director of the General Legal Division, in charge of the Office of Legal Affairs,

United Nations, New York, 14 March 1975

RESOLUTION 3166 (XXVIII) ADOPTED BY THE GENERAL ASSEMBLY ON 14 DECEMBER 1973[3]

Convention on the Prevention and Punishment of Crimes against Internationally Protected Persons, including Diplomatic Agents

The General Assembly,

Considering that the codification and progressive development of international law contributes to the implementation of the purposes and principles set forth in Articles 1 and 2 of the Charter of the United Nations,

---

3   Text of the resolution as reproduced in the Official Records of the General Assembly, Twenty-eighth Session, Supplement No. 30, p. 146 (see paragraph 6 of the resolution). [Footnote in the original.]

Recalling that in response to the request made in General Assembly resolution 2780 (XXVI) of 3 December 1971, the International Law Commission, at its twenty-fourth session, studied the question of the protection and inviolability of diplomatic agents and other persons entitled to special protection under international law and prepared draft articles on the prevention and punishment of crimes against such persons,

Having considered the draft articles and also the comments and observations thereon submitted by States and by specialized agencies and intergovernmental organizations in response to the invitation made in General Assembly resolution 2926 (XXVII) of 28 November 1972,

Convinced of the importance of securing international agreement on appropriate and effective measures for the prevention and punishment of crimes against diplomatic agents and other internationally protected persons in view of the serious threat to the maintenance and promotion of friendly relations and co-operation among States created by the commission of such crimes.

Having elaborated for that purpose the provisions contained in the Convention annexed hereto,

1. Adopts the Convention on the Prevention and Punishment of Crimes against Internationally Protected Persons, including Diplomatic Agents, annexed to the present resolution;

2. Re-emphasizes the great importance of the rules of international law concerning the inviolability of and special protection to be afforded to internationally protected persons and the obligations of States in relation thereto;

3. Considers that the annexed Convention will enable States to carry out their obligations more effectively;

4. Recognizes also that the provisions of the annexed Convention could not in any way prejudice the exercise of the legitimate right to self-determination and independence in accordance with the purposes and principles of the Charter of the United Nations and the Declaration on Principles of International Law concerning Friendly Relations and Co-operation among States in accordance with the Charter of the United Nations by peoples struggling against colonialism, alien domination, foreign occupation, racial discrimination and apartheid;

5. Invites States to become parties to the annexed Convention;

6. Decides that the present resolution, whose provisions are related to the annexed Convention, shall always be published together with it.

CRIMES AGAINST INTERNATIONALLY PROTECTED PERSONS

States which are currently parties:

Afghanistan
Albania
Algeria
Antigua and Barbuda
Argentina
Armenia
Australia
Austria
Azerbaijan
Bahamas
Barbados
Belarus
Belize
Benin
Bhutan
Bolivia
Bosnia and Herzegovina[1]
Botswana
Brazil
Brunei Darussalam
Bulgaria
Burkina Faso
Burundi
Cameroon
Canada
Cape Verde
Chile
China[2,3]
Colombia
Comoros
Costa Rica
Côte d'Ivoire
Croatia[1]
Cuba
Cyprus
Czech Republic[4]
Democratic People's Republic of Korea
Democratic Republic of the Congo

Denmark[5]
Dominican Republic
Ecuador
Egypt
El Salvador
Equatorial Guinea
Estonia
Ethiopia
Finland
France
Gabon
Georgia
Germany[6,7]
Ghana
Greece
Grenada
Guatemala
Haiti
Honduras
Hungary
Iceland
India
Iran (Islamic Republic of)
Iraq
Israel
Italy
Jamaica
Japan
Jordan
Kazakhstan
Kenya
Kuwait
Kyrgyzstan
Lao People's Democratic Republic
Latvia
Lebanon
Liberia
Libyan Arab Jamahiriya
Liechtenstein

CRIMES AGAINST INTERNATIONALLY PROTECTED PERSONS

Lithuania
Madagascar
Malawi
Malaysia
Maldives
Mali
Malta
Marshall Islands
Mauritania
Mauritius
Mexico
Monaco
Mongolia
Morocco
Mozambique
Nepal
Netherlands[8]
New Zealand[9]
Nicaragua
Niger
Norway
Oman
Pakistan
Palau
Panama
Papua New Guinea Paraguay
Peru
Philippines
Poland
Portugal[3]
Qatar
Republic of Korea
Republic of Moldova
Romania
Russian Federation

Rwanda
Saint Vincent and the Grenadines
Saudi Arabia
Serbia and Montenegro[1]
Seychelles
Sierra Leone
Slovakia[4]
Slovenia[1]
South Africa
Spain
Sri Lanka
Sudan
Swaziland
Sweden
Switzerland
Syrian Arab Republic
Tajikistan
The Former Yugoslav Republic of Macedonia[1]
Togo
Tonga
Trinidad and Tobago
Tunisia
Turkey
Turkmenistan
Uganda
Ukraine
United Arab Emirates
United Kingdom of Great Britain and Northern Ireland[2]
United States of America
Uruguay
Uzbekistan
Viet Nam
Yemen[10]

CRIMES AGAINST INTERNATIONALLY PROTECTED PERSONS

DECLARATIONS

Declarations and Reservations
(Unless otherwise indicated, the declarations and reservations were made upon ratification, accession or succession. For objections thereto see hereinafter.)

Algeria

Reservation:

The Government of the People's Democratic Republic of Algeria does not consider itself bound by the provisions of article 13, paragraph 1, of the Convention on the Prevention and Punishment of Crimes against Internationally Protected Persons, including Diplomatic Agents.

The Government of the People's Democratic Republic of Algeria states that in each individual case, a dispute may be submitted to arbitration or referred to the International Court of Justice only with the consent of all parties to the dispute.

Argentina

In accordance with article 13, paragraph 2, of the Convention, the Argentine Republic declares that it does not consider itself bound by the provisions of article 13, paragraph 1, of the Convention.

Belarus

Reservation made upon signature and confirmed upon ratification:

The Byelorussian Soviet Socialist Republic does not consider itself bound by the provisions of article 13, paragraph 1, of the Convention, under which any dispute between two or more States Parties concerning the interpretation or application of the Convention shall, at the request of one of them, be submitted to arbitration or to the International Court of Justice, and states that, in each individual case, the consent of all parties to such a dispute is necessary for submission of the dispute to arbitration or to the International Court of Justice.

Brazil

Reservation:

With the reservation provided for in paragraph 2 of article 13.

Bulgaria[11]

Burundi[12]

In respect of cases where the alleged offenders belong to a national liberation movement recognized by Burundi or by an international organization of which Burundi is a member, and their actions are part of their struggle for liberation, the Government of the Republic of Burundi reserves the right not to apply to them the provisions of article 2, paragraph 2, and article 6, paragraph 1.

China

[The People's Republic of China] declares that, in accordance with paragraph 2 of article 13 of the Convention, the People's Republic of China has reservations on paragraph 1 of article 13 of the Convention and does not consider itself bound by the provisions of the said paragraph.

Colombia[13]

Reservations:

...

3. Colombia enters a reservation to those provisions of the Convention, which are contrary to the guiding principles of the Colombian Penal Code and to article 29 of the Political Constitution of Colombia, the fourth paragraph of which states that:

Everyone shall be presumed innocent until proven guilty according to law. Anyone who is charged with an offence shall be entitled to defence and the assistance of counsel of his own choosing, or one appointed by the court, during the investigation and trial; to be tried properly, in public without undue delay; to present evidence and to refute evidence brought against him; to contest the sentence; and not to be tried twice for the same act.

Consequently, the expression "Alleged offender" shall be taken to mean "the accused".

Cuba

Declaration:

In accordance with article 13, paragraph 2 of the Convention, the Republic of Cuba declares that it does not consider itself bound by the provisions of article 13, paragraph 1, of the Convention.

Czech Republic[3]

Democratic People's Republic of Korea

Reservation:

The Government of the Democratic People's Republic of Korea does not consider itself bound by the provisions of article 13, paragraph 1, of the Convention, recognizing that any dispute between two or more States Parties concerning the interpretation or application of the Convention should not, without consent of both parties, be submitted to international arbitration and to the International Court of Justice.

Democratic Republic of the Congo

The Republic of Zaire does not consider itself bound by the provisions of article 13, paragraph 1, of the Convention, under which any dispute between two or more Contracting Parties concerning the interpretation or application of the Convention which is not settled by negotiation shall, at the request of one of them, be submitted to arbitration or referred to the International Court of Justice. In the light of its policy based on respect for the sovereignty of States, the Republic of Zaire is opposed to any form of compulsory arbitration and hopes that such disputes may be submitted to arbitration or referred to the International Court of Justice not at the request of one of the parties but with the consent of all the interested parties.

Ecuador

Upon signature:

Ecuador wishes to avail itself of the provisions of article 13, paragraph 2, of the Convention, declaring that it does not consider itself bound to refer disputes concerning the application of the Convention to the International Court of Justice.

El Salvador

The State of El Salvador does not consider itself bound by paragraph 1 of article 13 of the Convention.

CRIMES AGAINST INTERNATIONALLY PROTECTED PERSONS

Ethiopia

Reservation pursuant to article 13 (2):

"The Government of the Federal Democratic Republic of Ethiopia does not consider itself bound by the aforementioned provision of the Convention, under which any dispute between two or more States Parties concerning the interpretation or application of the Convention shall, at the request of one of them, be submitted to arbitration or to the International Court of Justice, and states that disputes concerning the interpretation or application of the Convention would be submitted to arbitration or to the Court only with the prior consent of all the parties concerned."

Finland

Reservation made upon signature and confirmed upon ratification:

"Finland reserves the right to apply the provision of article 8, paragraph 3, in such a way that extradition shall be restricted to offences which, under Finnish Law, are punishable by a penalty more severe than imprisonment for one year and, provided also that other conditions in the Finnish Legislation for extradition are fulfilled."

Declaration made upon signature:

"Finland also reserves the right to make such other reservations as it may deem appropriate if and when ratifying this Convention."

France

Déclarations:

France understands that only acts which may be defined as acts of terrorism constitute crimes within the meaning of article 2 of the Convention.

The application of the Convention shall be without prejudice to the Convention adopted at New York on 9 December 1994 on the Safety of United Nations and Associated Personnel.

Germany[6]

Upon signature:

"The Federal Republic of Germany reserves the right, upon ratifying this Convention, to state its views on the explanations of vote and declarations made by other States upon signing or ratifying or acceding to that Convention and to make reservations regarding certain provisions of the said Convention."

Ghana[14]

"(i) Paragraph 1 of article 13 of the Convention provides that disputes may be submitted to arbitration, failing which any of the parties to the dispute may refer it to the International Court of Justice by request. Since Ghana is opposed to any form of compulsory arbitration, she wishes to exercise her option under article 13 (2) to make a reservation on article 13 (1). It is noted that such a reservation can be withdrawn later under article 13 (3)."

Hungary[15]

India

"The Government of the Republic of India does not consider itself bound by paragraph 1 of article 13 which establishes compulsory arbitration or adjudication by the International Court of Justice concerning disputes between two or more States Parties relating to the interpretation or application of this Convention."

Iraq[12,16]

(1) The resolution of the United Nations General Assembly with which the above-mentioned Convention is enclosed shall be considered to be an integral part of the above-mentioned Convention.

(2) Sub-paragraph (b) of paragraph (1) of article 1 of the Convention shall cover the representatives of the national liberation movements recognized by the League of Arab States or the Organization of African Unity.

(3) The Republic of Iraq shall not bind itself by paragraph (1) of article 13 of the Convention.

(4) The accession of the Government of the Republic of Iraq to the Convention shall in no way constitute a recognition of Israel or a cause for the establishment of any relations of any kind therewith.

Israel[17]

Declarations:

"The Government of the State of Israel declares that its accession to the Convention does not constitute acceptance by it as binding of the provisions of any other international instrument, or acceptance by it of any other international instrument as being an instrument related to the Convention.

The Government of Israel reaffirms the contents of its communication of 11 May 1979 to the Secretary-General of the United Nations."

Reservation:

"The State of Israel does not consider itself bound by paragraph 1 of article 13 of the Convention."

Jamaica

"Jamaica avails itself of the provisions of article 13, paragraph 2, and declares that it does not consider itself bound by the provisions of paragraph 1 of this article under which any dispute between two or more States Parties concerning the interpretation or application of this Convention shall, at the request of one of them, be submitted to arbitration or referred to the International Court of Justice, and states that in each individual case, the consent of all parties to such a dispute is necessary for the submission of the dispute to arbitration or to the International Court of Justice."

Jordan[16]

Reservation:

The Government of the Hashemite Kingdom of Jordan declares that its accession [. . .] cannot give rise to relations with "Israel".

Kuwait[16]

Declaration:

[The Government of Kuwait] wishes to reiterate Kuwait's complete reservation on paragraph 1 of article 13 in the Convention, for its accession to it does not mean in any way a recognition of Israel by the Government of the State of Kuwait and does not engage them into any treaty relations as a result.

Lao People's Democratic Republic

Reservation:

"In accordance with paragraph 2, Article 13 of the Convention on the Prevention and Punishment of Crimes Against Internationally Protected Persons, including Diplomatic Agents, the Lao People's Democratic Republic does not consider itself bound by paragraph 1, article 13 of the present Convention. The Lao People's Democratic Republic declares that to refer to a dispute relating to interpretation and application of the present Convention to arbitration or International Court of Justice, the agreement of all parties concerned in the dispute is necessary."

Liechtenstein

Interpretative declaration:

The Principality of Liechtenstein construes articles 4 and 5, paragraph 1 of the Convention, to mean that the Principality of Liechtenstein undertakes to fulfil the obligations contained therein under the conditions laid down in its domestic legislation.

Lithuania

Reservation:

" . . . Whereas it is provided in paragraph 2 of Article 13 of the said Convention, the Seimas of the Republic of Lithuania declares that the Republic of Lithuania does not consider itself bound by paragraph 1 of Article 13 of the said Convention, providing that any dispute concerning the interpretation or application of this Convention shall be referred to the International Court of Justice."

Malawi

"The Government of the Republic of Malawi [declares], in accordance with the provisions of paragraph 2 of article 13, that it does not consider itself bound by the provisions of paragraph 1 of article 13 of the Convention."

Malaysia

Declarations:

"1. The Government of Malaysia understands the phrase "alleged offender" in Article 1(2) of the Convention to mean the accused.

2. The Government of Malaysia understands the phrase "or other attack" in Article 2(1)(a) of the Convention to mean acts that are recognized as offences under its domestic laws.

3. The Government of Malaysia understands Article 7 of the Convention to include the right of the competent authorities to decide not to submit any particular case for prosecution before the judicial authorities if the alleged offender is dealt with under national security and preventive detention laws.

4. (a) Pursuant to Article 13(2) of the Convention, the Government of Malaysia declares that it does not consider itself bound by Article 13(l) of the Convention; and

(b) the Government of Malaysia reserves the right specifically to agree in a particular case to follow the arbitration procedure set forth in Article 13(l) of the Convention or any other procedure for arbitration."

Mauritius

Reservation:

"In accordance with Article 13, paragraph 2, of the Convention on the Prevention and Punishment of Crimes against Internationally Protected Persons, including Diplomatic Agents, the Republic of Mauritius hereby declares that it does not consider itself bound by the provisions of Article 13, paragraph 1, of the Convention, and states that it considers that a dispute may be submitted or referred to the International Court of Justice only with the consent of all parties to the dispute."

Declaration:

"The Republic of Mauritius rejects the extension of the Convention by the Government of the United Kingdom and Northern Ireland to the Chagos Archipelago (so-called British Indian Ocean Territory) and reaffirms its sovereignty over the Chagos Archipelago which forms part of its national territory."

Mongolia

Declaration made upon signature and renewed upon ratification:

"The Mongolian People's Republic does not consider itself bound by the provisions of article 13, paragraph 1, of the Convention, under which any dispute between two or more States Parties of the Convention shall, at the request of one of them, be submitted to arbitration or to the International Court of Justice, and states that, in each individual case, the consent of all parties to such a dispute is necessary for submission of the dispute to arbitration or to the International Court of Justice."

Mozambique

Declaration:

" . . . with the following declaration in accordance with its article 13, paragraph 2:

"The Republic of Mozambique does not consider itself bound by the provisions of article 13, paragraph 1 of the Convention.

In this connection, the Republic of Mozambique states that, in each individual case, the consent of all Parties to such a dispute is necessary for the submission of the dispute to arbitration or to [the] International Court of Justice.

Furthermore, the Republic of Mozambique declares that: The Republic of Mozambique, in accordance with its Constitution and domestic laws, can not extradite Mozambique citizens.

Therefore, Mozambique citizens will be tried and sentenced in national courts."

Netherlands

Declaration:

"In view of the Government of the Kingdom of the Netherlands article 12 of the Convention, and in particular the second sentence of that Article, in no way affects the applicability of article 33 of the Convention of 28 July 1951 relating to the Status of Refugees".

Reservation:

"In cases where the judicial authorities of either the Netherlands, the Netherlands Antilles or Aruba cannot exercise jurisdiction pursuant to one of the principles mentioned in article 3, para. 1, the Kingdom accepts the aforesaid obligation [laid down in article 7] subject to the condition that it has received and rejected a request for extradition from another State party to the Convention."

New Zealand[8]

Reservation:

The Government of New Zealand reserves the right not to apply the provisions of the Convention to Tokelau pending the enactment of the necessary implementing legislation in Tokelau law.

Pakistan

"Pakistan shall not be bound by paragraph 1 of article 13 of the Convention".

Peru

With reservation as to article 13 (1).

CRIMES AGAINST INTERNATIONALLY PROTECTED PERSONS

Poland[18]

Portugal

Reservation:

> Portugal does not extradite anyone for crimes which carry the death penalty or life imprisonment under the law of the requesting State nor does it extradite anyone for violations which carry security measure for life.

Romania

Reservation made upon signature and confirmed upon ratification:

> The Socialist Republic of Romania declares that it does not consider itself bound by the provisions of article 13, paragraph 1, of the Convention, under which any dispute between two or more Contracting Parties concerning the interpretation or application of the Convention which is not settled by negotiation shall, at the request of one of them, be submitted to arbitration or referred to the International Court of Justice.
>
> The Socialist Republic of Romania considers that such disputes may be submitted to arbitration or referred to the International Court of Justice only with the consent of all parties to the dispute in each individual case.

Russian Federation

Reservation made upon signature and confirmed upon ratification:

> The Union of Soviet Socialist Republics does not consider itself bound by the provisions of article 13, paragraph 1, of the Convention, under which any dispute between two or more States Parties concerning the interpretation or application of the Convention shall, at the request of one of them, be submitted to arbitration or to the International Court of Justice, and states that, in each individual case, the consent of all parties to such a dispute is necessary for submission of the dispute to arbitration or to the International Court of Justice.

Saint Vincent and the Grenadines

Declaration:

> "Saint Vincent and the Grenadines avails itself of the provisions of article 13, paragraph 2 of the aforesaid Convention and declares that it does not consider itself bound by the provisions of paragraph 1 of that article under which any dispute between two or more States Parties concerning the interpretation or application of this Convention shall, at the request of one of them, be submitted to arbitration or referred to the International Court of Justice, and states that in each individual case, the consent of all Parties to such a dispute is necessary for the submission of the dispute to arbitration or to the International Court of Justice."

Saudi Arabia

Reservation:

> ... the Kingdom of Saudi Arabia does not consider itself obligated to observe paragraph 1 of Article 13 which deals with resolving any dispute arising from interpretation or implementation of the Convention .

Slovakia[3]

Switzerland

Declaration:

> The Swiss Federal Council interprets article 4 and article 5, paragraph 1, of the Convention to mean that Switzerland undertakes to fulfil the obligations contained therein in the conditions specified by its domestic legislation.

Syrian Arab Republic[16]

Declaration:

1. The Syrian Arab Republic does not consider itself bound by the provisions of article 13, paragraph 1, of the Convention, concerning arbitration and the results thereof.

2. Accession of the Syrian Arab Republic to this Convention in no way implies recognition of Israel or entry into any relations with Israel concerning any question regulated by this Convention.

Trinidad and Tobago

"The Republic of Trinidad and Tobago avails itself of the provisions of article 13, paragraph 2, and declares that it does not consider itself bound by the provisions of paragraph 1 of that article under which any dispute between two or more States Parties concerning the interpretation or application of this Convention shall, at the request of one of them, be submitted to arbitration or referred to the International Court of Justice, and states that in each individual case, the consent of all Parties to such a dispute is necessary for the submission of the dispute to arbitration or to the International Court of Justice."

Tunisia

Reservation made upon signature and confirmed upon ratification:

No dispute may be brought before the International Court of Justice unless by agreement between all parties to the dispute.

Ukraine

Reservation made upon signature and confirmed upon ratification:

The Ukrainian Soviet Socialist Republic does not consider it self bound by the provisions of article 13, paragraph 1, of the Convention, under which any dispute between two or more States Parties concerning the interpretation or application of the Convention shall, at the request of one of them, be submitted to arbitration or to the International Court of Justice, and states that, in each individual case, the consent of all parties to such a dispute is necessary for submission of the dispute to arbitration or to the International Court of Justice.

Viet Nam

Reservation:

"Acceding to this Convention, the Socialist Republic of Viet Nam makes its reservation to paragraph 1 of article 13 of the Convention."

Yemen[10,16]

Reservation:

In acceding to this Convention, the People's Democratic Republic of Yemen does not consider itself bound by article 13, paragraph 1, of the Convention, which states that disputes between States parties concerning the interpretation or application of this Convention may, at the request of anyone of the parties to the dispute, be referred to the International Court of Justice. It declares that the competence of the International Court of Justice with respect to disputes concerning the interpretation or application of the Convention shall in each case be subject to the express consent of all parties to the dispute.

Declaration

The People's Democratic Republic of Yemen declares that its accession to this Convention shall in no way signify recognition of Israel or serve as grounds for the establishment of relations of any sort with Israel.

CRIMES AGAINST INTERNATIONALLY PROTECTED PERSONS

Objections
(Unless otherwise indicated, the objections were made upon ratification, accession or succession.)

Germany[6]

30 November 1979

The statement by the Republic of Iraq on sub-paragraph (b) of paragraph (1) of article 1 of the Convention does not have any legal effects for the Federal Republic of Germany.

25 March 1981

The Government of the Federal Republic of Germany considers the reservation made by the Government of Burundi concerning article 2, paragraph 2, and article 6, paragraph 1, of the Convention on the Prevention and Punishment of Crimes against Internationally Protected Persons, including Diplomatic Agents, to be incompatible with the object and purpose of the Convention.

Israel

"The Government of the State of Israel does not regard as valid the reservation made by Iraq in respect of paragraph (1) (b) of article 1 of the said Convention."

28 June 1982

"The Government of the State of Israel regards the reservation entered by the Government of Burundi as incompatible with the object and purpose of the Convention and is unable to consider Burundi as having validly acceded to the Convention until such time as the reservation is withdrawn.

"In the view of the Government of Israel, the purpose of this Convention was to secure the world-wide repression of crimes against internationally protected persons, including diplomatic agents, and to deny the perpetrators of such crimes a safe haven."

Italy

(a) The Italian Government does not consider as valid the reservation made by Iraq on 28 February 1978 with regard to article 1, paragraph 1(b), of the said Convention;

(b) With regard to the reservation expressed by Burundi on 17 December 1980, [the Italian Government considers that] the purpose of the Convention is to ensure the punishment, world-wide, of crimes against internationally protected persons, including diplomatic agents, and to deny a safe haven to the perpetrators of such crimes. Considering therefore that the reservation expressed by the Government of Burundi is incompatible with the aim and purpose of the Convention, the Italian Government can not consider Burundi's accession to the Convention as valid as long as it does not withdraw that reservation.

United Kingdom of Great Britain and Northern Ireland

"The Government of the United Kingdom of Great Britain and Northern Ireland do not regard as valid the reservation made by Iraq in respect of paragraph (1) (b) of article 1 of the said Convention."

15 January 1982

"The purpose of this Convention was to secure the world-wide repression of crimes against internationally protected persons, including diplomatic agents, and to deny the perpetrators of such crimes a safe haven. Accordingly the Government of the United Kingdom of Great Britain and Northern Ireland regard the reservation entered by the Government of Burundi as incompatible with the object and purpose of the Convention, and are unable to consider Burundi as having validly acceded to the Convention until such time as the reservation is withdrawn."

CRIMES AGAINST INTERNATIONALLY PROTECTED PERSONS

Territorial Application

United Kingdom[2,19,20,21]

Bailiwick of Jersey, Bailiwick of Guernsey, Isle of Man, Belize, Bermuda, British Antarctic Territory, British Indian Ocean Territory, British Virgin Islands, Cayman Islands, Falkland Islands and Dependencies, Gibraltar, Gilbert Islands, Hong Kong, Montserrat, the Pitcairn, Henderson, Ducie and Oeno Islands, Saint Helena and Dependencies, Turks and Caicos Islands, United Kingdom Sovereign Base Areas of Akrotiri and Dhekelia in the Island of Cyprus. Anguilla

NOTES

1. The former Yugoslavia had signed and ratified the Convention on 17 December 1974 and 29 December 1976, respectively. See also note 1 under "Bosnia and Herzegovina", "Croatia", "former Yugoslavia", "The Former Yugoslav Republic of Macedonia" and "Yugoslavia" in the "Historical Information" section in the front matter of this volume.

2. The Secretary-General received, on 6 and 10 June 1999, communications concerning the status of Hong Kong from China and the United Kingdom (see also note 2 under "China" and note 2 under "United Kingdom of Great Britain and Northern Ireland" regarding Hong Kong in the "Historical Information" section in the front matter of this volume). Upon resuming the exercise of sovereignty over Hong Kong, China notified the Secretary-General that the Convention with reservation will also apply to the Hong Kong Special Administrative Region.

3. On 11 August 1999, the Government of Portugal informed the Secretary-General that the Convention will apply to Macao. Subsequently, the Secretary-General received, on 18 November 1999 and 13 December 1999, communications concerning the status of Macao from Portugal and China (see also note 3 under "China" and note 1 under "Portugal" regarding Macao in the "Historical Information" section in the front matter of this volume). Upon resuming the exercise of sovereignty over Macao, China notified the Secretary-General that the Convention with reservation will also apply to the Macao Special Administrative Region.

4. Czechoslovakia had signed and ratified the Convention on 11 October 1974 and 30 June 1975, respectively, with a reservation. Subsequently, by a notification received on 26 April 1991, the Government of Czechoslovakia notified the Secretary-General of its decision to withdraw the reservation to article 13 (1) made upon ratification. For the text of the reservation, see United Nations, Treaty Series, vol. 1035, p. 234. See also note 1 under "Czech Republic" and note 1 under "Slovakia" in the "Historical Information" section in the front matter of this volume.

5. In a notification received on 12 March 1980, the Government of Denmark informed the Secretary-General that it had decided to withdraw the reservation made upon ratification of the Convention, which specified that until further decision, the Convention would not apply to the Faeroe Islands or to Greenland. The notification indicates 1 April 1980 as the effective date of withdrawal.

6. The German Democratic Republic had signed and ratified the Convention, with reservation, on 23 May 1974 and 30 November 1976, respectively. For the text of the reservation, see United Nations, Treaty Series, vol. 1035, p. 230. See note 2 under "Germany" in the "Historical Information" section in the front matter of this volume.

7. See note 1 under "Germany" regarding Berlin (West) in the "Historical Information" section in the front matter of this volume.

8. For the Kingdom in Europe, the Netherlands Antilles and Aruba.

9. The instrument of accession specifies that the Convention will also apply to the Cook Islands and Niue. See also note 1 under "New Zealand" regarding Tokelau in the "Historical Information" section in the front matter of this volume.

10. The formality was effected by Democratic Yemen. See also note 1 under "Yemen" in the "Historical Information" section in the front matter of this volume.

11. On 24 June 1992, the Government of Bulgaria notified the Secretary-General of its decision to withdraw the reservation to article 13 (1) of the Convention, made upon signature and renewed upon ratification. For the text of the declaration, see United Nations, Treaty Series, vol. 1035, p. 228.

12. Upon depositing its instrument of accession, the Government of France made the following declaration with regard to declarations made by the following States:

Burundi upon accession:

France objects to the declaration made by Burundi on 17 December 1980 limiting the application of the provisions of article 2, paragraph 2 and article 6, paragraph 1.

Iraq upon accession:

France contests the interpretation made by Iraq on 28 February 1978 that the resolution of the United Nations General Assembly with which the above-mentioned Convention is enclosed should be considered to be an integral part of the Convention, and objects to Iraq's reservation relating to article 1, paragraph 1 (b) of the Convention.

13. On 1 March 2002, the Government of Colombia informed the Secretary-General that it had decided to withdraw the following reservations made upon accession:

1. Colombia enters a reservation to those provisions of the Convention, and particularly to article 8 (1), (2), (3) and (4) thereof, which are inconsistent with article 35 of the Basic Law in force which states that: Native-born Colombians may not be extradited. Aliens will not be extradited for political crimes or for their opinions. Any Colombian who has committed, abroad, crimes that are considered as such under national legislation, shall be tried and sentenced in Colombia.

2. Colombia enters a reservation to article 13 (1) of the Convention, inasmuch as it is contrary to the provisions of article 35 of its Political Constitution.

14. In a notification received on 18 November 1976, the Government of Ghana informed the Secretary-General that it had decided to withdraw the reservation contained in its instrument of accession, concerning article 3 (1)(c) of the Convention. For the text of the reservation, see United Nations, Treaty Series, vol. 1035, p. 235.

15. In a communication received on 8 December 1989, the Government of Hungary notified the Secretary-General that it had decided to withdraw the reservation in respect to article 13 (1) of the Convention made upon ratification. For the text of the reservation, see United Nations, Treaty Series, vol. 1035, p. 235.

16. The Secretary-General received on 11 May 1979 from the Government of Israel the following communication:

"The instrument deposited by the Government of Iraq contains a statement of a political character in respect to Israel. In the view of the Government of Israel, this is not the proper place for making such political pronouncements, which are, moreover, in flagrant contradiction to the principles, objects and purposes of the Organization. That pronouncement by the Government of Iraq cannot in any way affect whatever obligations are binding upon it under general international law or under particular treaties.

"The Government of Israel will, insofar as concerns the substance of the matter, adopt towards the Government of Iraq an attitude of complete reciprocity."

Identical communications, in essence, mutatis mutandis have been received by the Secretary-General from the Government of Israel on 11 March 1985 in respect of the reservation made by Jordan; on 21 August 1987 in respect of the declaration by Democratic Yemen; on 26 July 1988 in respect of the declaration made by the Syrian Arab Republic; and on 17 May 1989 in respect of the declaration made by Kuwait.

17. The communication of 11 May 1979 referred to in the second paragraph of the declaration made by Israel upon accession to the Convention, refers to the communication made with respect to the reservation made by Iraq upon its accession to the Convention. See note 14 in this chapter.

18. On 16 October 1997, the Government of Poland notified the Secretary-General that it had decided to withdraw its reservation with regard to article 13, paragraph 1 of the Convention made upon ratification. For the text of the reservation see United Nations, Treaty Series, vol. 1295, p. 394.

19. The Secretary-General received, on 25 May 1979 from the Government of Guatemala, the following communication:

> The Government of Guatemala [does] not accept [the extension by the United Kingdom of the Convention to the Territory of Belize] in view of the fact the said Territory is a territory concerning which a dispute exists and to which [Guatemala] maintains a claim that is the subject, by mutual agreement, of procedures for the peaceful settlement of disputes between the two Governments concerned.

In this respect, the Government of the United Kingdom of Great Britain and Northern Ireland in a communication received by the Secretary-General on 12 November 1979, stated the following:

> "The Government of the United Kingdom of Great Britain and Northern Ireland have no doubt as to their sovereignty over Belize and do not accept the reservation submitted by the Government of Guatemala."

20. On 3 October 1983, the Secretary-General received from the Government of Argentina the following objection:

> [The Government of Argentina makes a] formal objection to the [declaration] of territorial extension issued by the United Kingdom with regard to the Malvinas Islands [and dependencies], which that country is illegally occupying and refers to as the "Falkland Islands".

The Argentine Republic rejects and considers null and void the [said declaration] of territorial extension.

With reference to the above-mentioned objection, the Secretary-General received, on 28 February 1985, from the Government of the United Kingdom of Great Britain and Northern Ireland the following declaration:

> "The Government of the United Kingdom of Great Britain and Northern Ireland have no doubt as to their right, by notification to the Depositary under the relevant provisions of the above-mentioned Convention, to extend the application of the Convention in question to the Falkland Islands or to the Falkland Islands Dependencies, as the case may be.
>
> For this reason alone, the Government of the United Kingdom are unable to regard the Argentine [communication] under reference as having any legal effect."

21. The Government of the United Kingdom specified that the application of the Convention had been extended to Anguilla as from 26 March 1987.

CONVENTION ON THE PHYSICAL PROTECTION OF NUCLEAR MATERIAL

COMMENTARY

In a sense, the nations of the world moved (with a measured step) to ensure that international agreements relating to terrorism covered evolving threats prompted by scientific advances. This Convention, in large part, addresses the realization that nuclear proliferation opens the way for innovative and horrific terrorist attacks.

Apart from outlining requirements for the acquisition, transportation, and storage of nuclear materials, the Convention also defines (in Article 7) the unlawful acts which will be made punishable by each State under its national law. These offences include theft, robbery, or embezzlement to fraudulently obtain nuclear material and (for more direct relevance to terrorism):

"(e) A threat:

(i) To use nuclear material to cause death or serious injury to any person or substantial property damage, or

(ii) To commit an offence described in sub-paragraph (b) in order to compel a natural or legal person, international organization or State to do or to refrain from doing any act"

or an attempt to commit one of these offences.

The full text of the President's Message sending this Convention to the Senate follows:

"To the Senate of the United States:

I submit herewith, for Senate advice and consent to ratification, the Convention on the Physical Protection of Nuclear Material. This Convention was adopted at a Vienna meeting of government representatives on October 26, 1979, and was signed by the United States on March 3, 1980. The Convention establishes an international framework for improving the physical pro-

PHYSICAL PROTECTION OF NUCLEAR MATERIAL

tection of nuclear material during international transport as well as for international cooperation in recovering stolen nuclear material and in responding to serious offenses involving nuclear material.

The United States has been a leader in the international campaign to prevent the proliferation of nuclear explosive devices. The Congress and I have cooperated in enacting the Nuclear Non-Proliferation Act of 1978 to strengthen this critically important effort.

The Convention on the Physical Protection of Nuclear Material was a United States initiative called for by that Act. It complements our non-proliferation efforts by dealing with threats to nuclear material that may arise from terrorist groups. This is a gap in the current international structure, and I urge the Senate to act expeditiously in giving its advice and consent to ratification. I also transmit herewith, for the information of the Senate, the report of the Department of State concerning the Convention.

Jimmy Carter

The White House
May 9, 1980"

CONVENTION ON THE PHYSICAL PROTECTION OF NUCLEAR MATERIAL

Adopted at Vienna on 26 October 1979
Entered into force 8 February 1987*

THE STATES PARTIES TO THIS CONVENTION,

Recognizing the right of all States to develop and apply nuclear energy for peaceful purposes and their legitimate interests in the potential benefits to be derived from the peaceful application of nuclear energy.

Convinced of the need for facilitating international co-operation in the peaceful application of nuclear energy,

Desiring to avert the potential dangers posed by the unlawful taking and use of nuclear material,

Convinced that offences relating to nuclear material are a matter of grave concern and that there is an urgent need to adopt appropriate and effective measures to ensure the prevention, detection and punishment of such offences.

Aware of the Need for international co-operation to establish, in conformity with the national law of each State Party and with this Convention, effective measures for the physical protection of nuclear material,

Convinced that this Convention should facilitate the safe transfer of nuclear material.

Stressing also the importance of the physical protection of nuclear material in domestic use, storage and transport,

Recognizing the importance of effective physical protection of nuclear material used for military purposes, and understanding that such material is and will continue to be accorded stringent physical protection,

---

* Treaties and International Agreements Online, CTIA 8375.000 (Oceana Publications, Inc. <www.oceanalaw.com>.

HAVE AGREED as follows:

Article 1

For the purposes of this Convention:

(a) "nuclear material" means plutonium except that with isotopic concentration exceeding 80% in plutonium-238; uranium-233; uranium enriched in the isotopes 235 or 233; uranium containing the mixture of isotopes as occurring in nature other than in the form of ore or ore-residue; any material containing one or more of the foregoing;

(b) "uranium enriched in the 235 or 233" means uranium containing the isotopes 235 or 233 or both in an amount such that the abundance ratio of the sum of these isotopes to the isotope 238 is greater than the ratio of the isotope 235 to the isotope 238 occurring in nature;

(c) "international nuclear transport" means the carriage of a consignment of nuclear material by any means of transportation intended to go beyond the territory of the State where the shipment originates beginning with the departure from a facility of the shipper in that State and ending with the arrival at a facility of the receiver within the State of ultimate destination.

Article 2

1. The Convention shall apply to nuclear material used for peaceful purposes while in international nuclear transport.

2. With the exception of articles 3 and 4 and paragraph 3 of article 5, this Convention shall also apply to nuclear material used for peaceful purposes while in domestic use, storage and transport.

3. Apart from the commitments expressly undertaken by States Parties in the articles covered by paragraph 2 with respect to nuclear material used for peaceful purposes while in domestic use, storage and transport, nothing in this Convention shall be interpreted as affecting the sovereign rights of a State regarding the domestic use, storage and transport of such nuclear material.

Article 3

Each State Party shall take appropriate steps within the framework of its national law and consistent with international law to ensure as far as practicable that, during international nuclear transport, nuclear material within its territory, or on board a ship or aircraft under its jurisdiction insofar as such ship or aircraft is engaged in the transport to or from that State, is protected at the levels described in Annex I.

Article 4

1. Each State Party shall not export or authorize the export of nuclear material unless the State Party has received assurances that such material will be protected during the international nuclear transport at the levels described in Annex I.

2. Each State Party shall not import or authorize the import of nuclear material from a State not party to this Convention unless the State Party has received assurances that such material will during the international nuclear transport be protected at the levels described in Annex I.

3. A State Party shall not allow the transit of its territory by land or internal waterways or through its airports or seaports of nuclear material between States that are not parties to this Convention unless the State Party has received assurances as far as practicable that this nuclear material will be protected during international nuclear transport at the levels described in Annex I.

4. Each State Party shall apply within the framework of its national law the levels of physical protection described in Annex I to nuclear material being transported from a part of that State to another part of the same State through international waters or airspace.

5. The State Party responsible for receiving assurances that the nuclear material will be protected at the levels described in Annex I according to paragraphs 1 to 3 shall identify and inform in advance States which the nuclear material is expected to transit by land or internal waterways, or whose airports or seaports it is expected to enter.

6. The responsibility for obtaining assurances referred to in paragraph 1 may be transferred, by mutual agreement, to the State Party involved in the transport as the importing State.

7. Nothing in this article shall be interpreted as in any way affecting the territorial sovereignty and jurisdiction of a State, including that over its airspace and territorial sea.

Article 5

1. States Parties shall identify and make known to each other directly or through the International Atomic Energy Agency their central authority and point of contact having responsibility for physical protection of nuclear material and for co-ordinating recovery and response operations in the event of any unauthorized removal, use or alteration of nuclear material or in the event of credible threat thereof.

2. In the case of theft, robbery or any other unlawful taking of nuclear material or of credible threat thereof, States Parties shall, in accordance with their national law, provide co-operation and assistance to the maximum

feasible extent in the recovery and protection of such material to any State that so requests. In particular:

(a) a State Party shall take appropriate steps to inform as soon as possible other States, which appear to it to be concerned, of any theft, robbery or other unlawful taking of nuclear material or credible threat thereof and to inform, where appropriate, international organizations;

(b) as appropriate, the States Parties concerned shall exchange information with each other or international organizations with a view to protecting threatened nuclear material, verifying the integrity of the shipping container, or recovering unlawfully taken nuclear material and shall:

(i) co-ordinate their efforts through diplomatic and other agreed channels;

(ii) render assistance, if requested; (iii) ensure the return of nuclear material stolen or missing as a consequence of the above-mentioned events. The means of implementation of this co-operation shall be determined by the States Parties concerned.

3. States Parties shall co-operate and consult as appropriate, with each other directly or through international organizations, with a view to obtaining guidance on the design, maintenance and improvement of systems of physical protection of nuclear material in international transport.

Article 6

1. States Parties shall take appropriate measures consistent with their national law to protect the confidentiality of any information which they receive in confidence by virtue of the provisions of this Convention from another State Party or through participation in an activity carried out for the implementation of this Convention. If States Parties provide information to international organizations in confidence, steps shall be taken to ensure that the confidentiality of such information is protected.

2. States Parties shall not be required by this Convention to provide any information which they are not permitted to communicate pursuant to national law or which would jeopardize the security of the State concerned or the physical protection of nuclear material.

Article 7

1. The intentional commission of:

(a) an act without lawful authority which constitutes the receipt, possession, use, transfer, alteration, disposal or dispersal of nuclear material and which causes or is likely to cause death or serious injury to any person or substantial damage to property;

(b) a theft or robbery of nuclear material;

(c) an embezzlement or fraudulent obtaining of nuclear material;

(d) an act constituting a demand for nuclear material by threat or use of force or by any other form of intimidation;

(e) a threat:

(i) to use nuclear material to cause death or serious injury to any person or substantial property damage, or

(ii) to commit an offense described in subparagraph (b) in order to compel a natural or legal person, international organization or State to do or to refrain from doing any act;

(f) an attempt to commit any offense described in paragraphs (a), (b) or (c); and

(g) an act which constitutes participation in any offense described in paragraphs (a) to (f)

shall be made a punishable offense by each State Party under its national law.

2. Each State Party shall make the offenses described in this article, punishable by appropriate penalties which take into account their grave nature.

Article 8

1. Each State Party shall take such measures as may be necessary to establish its jurisdiction over the offenses set forth in article 7 in the following cases:

(a) when the offense is committed in the territory of that State or on board a ship or aircraft registered in that State;

(b) when the alleged offender is a national of that State.

2. Each State Party shall likewise take such measures as may be necessary to establish its jurisdiction over these offenses in cases where the alleged offender is present in its territory and it does not extradite him pursuant to article 11 to any of the States mentioned in paragraph 1.

3. This Convention does not exclude any criminal jurisdiction exercised in accordance with national law.

4. In addition to the State Parties mentioned in paragraph 1 and 2, each State Party may, consistent with international law, establish its jurisdiction over the offenses set forth in article 7 when it is involved in international nuclear transport as the exporting or importing State.

Article 9

Upon being satisfied that the circumstances so warrant, the State Party in whose territory the alleged offender is present shall take appropriate measures, including detention, under its national law to ensure his presence for the purpose of prosecution or extradition. Measures taken according to this article shall be notified without delay to the States required to establish jurisdiction pursuant to article 8 and, where appropriate, all other States concerned.

Article 10

The State Party in whose territory the alleged offender is present shall, if it does not extradite him, submit, without exception what soever and without undue delay, the case to its competent authorities for the purpose of prosecution, through proceedings in accordance with the laws of that State.

Article 11

1. The offences in article 7 shall be deemed to be included as extraditable offences in any extradition treaty existing between States Parties. States Parties undertake to include those offences as extraditable offenses in every future extradition treaty to be concluded between them.

2. If a State Party which makes extradition conditional on the existence of a treaty receives a request for extradition from another State Party with which it has no extradition treaty, it may at its option consider this Convention as the legal basis for extradition in respect of those offences. Extradition shall be subject to the other conditions provided by the law of the requested State.

3. States Parties which do not make extradition conditional on the existence of a treaty shall recognized those offences as extraditable offences between themselves subject to the conditions provided by the law of the requested State.

4. Each of the offences shall be treated, for the purpose of extradition between States Parties, as if it had been committed not only in the place in which it occurred but also in the territories of the States Parties required to establish their jurisdiction in accordance with paragraph 1 of article 8.

Article 12

Any person regarding whom proceedings are being carried out in connection with any of the offences set forth in article 7 shall be guaranteed fair treatment at all stages of the proceedings.

Article 13

1. States Parties shall afford one another the greatest measure of assistance in connection with criminal proceedings brought in respect of the offenses set forth in article 7, including the supply of evidence at their disposal necessary for the proceedings. The law of the State requested shall apply in all cases.

2. The provisions of paragraph 1 shall not affect obligations under any other treaty, bilateral or multilateral, which governs or will govern, in whole or in part, mutual assistance in criminal matters.

Article 14

1. Each State Party shall inform the depositary of its laws and regulations which give effect to this Convention. The depositary shall communicate such information periodically to all States Parties.

2. The State Party where an alleged offender is prosecuted shall, wherever practicable, first communicate the final outcome of the proceedings to the State directly concerned. The State Party shall also communicate the final outcome to the depositary who shall inform all States.

3. Where an offence involves nuclear material used for peaceful purposes in domestic use, storage or transport, and both the alleged offender and the nuclear material remain in the territory of the State Party in which the offence was committed, nothing in this Convention shall be interpreted as requiring that State Party to provide information concerning criminal proceedings arising out of such an offense.

Article 15

The Annexes constitute an integral part of this Convention.

Article 16

1. A conference of States Parties shall be convened by the depositary five years after the entry into force of this Convention to review the implementation of the Convention and its adequacy as concerns the preamble, the whole of the operative part and the annexes in the light of the then prevailing situation.

2. At intervals of not less than five years thereafter, the majority of States Parties may obtain, by submitting a proposal to this effect to the depositary, the convening of further conferences with the same objective.

Article 17

1. In the event of a dispute between two or more States Parties concerning the interpretation or application of this Convention, such States Parties shall consult with a view to the settlement of the dispute by negotiation, or by any other peaceful means of settling disputes acceptable to all parties to the dispute.

2. Any dispute of this character which cannot be settled in the manner prescribed in paragraph 1 shall, at the request of any party to such dispute, be submitted to arbitration or referred to the International Court of Justice for decision. Where a dispute is submitted to arbitration, if, within six months

from the date of the request, the parties to the dispute are unable to agree on the organization of the arbitration, a party may request the President of the International Court of Justice or the Secretary-General of the United Nations to appoint one or more arbitrators. In case of conflicting requests by the parties to the dispute, the request to the Secretary-General of the United Nations shall have priority.

3. Each State Party may at the time of signature, ratification, acceptance or approval of this Convention or accession thereto declare that it does not consider itself bound by either or both of the dispute settlement procedures provided for in paragraph 2. The other States Parties shall not be bound by a dispute settlement procedure provided for in paragraph 2, with respect to a State Party which has made a reservation to that procedure.

4. Any State Party which has made a reservation in accordance with paragraph 3 may at any time withdraw that reservation by notification to the depositary.

Article 18

1. This Convention shall be open for signature by all States at the Headquarters of the International Atomic Energy Agency in Vienna and at the Headquarters of the United Nations in New York from 3 March 1980 until its entry into force.

2. This Convention is subject to ratification, acceptance or approval by the signatory States.

3. After its entry into force, this Convention will be open for accession by all States.

4. (a) This Convention shall be open for signature or accession by international organizations and regional organizations of an integration or other nature, provided that any such organization is constituted by sovereign States and has competence in respect of the negotiation, conclusion and application of international agreements in matters covered by this Convention.

(b) In matters within their competence, such organizations shall, on their own behalf, exercise the rights and fulfill the responsibilities which this Convention attributes to States Parties.

(c) When becoming party to this Convention such an organization shall communicate to the depositary a declaration indicating which States are members thereof and which articles of this Convention do not apply to it.

(d) Such an organization shall not hold any vote additional to those of its Member States.

5. Instruments of ratification, acceptance, approval or accession shall be deposited with the depositary.

Article 19

1. This Convention shall enter into force on the thirtieth day following the date of deposit of the twenty first instrument of ratification, acceptance or approval with the depositary.

2. For each State ratifying, accepting, approving or acceding to the Convention after the date of deposit of the twenty first instrument of ratification, acceptance or approval, the Convention shall enter into force on the thirtieth day after the deposit by such State of its instrument of ratification, acceptance, approval or accession.

Article 20

1. Without prejudice to article 16 a State Party may propose amendments to this Convention. The proposed amendment shall be submitted to the depositary who shall circulate it immediately to all States Parties. If a majority of States Parties request the depositary to convene a conference to consider the proposed amendments, the depositary shall invite all States Parties to attend such a conference to begin not sooner than thirty days after the invitations are issued. Any amendment adopted at the conference by a two-thirds majority of all States Parties shall be promptly circulated by the depositary to all States Parties.

2. The amendment shall enter into force for each State Party that deposits its instrument of ratification, acceptance or approval of the amendment on the thirtieth day after the date on which two thirds of the States Parties have deposited their instruments of ratification, acceptance or approval with the depositary. Thereafter, the amendment shall enter into force for any other State Party on the day on which that State Party deposits its instrument of ratification, acceptance or approval of the amendment.

Article 21

1. Any State Party may denounce this Convention by written notification to the depositary.

2. Denunciation shall take effect one hundred and eighty days following the date on which notification is received by the depositary.

Article 22

The depositary shall promptly notify all States of:

(a) each signature of this Convention;

(b) each deposit of an instrument of ratification, acceptance, approval or accession;

(c) any reservation or withdrawal in accordance with article 17;

(d) any communication made by an organization in accordance with paragraph 4 (c) of article 18;

(e) the entry into force of this Convention;

(f) the entry into force of any amendment to this Convention; and

(g) any denunciation made under article 21.

Article 23

The original of this Convention, of which the Arabic, Chinese, English, French, Russian and Spanish texts are equally authentic, shall be deposited with the Director General of the International Atomic Energy Agency who shall send certified copies thereof to all States.

ANNEX I
LEVELS OF PHYSICAL PROTECTION TO BE APPLIED IN INTERNATIONAL TRANSPORT OF NUCLEAR MATERIAL AS CATEGORIZED IN ANNEX II

1. Levels of physical protection for nuclear material during storage incidental to international nuclear transport include:

(a) For Category III materials, storage within an area to which access is controlled;

(b) For Category II materials, storage within an area under constant surveillance by guards or electronic devices, surrounded by a physical barrier with a limited number of points of entry under appropriate control or any area with an equivalent level of physical protection;

(c) For Category I material, storage within a protected area as defined for Category II above, to which, in addition, access is restricted to persons whose trustworthiness has been determined, and which is under surveillance by guards who are in close communication with appropriate response forces. Specific measures taken in this context should have as their object the detection and prevention of any assault, unauthorized access or unauthorized removal of material.

2. Levels of physical protection for nuclear material during international transport include:

(a) For Category II and III materials, transportation shall take place under special precautions including prior arrangements among sender, receiver, and carrier, and prior agreement between natural or legal persons subject to the jurisdiction and regulation of exporting and importing States, specifying time, place and procedures for transferring transport responsibility;

(b) For Category I materials, transportation shall take place under special precautions identified above for transportation of Category II and III materials, and in addition, under constant surveillance by escorts and under conditions which assure close communication with appropriate response forces;

(c) For natural uranium other than in the form of ore or ore-residue, transportation protection for quantities exceeding 500 kilograms U shall include advance notification of shipment specifying mode of transport, expected time of arrival and confirmation of receipt of shipment.

IN WITNESS WHEREOF, the undersigned, being duly authorized, have signed this Convention; opened for signature at Vienna and at New York on 3 March 1980.

ANNEX II
TABLE: CATEGORIZATION OF NUCLEAR MATERIAL

Material	Form	Category		
		I	II	III[c]
1. Plutonium[a]	Unirradiated[b]	2 kg or more	Less than 2 kg but more than 500 g	500 g or less but more than 15 g.
2. Uranium-235	Unirradiated[b]			
	-uranium enriched to 20% U235 or more	5 kg or more	Less than 5 kg but more than 1kg	1 kg or less but more than 15 g
	uranium enriched to 10% 235U but less than 20%		10 kg or more	Less than 10 kg but more than 1 kg
	-uranium enriched above natural but less than 10% 235U			10 kg or more
3. Uranium-233	Unirradiated[b]	2 kg or more	Less than 2 kg but more than 500 g.	500 g or less but more than 15 g.
4. Irradiated fuel			Depleted or natural uranium thorium or low-enriched fuel (less than 10% fissile content).[d, e]	

[a] All plutonium except that with isotopic concentration exceeding 80% in plutonium-238.

[b] Material not irradiated in a reactor or material irradiated in a reactor but with a radiation level equal to or less than 100 rads/hour at one metre unshielded.

[c] Quantities not falling in Category III and natural uranium should be protected in accordance with prudent management practice.

[d] Although this level of protection is recommended, it would be open to States, upon evaluation of the specific circumstances, to assign a different category of physical protection.

[e] Other fuel which by virtue of its original fissile material content is classified as Category I and II before may be reduced one category level while the radiation level from the fuel exceeds 100 rads/hour at one metre unshielded.

PHYSICAL PROTECTION OF NUCLEAR MATERIAL

[Original signatories omitted]

States which are currently parties:

Afghanistan
Albania
Algeria
Antigua and Barbuda
Argentina
Armenia
Australia
Austria[a]
Azerbaijan
Belarus
Belgium *,[a]
Bolivia
Bosnia and Herzegovina
Botswana
Brazil
Bulgaria
Burkina Faso
Canada
Chile
China
Colombia
Costa Rica
Croatia
Cuba
Cyprus
Czech Republic
Denmark *
Dominican Republic
Ecuador
Equatorial Guinea
Estonia
Finland [a]
France *,[a]
Germany *,[a]
Ghana
Greece*,[a]
Grenada
Guatemala

Haiti
Honduras
Hungary
Iceland
India
Indonesia
Ireland *,[a]
Israel
Italy *,[a]
Japan
Kenya
Korea, Republic of
Kuwait
Latvia
Lebanon
Libyan Arab Jamahiriya
Liechtenstein
Lithuania
Luxembourg *,[a]
Madagascar
Mali
Malta
Marshall Islands
Mexico
Monaco
Mongolia
Morocco
Mozambique
Namibia
Netherlands *,[a]
New Zealand
Niger
Norway [a]
Oman
Pakistan
Panama
Paraguay
Peru

PHYSICAL PROTECTION OF NUCLEAR MATERIAL

Philippines	Sweden [a]
Poland	Switzerland [a]
Portugal [*, a]	Tajikistan
Qatar	The Frmr. Yug. Rep. of Macedonia
Republic of Moldova	Tonga
Romania	Trinidad and Tobago
Russian Federation	Tunisia
Senegal	Turkey
Serbia and Montenegro	Uganda
Seychelles	Ukraine
Slovakia	United Arab Emirates
Slovenia	United Kingdom [*, a]
South Africa	United States of America
Spain [*, a]	Uruguay
Sudan	Uzbekistan
Swaziland	EURATOM [a]

[*] signed/ratified as a EURATOM Member State

[a] Deposited an objection to the declaration of Pakistan.

Declarations/reservations made upon expressing consent to be bound and objections thereto

Algeria, People's Democratic Republic of

"The Government of the People's Democratic Republic of Algeria does not consider itself bound by the provisions of Article 17, paragraph 2, of this Convention. The Government of the People's Democratic Republic of Algeria declares that any dispute can only be submitted to arbitration or referred to the International Court of Justice with the prior consent of all parties concerned."

acceded 30 Apr 2003

Argentina (Argentine Republic)

ratified 06 Apr 1989

[6 April 1989]

"In accordance with the provisions of Article 17.3 of the Convention, Argentina does not consider itself bound by either of the dispute settlement procedures provided for in Article 17.2 of the Convention."

(Original in Spanish; translation by the Secretariat)

Austria, Republic of

ratified 22 Dec 1988

[Objection to the declaration of Pakistan—received on 12 October 2001]

"Austria has carefully examined the declaration made by the Government of the Islamic Republic of Pakistan at the time of its accession to the Convention on the Physical Protection of Nuclear Material, regarding article 2, paragraph 2.

PHYSICAL PROTECTION OF NUCLEAR MATERIAL

Austria objects to the aforesaid declaration by the Government of the Islamic Republic of Pakistan to the Convention on the Physical Protection of Nuclear Material, which raises doubts with regard to the commitment of the Islamic Republic of Pakistan to the object and purpose of the Convention.

Although the declaration made by the Government of the Islamic Republic of Pakistan refers to the area "beyond the scope of the said Convention" the purpose of that declaration could be interpreted as if it also related to obligations within the framework of that Convention, such as obligations to make the offences described in article 7 of the Convention punishable under its national law or to cooperate with other States Parties in the field of criminal prosecution. Such interpretation would be incompatible with the object and purpose of the Convention.

This objection does not preclude the entry into force of the Convention between the Republic of Austria and the Islamic Republic of Pakistan."

(Original in English)

Azerbaijan, Republic of

acceded 19 Jan 2004

"In accordance with paragraph 3 of Article 17 of the Convention, the Republic of Azerbaijan declares that it does not consider itself bound by paragraph 2 of Article 17."

Belarus, Republic of

succeded 09 Sep 1993

[9 September 1993]

" . . . does not consider itself bound by the provisions of Article 17, paragraph 2 of the Convention that any dispute concerning the interpretation or application of the Convention shall be submitted to arbitration or referred to the International Court of Justice at the request of any party to such dispute."

(Original in Russian; translation by the Secretariat)

Belgium, Kingdom of

ratified 06 Sep 1991

[Objection to the declaration of Pakistan—received on 16 October 2001]

" . . . the Government of the Kingdom of Belgium has examined the reservation expressed by the Government of the Islamic Republic of Pakistan on its accession to the Convention on the Physical Protection of Nuclear Material with regard to paragraph 2 of article 2 thereof.

The Government of the Kingdom of Belgium objects to the aforementioned reservation of the Government of the Islamic Republic of Pakistan which raises a doubt with regard to Pakistan's commitment to the object and purpose of the Convention.

This objection shall not preclude the entry into force of the Convention between the Government of the Kingdom of Belgium and the Government of the Islamic Republic of Pakistan."

(Original in French; translation by the Secretariat)

China, People's Republic of

acceded 10 Jan 1989

[10 January 1989]

"China will not be bound by the two dispute settlement procedures as stipulated in Paragraph 2, Article 17 of the said Convention."

PHYSICAL PROTECTION OF NUCLEAR MATERIAL

(Original in Chinese; translation by the Secretariat)

Cuba, Republic of

acceded 26 Sep 1997

"The Republic of Cuba declares with respect to the content of Article 17 of the Convention on the Physical Protection of Nuclear Material that any dispute that may arise concerning the interpretation or application of the Convention shall be settled by diplomatic means among the parties to the dispute. By the same token, it does not consider itself bound by the procedure involving the International Court of Justice".

Cyprus, Republic of

acceded 23 Jul 1998

"The Republic of Cyprus declares that in accordance with the provisions of Article 17.3 of the Convention Cyprus does not consider itself bound by either of the dispute settlement procedures provided for in Article 17.2 of the Convention".

EURATOM

confirmed 06 Sep 1991

[6 September 1991]

"Pursuant to Article 18 (4)(c) of the Convention, [the European Atomic Energy Community] would like to declare:

(a) that the Member States of the Community are at present Belgium, Denmark, France, Germany, Greece, Ireland, Italy, Luxembourg, the Netherlands, Portugal, Spain, and the United Kingdom of Great Britain and Northern Ireland;

(b) that Articles 7 to 13 of the Convention are not applicable to the Community.

"Further, pursuant to Article 17 (3) of the Convention, [the European Atomic Energy Community] declare[s] that, since only States may be parties in cases before the International Court of Justice, the Community considers itself exclusively bound by the arbitration procedures provided for in Article 17 (2)."

(Original in English)

[Objection to the declaration of Pakistan—received on 19 October 2001]

"The European Atomic Energy Community has carefully examined the declaration made by the Islamic Republic of Pakistan at the time of its accession to the Convention on the Physical Protection of Nuclear Material, with regard to article 2, paragraph 2.

The European Atomic Energy Community objects to the aforesaid reservation by the Government of the Islamic Republic of Pakistan to the Convention on the Physical Protection of Nuclear Material, which puts in question Pakistan's commitment to the object and purpose of the Convention.

This objection does not preclude the entry into force of the Convention between the European Atomic Energy Community and the Islamic Republic of Pakistan."

(Original in English)

Finland, Republic of

accepted 22 Sep 1989

[Objection to the declaration of Pakistan—received on 18 October 2001]

"The Government of the Finland has carefully examined the reservation made by the Government of the Islamic Republic of Pakistan at the time of its accession to the Convention on the Physical Protection of Nuclear Material, regarding article 2, paragraph 2.

PHYSICAL PROTECTION OF NUCLEAR MATERIAL

The Government of Finland objects to the aforesaid reservation by the Government of the Islamic Republic of Pakistan to the Convention on the Physical Protection of Nuclear Material, which puts in question Pakistan's commitment to the object and purpose of the Convention.

This objection does not preclude the entry into force of the Convention between the Government of Finland and the Islamic Republic of Pakistan."

(Original in English)

France (French Republic)

approved 06 Sep 1991

[6 September 1991]

"(1) In approving the Convention, the French Government expresses the following reservation: the offences described in sub-paragraphs 1(e) and 1(f) of Article 7 of the Convention shall be punished in accordance with the provisions of French penal legislation.

"(2) The French Government declares that the jurisdiction referred to in Article 8, paragraph 4 may not be invoked against it, since the criterion of jurisdiction based on involvement in international nuclear transport as the exporting or importing State is not expressly recognized in international law and is not provided for in French national legislation.

"(3) In accordance with Article 17, paragraph 3, France declares that it does not accept the competence of the International Court of Justice in the settlement of the disputes referred to in paragraph 2 of this article, nor that of the President of the International Court of Justice to appoint one or more arbitrators."

(Original in French; translation by the Secretariat)

[Objection to the declaration of Pakistan—received on 12 October 2001]

"The Government of the French Republic has examined the reservation expressed by the Islamic Republic of Pakistan on its accession to the Convention on the Physical Protection of Nuclear Material, with regard to paragraph 2 of article 2 thereof.

The Government of the French Republic objects to the aforementioned reservation of the Islamic Republic of Pakistan which raises a doubt with regard to Pakistan's commitment to the object and purposes of the Convention.

This objection shall not preclude the entry into force of the Convention between France and the Islamic Republic of Pakistan."

(Original in French; translation by the Secretariat)

Germany, Federal Republic of

ratified 06 Sep 1991

[Objection to the declaration of Pakistan—received on 20 September 2001]

"The Government of the Federal Republic of Germany has examined the declaration made by the Government of the Islamic Republic of Pakistan upon its accession to the Convention on the Physical Protection of Nuclear Material, regarding paragraph 2 of Article 2. The Government of the Federal Republic of Germany objects to the aforesaid declaration by the Government of the Islamic Republic of Pakistan which raises doubts with regard to the commitment of the Islamic Republic of Pakistan to the object and purpose of the Convention.

It is in the common interest that treaties are respected as to their object and purpose by all parties.

This objection does not preclude the entry into force of the Convention between the Federal Republic of Germany and the Islamic Republic of Pakistan".

(Original in English)

PHYSICAL PROTECTION OF NUCLEAR MATERIAL

Greece (Hellenic Republic)

ratified 06 Sep 1991

[Objection to the declaration of Pakistan—received on 26 November 2001]

"The Government of Greece has carefully examined the reservation made by the Government of the Islamic Republic of Pakistan at the time of its accession to the Convention on the Physical Protection of Nuclear Material, regarding article 2, paragraph 2.

The Government of Greece objects to the aforesaid reservation by the Government of the Islamic Republic of Pakistan to the Convention on the Physical Protection of Nuclear Material, which puts in question Pakistan's commitment to the object and purpose of the Convention.

This objection does not preclude the entry into force of the Convention between the Government of Greece and the Islamic Republic of Pakistan."

(Original in English)

Guatemala, Republic of

ratified 23 Apr 1985

[23 April 1985]

"The Republic of Guatemala does not consider itself bound by any of the dispute settlement procedures set out in paragraph 2 of Article 17 of the Convention, which provide for the submission of disputes to arbitration or their referral to the International Court of Justice for decision."

(Original in Spanish; translation by the Secretariat)

India, Republic of

acceded 12 Mar 2002

"In accordance with Article 17, paragraph 3, the Government of the Republic of India does not consider itself bound by the procedure for the settlement of disputes provided for under Article 17, paragraph 2 of the Convention".

Indonesia, Republic of

ratified 05 Nov 1986

[5 November 1986]

"The Government of the Republic of Indonesia does not consider itself bound by the provision of Article 17, paragraph 2 of this Convention and take the position that any dispute relating to the interpretation or application of the Convention may only be submitted to arbitration or to the International Court of Justice with the agreement of all the parties to the dispute."

(Originals in English and Indonesian; supplied by the Government)

Ireland

ratified 06 Sep 1991

[Objection to the declaration of Pakistan—received on 28 September 2001] "The Government of Ireland has carefully examined the reservation made by the Government of the Islamic Republic of Pakistan upon its accession to the Convention on the Physical Protection of Nuclear Material, regarding paragraph 2 of Article 2.

The Government of Ireland objects to the aforesaid reservation by the Government of the Islamic Republic of Pakistan to the Convention on the Physical Protection of Nuclear Material, which raises doubts with regard to the commitment of the Islamic Republic of Pakistan to the object and purpose of the Convention.

It is in the common interest that treaties are respected as to their object and purpose by all parties.

This objection does not preclude the entry into force of the convention between Ireland and the Islamic Republic of Pakistan."

(Original in English)

Israel, State of

ratified 22 Jan 2002

[22 January 2002]

"In accordance with Article 17 paragraph 3, the Government of the State of Israel declares that it does not consider itself bound by the dispute settlement procedures provided for in paragraph 2 of Article 17."

(Original in English)

Italy (Italian Republic)

ratified 06 Sep 1991

[6 September 1991]

Confirms the reservations and declaration made upon signature. (Original in English)

[Objection to the declaration of Pakistan—received on 15 October 2001]

"The Government of the Republic of Italy has carefully examined the reservation made by the Government of the Islamic Republic of Pakistan at the time of its accession to the Convention on the Physical Protection of Nuclear Material, regarding article 2, paragraph 2 of the aforesaid Convention.

The Government of the Republic of Italy objects to the aforesaid reservation by the Government of the Islamic Republic of Pakistan, which raises doubts with regard to the commitment of the Islamic Republic of Pakistan to the object and the purpose of the Convention.

This objection does not preclude the entry into force of the Convention between the Republic of Italy and the Islamic Republic of Pakistan."

(Original in English)

Korea, Republic of

ratified 07 Apr 1982

[7 April 1982]

Confirms the reservation made upon signature.

(Original in English)

Kuwait, State of

acceded 23 Apr 2004

"Having considered the Convention on the Physical Protection of Nuclear Material signed on 3 March 1980, and having considered Law No. 12 of 2004, issued on (14 Dhu Al-Qa'da 1424—year of the Hegira) 6 January 2004 pertaining to approval of it with a reservation on paragraph 2 of Article 17 declaring nonobligation to be bound by it, we hereby announce our accession to the said Convention and pledge to comply with it and ensure its observance."

PHYSICAL PROTECTION OF NUCLEAR MATERIAL

Luxembourg, Grand Duchy of

ratified 06 Sep 1991

[Objection to the declaration of Pakistan—received on 23 October 2001]

"The Government of the Grand Duchy of Luxembourg has examined the reservation expressed by the Government of the Islamic Republic of Pakistan on its accession to the Convention on the Physical Protection of Nuclear Material with regard to paragraph 2 of article 2 thereof.

The Government of the Grand Duchy of Luxembourg objects to the aforementioned reservation of the Government of the Islamic Republic of Pakistan which raises a doubt with regard to Pakistan's commitment to the object and purpose of the Convention.

This objection shall not preclude the entry into force of the Convention between the Government of the Grand Duchy of Luxembourg and the Government of the Islamic Republic of Pakistan."

(Original in French; translation by the Secretariat)

Mozambique, Republic of

acceded 03 Mar 2003

"The Republic of Mozambique does not consider itself bound by the provisions of article 17, paragraph 2 of the Convention. In this connection, the Republic of Mozambique states that, in each individual case, the consent of all Parties to such a dispute is necessary for the submission of the dispute to arbitration or to International Court of Justice."

Netherlands, Kingdom of the

accepted 06 Sep 1991

[6 September 1991]

"With regard to the obligation to exercise jurisdiction referred to in Article 10 of the Convention on the Physical Protection of Nuclear Material, done at Vienna/New York on 3 March 1980, the Kingdom of the Netherlands makes the reservation, that in cases where the judicial authorities of the Netherlands are unable to exercise jurisdiction on the grounds of one of the principles referred to in Article 8, paragraph 1, of the Convention, the Kingdom shall be bound by this obligation only if it has received an extradition request from a Party to the Convention and the said request has been rejected."

(Original in English)

[Objection to the declaration of Pakistan—received on 9 October 2001]

"The Government of the Kingdom of the Netherlands has examined the reservation made by the Government of the Islamic Republic of Pakistan at the time of its accession to the Convention on the Physical Protection of Nuclear Material, regarding article 2, paragraph 2.

The Government of the Kingdom of the Netherlands objects to the aforesaid reservation by the Government of the Islamic Republic of Pakistan to the Convention on Physical Protection of Nuclear Material, which raises doubts as to Pakistan's commitment to the object and purpose of the Convention.

It is in the common interest of States that treaties to which they have chosen to become party should be respected, as to object and purpose, by all parties.

The Government of the Kingdom of the Netherlands therefore objects to the aforesaid reservation made by the Government of the Islamic Republic of Pakistan to the Convention on the Physical Protection of Nuclear Material.

This objection shall not preclude the entry into force of the Convention between the Kingdom of the Netherlands and the Islamic Republic of Pakistan."

(Original in English)

Norway, Kingdom of

ratified 15 Aug 1985

[Objection to the declaration of Pakistan—received on 17 October 2001]

"The Government of Norway has examined the contents of the reservation made by the Islamic Republic of Pakistan upon accession to the Convention on the Physical Protection of Nuclear Material.

According to paragraph 1 of the reservation, Pakistan does not consider itself bound by paragraph 2 of article 2 of the Convention. This paragraph extends the obligation of protection of nuclear material to such material while in domestic use, storage and transport. The provision aims at averting the potential dangers posed by the unlawful taking and use of nuclear material. Norway therefore objects to paragraph 1 of the reservation, as it is contrary to the object and purpose of the Convention and thus impermissible according to well established treaty law.

This objection does not preclude the entry into force in its entirety of the Convention between the Kingdom of Norway and the Islamic Republic of Pakistan. The Convention thus becomes operative between Norway and Pakistan without Pakistan benefiting from the said part of the reservation."

(Original in English)

Oman, Sultanate of

acceded 11 Jun 2003

"1. Reservation with respect to Article 8, paragraph 4, the text of which states that "each State Party may, consistent with international law, establish its jurisdiction over the offences set forth in Article 7 when it is involved in international nuclear transport as the exporting or importing State.

2. In accordance with Article 17, paragraph 3 of the Convention, the Sultanate does not consider itself bound by the dispute settlement procedures provided for in Article 17, paragraph 2."

(Original in Arabic, translation by the Secretariat)

Upon a request by the Secretariat, the following specification of the nature of the reservation made with respect to Article 8, paragraph 4, was received from the Sultanate of Oman:

> "The reservation made by the Sultanate of Oman to Article 8, paragraph 4 of the Convention is due to the fact that it is inconsistent with the principle of the sovereignty of national jurisdiction, as well as with the principles of international law. This is because it establishes jurisdiction by exporting or importing States over offences committed outside their territories when they are involved in international nuclear transport."

(Original in Arabic, translation by the Secretariat)

Pakistan, Islamic Republic of

acceded 12 Sep 2000

[12 September 2000]

"1. The Government of the Islamic Republic of Pakistan does not consider itself bound by paragraph 2 of Article 2, as it regards the question of domestic use, storage and transport of nuclear material beyond the scope of the said Convention.

2. The Government of the Islamic Republic of Pakistan does not consider itself bound by either of the dispute settlement procedures provided for in paragraph 2 of Article 17 of the said Convention."

PHYSICAL PROTECTION OF NUCLEAR MATERIAL

(Original in English)

Peru, Republic of

acceded 11 Jan 1995

[11 January 1995]

"In accordance with the provisions of Article 17.3 of the Convention, Peru does not consider itself bound by any of the dispute settlement procedures provided for in the convention."

A Note explaining the reservation reads as follows:

"The reservation made by Peru in the instrument of accession ... refers only to the dispute settlement procedures provided for in paragraph 2 of Article 17, in accordance with paragraph 3 of the same article."

(Original in Spanish; translation by the Secretariat)

Portugal (Portuguese Republic)

ratified 06 Sep 1991

[Objection to the declaration of Pakistan—received on 18 October 2001]

"The Government of the Portuguese Republic has carefully examined the reservation made by the Government of the Islamic Republic of Pakistan at the time its accession to the Convention on the Physical Protection of Nuclear Material, regarding article 2, paragraph 2.

The Government of the Portuguese Republic objects to the aforesaid reservation made by the Government of the Islamic Republic of Pakistan to the Convention on the Physical Protection of Nuclear Material, which raises doubts regarding the commitment of the Islamic Republic of Pakistan to the object and purpose of the Convention.

This objection does not preclude the entry into force of the Convention between the Portuguese Republic and the Islamic Republic of Pakistan."

(Original in English)

Qatar, State of

acceded 09 Mar 2004

"The State of Qatar does not consider itself bound by either of the dispute settlement procedures provided for in paragraph (2) of Article (17)."

Russian Federation

ratified 25 May 1983

[25 May 1983]

Confirms the reservation made upon signature.

(Original in Russian; translation by the Secretariat)

Spain, Kingdom of

ratified 06 Sep 1991

[6 September 1991]

"The Kingdom of Spain declares, in accordance with paragraph 3 of Article 17 of the Convention, that it does not consider itself bound by the procedure for the settlement of disputes stipulated in paragraph 2 of Article 17."

(Original in Spanish; translation by the Secretariat)

[Objection to the declaration of Pakistan—received on 4 October 2001]

"The Government of the Kingdom of Spain has carefully examined the reservation made by the Government of the Islamic Republic of Pakistan at the time of its accession to the Convention on the Physical Protection of Nuclear Material, regarding Article 2, Paragraph 2.

The Government of the Kingdom of Spain objects to the aforesaid reservation by the Government of the Islamic Republic of Pakistan to the Convention on the Physical Protection of Nuclear Material, which puts in question Pakistan's commitment to the object and purpose of the Convention.

This object does not preclude the entry into force of the Convention between the Government of the Kingdom of Spain and the Islamic Republic of Pakistan."

(Original in English)

Sweden, Kingdom of

ratified 01 Aug 1980

[Objection to the declaration of Pakistan—received on 8 October 2001]

"The Government of Sweden has carefully examined the reservation made by the Government of the Islamic Republic of Pakistan at the time of its accession to the Convention on the Physical Protection of Nuclear Material, regarding article 2, paragraph 2.

The Government of Sweden objects to the aforesaid reservation by the Government of the Islamic Republic of Pakistan to the Convention on the Physical Protection of Nuclear Material, which puts in question Pakistan's commitment to the object and purpose of the Convention.

This objection does not preclude the entry into force of the convention between the Government of Sweden and the Islamic Republic of Pakistan."

(Original in English)

Switzerland (Swiss Confederation)

ratified 09 Jan 1987

[Objection to the declaration of Pakistan—received on 19 October 2001]

"The Government of Switzerland has carefully examined the declaration made by the Government of the Islamic Republic of Pakistan at the time of its accession to the Convention on the Physical Protection of Nuclear Material, regarding article 2, paragraph 2 of this Convention.

The name assigned to a statement whereby the legal effect of certain provisions of a treaty is excluded or modified does not determine its status as a reservation to the treaty. The Government of Switzerland considers the declaration of the Government of the Islamic Republic of Pakistan in its substance as a reservation.

According to international law a reservation incompatible with the object and purpose of the treaty is not permitted. The Government of Switzerland is of the view that the aforesaid reservation raises doubts as to the commitment of the Islamic Republic of Pakistan to the object and purpose of the Convention. The Government of Switzerland therefore objects to this reservation.

This objection does not preclude the entry into force of the Convention between Switzerland and the Islamic Republic of Pakistan. The Convention enters into force in its entirety between the two States, without the Islamic Republic of Pakistan benefiting from its reservation."

(Original in English)

PHYSICAL PROTECTION OF NUCLEAR MATERIAL

Turkey, Republic of
ratified 27 Feb 1985

[27 February 1985]

Confirms the reservation made upon signature.

(Original in English)

United Kingdom of Great Britain and Northern Ireland
ratified 06 Sep 1991

[11 December 1991]

" ... the Convention was extended to cover the Bailiwicks of Jersey and Guernsey and the Isle of Man with effect from 6 October 1991. The United Kingdom's Instrument of Ratification should accordingly be construed to extend to them."

(Original in English)

[Objection to the declaration of Pakistan—received on 16 October 2001]

"The Permanent Mission of the United Kingdom of Great Britain and Northern Ireland to the United Nations and other International Organizations in Vienna ... has the honour to refer to the reservation made by the Government of the Islamic Republic of Pakistan at the time of its accession to the Convention on the Physical Protection of Nuclear Material, regarding article 2, paragraph 2.

The Government of the United Kingdom of Great Britain and Northern Ireland objects to the aforesaid reservation by the Government of the Islamic Republic of Pakistan to the Convention on the Physical Protection of Nuclear Material, which puts in question Pakistan's commitment to the object and purpose of the Convention.

This objection does not preclude the entry into force of the Convention between the Government of the United Kingdom of Great Britain and Northern Ireland and the Islamic Republic of Pakistan."

(Original in English)

Declarations/reservations made upon signature

Argentina (Argentine Republic)
28 Feb 1986

[28 February 1986]

"In accordance with the provision of Article 17.3, the Republic of Argentina does not consider itself bound by any of the arbitration procedures laid down in Article 17.2 of the Convention."

(Original in Spanish; translation by the Secretariat)

EURATOM
13 Jun 1980

[13 June 1980]

"At present the following States are members of the European Atomic Energy Community: Belgium, Denmark, France, the Federal Republic of Germany, Ireland, Italy, Luxembourg, the Netherlands and the United Kingdom.

"In signing the Convention, the Community declares that, when it has deposited the instrument of approval or acceptance pursuant to Article 18 and the Convention has entered into force for the Community pursuant to Article 19, Articles 7 to 13 of the Convention will not apply to it.

"Furthermore, the Community declares that, because under Article 34 of the Statute of the International Court of Justice only States may be parties in cases before the Court, it can only be bound by the arbitration procedure set out in Article 17(2)."

(Original in English)

France (French Republic)

13 Jun 1980

[13 June 1980]

"Recalling its statement contained in document CPNM/90 of 25 October 1979, the French Government declares that the jurisdiction referred to in Article 8, paragraph 4 may not be invoked against it, since the criterion of jurisdiction based on involvement in international nuclear transport as the exporting or importing State is not expressly recognized in international law and is not provided for in French national legislation."

"In accordance with Article 17, paragraph 3, France declares that it does not accept the competence of the International Court of Justice in the settlement of the disputes referred to in paragraph 2 of this article, nor that of the President of the International Court of Justice to appoint one or more arbitrators."

(Original in French; translation by the Secretariat)

Israel, State of

17 Jun 1983

[17 June 1983]

"In accordance with Article 17, paragraph 3, Israel declares that it does not consider itself bound by the dispute settlement procedures provided for in paragraph 2 of Article 17."

(Original in English)

Italy (Italian Republic)

13 Jun 1980

[13 June 1980]

"1) In connection with Art. 4.2

Italy considers that if assurances as to the levels of physical protection described in annex I have not been received in good time the importing state party may take appropriate bilateral steps as far as practicable to assure itself that the transport will take place in compliance with the aforesaid levels.

"2) In connection with Art. 10

The last words 'through proceedings in accordance with the laws of the state' are to be considered as referring to the whole Article 10.

"Italy considers that international co-operation and assistance for physical protection and recovery of nuclear materials as well as criminal rules and extradition will apply also to the domestic use, storage and transport of nuclear material used for peaceful purposes. Italy also considers that no provision contained in this convention shall be interpreted as precluding the possibility to widen the scope of the convention at the review conference foreseen in Art. 16."

(Original in English)

PHYSICAL PROTECTION OF NUCLEAR MATERIAL

Korea, Republic of

29 Dec 1981

[29 December 1981]

" ... the Government of the Republic of Korea does not consider itself bound by the dispute settlement procedures provided for in Paragraph 2 of Article 17."

(Original in English)

Romania

15 Jan 1981

[15 January 1981]

"The Socialist Republic of Romania declares that it does not consider itself bound by the provisions of Article 17, paragraph 2 of the Convention on the Physical Protection of Nuclear Material, which state that any dispute concerning the interpretation or application of the Convention which cannot be settled by negotiation or by any other peaceful means of settling disputes shall, at the request of any party to such dispute, be submitted to arbitration or referred to the International Court of Justice for decision.

"The Socialist Republic of Romania considers that such disputes can be submitted to arbitration or to the International Court of Justice only with the consent of all parties to the dispute in each individual case.

"In signing the Convention on the Physical Protection of Nuclear Material, the Socialist Republic of Romania declares that, in its interpretation, the provisions of Article 18, paragraph 4 refer exclusively to organizations to which the Member States have transferred competence to negotiate, conclude and apply international agreements on their behalf and to exercise the rights and fulfil the responsibilities entailed by such agreements including the right to vote."

(Original in French; translation by the Secretariat)

Russian Federation

22 May 1980

[22 May 1980]

"The Union of Soviet Socialist Republics does not consider itself bound by the provisions of Article 17, paragraph 2 of the Convention that any dispute concerning the interpretation or application of the Convention shall be submitted to arbitration or referred to the International Court of Justice at the request of any party to such dispute."

(Original in Russian; translation by the Secretariat)

South Africa, Republic of

18 May 1981

[18 May 1981]

"In accordance with Article 17, paragraph 3, the Republic of South Africa declares that it does not consider itself bound by the dispute settlement procedures provided for in paragraph 2 of Article 17."

(Original in English)

Spain, Kingdom of

07 Apr 1986

[7 April 1986]

" . . . in accordance with paragraph 3 of Article 17 of the Convention, Spain does not consider itself bound by the procedure for the settlement of disputes stipulated in paragraph 2 of Article 17."

(Original in Spanish; translation by the Secretariat)

Turkey, Republic of

23 Aug 1983

[23 August 1983]

"Turkey, in accordance with Article 17, Paragraph 3, of the Convention does not consider itself bound by Article 17, Paragraph 2 of the Convention."

(Original in English)

INTERNATIONAL CONVENTION AGAINST THE TAKING OF HOSTAGES

COMMENTARY

In November of 1979 the world was shocked to witness the attack on the Embassy of the United States in Iran and the taking of 66 American diplomats as hostage. Later in that same month hundreds of hostages were taken in Mecca and, in the end, 250 people were killed and 600 wounded when authorities tried to free the hostages.

Once again, the international community responded to a method of terrorism with a new Convention. The purpose of this convention was to structure a framework of understandings which would, on an international scale, govern the response of nations to terrorist acts.

Article I sets out the definition of a "hostage" stating:

> "1. Any person who seizes or detains and threatens to kill, to injure or to continue to detain another person ... in order to compel a third party, namely, a State, an international intergovernmental organization, a natural or juridical person, or a group of persons, to do or abstain from doing any act as an explicit or implicit condition for the release of the hostage commits the offence of taking of hostages ... within the meaning of this Convention."

Not only does the Convention address the taking of hostages, but it also describes what the States who are Party to the Convention should do to prevent such offences, to include ". . . Taking all practicable measures to prevent preparations in their respective territories for the commission of those offences within or outside their territories ..." and to exchange ". . . information and co-ordinating the taking of administrative and other measures as appropriate to prevent the commission of those offences."

The full text of the President's Message sending this Convention to the Senate follows:

> *"To the Senate of the United States:*
>
> With a view to receiving the advice and consent of the Senate to ratification, I transmit herewith a copy of the International Convention Against the Tak-

ing of Hostages, adopted by the United Nations General Assembly on December 17, 1979 and signed on behalf of the United States of America on December 21, 1979. The report of the Department of State with respect to the Convention is also transmitted for the information of the Senate.

In recent years, we have witnessed an unprecedented and intolerable increase in acts of terrorism involving the taking of hostages in various parts of the world. Events have clearly demonstrated that no country or region is exempt from the human tragedy and immense costs which almost invariably result from such criminal acts. Consequently, the urgent need to take positive action against these manifestations of international terrorism has become readily apparent. Although the penal codes of most States contain provisions proscribing assault, extortion, kidnapping, and other serious crimes inherent in hostage-taking incidents and ensuring punishment of offenders, wherever found, has not previously existed.

The Convention creates a legal mechanism where persons alleged to have committed offenses under the Convention will be prosecuted or extradited if apprehended within the jurisdiction of a State Party, wherever the offense was committed. In essence, the Convention imposes binding legal obligations upon States Parties either to submit for prosecution or to extradite any person within their jurisdiction who commits an act of hostage taking (as defined in Article 1), attempts to commit such an act, or participates as an accomplice of anyone who commits or attempts to commit such an act. A State Party is subject to these obligations without regard to the place where the alleged act covered by Article 1 was committed.

Article 1 of the convention declares that the act or offense of taking of hostages is committed by any person who seizes or detains and threatens to kill, injure, or continue to detain another person (the "hostage") in order to compel a third party (a State, an international intergovernmental organization, a natural or juridical person, or a group of persons) to do or abstain from doing any act as an explicit or implicit condition for the release of the hostage. States Parties to the convention will also be obligated to cooperate in preventing hostage-taking offenses by means of internal preventive measures, exchange of information, and coordination of enforcement activities.

This Convention is a vitally important new element in the campaign against the scourge of international terrorism in general and the heinous crime of hostage-taking in particular. I hope that all States will become Parties to this Convention, and that it will be applied universally. I recommend, therefore, that the Senate give early and favorable consideration to this Convention.

Jimmy Carter
The White House
August 4, 1980"

INTERNATIONAL CONVENTION AGAINST THE TAKING OF HOSTAGES

Adopted by the United Nations on 17 December, 1979
Entered into force 3 June 1983*

BY THE PRESIDENT OF THE UNITED STATES OF AMERICA
A PROCLAMATION

CONSIDERING THAT:

The International Convention Against the Taking of Hostages was adopted by the United Nations General Assembly on December 17, 1979, and was signed on behalf of the United States of America on December 21, 1979, a certified copy of which Convention is hereto annexed;

The Senate of the United States of America by its resolution of July 30, 1981, two-thirds of the Senators present concurring therein, gave its advice and consent to ratification of the Convention;

The President of the United States of America ratified the Convention on September 4, 1981, in pursuance of the advice and consent of the Senate;

The United States of America deposited its instrument of ratification on December 7, 1984, in accordance with the provisions of Article 17 of the Convention;

Pursuant to the provisions of Article 18, the Convention entered into force for the United States of America on January 6, 1985;

NOW THEREFORE, I, Ronald Reagan, President of the United States of America, proclaim and make public the Convention, to the end that it be observed and fulfilled with good faith on and after January 6, 1985, by the United States of America and by the citizens of the United States of America and all other persons subject to the jurisdiction thereof.

---

* Treaties and International Agreements Online, CTIA 8465.000 (Oceana Publications, Inc. <www.oceanalaw.com>.

IN TESTIMONY WHEREOF, I have signed this proclamation and caused the Seal of the United States of America to be affixed.

DONE at the city of Washington this third day of October in the year of our Lord one thousand nine hundred eighty-six and of the Independence of the United States of America the two hundred eleventh.

By the President:

Secretary of State

THE STATES PARTIES TO THIS CONVENTION,

Having in mind the purposes and principles of the Charter of the United Nations concerning the maintenance of international peace and security and the promotion of friendly relations and co-operating among States,

Recognizing in particular that everyone has right to life, liberty and security of person, as set out in the Universal Declaration of Human Rights and the International Covenant on Civil and Political Rights,

Reaffirming the principle of equal rights and self-determination of peoples as enshrined in the Charter of the United Nations and the Declaration on Principles of International Law concerning Friendly Relations and Co-operation among States in accordance with the Charter of the United Nations, as well as in other relevant resolutions of the General Assembly,

Considering that the taking of hostages is an offence of grave concern to the international community and that, in accordance with the provisions of this Convention, any person committing an act of hostage taking shall either be prosecuted or extradited.

Being convinced that it is urgently necessary to develop international co-operation between States in devising and adopting effective measures for the prevention, prosecution and punishment of all acts of taking of hostages as manifestations of international terrorism,

HAVE AGREED as follows:

Article 1

1. Any person who seizes or detains and threatens to kill, to injure or to continue to detain another person (hereinafter referred to as the "hostage") in order to compel a third party, namely, a State, an international intergovernmental organization, a natural or juridical person, or a group of persons, to do or abstain from doing any act as an explicit or implicit condition for the release of the hostage commits the offence of taking hostages ("hostage-taking") within the meaning of this Convention.

2. Any person who:

(a) attempts to commit an act of hostage-taking, or

(b) participates as an accomplice of anyone who commits or attempts to commit an act of hostage-taking likewise commits an offence for the purposes of this Convention.

Article 2

Each State Party shall make the offences set forth in article 1 punishable by appropriate penalties which take into account the grave nature of those offences.

Article 3

1. The State Party in the territory of which the hostage is held by the offender shall take all measures it considers appropriate to ease the situation of the hostage, in particular, to secure his release and, after his release, to facilitate, when relevant, his departure.

2. If any object which the offender has obtained as a result of the taking of hostages comes into the custody of a State Party, that State Party shall return it as soon as possible to the hostage or the third party referred to in article 1, as the case may be, or to the appropriate authorities thereof.

Article 4

States Parties shall co-operate in the prevention of the offences set forth in article 1, particularly by:

(a) taking all practicable measures to prevent preparations in their respective territories for the commission of those offences within or outside their territories, including measures to prohibit in their territories illegal activities of persons, groups and organizations that encourage, instigate, organize or engage in the perpetration of acts of taking of hostages;

(b) exchanging information and co-ordinating the taking of administrative and other measures as appropriate to prevent the commission of those offences.

Article 5

1. Each State Party shall take such measures as may be necessary to establish its jurisdiction over any of the offences set forth in article 1 which are committed:

(a) in its territory or on board a ship or aircraft registered in that State;

(b) by any of its nationals or, if the State considers it appropriate, by those stateless persons who have their habitual residence in its territory;

(c) in order to compel that State to do or abstain from doing any act; or

(d) with respect to a hostage who is a national of that State, if that State considers it appropriate.

2. Each State Party shall likewise take such measures as may be necessary to establish its jurisdiction over the offences set forth in article 1 in cases where the alleged offender is present in its territory and it does not extradite him to any of the States mentioned in paragraph 1 of this article.

3. This Convention does not exclude any criminal jurisdiction exercised in accordance with internal law.

Article 6

1. Upon being satisfied that the circumstances so warrant, any State Party in the territory of which the alleged offender is present shall, in accordance with its laws, take him into custody or take other measures to ensure his presence for such time as is necessary to enable any criminal or extradition proceedings to be instituted. That State Party shall immediately make a preliminary inquiry into the facts.

2. The custody or other measures referred to in paragraph 1 of this article shall be notified without delay directly or through the Secretary-General of the United Nations to:

(a) the State where the offense was committed;

(b) the State against which compulsion has been directed or attempted;

(c) the State of which the natural or juridical person against whom compulsion has been directed or attempted is a national;

(d) the State of which the hostage is a national or in the territory of which he has his habitual residence;

(e) the State of which the alleged offender is a national or, if he is a stateless person, in the territory of which he has his habitual residence;

(f) the international intergovernmental organization against which compulsion has been directed or attempted;

(g) all other States concerned.

3. Any person regarding whom the measures referred to in paragraph 1 of this article are being taken shall be entitled;

(a) to communicate without delay with the nearest appropriate representative of the State of which he is a national or which is otherwise entitled to establish such communication or, if he is a stateless person, the State in the territory of which he has his habitual residence;

(b) to be visited by a representative of that State.

4. The rights referred to in paragraph 3 of this article shall be exercised in conformity with the laws and regulations of the State in the territory of which the alleged offender is present subject to the proviso, however, that the said laws and regulations must enable full effect to be given to the purposes for which the rights accorded under paragraph 3 of this article are intended.

5. The provisions of paragraphs 3 and 4 of this article shall be without prejudice to the right of any State Party having a claim to jurisdiction in accordance with paragraph 1(b) of article 5 to invite the International Committee of the Red Cross to communicate with and visit the alleged offender.

6. The State which makes the preliminary inquiry contemplated in paragraph 1 of this article shall promptly report its findings to the States or organization referred to in paragraph 2 of this article and indicate whether it intends to exercise jurisdiction.

Article 7

The State Party where the alleged offender is prosecuted shall in accordance with its laws communicate the final outcome of the proceedings to the Secretary-General of the United Nations, who shall transmit the information to the other States concerned and the international intergovernmental organizations concerned.

Article 8

1. The State Party in the territory of which the alleged offender is found shall, if it does not extradite him, be obliged, without exception Whatsoever and whether or not the offence was committed in its territory, to submit the case to its competent authorities for the purpose of prosecution, through proceedings in accordance with the laws of that State. Those authorities shall take their decision in the same manner as in the case of any ordinary offence of a grave nature under the law of that State.

2. Any person regarding whom proceedings are being carried out in connexion with any of the offences set forth in article 1 shall be guaranteed fair treatment at all stages of the proceedings, including enjoyment of all the rights and guarantees provided by the law of the State in the territory of which he is present.

Article 9

1. A request for the extradition of an alleged offender, pursuant to this Convention, shall not be granted if the requested State Party has substantial grounds for believing:

>(a) that the request for extradition for an offence set forth in article 1 has been made for the purpose of prosecuting or punishing a person on ac-

count of his race, religion, nationality, ethnic origin or political opinion; or

(b) that the person's position may be prejudiced:

(i) for any of the reasons mentioned in subparagraph (a) of this paragraph, or

(ii) for the reason that communication with him by the appropriate authorities of the State entitled to exercise rights of protection cannot be effected.

2. With respect to the offences as defined in this Convention, the provisions of all extradition treaties and arrangements applicable between States Parties are modified as between States Parties to the extent that they are incompatible with this Convention.

Article 10

1. The offences set forth in article 1 shall be deemed to be included as extraditable offences in any extradition treaty existing between States Parties. States Parties undertake to include such offences as extraditable offences in every extradition treaty to be concluded between them.

2. If a State Party which makes extradition conditional on the existence of a treaty receives a request for extradition from another State Party with which it has no extradition treaty, the requested State may at its option consider this Convention as the legal basis for extradition in respect of the offences set forth in article 1. Extradition shall be subject to the other conditions provided by the law of the requested State.

3. States Parties which do not make extradition conditional on the existence of a treaty shall recognize the offences set forth in article 1 as extraditable offences between themselves subject to the conditions provided by the law of the requested State.

4. The offences set forth in article 1 shall be treated, for the purpose of extradition between States Parties, as if they had been committed not only in the place in which they occurred but also in the territories of the States required to establish their jurisdiction in accordance with paragraph 1 of article 5.

Article 11

1. States Parties shall afford one another the greatest measure of assistance in connexion with criminal proceedings brought in respect of the offences set forth in article 1, including the supply of all evidence at their disposal necessary for the proceedings.

2. The provisions of paragraph 1 of this article shall not affect obligations concerning mutual judicial assistance embodied in any other treaty.

Article 12

In so far as the Geneva Conventions of 1949 for the protection of war victims or the Protocols Additional to those Conventions are applicable to a particular act of hostage-taking, and in so far as States Parties to this Convention are bound under those conventions to prosecute or hand over the hostage-taker, the present Convention shall not apply to an act of hostage-taking committed in the course of armed conflicts as defined in the Geneva Conventions of 1949 and the Protocols thereto, including armed conflicts mentioned in article 1, paragraph 4, Additional Protocol I of 1977, in which peoples are fighting against colonial domination and alien occupation and against racist regimes in the exercise of their right of self-determination, as enshrined in the Charter of the United Nations and the Declaration on Principles of International Law concerning Friendly Relations and Co-operation among States in accordance with the Charter of the United Nations.

Article 13

This Convention shall not apply where the offence is committed within a single State, the hostage and the alleged offender are nationals of that State and the alleged offender is found in the territory of that State.

Article 14

Nothing in this Convention shall be construed as justifying the violation of the territorial integrity or political independence of a State in contravention of the Charter of the United Nations.

Article 15

The provisions of this Convention shall not affect the application of the Treaties on Asylum, in force at the date of the adoption of this Convention, as between the States which are parties to those Treaties; but a State Party to this Convention may not invoke those Treaties with respect to another State Party to this Convention which is not a party to those treaties.

Article 16

1. Any dispute between two or more States Parties concerning the interpretation or application of this Convention which is not settled by negotiation shall, at the request of one them, be submitted to arbitration. If within six months from the date of the request for arbitration the parties are unable to agree on the organization of the arbitration, any one of those parties may refer the dispute to the International Court of Justice by request in conformity with the Statute of the Court.

2. Each State may at the time of signature or ratification of this Convention or accession thereto declare that it does not consider itself bound by para-

graph 1 of this article. The other States Parties shall not be bound by paragraph 1 of this article with respect to any State Party which has made such a reservation.

3. Any State Party which has made a reservation in accordance, with paragraph 2 of this article may at any time withdraw that reservation by notification to the Secretary-General of the United Nations.

Article 17

1. This Convention is open for signature by all States until 31 December 1980 at United Nations Headquarters in New York.

2. This Convention is subject to ratification. The instruments of ratification shall be deposited with the Secretary-General of the United Nations.

3. This Convention is open for accession by any State. The instruments of accession shall be deposited with the Secretary-General of the United Nations.

Article 18

1. This Convention shall enter into force on the thirtieth day following the date of deposit of the twenty-second instrument of ratification or accession with the Secretary-General of the United Nations.

2. For each State ratifying or acceding to the Convention after the deposit of the twenty-second instrument of ratification or accession, the Convention shall enter into force on the thirtieth day after deposit by such State of its instrument of ratification or accession.

Article 19

1. Any State Party may denounce this Convention by written notification to the Secretary-General of the United Nations.

2. Denunciation shall take effect one year following the date on which notification is received by the Secretary-General of the United Nations.

Article 20

The original of this Convention, of which the Arabic, Chinese, English, French, Russian and Spanish texts are equally authentic, shall be deposited with the Secretary-General of the United Nations, who shall send certified copies thereof to all States.

IN WITNESS WHEREOF, the undersigned, being duly authorized thereto by their respective Governments, have signed this Convention, opened for signature at New York on 18 December 1979.

I hereby certify that the foregoing text is a true copy of the International Convention against the taking of hostages, adopted by the General Assembly of the United Nations on 17 December 1979, the original of which is deposited with the Secretary-General of the United Nations.

THE TAKING OF HOSTAGES

For the Secretary-General: The Legal Counsel.

United Nations, New York, March 24, 1980.

The Convention was adopted by resolution 34/146[1] of the General Assembly of the United Nations dated 17 December 1979. It was opened for signature from 18 December 1979 to 31 December 1980.

States which are currently parties:

Afghanistan
Albania
Algeria
Antigua and Barbuda
Argentina
Armenia
Australia
Austria
Azerbaijan
Bahamas
Barbados
Belarus
Belgium
Belize
Benin
Bhutan
Bolivia
Bosnia and Herzegovina[2]
Botswana
Brazil
Brunei Darussalam
Bulgaria
Burkina Faso
Cameroon
Canada
Cape Verde
Chile
China[3,4]
Comoros
Costa Rica
Côte d'Ivoire
Croatia
Cuba
Cyprus
Czech Republic[5]
Democratic People's Republic of Korea
Democratic Republic of the Congo
Denmark
Dominica
Dominican Republic
Ecuador
Egypt
El Salvador
Equatorial Guinea
Estonia
Ethiopia
Finland
France
Gabon
Georgia
Germany[6,7]
Ghana
Greece
Grenada
Guatemala
Haiti
Honduras
Hungary
Iceland
India
Iraq
Israel
Italy
Jamaica
Japan

THE TAKING OF HOSTAGES

Jordan
Kazakhstan
Kenya
Kuwait
Kyrgyzstan
Lao People's Democratic Republic
Latvia
Lebanon
Lesotho
Liberia
Libyan Arab Jamahiriya
Liechtenstein
Lithuania
Luxembourg
Madagascar
Malawi
Mali
Malta
Marshall Islands
Mauritania
Mauritius
Mexico
Monaco
Mongolia
Mozambique
Nepal
Netherlands[8]
New Zealand[9]
Nicaragua
Norway
Oman
Pakistan
Palau
Panama
Papua New Guinea
Peru
Philippines
Poland
Portugal[4]
Republic of Korea

Republic of Moldova
Romania
Russian Federation
Rwanda
Saint Kitts and Nevis
Saint Vincent and the Grenadines
Saudi Arabia
Senegal
Serbia and Montenegro[2]
Seychelles
Sierra Leone
Slovakia[5]
Slovenia[2]
South Africa
Spain
Sri Lanka
Sudan
Suriname
Swaziland
Sweden
Switzerland
Tajikistan
The Former Yugoslav Republic of Macedonia[2]
Togo
Tonga
Trinidad and Tobago
Tunisia
Turkey
Turkmenistan
Uganda
Ukraine
United Arab Emirates
United Kingdom of Great Britain and Northern Ireland[3,10]
United Republic of Tanzania
United States of America
Uruguay
Uzbekistan
Venezuela
Yemen

DECLARATIONS

Declarations and Reservations

(Unless otherwise indicated, the declarations and reservations were made upon ratification, accession or succession.)

Algeria

Reservation:

> The Government of the People's Democratic Republic of Algeria does not consider itself bound by the provisions of article 16, paragraph 1, of the [said Convention].
>
> These provisions are not in accordance with the view of the Government of the People's Democratic Republic of Algeria that the submission of a dispute to the International Court of Justice requires the prior agreement of all the parties concerned in each case.

Belarus

The Byelorussian Soviet Socialist Republic does not consider itself bound by article 16, paragraph 1, of the International Convention against the Taking of Hostages and declares that, in order for any dispute between parties to the Convention concerning the interpretation or application thereof to be referred to arbitration or to the International Court of Justice, the consent of all parties to the dispute must be secured in each individual case.

The Byelorussian Soviet Socialist Republic condemns international terrorism, which takes the lives of innocent people, constitutes a threat to their freedom and personal inviolability and destabilizes the international situation, whatever the motives used to explain terrorist actions. Accordingly, the Byelorussian Soviet Socialist Republic considers that article 9, paragraph 1, of the Convention should be applied in a manner consistent with the stated aims of the Convention, which include the development of international co-operation in adopting effective measures for the prevention, prosecution and punishment of all acts of hostage-taking as manifestations of international terrorism through, inter alia, the extradition of alleged offenders.

Brazil

Reservation:

> With the reservation provided under article 16 (2).

Bulgaria[11]

Declaration on article 9, paragraph 1:

> The People's Republic of Bulgaria condemns all acts of international terrorism, whose victims are not only governmental and public officials but also many innocent people, including mothers, children, old-aged, and which exerts an increasingly destabilizing impact on international relations, complicates considerably the political solution of crisis situations, irrespective of the reasons invoked to explain terrorist acts. The People's Republic of Bulgaria considers that article 9, paragraph 1 of the Convention should be applied in a manner consistent with the stated aims of the Convention, which include the development of international co-operation in adopting effective measures for the prevention, prosecution and punishment of all acts of hostage-taking as manifestations of international terrorism, including extradition of alleged offenders.

THE TAKING OF HOSTAGES

Chile

The Government of the Republic [of Chile], having approved this Convention, states that such approval is given on the understanding that the aforesaid Convention prohibits the taking of hostages in any circumstances, even those referred to in article 12.

China

Reservation:

> The People's Republic of China makes its reservation to article 16, paragraph 1, and does not consider itself bound by the provisions of article 16, paragraph 1, of the Convention.

Cuba

Reservation:

> The Republic of Cuba declares, pursuant to article 16, paragraph 2, that it does not consider itself bound by paragraph 1 of the said article, concerning the settlement of disputes arising between States Parties, inasmuch as it considers that such disputes must be settled through amicable negotiation. In consequence, it reiterates that it does not recognize the compulsory jurisdiction of the International Court of Justice.

Czech Republic[3]

Democratic People's Republic of Korea

Reservations: . . . with the following reservations:

> 1. The Democratic People's Republic of Korea does not consider itself bound by the provisions of article 16, paragraph 1 of the Convention.
>
> 2. The Democratic People's Republic of Korea does not consider itself bound by the provisions of article 5, paragraph 3 of the Convention.

Dominica

Understanding:

> "The aforesaid Convention prohibits the taking of hostages in any circumstances, even those referred to in article 12."

El Salvador

Upon signature:

> With the reservation permitted under article 16 (2) of the said Convention.

Upon ratification:

> Reservation with respect to the application of the provisions of article 16, paragraph 1 of the Convention.

Ethiopia

Reservation pursuant to article 16 (2):

> "The Government of the Federal Democratic Republic of Ethiopia does not consider itself bound by the aforementioned provision of the Convention, under which any dispute between two or more States Parties concerning the interpretation or application of the Convention shall, at the request of one of them, be submitted to arbitration or to the International Court of Justice, and states that disputes concerning the interpretation or application of the Convention would be submitted to arbitration or to the Court only with the prior consent of all the parties concerned."

France

Declarations:

1. France considers that the act of hostage-taking is prohibited in all circumstances.

2. With regard to the application of article 6, France, in accordance with the principles of its penal procedure, does not intend to take an alleged offender into custody or to take any other coercive measures prior to the institution of criminal proceedings, except in cases where pre-trial detention has been requested.

3. With regard to the application of article 9, extradition will not be granted if the person whose extradition is requested was a French national at the time of the events or, in the case of a foreign national, if the offence is punishable by the death penalty under the laws of the requesting State, unless that State gives what are deemed to be adequate assurances that the death penalty will not be imposed or, if a death sentence is passed, that it will not be carried out.

Hungary[12]

India

Reservation:

"The Government of the Republic of India declares that it does not consider itself bound by paragraph 1 of article 16 which establishes compulsory arbitration or adjudication by the International Court of Justice concerning disputes between two or more States Parties relating to the interpretation or application of this Convention at the request of one of them."

Israel

Upon signature:

"1. It is the understanding of Israel that the Convention implements the principle that hostage taking is prohibited in all circumstances and that any person committing such an act shall be either prosecuted or extradited pursuant to article 8 of this Convention or the relevant provisions of the Geneva Conventions of 1949 or their additional Protocols, without any exception whatsoever.

"2) The Government of Israel declares that it reserves the right, when depositing the instrument of ratification, to make reservations and additional declarations and understandings."

Italy

Upon signature:

The Italian Government declares that, because of the differing interpretations to which certain formulations in the text lend themselves, Italy reserves the right, when depositing the instrument of ratification, to invoke article 19 of the Vienna Convention on the Law of Treaties of 23 May 1969 in conformity with the general principles of international law.

Jordan

"The Government of the Hashemite Kingdom of Jordan declares that their accession to the International Convention against the Taking of Hostages can in no way be construed as constituting recognition of, or entering into treaty relations with the 'state of Israel'.

Kenya

"The Government of the Republic of Kenya does not consider herself bound by the provisions of paragraph (1) of the article 16 of the Convention."

THE TAKING OF HOSTAGES

Kuwait[13]

Declaration:

> It is understood that the accession to this Convention does not mean in any way a recognition of Israel by the Government of the State of Kuwait.
>
> Furthermore, no treaty relations will arise between the State of Kuwait and Israel.

Lao People's Democratic Republic

Reservation:

> "In accordance with paragraph 2, Article 16 of the International Convention Against the Taking of Hostages, the Lao People's Democratic Republic does not consider itself bound by paragraph 1, article 16 of the present Convention. The Lao People's Democratic Republic declares that to refer a dispute relating to interpretation and application of the present Convention to arbitration or International Court of Justice, the agreement of all parties concerned in the dispute is necessary."

Lebanon

Declaration:

> 1. The accession of the Lebanese Republic to the Convention shall not constitute recognition of Israel, just as the application of the Convention shall not give rise to relations or cooperation of any kind with it.
>
> 2. The provisions of the Convention, and in particular those of its article 13, shall not affect the Lebanese Republic's stance of supporting the right of States and peoples to oppose and resist foreign occupation of their territories.

Liechtenstein

Interpretative declaration:

> The Principality of Liechtenstein construes article 4 of the Convention to mean that the Principality of Liechtenstein undertakes to fulfil the obligations contained therein under the conditions laid down in its domestic legislation.

Malawi

"While the Government of the Republic of Malawi accepts the principles in article 16, this acceptance would nonetheless be read in conjunction with [the] declaration [made by the President and the Minister for Foreign Affairs of Malawi] of 12 December, 1966 upon recognition as compulsory, the jurisdiction of the International Court of Justice under article 36, paragraph 2, of the State of the Court."

Mexico

In relation to article 16, the United Mexican States adhere to the scope and limitations established by the Government of Mexico on 7 November 1945, at the time when it ratified the Charter of the United Nations and the Statute of the International Court of Justice.

6 August 1987

The Government of Mexico subsequently specified that the said declaration should be understood to mean that, in so far as article 16 is concerned, the United Mexican States accede subject to the limits and restrictions laid down by the Mexican Government when recognizing, on 23 October 1947, the compulsory jurisdiction of the International Court of Justice in accordance with article 36, paragraph 2, of the State of the Court.

THE TAKING OF HOSTAGES

Mozambique

Declaration:

" . . . with the following declaration in accordance with its article 16, paragraph 2:

"The Republic of Mozambique does not consider itself bound by the provisions of article 16 paragraph 1 of the Convention.

In this connection, the Republic of Mozambique states that, in each individual case, the consent of all Parties to such a dispute is necessary for the submission of the dispute to arbitration or to [the] International Court of Justice."

Furthermore, the Republic of Mozambique declares that:

"The Republic of Mozambique, in accordance with its Constitution and domestic laws, can not extradite Mozambique citizens.

Therefore, Mozambique citizens will be tried and sentenced in national courts."

Netherlands

Reservation:

"In cases where the judicial authorities of either the Netherlands, the Netherlands Antilles or Aruba cannot exercise jurisdiction pursuant to one of the principles mentioned in article 5, paragraph 1, the Kingdom accepts the aforesaid obligation [laid down in article 8] subject to the condition that it has received and rejected a request for extradition from another State party to the Convention."

Declaration:

"In the view of the Government of the Kingdom of the Netherlands article 15 of the Convention, and in particular the second sentence of that article, in no way affects the applicability of article 33 of the Convention of 28 July 1951 relating to the Status of Refugees."

Republic of Moldova

Reservation:

Pursuant to article 16, paragraph 2 of the International Convention against the Taking of Hostages, the Republic of Moldova declares that it does not consider itself bound by the provisions of article 16, paragraph 1 of the Convention.

Russian Federation

[Same reservation and declaration identical in substance, mutatis mutandis, as those made by Belarus.]

Saudi Arabia[13]

Reservation:

1. The Kingdom of Saudi Arabia does not consider itself obligated with the provision of paragraph 1, of article 16, of the Convention concerning arbitration.

Declaration:

2. The accession of the Kingdom of Saudi Arabia to this Convention does not constitute a recognition of Israel and does not lead to entering into any transactions or the establishment of any relations based on this Convention.

Serbia and Montenegro[2]

Confirmed upon succession:

Declaration:

"The [Government of Yugoslavia] herewith states that the provisions of Article 9 of the Convention should be interpreted and applied in practice in the way which would not

DOCUMENTS AND COMMENTARY

THE TAKING OF HOSTAGES

bring into question the goals of the Convention, i.e. undertaking of efficient measures for the prevention of all acts of the taking of hostages as a phenomenon of international terrorism, as well as the prosecution, punishment and extradition of persons considered to have perpetrated this criminal offence."

Slovakia[3]

Switzerland

Declaration:

The Swiss Federal Council interprets article 4 of the Convention to mean that Switzerland undertakes to fulfil the obligations contained therein in the conditions specified by its domestic legislation.

Tunisia

Reservation:

[The Government of the Republic of Tunisia] declares that it does not consider itself bound by the provisions of paragraph 1 of article 16 and states that disputes concerning the interpretation or application of the Convention can only be submitted to arbitration or to the International Court of Justice with the prior consent of all the Parties concerned.

Turkey

Reservation:

In acceding to the Convention the Government of the Republic of Turkey, under article 16 (2) of the Convention declares that it doesn't consider itself bound by the provisions of paragraph (1) of the said article.

Ukraine

[Same reservation and declaration identical in substance, mutatis mutandis, as those made by Belarus.]

Venezuela

Declaration:

The Republic of Venezuela declares that it is not bound by the provisions of article 16, paragraph 1, of the Convention.

Objections

(Unless otherwise indicated, the objections were received upon ratification, accession, acceptance, approval, formal confirmation or succession.)

Israel

9 September 1998

With regard to declarations made by Lebanon upon accession:

" ... The Government of Israel refers in particular to the political declaration "[see declaration "1" made under "Lebanon"] made by the Lebanese Republic on acceding to the [said] Convention.

"In the view of the Government of Israel, this Convention is not the proper place for making declarations of a political character. The Government of Israel will, in so far as concerns the substance of the matter adopt towards the Lebanese Republic an attitude of complete reciprocity.

"Moreover, in view of the Government of Israel, the Lebanese understanding of certain of the Convention's provisions [see declaration "2" made under "Lebanon"] is incompatible with and contradictory to the object and purpose of the Convention and in effect defeats that object and purpose.""

Communications made under article 7 of the Convention

Saudi Arabia

11 December 2001

[For the text of the communication see depositary notification C.N.1500.2001.TREATIES of 8 January 2002]

NOTES

1. Official Records of the General Assembly, Thirty-fourth Session, Supplement No. 46 (A/34/46), p. 245.

2. The former Yugoslavia had signed and ratified the Convention on 29 December 1980 and 19 April 1985, respectively, with the following reservation (made upon signature) and declaration (made upon ratification):

"With the reservation with regard to article 9, subject to subsequent approval pursuant to the constitutional provisions in force in Socialist Federal Republic of Yugoslavia".

Declaration:

"The Government of the Yugoslavia herewith states that the provisions of Article 9 of the Convention should be interpreted and applied in practice in the way which would not bring into question the goals of the Convention, i.e. undertaking of efficient measures for the prevention of all acts of the taking of hostages as a phenomenon of international terrorism, as well as the prosecution, punishment and extradition of persons considered to have perpetrated this criminal offence."

See also note 1 under "Bosnia and Herzegovina", "Croatia", "former Yugoslavia", "Slovenia", "The Former Yugoslav Republic of Macedonia" and "Yugoslavia" in the "Historical Information" section in the front matter of this volume.

3. The Secretary-General received, on 6 and 10 June 1999, communications concerning the status of Hong Kong from China and the United Kingdom (see also note 2 under "China" and note 2 under "United Kingdom of Great Britain and Northern Ireland" regarding Hong Kong in the "Historical Information" section in the front matter of this volume). Upon resuming the exercise of sovereignty over Hong Kong, China notified the Secretary-General that the Convention with reservation will also apply to the Hong Kong Special Administrative Region.

4. On 28 June 1999, the Government of Portugal informed the Secretary-General that the Convention would also apply to Macao. Subsequently, the Secretary-General received, on 27 October and 3 December 1999, communications concerning the status of Macao from Portugal and China (see also note 3 under "China" and note 1 under "Portugal" regarding Macao in the "Historical Information" section in the front matter of this volume). Upon resuming the exercise of sovereignty over Macao, China notified the Secretary-General that the Convention will also apply to the Macao Special Administrative Region.

5. Czechoslovakia had acceded to the Convention on 27 January 1988, with the following reservation to article 16 (1):

The Czechoslovak Socialist Republic does not consider itself bound by the provision of its article 16, paragraph 1, and states that, in accordance with the principle of sovereign equality of States, for any dispute to be submitted to a conciliation procedure or to the International Court of Justice the consent of all the parties to the dispute is required in each separate case.

Subsequently, on 26 April 1991, the Government of Czechoslovakia notified the Secretary-General of its decision to withdraw the said reservation.

See also note 1 under "Czech Republic" and note 1 under "Slovakia" in the "Historical Information" section in the front matter of this volume.

6. See note 1 under "Germany" regarding Berlin (West) in the "Historical Information" section in the front matter of this volume.

7. The German Democratic Republic had acceded to the Convention on 2 May 1988 with the following reservation and declaration:

Reservation regarding article 16, paragraph 1:

> The German Democratic Republic does not consider itself bound by the provisions of article 16, paragraph 1, of the International Convention against the Taking of Hostages and declares that in every single case the consent of all parties in the dispute is necessary to submit to arbitration or refer to the International Court of Justice any dispute between the States Parties to the Convention concerning the interpretation or application of the Convention.

Declaration regarding article 9, paragraph 1:

> The German Democratic Republic decisively condemns any act of international terrorism. Therefore, the German Democratic Republic holds the opinion that article 9, paragraph 1, of the Convention shall be applied in such a way as to be in correspondence with the declared aims of the Convention which embrace the taking of effective measures for the prevention, prosecution and punishment of all acts of international terrorism, including the taking of hostages.

See also note 2 under "Germany" in the "Historical Information" section in the front matter of this volume.

8. For the Kingdom in Europe, the Netherlands Antilles and Aruba.

9. For New Zealand (except Tokelau), Cook Islands and Niue.

10. In respect of the United Kingdom of Great Britain and Northern Ireland and the Territories under the territorial sovereignty of the United Kingdom. See also note 3.

11. On 24 June 1992, the Government of Bulgaria notified the Secretary-General of its decision to withdraw the reservation to article 16 (1) of the Convention, made upon accession which reads as follows:

The People's Republic of Bulgaria does not consider itself bound by the provisions of article 16, paragraph 1 of the International Convention against the Taking of Hostages and declares that submission of any dispute concerning interpretation and application of the Convention between parties to the Convention to arbitration or to the International Court of Justice requires the consent of all parties to the dispute in each individual case.

12. In a communication received on 8 December 1989, the Government of Hungary notified the Secretary-General that it had decided to withdraw its reservation with respect to article 16 made upon accession which reads as follows:

> The Hungarian People's Republic does not consider itself bound by the dispute settlement procedures provided for in article 16, paragraph ,1 of the Convention, since in its opinion, the jurisdiction of any arbitral tribunal or of the International Court of Justice can be founded only on the voluntary prior acceptance of such jurisdiction by all the Parties concerned.

13. On 17 May 1989, the Secretary-General received from the Government of Israel the following communication:

"The Government of the State of Israel has noted that the instrument of accession by the Government of Kuwait to the above-mentioned Convention contains a declaration in respect to Israel. In the view of the Government of the State of Israel, such declaration, which is explicitly of a political character, is incompatible with the purposes and objectives of this Convention and cannot in any way affect whatever obligations are binding upon the Government of Kuwait under general international law or under particular Conventions.

"The Government of the State of Israel, will insofar as concerns the substance of the matter, adopt towards the Government of Kuwait an attitude of complete reciprocity."

On 22 May 1991, the Secretary-General received from the Government of Israel a communication, identical in essence, mutatis mutandis , with regard to the declaration made by Saudi Arabia upon accession.

PROTOCOL FOR THE SUPPRESSION OF UNLAWFUL ACTS OF VIOLENCE AT AIRPORTS SERVING INTERNATIONAL CIVIL AVIATION

COMMENTARY

The 1971 Tokyo Convention addressed instances where an unlawful act was committed against civil aviation. This Protocol extended coverage to offences which involved violent acts against persons in an international airport. Not surprisingly, adoption of the Protocol was preceded by a series of terrorist acts that included the Rome and Vienna airports during 1985 and the Seoul airport in 1986.

In the United States, the Protocol has been implemented through the provisions of Title 18, Section 37 of the United States Code. As pointed out by the Department of Justice, Section 37

> ". . . makes it a Federal crime, using any device, substance or weapon, to intentionally perform an act of violence against any person at an airport serving international aviation or to destroy or seriously damage the facilities of such an airport . . . "

Furthermore, " . . . the Antiterrorism and Effective Death Penalty Act of 1996 expanded its extraterritorial jurisdiction to also cover the prohibited activity occurring overseas when either a national of the United States is a victim or a perpetrator of the offense."

PROTOCOL FOR THE SUPPRESSION OF UNLAWFUL ACTS OF VIOLENCE AT AIRPORTS SERVING INTERNATIONAL CIVIL AVIATION

Adopted at Montreal 24 February 1988
Entered into force 6 August 1989*

PROTOCOL

THE STATES PARTIES TO THIS PROTOCOL:

Considering that unlawful acts of violence which endanger or are likely to endanger the safety of persons at airports serving international civil aviation or which jeopardize the safe operation of such airports undermine the confidence of the peoples of the world in safety at such airports and disturb the safe and orderly conduct of civil aviation for all States;

Considering that the occurrence of such acts is a matter of grave concern to the international community and that, for the purpose of deterring such acts, there is an urgent need to provide appropriate measures for punishment of offenders;

Considering that it is necessary to adopt provisions supplementary to those of the Convention for the Suppression of Unlawful Acts against the Safety of Civil Aviation,** done at Montreal on 23 September 1971, to deal with such unlawful acts of violence at airports serving international civil aviation;

---

*   Treaties and International Agreements Online, CTIA 8071.001 (Oceana Publications, Inc. <www.oceanalaw.com>.

** Reproduced at page 43.

HAVE AGREED as follows:

Article I

This Protocol supplements the Convention for the Suppression of Unlawful Acts against the Safety of Civil Aviation, done at Montreal on 23 September 1971 (hereinafter referred to as "the Convention"), and, as between the Parties to this Protocol, the Convention and the Protocol shall be read and interpreted together as one single instrument.

Article II

1. In Article 1 of the Convention, the following shall be added as new paragraph 1 bis:

> "1 bis. Any person commits an offense if he unlawfully and intentionally using any device, substance or weapon:
>
> (a) performs an act of violence against a person at an airport serving international civil aviation which causes or is likely to cause serious injury or death; or
>
> (b) destroys or seriously damages the facilities of an airport serving international civil aviation or aircraft not in service located thereon or disrupts the services of the airport.
>
> if such an act endangers or is likely to endanger safety at that airport."

2. In paragraph 2 (a) of Article 1 of the Convention, the following words shall be inserted after the words "paragraph 1":

> "or paragraph 1 bis".

Article III

In Article 5 of the Convention, the following shall be added as paragraph 2 bis:

> "2 bis. Each Contracting State shall likewise take such measures as may be necessary to establish its jurisdiction over the offences mentioned in Article 1, paragraph 1 bis, and in Article 1, paragraph 2, in so far as that paragraph relates to those offences, in the case where the alleged offender is present in its territory and it does not extradite him pursuant to Article 8 to the State mentioned in paragraph 1 (a) of this Article."

Article IV

This Protocol shall be open for signature at Montreal on 24 February 1988 by States participating in the International Conference on Air Law held at Montreal from 9 to 24 February 1988. After 1 March 1988, the Protocol shall be open for signature to all States in London, Moscow, Washington and Montreal, until it enters into force in accordance with Article VI.

Article V

1. This Protocol shall be subject to ratification by the signatory States.

2. Any State which is not a Contracting State to the Convention may ratify this Protocol if at the same time it ratifies or accedes to the Convention in accordance with Article 15 thereof.

3. Instruments of ratification shall be deposited with the Governments of the Union of Soviet Socialist Republics, the United Kingdom of Great Britain and Northern Ireland and the United States of America or with the International Civil Aviation Organization, which are hereby designated the Depositaries.

Article VI

1. As soon as ten of the signatory States have deposited their instruments of ratification of this Protocol, it shall enter into force between them on the thirtieth day after the date of the deposit of the tenth instrument of ratification. It shall enter into force for each State which deposits its instrument of ratification after that date on the thirtieth day after deposit of its instrument of ratification.

2. As soon as this Protocol enters into force, it shall be registered by the Depositaries pursuant to Article 102 of the Charter of the United Nations and pursuant to Article 83 of the Convention on International Civil Aviation (Chicago, 1944).

Article VII

1. This Protocol shall, after it has entered into force, be open for accession by any non-signatory State.

2. Any State which is not a Contracting State to the Convention may accede to this Protocol if at the same time it ratifies or accedes to the Convention in accordance with Article 15 thereof.

3. Instruments of accession shall be deposited with the Depositaries and accession shall take effect on the thirtieth day after the deposit.

Article VIII

1. Any Party to this Protocol may denounce it by written notification addressed to the Depositaries.

2. Denunciation shall take effect six months following the date on which notification is received by the Depositaries.

3. Denunciation of this Protocol shall not of itself have the effect of denunciation of the Convention.

4. Denunciation of the Convention by

Contracting State to the Convention as supplemented by this Protocol shall also have the effect of denunciation of this Protocol.

Article IX

1. The Depositaries shall promptly inform all signatory and acceding States to this Protocol and all signatory and acceding States to the Convention:

(a) of the date of each signature and the date of deposit of each instrument of ratification of, or accession to, this Protocol, and

(b) of the receipt of any notification of denunciation of this Protocol and the date thereof. 2. The Depositaries shall also notify the States referred to in paragraph 1 of the date on which this Protocol enters into force in accordance with Article VI.

IN WITNESS WHEREOF the undersigned Plenipotentiaries, being duly authorized thereto by their Governments, have signed this Protocol.

DONE at Montreal on the twenty-fourth day of February of the year One Thousand Nine Hundred and Eighty-eight, in four originals, each being drawn up in four authentic texts in the English, French, Russian and Spanish languages.

ACTS OF VIOLENCE AT AIRPORTS

Parties:

Albania
Algeria
Argentina
Armenia
Australia
Austria
Azerbaijan
Bahrain
Barbados
Belarus
Belgium
Belize
Benin
Bolivia
Bosnia and Herzegovina[1]
Botswana
Brazil
Brunei Darussalam
Bulgaria
Burkina Faso
Cambodia
Cameroon
Canada
Cape Verde
Central African Republic
Chile
China[2,18]
Colombia
Congo
Costa Rica
Côte d'Ivoire
Croatia[3]
Cuba
Cyprus
Czech Republic[4]
Democratic People's Republic of Korea
Democratic Republic of the Congo
Denmark[5]

Djibouti
Ecuador
Egypt
El Salvador
Equatorial Guinea
Estonia
Ethiopia
Fiji
Finland
France[6]
Gabon
Gambia
Georgia
Germany[7]
Ghana
Greece
Grenada
Guatemala
Guinea
Guyana
Honduras
Hungary
Iceland
India
Indonesia
Iran (Islamic Republic of)
Iraq
Ireland
Israel
Italy
Jamaica
Japan
Jordan
Kazakhstan
Kenya
Kuwait[8]
Kyrgyzstan
Lao People's Democratic Republic
Latvia

ACTS OF VIOLENCE AT AIRPORTS

Lebanon	Russian Federation
Liberia	Rwanda
Libyan Arab Jamahiriya	Saint Lucia
Liechtenstein	Saint Vincent and the Grenadines
Lithuania	Samoa
Luxembourg	Saudi Arabia
Madagascar	Senegal
Malawi	Serbia and Montenegro[16]
Malaysia	Seychelles
Maldives	Singapore
Mali	Slovakia[10]
Malta	Slovenia[11]
Marshall Islands	South Africa
Mauritania	Spain
Mauritius	Sri Lanka
Mexico	Sudan
Micronesia (Federated States of)	Suriname
Monaco	Sweden
Mongolia	Switzerland
Morocco	Syrian Arab Republic[17]
Mozambique	Tajikistan
Myanmar	Thailand
Netherlands[9]	The former Yugoslav Republic of Macedonia[12]
New Zealand	
Nicaragua	Togo
Niger	Tonga
Nigeria	Trinidad and Tobago
Norway	Tunisia
Oman	Turkey
Pakistan	Turkmenistan
Palau	Uganda
Panama	Ukraine
Papua New Guinea	United Arab Emirates
Paraguay	United Kingdom[13,14,15]
Peru	United Republic of Tanzania
Philippines	United States
Poland	Uruguay
Portugal	Uzbekistan
Republic of Korea	Venezuela
Republic of Moldova	Viet Nam
Romania	

ACTS OF VIOLENCE AT AIRPORTS

Notes

(1) An instrument of succession by the Government of Bosnia and Herzegovina to the Protocol was deposited with the Government of the United States on 15 August 1994.

(2) Notification issued by the Government of the People's Republic of China dated 12 June 1997:

> "It is provided both in Section XI of Annex 1 to the Joint Declaration, 'Elaboration by the Government of the People's Republic of China of its Basic Policies Regarding Hong Kong', and Article 153 of the Basic Law of the Hong Kong Special Administrative Region of the People's Republic of China, . . . , that international agreements to which the People's Republic of China is not a party but which are implemented in Hong Kong may continue to be implemented in the Hong Kong Special Administrative Region.
>
> In accordance with the above provisions, I am instructed by the Minister of Foreign Affairs of the People's Republic of China to make the following notification: The Protocol . . . , which applies to Hong Kong at present, will continue to apply to the Hong Kong Special Administrative Region with effect from 1 July 1997.
>
> Within the above ambit, responsibility for the international rights and obligations of a party to the Protocol will be assumed by the Government of the People's Republic of China."

The Government of the People's Republic of China made the following reservation at the time of ratification of the Protocol: "the reservation made by the People's Republic of China, when it adhered to the Convention, on paragraph 1 of Article 14 of the 'Convention for the Suppression of Unlawful Acts against the Safety of Civil Aviation' done at Montreal on 23 September 1971 is also applicable to this Protocol."

(3) An instrument of succession by the Government of Croatia to the Protocol was deposited with the Government of the United States on 8 June 1993.

(4) By a Note dated 8 March 1993, received on 25 March 1993, the Government of the Czech Republic informed the International Civil Aviation Organization that, as a successor State created as a result of the dissolution of the Czech and Slovak Federal Republic, it considered itself bound by the Protocol with effect from 1 January 1993.

(5) The Government of Denmark made the following reservation at the time of ratification of the Protocol: "Until later decision, the Protocol will not be applied to the Faroe Islands."

Note: On 27 September 1994, a declaration dated 22 September 1994 was deposited with the International Civil Aviation Organization by the Government of Denmark whereby that Government withdraws the above reservation, with effect from 1 October 1994.

(6) The Government of France made the following declaration at the time of signature of the Protocol:

> "The French Republic recalls the declaration made at the time of its accession to the Convention for the Suppression of Unlawful Acts against the Safety of Civil Aviation of 23 September 1971, when it stated that: 'In accordance with Article 14, paragraph 2, the French Republic does not consider itself bound by the provisions of paragraph 1 of that Article under which any dispute between two or more Contracting States concerning the interpretation or application of this Convention which cannot be settled through negotiation, shall, at the request of one of them, be submitted to arbitration. If within six months from the date of the request for arbitration the Parties are unable to agree on the organization of the arbitration, any one of those Parties may refer the dispute to the International Court of Justice by request in conformity with the Statute of the Court.'
>
> The above declaration is applicable to the Protocol for the Suppression of Unlawful Acts of Violence at Airports Serving International Civil Aviation, Supplementary to the Convention for the Suppression of Unlawful Acts against the Safety of Civil Aviation of 23 September 1971."

In addition, the following declaration was made by that Government at the time of ratification:

"In depositing its instrument of ratification of the Protocol of 24 February 1988 for the Suppression of Unlawful Acts of Violence at Airports Serving International Civil Aviation, Supplementary to the Convention for the Suppression of Unlawful Acts against the Safety of Civil Aviation done at Montreal on 23 September 1971, the French Republic recalls and confirms the declaration made at the time of its accession to the said Convention, when it stated that: 'In accordance with Article 14, paragraph 2, the French Republic does not consider itself bound by the provisions of paragraph 1 of that Article under which any dispute between two or more Contracting States concerning the interpretation or application of this Convention which cannot be settled through negotiation, shall, at the request of one of them, be submitted to arbitration. If within six months from the date of the request for arbitration the Parties are unable to agree on the organization of the arbitration, any one of those Parties may refer the dispute to the International Court of Justice by request in conformity with the Statute of the Court.'

The above declaration is applicable to the Protocol for the Suppression of Unlawful Acts of Violence at Airports Serving International Civil Aviation, Supplementary to the Convention for the Suppression of Unlawful Acts against the Safety of Civil Aviation of 23 September 1971."

(7) The German Democratic Republic, which ratified the Protocol on 31 January 1989, acceded to the Federal Republic of Germany on 3 October 1990.

(8) It is understood that the ratification of this Protocol does not mean in any way a recognition of Israel by the Government of the State of Kuwait. Furthermore, no treaty relations will arise between the State of Kuwait and Israel.

(9) The Government of the Kingdom of the Netherlands made the following interpretative statement at the time of signature of the Protocol:

"The Government of the Kingdom of the Netherlands hereby declares that, in the light of the preamble, it understands the provisions laid down in Articles II and III of the Protocol to signify the following:

- only those acts which, in view of the nature of the weapons used and the place where they are committed, cause or are likely to cause incidental loss of life or serious injury among the general public or users of international civil aviation in particular, shall be classed as acts of violence within the meaning of the new paragraph 1 bis (a), as contained in Article II of the Protocol;

- only those acts which, in view of the damage which they cause to buildings or aircraft at the airport or their disruption of the services provided by the airport, endanger or are likely to endanger the safe operation of the airport in relation to international civil aviation, shall be classed as acts of violence within the meaning of the new paragraph 1 bis (b), as contained in Article II of the Protocol."

On depositing its instrument of ratification, the Kingdom of the Netherlands made the following declaration:

"The Government of the Kingdom of the Netherlands hereby declares that, in the light of the preamble, it understands the provisions laid down in Article II and III of the Protocol to signify the following:

- only those acts which, in the view of the nature of the weapons used and the place where they are committed, cause or are likely to cause incidental loss of life or serious injury among the general public or users of international civil law aviation in particular, shall be classed as acts of violence within the meaning of the new paragraph 1 bis (a), as contained in Article II of the Protocol;

- only those acts which, in view of the damage which they cause to buildings or aircraft at the airport or their disruption of the services provided by the airport, endanger or are likely to endanger the safe operation of the airport in relation to international civil aviation, shall be classed as acts of violence within the meaning of the new paragraph 1 bis (b), as contained in Article II of the Protocol."

(10) By a Note dated 16 February 1995, received on 20 March 1995, the Government of Slovakia informed the International Civil Aviation Organization that, as a successor State, born from the dissolution of the Czech and Slovak Federal Republic, it considered itself bound by the Protocol with effect from 1 January 1993.

(11) An instrument of succession by the Government of Slovenia to the Protocol was deposited with the Government of the United Kingdom on 27 May 1992.

(12) An instrument of succession by the Government of the former Yugoslav Republic of Macedonia to the Protocol was deposited with the Government of the United States on 4 January 1995.

(13) The Government of the United Kingdom made the following declaration at the time of ratification of the Protocol: " . . . the United Kingdom declares that until consultations with various territories under the territorial sovereignty of the United Kingdom are completed, the Protocol will apply in respect of the United Kingdom of Great Britain and Northern Ireland only. Consultations with the territories are in hand and are expected to be completed by the end of 1991."

(14) Declaration made at the time of ratification by the Isle of Man: " . . . subsequent to the deposit of the United Kingdom's Instrument of Ratification in the Treaty Archives on 15 November 1990 The Isle of Man, for whose international relations the United Kingdom is responsible and whose Government has informed the Government of the United Kingdom that they wish to participate in the Protocol, has been included under the United Kingdom's ratification of the Protocol . . . to take effect from 14 February 1997."

(15) Statement issued by the Government of the United Kingdom of Great Britain and Northern Ireland, dated 18 June 1997:

" . . . in accordance with the Joint Declaration of the Government of the United Kingdom of Great Britain and Northern Ireland and the Government of the People's Republic of China on the Question of Hong Kong, signed on 19 December 1984, the Government of the United Kingdom will restore Hong Kong to the People's Republic of China with effect from 1 July 1997. The Government of the United Kingdom will continue to have international responsibility for Hong Kong until that date. Therefore, from that date the Government of the United Kingdom will cease to be responsible for the international rights and obligations arising from the application of the Protocol to Hong Kong."

(16) On 4 February 2003, the name of the State of the Federal Republic of Yugoslavia was changed to Serbia and Montenegro.

By a Note dated 17 July 2001, deposited on 6 September 2001 with ICAO, the Government of the Federal Republic of Yugoslavia declared itself bound, as a successor State to the Socialist Federal Republic of Yugoslavia, by the provisions of, inter alia, this Protocol, with effect from 27 April 1992, the date of State succession. (The former Socialist Federal Republic of Yugoslavia had signed the Protocol on 24 February 1988 and ratified it on 21 December 1989.)

(17) In its instrument of accession deposited on 18 July 2002 with ICAO, the Government of the Syrian Arab Republic made the following reservation: "the Syrian Arab Republic will not be bound by paragraph 1 of Article 14 of the Montreal Convention signed on 23 September 1971."

(18) By a note from the Ambassador of the People's Republic of China to the U.S. Secretary of State, dated 19 September 2002, the People's Republic of China extended the Protocol to the Macao Special Administrative Region of the People's Republic of China.

CONVENTION FOR THE SUPPRESSION OF UNLAWFUL ACTS AGAINST THE SAFETY OF MARITIME NAVIGATION

COMMENTARY

The negotiation and adoption of this Convention was tied directly to the October, 1985 Achille Lauro terrorist attack which resulted in the murder of an American citizen. It establishes, under international law, a new basis for combating acts of terrorism, whether on board a ship or on a fixed platform. Though sovereign immunity for warships is preserved (and a few other exceptions are noted), the Convention applies directly to any ship which is navigating or is scheduled to navigate beyond the territorial waters of any State.

President Reagan described, with clarity, the purpose of the Convention in his letter to the Congress:

> "The principal purpose of the Convention and Protocol is to ensure that individuals who commit acts of terrorist violence which endanger the safe navigation of a ship or the safety of a platform are either prosecuted in the state in which they are found or extradited to another state for prosecution" He went on to point out that as with the Hague and Montreal Conventions covering aircraft, the new Convention requires " . . . states to establish certain offenses under their criminal law, to provide a basis for the exercise of criminal jurisdiction in specified circumstances, and to extradite or prosecute any alleged offender found within their territory . . . "

The full text of the President's Message sending this Convention to the Senate follows:

"LETTER OF TRANSMITTAL

THE WHITE HOUSE,
January 3, 1989.

To the Senate of the United States:

With a view to receiving the advice and consent of the Senate to ratification, I transmit herewith the Convention for the Suppression of Unlawful Acts against the Safety of Maritime Navigation, and the related Protocol for the Suppression of Unlawful Acts against the Safety of Fixed Platforms Located on the Continental Shelf, signed at Rome on March 10, 1988. I also transmit, for the information of the Senate, the report of the Department of State with respect to the Convention and Protocol.

The seizure of the Italian cruise ship Achille Lauro in 1985, and the murder of American passenger Leon Klinghoffer, demonstrated that no country, or form of transportation, is immune from the criminal savagery of those who engage in terrorist acts. This Convention is aimed at ensuring that those who engage in such acts on board or against ships engaged in navigation are brought to justice. The Protocol would do the same with respect to acts on or against fixed platforms on the continental shelf. Modeled on earlier conventions dealing with aircraft hijacking and sabotage (to which the United States is a party), they include provisions requiring States to provide severe punishment for such offenses, and to extradite or prosecute those who commit them.

Work on the Convention and Protocol began in 1986 under the auspices of the International Maritime Organization on the basis of an initial draft co-sponsored by the Governments of Italy, Austria and Egypt. That work was completed, and the Convention and Protocol adopted by consensus, at an international conference in Rome in March 1988. The United States and 22 other States signed the Convention at that time, and the United States and 20 other States signed the Protocol. It is clear that the Convention already has broad support in the international community, and it is hoped that all States will join in this major step to deter acts against the safety of maritime navigation.

I recommend, therefore, that the Senate give early and favorable consideration to this Convention and Protocol and give its advice and consent to ratification.

RONALD REAGAN."

CONVENTION FOR THE SUPPRESSION OF UNLAWFUL ACTS AGAINST THE SAFETY OF MARITIME NAVIGATION

Adopted at Rome on 10 March 1988
Entered into force 1 March 1992*

THE STATES PARTIES TO THIS CONVENTION:

Having in mind the purposes and principles of the Charter of the United Nations concerning the maintenance of international peace and security and the promoting of friendly relations and co-operation among States,

Recognizing in particular that everyone has the right to life, liberty and security of person, as set out in the University Declaration of Human Rights and the International Covenant on Civil and Political Rights,

Deeply concerned about the world-wide escalation of acts of terrorism in all its forms, which endanger or take innocent human lives, jeopardize fundamental freedoms and seriously impair the dignity of human beings,

Considering that unlawful acts against the safety of maritime navigation jeopardize the safety of persons and property, seriously affect the operation of maritime services, and undermine the confidence of the people of the world in the safety of maritime navigation,

Considering that the occurrence of such acts is a matter of grave concern to the international community as a whole,

Being convinced of the urgent need to develop international co-operation between States in devising and adopting effective and practical measures for the prevention of all unlawful acts against the safety of maritime navigation, and the prosecution and punishment of their perpetrators,

---

* Treaties and International Agreements Online, CTIA 9285.000 (Oceana Publications, Inc. <www.oceanalaw.com>.

Recalling resolution 40/61 of the General Assembly of the United Nations of 9 December 1985 which, *inter alia*, "urges all States unilaterally and in co-operation with other States, as well as relevant United Nations organs, to contribute to the progressive elimination of causes underlying international terrorism and to pay special attention to all situations, including colonialism, racism and situations involving mass and flagrant violations of human rights and fundamental freedoms and those involving alien occupation, that may give rise to international terrorism and may endanger international peace and security".

Recalling further that resolution 40/61 "unequivocally condemns, as criminal, all acts, methods and practices of terrorism wherever and by whomever committed, including those which jeopardize friendly relations among States and their security",

Recalling also that by resolution 40/61, the International Maritime Organization was invited to "study the problem of terrorism aboard or against ships with a view to making recommendations on appropriate measures",

Having in mind resolution A.584(14) of 20 November 1985, of the Assembly of the International Maritime Organization, which called for development of measures to prevent unlawful acts which threaten the safety of ships and the security of their passengers and crews,

Noting that acts of the crews which are subject to normal shipboard discipline are outside the purview of this Convention,

Affirming the desirability of monitoring rules and standards relating to the prevention and control of unlawful acts against ships and persons on board ships, with a view to updating them as necessary, and, to this effect, taking note with satisfaction of the Measures to Prevent Unlawful Acts Against Passengers and Crews on Board Ships, recommended by the Maritime Safety Committee of the International Maritime Organization,

Affirming further that matters not regulated by this Convention continue to be governed by the rules and principles of general international law,

Recognizing the need for all States, in combating unlawful acts against the safety of maritime navigation, strictly to comply with rules and principles of general international law.

HAVE AGREED as follows:

Article 1

For the purposes of this Convention, "ship" means a vessel of any type whatsoever not permanently attached to the sea-bed, including dynamically supported craft, submersibles, or any other floating craft.

Article 2

1. This Convention does not apply to:

(a) a warship; or

(b) a ship owned or operated by a State when being used as a naval auxiliary or for customs or police purposes; or

(c) a ship which has been withdrawn from navigation or laid up.

2. Nothing in this Convention affects the immunities of warships and other government ships operated for non-commercial purposes.

Article 3

1. Any person commits an offence if that person unlawfully and intentionally:

(a) seizes or exercises control over a ship by force or threat thereof or any other form of intimidation; or

(b) performs an act of violence against a person on board a ship if that act is likely to endanger the safe navigation of that ship; or

(c) destroys a ship or causes damage to a ship or to its cargo which is likely to endanger the safe navigation of that ship; or

(d) places or causes to be placed on a ship, by any means whatsoever, a device or substance which is likely to destroy that ship, or cause damage to that ship or its cargo which endangers or is likely to endanger the safe navigation of that ship; or

(e) destroys or seriously damages maritime navigational facilities or seriously interferes with their operation, if any such act is likely to endanger the safe navigation of a ship; or

(f) communicates information which he knows to be false, thereby endangering the safe navigation of a ship; or

(g) injures or kills any person, in connection with the commission or the attempted commission of any of the offences set forth in subparagraphs (a) to (f).

2. Any person also commits an offence if that person:

(a) attempts to commit any of the offences set forth in paragraph 1; or

(b) abets the commission of any of the offences set forth in paragraph 1 perpetrated by any person or is otherwise an accomplice of a person who commits such an offence; or

(c) threatens, with or without a condition, as is provided for under national law, aimed at compelling a physical or juridical person to do or refrain from doing any act, to commit any of the offences set forth in paragraph 1, subparagraphs (b), (c) and (e), if that threat is likely to endanger the safe navigation of the ship in question.

Article 4

1. This Convention applies if the ship is navigating or is scheduled to navigate into, through or from waters beyond the outer limit of the territorial sea of a single State, or the lateral limits of its territorial sea with adjacent States.

2. In cases where the Convention does not apply pursuant to paragraph 1, it nevertheless applies when the offender or the alleged offender is found in the territory of a State Party other than the State referred to in paragraph 1.

Article 5

Each State Party shall make the offences set forth in article 3 punishable by appropriate penalties which take into account the grave nature of those offences.

Article 6

1. Each State Party shall take such measures as may be necessary to establish its jurisdiction over the offences set forth in article 3 when the offence is committed:

(a) against or on board a ship flying the flag of the State at the time the offence is committed; or

(b) in the territory of that State, including its territorial sea; or

(c) by a national of that State.

2. A State Party may also establish its jurisdiction over any such offence when:

(a) it is committed by a stateless person whose habitual residence is in that State; or

(b) during its commission a national of that State is seized, threatened, injured or killed; or

(c) it is committed in an attempt to compel that State to do or abstain from doing any act.

3. Any State Party which has established jurisdiction mentioned in paragraph 2 shall notify the Secretary-General of the International Maritime Organization (hereinafter referred to as "the Secretary-General"). If such State Party subsequently rescinds that jurisdiction, it shall notify the Secretary-General.

4. Each State Party shall take such measures as may be necessary to establish its jurisdiction over the offences set forth in article 3 in cases where the

alleged offender is present in its territory and it does not extradite him to any of the States Parties which have established their jurisdiction to accordance with paragraphs 1 and 2 of this article.

Article 7

1. Upon being satisfied that the circumstances so warrant, any State Party in the territory of which the offender or the alleged offender is present shall, in accordance with its law, take him into custody or take other measures to ensure his presence for such time as is necessary to enable any criminal or extradition proceedings to be instituted.

2. Such State shall immediately make a preliminary inquiry into the facts, in accordance with its own legislation.

3. Any person regarding whom the measures referred to in paragraph 1 are being taken shall be entitled to:

> (a) communicate without delay with the nearest appropriate representative of the State of which he is a national or which is otherwise entitled to establish such communication or, if he is a stateless person, the State in the territory of which he has his habitual residence;

> (b) be visited by a representative of that State.

4. The rights referred to in paragraph 3 shall be exercised in conformity with the laws and regulations of the State in the territory of which the offender or the alleged offender is present, subject to the provision that the said laws and regulations must enable full effect to be given to the purposes for which the rights accorded under paragraph 3 are intended.

5. When a State Party, pursuant to this article, has taken a person into custody, it shall immediately notify the States which have established jurisdiction in accordance with article 6, paragraph 1 and, if it considers it advisable, any other interested States, of the fact that such person is in custody and of the circumstances which warrant his detention. The State which makes the preliminary inquiry contemplated in paragraph 2 of this article shall promptly report its findings to the said States and shall indicate whether it intends to exercise jurisdiction.

Article 8

1. The master of a ship of a State Party (the "flag State") may deliver to the authorities of any other State Party (the "receiving State") any person who he has reasonable grounds to believe has committed one of the offences set forth article 3.

2. The flag State shall ensure that the master of its ship is obliged, whenever practicable, and if possible before entering the territorial sea of the receiving State carrying on board any person whom the master intends to deliver in accordance with paragraph 1, to give notification to the authorities of the

receiving State of his intention to deliver such person and the reasons therefor.

3. The receiving State shall accept the delivery, except where it has grounds to consider that the Convention is not applicable to the acts giving rise to the delivery, and shall proceed in accordance with the provisions of article 7. Any refusal to accept a delivery shall be accompanied by a statement of the reasons for refusal.

4. The flag State shall ensure that the master of its ship is obliged to furnish the authorities of the receiving State with the evidence in the master's possession which pertains to the alleged offence.

5. A receiving State which has accepted the delivery of a person in accordance with paragraph 3 may, in turn, request the flag State to accept delivery of that person. The flag State shall consider any such request, and if it accedes to the request it shall proceed in accordance with article 7. If the flag State declines a request, it shall furnish the receiving State with a statement of the reasons therefor.

Article 9

Nothing in this Convention shall affect in any way the rules of international law pertaining to the competence of States to exercise investigative or enforcement jurisdiction on board ships not flying their flag.

Article 10

1. The State Party in the territory of which the offender or the alleged offender is found shall, in cases to which article 6 applies, if it does not extradite him, be obliged, without exception whatsoever and whether or not the offence was committed in its territory, to submit the case without delay to its competent authorities for the purpose of prosecution, through proceedings in accordance with the laws of that State. Those authorities shall take their decision in the same manner as in the case of any other offence of a grave nature under the law of that State.

2. Any person regarding whom proceedings are being carried out in connection with any of the offences set forth in article 3 shall be guaranteed fair treatment at all stages of the proceedings, including enjoyment of all the rights and guarantees provided for such proceedings by the law of the State in the territory of which he is present.

Article 11

1. The offences set forth in article 3 shall be deemed to be included as extraditable offences in any extradition treaty existing between any of the States Parties. States Parties undertake to include such offences as extraditable offences in every extradition treaty to be concluded between them.

2. If a State Party which makes extradition conditional on the existence of a treaty receives a request for extradition from another State Party with which it has no extradition treaty, the requested State Party may, at its option, consider this Convention as a legal basis for extradition in respect of the offences set forth in article 3. Extradition shall be subject to the other conditions provided by the law of the requested State Party.

3. States Parties which do not make extradition conditional on the existence of a treaty shall recognize the offences set forth in article 3 as extraditable offences between themselves, subject to the conditions provided by the law of the requested State.

4. If necessary, the offences set forth in article 3 shall be treated, for the purposes of extradition between States Parties, as if they had been committed not only in the place in which they occurred but also in a place within the jurisdiction of the State Party requesting extradition.

5. A State Party which receives more than one request for extradition from States which have established jurisdiction in accordance with article 7 and which decides not to prosecute shall, in selecting the State to which the offender or alleged offender is to be extradited, pay due regard to the interests and responsibilities of the State Party whose flag the ship was flying at the time of the commission of the offence.

6. In considering a request for the extradition of an alleged offender pursuant to this Convention, the requested State shall pay due regard to whether his rights as set forth in article 7, paragraph 3, can be effected in the requesting State.

7. With respect to the offences as defined in this Convention, the provisions of all extradition treaties and arrangements applicable between States Parties are modified as between States Parties to the extent that they are incompatible with this Convention.

Article 12

1. State Parties shall afford one another the greatest measure of assistance in connection with criminal proceedings brought in respect of the offences set forth in article 3 including assistance in obtaining evidence at their disposal necessary for the proceedings.

2. States Parties shall carry out their obligations under paragraph 1 in conformity with any treaties on mutual assistance that may exist between them. In the absence of such treaties, States Parties shall afford each other assistance in accordance with their national law.

Article 13

1. States Parties shall co-operate in the prevention of the offences set forth in article 3, particularly by:

(a) taking all practicable measures to prevent preparations in their respective territories for the commission of those offences within or outside their territories;

(b) exchanging information in accordance with their national law, and co-ordinating administrative and other measures taken as appropriate to prevent the commission of offences set forth in article 3.

2. When, due to the commission of an offence set forth in article 3, the passage of a ship has been delayed or interrupted, any State Party in whose territory the ship or passengers or crew are present shall be bound to exercise all possible efforts to avoid a ship, its passengers, crew or cargo being unduly detained or delayed.

Article 14

Any State Party having reason to believe that an offence set forth in article 3 will be committed shall, in accordance with its national law, furnish as promptly as possible any relevant information in its possession to those States which it believes would be the States having established jurisdiction in accordance with article 6.

Article 15

1. Each State Party shall, in accordance with its national law, provide to the Secretary-General, as promptly as possible, any relevant information in its possession concerning:

(a) the circumstances of the offence;

(b) the action taken pursuant to article 13, paragraph 2;

(c) the measures taken in relation to the offender or the alleged offender and, in particular, the results of any extradition proceedings or other legal proceedings.

2. The State Party where the alleged offender is prosecuted shall, in accordance with its national law, communicate the final outcome of the proceedings to the Secretary-General.

3. The information transmitted in accordance with paragraphs 1 and 2 shall be communicated by the Secretary-General to all States Parties, to Members of the International Maritime Organization (hereinafter referred to as "the Organization"), to the other States concerned, and to the appropriate international intergovernmental organizations.

Article 16

1. Any dispute between two or more States Parties concerning the interpretation or application of this Convention which cannot be settled through negotiation within a reasonable time shall, at the request of one of them, be submitted to arbitration. If, within six months from the date of the request for arbitration, the parties are unable to agree on the organization of the arbitration any one of those parties may refer the dispute to the International Court of Justice by request in conformity with the Statute of the Court.

2. Each State may at the time of signature or ratification, acceptance or approval of this Convention or accession thereto, declare that it does not consider itself bound by any or all of the provisions of paragraph 1. The other States Parties shall not be bound by those provisions with respect to any State Party which has made such a reservation.

3. Any State which has made a reservation in accordance with paragraph 2 may, at any time, withdraw that reservation by notification to the Secretary-General.

Article 17

1. This Convention shall be open for signature at Rome on 10 March 1988 by States participating in the International Conference on the Suppression of Unlawful Acts against the Safety of Maritime Navigation and at the Headquarters of the Organization by all States from 14 March 1988 to 9 March 1989. It shall thereafter remain open for accession.

2. States may express their consent to be bound by this Convention by:

(a) signature without reservation as to ratification, acceptance or approval; or

(b) signature subject to ratification, acceptance or approval, followed by ratification, acceptance or approval; or

(c) accession.

3. Ratification, acceptance, approval or accession shall be effected by the deposit of an instrument to that effect with the Secretary-General.

Article 18

1. This Convention shall enter into force ninety days following the date on which fifteen States have either signed it without reservation as to ratification, acceptance or approval, or have deposited an instrument of ratification, acceptance, approval or accession in respect thereof.

2. For a State which deposits an instrument of ratification, acceptance, approval or accession in respect of this Convention after the conditions for entry into force thereof have been met, the ratification, acceptance, approval or accession shall take effect ninety days after the date of such deposit.

Article 19

1. This Convention may be denounced by any State Party at any time after the expiry of one year from the date on which this Convention enters into force for that State.

2. Denunciation shall be effected by the deposit of an instrument of denunciation with the Secretary-General.

3. A denunciation shall take effect one year, or such longer period as may be specified in the instrument of denunciation, after the receipt of the instrument of denunciation by the Secretary-General.

Article 20

1. A conference for the purpose of revising or amending this Convention may be convened by the Organization.

2. The Secretary-General shall convene a conference of the States Parties to this Convention for revising or amending the Convention, at the request of one third of the States Parties, or ten States Parties, whichever is the higher figure.

3. Any instrument of ratification, acceptance, approval or accession deposited after the date of entry into force of an amendment to this Convention shall be deemed to apply to the Convention as amended.

Article 21

1. This Convention shall be deposited with the Secretary-General.

2. The Secretary-General shall:

(a) inform all States which have signed this Convention or acceded thereto, and all Members of the Organization, of:

(i) each new signature or deposit of an instrument of ratification, acceptance, approval or accession together with the date thereof;

(ii) the date of the entry into force of this Convention;

(iii) the deposit of any instrument of denunciation of this Convention together with the date on which it is received and the date on which the denunciation takes effect;

(iv) the receipt of any declaration or notification made under this Convention;

(b) transmit certified true copies of this Convention to all States which have signed this Convention or acceded thereto.

3. As soon as this Convention enters into force, a certified true copy thereof shall be transmitted by the Depositary to the Secretary-General of the

United Nations for registration and publication in accordance with Article 102 of the Charter of the United Nations.

Article 22

This Convention is established in a single original in the Arabic, Chinese, English, French, Russian and Spanish languages, each text being equally authentic.

In witness whereof the undersigned being duly authorized by their respective Governments for that purpose have signed this Convention.

Done at Rome this tenth day of March one thousand nine hundred and eighty-eight.

Certified true copy in the English, French and Spanish languages of the Convention for the Suppression of Unlawful Acts against the Safety of Maritime Navigation, done at Rome on 10 March 1988, the original of which is deposited with the Secretary-General of the International Maritime Organization.

For the Secretary-General of the International Maritime Organization:

Parties:

Albania
Algeria
Argentina
Australia
Austria
Barbados
Bolivia
Botswana
Bulgaria
Canada
Chile
China
Cuba
Cyprus
Denmark
Dominica
Egypt
El Salvador
Estonia
Finland
France

Gambia
Germany
Ghana
Greece
Grenada
Hungary
Iceland
India
Italy
Japan
Kenya
Lebanon
Liberia
Libya
Liechtenstein
Mali
Malta
Marshall Is.
Mexico
Monaco
Morocco

THE SAFETY OF MARITIME NAVIGATION

Netherlands	Sri Lanka
New Zealand	Sudan
Norway	Sweden
Oman	Switzerland
Pakistan	Trinidad & Tobago
Palau	Tunisia
Panama	Turkey
Peru	Turkmenistan
Poland	Ukraine
Portugal	United Kingdom
Romania	United States
Russian Fed.	Uruguay
St. Kitts & Nevis	Uzbekistan
St. Vincent & the Grenadines	Vanuatu
Seychelles	Vietnam
Slovak Rep.	Yemen
Spain	

PROTOCOL FOR THE SUPPRESSION OF UNLAWFUL ACTS AGAINST THE SAFETY OF FIXED PLATFORMS LOCATED ON THE CONTINENTAL SHELF

COMMENTARY

This Protocol supplements the Convention for the Suppression of Unlawful Acts Against the Safety of Maritime Navigation. It incorporates certain provisions from that Convention into the Protocol and then adds specific terms which apply to "fixed platforms". A fixed platform refers to "an artificial island, installation or structure permanently attached to the sea-bed for the purpose of exploration or exploitation of resources or for other economic purposes."

Undoubtedly considering the special circumstances of petroleum installations, the Protocol covers the seizing, the destroying, or the threat to seize such an installation and also acts of violence against persons on board such structures.

PROTOCOL FOR THE SUPPRESSION OF UNLAWFUL ACTS AGAINST THE SAFETY OF FIXED PLATFORMS LOCATED ON THE CONTINENTAL SHELF

Adopted at Rome on 10 March 1988
Entered into force 1 March 1992*

THE STATES PARTIES TO THIS PROTOCOL,

Being parties to the Convention for the Suppression of Unlawful Acts against the Safety of Maritime Navigation,**

Recognizing that the reasons for which the Convention was elaborated also apply to fixed platforms located on the continental shelf,

Taking account of the provisions of that Convention,

Affirming that matters not regulated by this Protocol continue to be governed by the rules and principles of general international law,

HAVE AGREED as follows:

Article 1

1. The provisions of articles 5 and 7 and of articles 10 to 16 of the Convention for the Suppression of Unlawful Acts against the Safety of Maritime Navigation (hereinafter referred to as "the Convention") shall also apply *mutatis mutandis* to the offences set forth in article 2 of this Protocol where such offences are committed on board or against fixed platforms located on the continental shelf.

---

* Treaties and International Agreements Online, CTIA 9285.000 (Oceana Publications, Inc. <www.oceanalaw.com>.

** Reproduced at page 155.

2. In cases where this Protocol does not apply pursuant to paragraph 1, it nevertheless applies when the offender or the alleged offender is found in the territory of a State Party other than the State in whose internal waters or territorial sea the fixed platform is located.

3. For the purposes of this Protocol, "fixed platform" means an artificial island, installation or structure permanently attached to the sea-bed for the purpose of exploration or exploitation of resources or for other economic purposes.

Article 2

1. Any person commits an offence if that person unlawfully and intentionally:

(a) seizes or exercises control over a fixed platform by force or threat thereof or any other form of intimidation; or

(b) performs an act of violence against a person on board a fixed platform if that act is likely to endanger its safety; or

(c) destroys a fixed platform or causes damage to it which is likely to endanger its safety; or

(d) places or causes to be placed on a fixed platform, by any means whatsoever, a device or substance which is likely to destroy that fixed platform or likely to endanger its safety; or

(e) injures or kills any person in connection with the commission or the attempted commission of any of the offences set forth in subparagraphs (a) to (d).

2. Any person also commits an offence if that person:

(a) attempts to commit any of the offences set forth in paragraph 1; or

(b) abets the commission of any such offences perpetrated by any person or is otherwise an accomplice of a person who commits such an offence; or

(c) threatens, with or without a condition, as is provided for under national law, aimed at compelling a physical or juridical person to do or refrain from doing any act, to commit any of the offences set forth in paragraph 1, subparagraphs (b) and (c), if that threat is likely to endanger the safety of the fixed platform.

Article 3

1. Each State Party shall take such measures as may be necessary to establish its jurisdiction over the offences set forth in article 2 when the offence is committed:

(a) against or on board a fixed platform while it is located on the continental shelf of that State; or

(b) by a national of that State.

2. A State Party may also establish its jurisdiction over any such offence when:

(a) it is committed by a stateless person whose habitual residence is in that State;

(b) during its commission a national of that State is seized, threatened, injured or killed; or

(c) it is committed in an attempt to compel that State to do or abstain from doing any act.

3. Any State Party which has established jurisdiction mentioned in paragraph 2 shall notify the Secretary-General of the International Maritime Organization (hereinafter referred to as "the Secretary-General"). If such State Party subsequently rescinds that jurisdiction, it shall notify the Secretary-General.

4. Each State Party shall take such measures as may be necessary to establish its jurisdiction over the offences set forth in article 2 in cases where the alleged offender is present in its territory and it does not extradite him to any of the States Parties which have established their jurisdiction in accordance with paragraphs 1 and 2 of this article.

5. This Protocol does not exclude any criminal jurisdiction exercised in accordance with national law.

Article 4

Nothing in this Protocol shall affect in any way the rules of international law pertaining to fixed platforms located on the continental shelf.

Article 5

1. This Protocol shall be open for signature at Rome on 10 March 1988 and at the Headquarters of the International Maritime Organization (hereinafter referred to as "the Organization") from 14 March 1988 to 9 March 1989 by any State which has signed the Convention. It shall thereafter remain open for accession.

2. States may express their consent to be bound by this Protocol by:

(a) signature without reservation as to ratification, acceptance or approval; or

(b) signature subject to ratification, acceptance or approval, followed by ratification, acceptance or approval; or

(c) accession.

3. Ratification, acceptance, approval or accession shall be effected by the deposit of an instrument to that effect with the Secretary-General.

4. Only a State which has signed the Convention without reservation as to ratification, acceptance or approval, or has ratified, accepted, approved or acceded to the Convention may become a Party to this Protocol.

Article 6

1. This Protocol shall enter into force ninety days following the date on which three States have either signed it without reservation as to ratification, acceptance or approval, or have deposited an instrument of ratification, acceptance, approval or accession in respect thereof. However, this Protocol shall not enter into force before the Convention has entered into force.

2. For a State which deposits an instrument of ratification, acceptance, approval or accession in respect of this Protocol after the conditions for entry into force thereof have been met, the ratification, acceptance, approval or accession shall take effect ninety days after the date of such deposit.

Article 7

1. This Protocol may be denounced by any State Party at any time after the expiry of one year from the date on which this Protocol enters into force for that State.

2. Denunciation shall be effected by the deposit of an instrument of denunciation with the Secretary-General.

3. A denunciation shall take effect one year, or such longer period as may be specified in the instrument of denunciation, after the receipt of the instrument of denunciation by the Secretary-General.

4. A denunciation of the Convention by a State Party shall be deemed to be a denunciation of this Protocol by that Party.

Article 8

1. A conference for the purpose of revising or amending this Protocol may be convened by the Organization.

2. The Secretary-General shall convene a conference of the States Parties to this Protocol for revising or amending the Protocol, at the request of one third of the States Parties, or five States Parties, whichever is the higher figure.

3. Any instrument of ratification, acceptance, approval or accession deposited after the date of entry into force of an amendment to this Protocol shall be deemed to apply to the Protocol as amended.

Article 9

1. This Protocol shall be deposited with the Secretary-General.

2. The Secretary-General shall:

(a) inform all States which have signed this Protocol or acceded thereto, and all Members of the Organization, of:

(i) each new signature or deposit of an instrument of ratification, acceptance, approval or accession, together with the date thereof;

(ii) the date of entry into force of this Protocol;

(iii) the deposit of any instrument of denunciation of this Protocol together with the date on which it is received and the date on which the denunciation takes effect;

(iv) the receipt of any declaration or notification made under this Protocol or under the Convention, concerning this Protocol;

(b) transmit certified true copies of this Protocol to all States which have signed this Protocol or acceded thereto.

3. As soon as this Protocol enters into force, a certified true copy thereof shall be transmitted by the Depositary to the Secretary-General of the United States for registration and publication in accordance with Article 102 of the Charter of the United Nations.

Article 10

This Protocol is established in a single original in the Arabic, Chinese, English, French, Russian and Spanish languages, each text being equally authentic.

In witness whereof the undersigned, being duly authorized by their respective Governments for that purpose, have signed this Protocol.

Done at Rome this tenth day of March one thousand nine hundred and eighty-eight.

Certified true copy in the English, French and Spanish languages of the Protocol for the Suppression of Unlawful Acts against the Safety of Fixed Platforms Located on the Continental Shelf, done at Rome on 10 March 1988, the original of which is deposited with the Secretary-General of the International Maritime Organization.

For the Secretary-General of the International Maritime Organization.

MARITIME NAVIGATION—THE SAFETY OF FIXED PLATFORMS

Parties:

- Albania
- Algeria
- Argentina
- Australia
- Austria
- Barbados
- Bolivia
- Botswana
- Bulgaria
- Canada
- Chile
- China
- Cuba
- Cyprus
- Denmark
- Dominica
- Egypt
- El Salvador
- Estonia
- Finland
- France
- Gambia
- Germany
- Ghana
- Greece
- Grenada
- Hungary
- Iceland
- India
- Italy
- Japan
- Kenya
- Lebanon
- Liberia
- Libya
- Liechtenstein
- Mali
- Malta
- Marshall Is.
- Mexico
- Monaco
- Morocco
- Netherlands
- New Zealand
- Norway
- Oman
- Pakistan
- Palau
- Panama
- Peru
- Poland
- Portugal
- Romania
- Russian Fed.
- St. Kitts & Nevis
- St. Vincent & the Grenadines
- Seychelles
- Slovak Rep.
- Spain
- Sri Lanka
- Sudan
- Sweden
- Switzerland
- Trinidad & Tobago
- Tunisia
- Turkey
- Turkmenistan
- Ukraine
- United Kingdom
- United States
- Uruguay
- Uzbekistan
- Vanuatu
- Vietnam
- Yemen

MARITIME NAVIGATION—THE SAFETY OF FIXED PLATFORMS

LETTER OF SUBMITTAL

DEPARTMENT OF STATE,
Washington, DC, November 21, 1988.

The PRESIDENT, The White House.

THE PRESIDENT: I have the honor to submit to you the Convention for the Suppression of Unlawful Acts against the Safety of Maritime Navigation, and the accompanying protocol for the Suppression of Unlawful Acts against the Safety of Fixed Platforms Located on the Continental Shelf, both signed at Rome on March 10, 1988. I recommend that the Treaty and Protocol be transmitted to the Senate for its advice and consent to ratification.

The Convention and Protocol provide an important new basis under international law for combatting acts of terrorist violence on board ships and fixed platforms. Negotiation of the Convention began in mid-1986, after the Assembly of the International Maritime Organization (IMO) called for development of a new international instrument for the suppression of unlawful acts of violence which endanger the safety of maritime navigation. The Assembly's action was taken in the wake of the October 1985 Achille Lauro incident, which resulted in the murder of an American citizen, Leon Klinghoffer.

At the IMO's Council's direction, an Ad Hoc Preparatory Committee was convened within the IMO to consider an initial draft of the Convention co-sponsored by the Governments of Italy, Austria and Egypt. The Ad Hoc Preparatory Committee met in March and May of 1987 and agreed upon a revised draft of the Convention, as well as upon the adoption of a separate Protocol concerning fixed platforms located on the continental shelf. These texts were further reviewed by the Assembly, as well as the IMO's Legal Committee and the Council. The final texts were adopted by consensus by the 76 nations represented at an International Conference on the Suppression of Unlawful Acts against the Safety of Maritime Navigation, held in Rome from March 1-10, 1988 under the auspices of the IMO. The positions taken by the U.S. delegation to the Conference, which were for the most part adopted, were coordinated with interested agencies and reviewed by interested members of the public.

The principal purpose of the Convention and Protocol is to ensure that individuals who commit acts of terrorist violence which endanger the safe navigation of a ship or the safety of a platform are either prosecuted in the state in which they are found or extradited to another state for prosecution. Following the essential structure and approach of The Hague and Montreal Conventions in the aviation field, the Convention and Protocol require states to establish certain offenses under their criminal law, to provide a basis for the exercise of criminal jurisdiction in specified circumstances, and to extradite or prosecute any alleged offender found within their territory. The Convention and Protocol thus fill a gap in the international legal regime governing acts of violence on board or against ships engaged in international maritime navigation as well as fixed platforms located on the continental shelf.

The major provisions of the Convention are as follows:

(1) Scope of the Convention.—The Convention applies to any ship (broadly defined to include vessels of any type not permanently attached to the seabed) which is navigating or is scheduled to navigate beyond the territorial waters of a single State. Exceptions are made for warships, State-owned or operated ships used for customs or police purposes or as naval auxiliaries, and ships which have been withdrawn from navigation or laid up. The sovereign immunity of warships and other public vessels is preserved. The Convention makes it an offense for a person unlawfully and intentionally to seize or exercise control over a ship by force, threat or intimidation; to perform an act of violence against a person on board a ship if that act is likely to endanger the safe navigation of the ship; to destroy a ship or damage a ship or its cargo; to place a destructive device or substance on a ship; to damage or destroy maritime navigational facilities; to communicate information known to be false, thereby endangering the safe navigation of a ship; or to kill or injure any person in connection with the commission or attempted commission of any of these offenses. A person also commits an offense by attempting or abetting the commission of any of these offenses, or by threatening to commit certain of them.

(2) Penalties and Jurisdiction.—Each State Party is obliged to make the acts covered by the Convention punishable by appropriate penalties which take into account the grave nature of the offenses. Each State is required to establish its jurisdiction over offenses committed against or on board a ship flying its flag, in its territory including its territorial sea, and by its nationals. Each State may, at its option, also establish jurisdiction over offenses: which are committed by stateless persons habitually resident in its territory; during which one of its nationals is seized, threatened, killed or injured; or which are committed in an attempt to compel that State to do or abstain from doing any act.

(3) Custody.—Each State is obliged to take into custody an offender or alleged offender found in its territory or to take other measures to ensure that person's presence for such time as is necessary to enable criminal or extradition proceedings to be instituted. States Party are also obliged to take custody from the master of a ship of another State Party of any person reasonably believed to have committed one of the covered offenses; such States may, in turn, request that the flag State accept delivery of the person.

(4) Extradition or Prosecution.—The Convention amends existing extradition treaties between Parties to include the covered offenses as extra-

ditable offenses and provides that they shall be extraditable offenses between States which do not make extradition conditional on an extradition treaty. If a State in which an offender is found does not extradite that person or deliver him or her to another State Party for purposes of prosecution, that State is obliged "without exception whatsoever and whether or not the offence was committed in its territory, to submit the case without delay to its competent authorities for the purpose of prosecution".

(5) Reports.—When a State has taken a person into custody, it must immediately notify those States which have established the required jurisdiction over the offenses, and any other interested States. States Party having reason to believe that a covered offense will be committed must immediately inform those States it believes would have established jurisdiction over such an offense. States Party must also inform the Secretary-General of any relevant information concerning the circumstances of an offense and measures taken in relation to an offender, including the results of any extradition or other legal proceeding.

(6) Cooperation.—The Convention requires States Party to afford each other the greatest measure of assistance in connection with criminal proceedings brought in respect of covered offenses, and to cooperate in the prevention of such offenses by taking practicable measure to prevent preparations in their territories for those offenses, by exchanging information, and by coordinating administrative and other preventative measures.

(7) Limitations.—The Convention explicitly provides that its provisions do not affect the immunities of warships and other Government ships operated for non-commercial purposes, or the rules of international law pertaining to the competence of States to exercise investigative or enforcement jurisdiction on board ships not flying their flag. In addition, the Convention does not exclude any criminal jurisdiction that may be exercised in accordance with national law.

Article 16 of the Convention, concerning dispute settlement, permits States Parties to submit disputes to the International Court of Justice in the event that those disputes cannot be settled by arbitration. It is my recommendation that, at the time of ratification, the United States exercise its right under paragraph 2 of that Article to declare, by means of reservation, that it does not consider itself bound to submit to the compulsory jurisdiction of the Court in respect of disputes arising under this Convention.

The Protocol applies the provisions of the Convention to offenses committed on board or against fixed platforms located on the continental shelf. The term "fixed platform" is defined to include an artificial island, installation or structure permanently attached to the sea-bed for the purpose of exploration or exploitation of resources, or for other economic purposes. Thus, oil rigs, floating hotels, and similar platforms will be afforded the same protection by the Protocol as ships are afforded by the Convention.

The Convention will enter into force ninety days after the date on which fifteen States have signed without reservation or have deposited instruments of ratification, acceptance, approval or accession. The Protocol may enter into force ninety days after the date on which three States have signed without reservation or deposited similar instruments, provided that the Convention must first be in force. A State may only become Party to the Protocol if it has become Party to the Convention.

Proposed legislation necessary to implement the Convention will be submitted to the Congress in the near future.

Respectfully submitted,
GEORGE P. SHULTZ.

CONVENTION ON THE MARKING OF PLASTIC EXPLOSIVES FOR THE PURPOSE OF DETECTION

COMMENTARY

A clear impediment to identifying those responsible for terrorist attacks where plastic explosives are used (and such explosives are favored by terrorists) was the lack of any universal requirements to mark their origin. The Convention was negotiated following the bombing of PanAm 103 and it mandates the use of selected chemical marking agents in the manufacture of plastic explosives. According to a spokesman for the U.S. State Department when the Convention entered into force: ". . . parties to the convention are committed to an international control regime aimed at diminishing and eliminating the availability of very difficult-to-detect explosives—unmarked plastic explosives—that have been attractive to terrorists over the years." The Convention is regulatory in nature and has no penal provisions.

As in other States who are party to the Convention, the United States has regulations which implement the requirements defined in the Convention. According to the State Department, the Convention ". . . signals the intention of the international community to cooperate in practical ways to begin to address the problem posed specifically by plastic explosives, and by explosives in general."

The U.S. implementing legislation for the Convention is contained in Title VI of the Antiterrorism and Effective Death Penalty Act which took effect in the United States on April 24, 1997.

"LETTER OF TRANSMITTAL

THE WHITE HOUSE,
June 29, 1993.

To the Senate of the United States:

I transmit herewith, for the advice and consent of the Senate to ratification, the Convention on the Marking of Plastic Explosives for the Purpose of Detection with Technical Annex, done at Montreal on March 1, 1991. The report of the Department of State is also enclosed for the information of the Senate.

The terrorist bombing of Pan Am 103 in December 1988 with the resultant deaths of 270 (including 189 Americans), and the terrorist bombing of UTA flight 772 in September 1989 with the resultant deaths of 171 (including 7 Americans), dramatically demonstrate the threat posed by virtually undetectable plastic explosives in the hands of those nations and groups that engage in terrorist savagery.

This Convention is aimed at precluding such incidents from recurring, as well as others where plastic explosives are utilized, by requiring States that produce plastic explosives to mark them at the time of manufacture with a substance to enhance their detectability by commercially available mechanical or canine detectors. States are also required to ensure that controls are implemented over the sale, use, and disposition of marked and unmarked plastic explosives.

Work on the Convention began in January 1990 under the auspices of the International Civil Aviation Organization (ICAO) on the basis of an initial draft prepared by a special subcommittee of the ICAO Legal Committee. That work was completed, and the Convention was adopted by consensus, at an international conference in Montreal in March 1991. The United States and 50 other States signed the Convention. Early ratification by the United States should encourage other nations to become party to the Convention.

I recommend that the Senate give early and favorable consideration to the Convention and give its advice and consent to ratification, subject to the declaration described in the accompanying report of the Secretary of State.

WILLIAM J. CLINTON"

CONVENTION ON THE MARKING OF PLASTIC EXPLOSIVES FOR THE PURPOSE OF DETECTION

Signed in Montreal on 1 March 1991
Entered into force 21 June 1998*

THE STATES PARTIES TO THIS CONVENTION,

CONSCIOUS of the implications of acts of terrorism for international security;

EXPRESSING deep concern regarding terrorist acts aimed at destruction of aircraft, other means of transportation and other targets;

CONCERNED that plastic explosives have been used for such terrorist acts;

CONSIDERING that the marking of such explosives for the purpose of detection would contribute significantly to the prevention of such unlawful acts;

RECOGNIZING that for the purpose of deterring such unlawful acts there is an urgent need for an international instrument obliging States to adopt appropriate measures to ensure that plastic explosives are duly marked;

CONSIDERING United Nations Security Council Resolution 635 of 14 June 1989, and United Nations General Assembly Resolution 44/29 of 4 December 1989 urging the International Civil Aviation Organization to intensify its work on devising an international regime for the marking of plastic or sheet explosives for the purpose of detection;

BEARING IN MIND Resolution A27-8 adopted unanimously by the 27th Session of the Assembly of the International Civil Aviation Organization which endorsed with the highest and overriding priority the preparation of a new international instrument regarding the marking of plastic or sheet explosives for detection;

---

* Treaties and International Agreements Online, CTIA 9286.000 (Oceana Publications, Inc. <www.oceanalaw.com>.

NOTING with satisfaction the role played by the Council of the International Civil Aviation Organization in the preparation of the Convention as well as its willingness to assume functions related to its implementation;

HAVE AGREED AS FOLLOWS:

Article I

For the purposes of this Convention:

1. "Explosives" means explosive products, commonly known as "plastic explosives", including explosives in flexible or elastic sheet form, as described in the Technical Annex to this Convention.

2. "Detection agent" means a substance as described in the Technical Annex to this Convention which is introduced into an explosive to render it detectable.

3. "Marking" means introducing into an explosive a detection agent in accordance with the Technical Annex to this Convention.

4. "Manufacture" means any process, including reprocessing, that produces explosives.

5. "Duly authorized military devices" include, but are not restricted to, shells, bombs, projectiles, mines, missiles, rockets, shaped charges, grenades and perforators manufactured exclusively for military or police purposes according to the laws and regulations of the State Party concerned.

6. "Producer State" means any State in whose territory explosives are manufactured.

Article II

Each State Party shall take the necessary and effective measures to prohibit and prevent the manufacture in its territory of unmarked explosives.

Article III

1. Each State Party shall take the necessary and effective measures to prohibit and prevent the movement into or out of its territory of unmarked explosives.

2. The preceding paragraph shall not apply in respect of movements for purposes not inconsistent with the objectives of this Convention, by authorities of a State Party performing military or police functions, of unmarked explosives under the control of that State Party in accordance with paragraph 1 of Article IV.

Article IV

1. Each State Party shall take the necessary measures to exercise strict and effective control over the possession and transfer of possession of unmarked explosives which have been manufactured in or brought into its territory prior to the entry into force of this Convention in respect of that State, so as to prevent their diversion or use for purposes inconsistent with the objectives of this Convention.

2. Each State Party shall take the necessary measures to ensure that all stocks of those explosives referred to in paragraph 1 of this Article not held by its authorities performing military or police functions are destroyed or consumed for purposes not inconsistent with the objectives of this Convention, marked or rendered permanently ineffective, within a period of three years from the entry into force of this Convention in respect of that State.

3. Each State Party shall take the necessary measures to ensure that all stocks of those explosives referred to in paragraph 1 of this Article held by its authorities performing military or police functions and that are not incorporated as an integral part of duly authorized military devices are destroyed or consumed for purposes not inconsistent with the objectives of this Convention, marked or rendered permanently ineffective, within a period of fifteen years from the entry into force of this Convention in respect of that State.

4. Each State Party shall take the necessary measures to ensure the destruction, as soon as possible, in its territory of unmarked explosives which may be discovered therein and which are not referred to in the preceding paragraphs of this Article, other than stocks of unmarked explosives held by its authorities performing military or police functions and incorporated as an integral part of duly authorized military devices at the date of the entry into force of this Convention in respect of that State.

5. Each State Party shall take the necessary measures to exercise strict and effective control over the possession and transfer of possession of the explosives referred to in paragraph II of Part I of the Technical Annex to this Convention so as to prevent their diversion or use for purposes inconsistent with the objectives of this Convention.

6. Each State Party shall take the necessary measures to ensure the destruction, as soon as possible, in its territory of unmarked explosives manufactured since the coming into force of this Convention in respect of that State that are not incorporated as specified in paragraph II d) of Part 1 of the Technical Annex to this Convention and of unmarked explosives which no longer fall within the scope of any other sub-paragraphs of the said paragraph II.

Article V

1. There is established by this Convention an International Explosives Technical Commission (hereinafter referred to as "the Commission") consisting

of not less than fifteen nor more than nineteen members appointed by the Council of the International Civil Aviation Organization (hereinafter referred to as "the Council") from among persons nominated by States Parties to this Convention.

2. The members of the Commission shall be experts having direct and substantial experience in matters relating to the manufacture or detection of, or research in, explosives.

3. Members of the Commission shall serve for a period of three years and shall be eligible for re-appointment.

4. Sessions of the Commissions shall be convened, at least once a year at the Headquarters of the International Civil Aviation Organization, or at such places and times as may be directed or approved by the Council.

5. The Commission shall adopt its rules of procedure, subject to the approval of the Council.

Article VI

1. The Commission shall evaluate technical developments relating to the manufacture, marking and detection of explosives.

2. The Commission, through the Council, shall report its findings to the States Parties and international organizations concerned.

3. Whenever necessary, the Commission shall make recommendations to the Council for amendments to the Technical Annex to this Convention. The Commission shall endeavour to take its decisions on such recommendations by consensus. In the absence of consensus the Commission shall take such decisions by a two-thirds majority vote of its members.

4. The Council may, on the recommendation of the Commission, propose to States Parties amendments to the Technical Annex to this Convention.

Article VII

1. Any State Party may, within ninety days from the date of notification of a proposed amendment to the Technical Annex to this Convention, transmit to the Council its comments. The Council shall communicate these comments to the Commission as soon as possible for its consideration. The Council shall invite any State Party which comments on or objects to the proposed amendment to consult the Commission.

2. The Commission shall consider the views of States Parties made pursuant to the preceding paragraph and report to the Council. The Council, after consideration of the Commission's report, and taking into account the nature of the amendment and the comments of States Parties, including producer States, may propose the amendment to all States Parties for adoption.

3. If a proposed amendment has not been objected to by five or more States Parties by means of written notification to the Council within ninety days from the date of notification of the amendment by the Council, it shall be deemed to have been adopted, and shall enter into force one hundred and eighty days thereafter or after such other period as specified in the proposed amendment for States Parties not having expressly objected thereto.

4. States Parties having expressly objected to the proposed amendment may, subsequently, by means of the deposit of an instrument of acceptance or approval, express their consent to be bound by the provisions of the amendment.

5. If five or more States Parties have objected to the proposed amendment, the Council shall refer it to the Commission for further consideration.

6. If the proposed amendment has not been adopted in accordance with paragraph 3 of this Article, the Council may also convene a conference of all States Parties.

Article VIII

1. States Parties shall, if possible, transmit to the Council information that would assist the Commission in the discharge of its functions under paragraph 1 of Article VI.

2. States Parties shall keep the Council informed of measures they have taken to implement the provisions of this Convention. The Council shall communicate such information to all States Parties and international organizations concerned.

Article IX

The Council shall, in co-operation with States Parties and international organizations concerned, take appropriate measures to facilitate the implementation of this Convention, including the provision of technical assistance and measures for the exchange of information relating to technical developments in the marking and detection of explosives.

Article X

The Technical Annex to this Convention shall form an integral part of this Convention.

Article XI

1. Any dispute between two or more States Parties concerning the interpretation or application of this Convention which cannot be settled through negotiation shall, at the request of one of them, be submitted to arbitration. If within six months from the date of the request for arbitration the Parties are unable to agree on the organization of the arbitration, any one of those

Parties may refer the dispute to the International Court of Justice by request in conformity with the Statute of the Court.

2. Each State Party may, at the time of signature, ratification, acceptance or approval of this Convention or accession thereto, declare that it does not consider itself bound by the preceding paragraph. The other States Parties shall not be bound by the preceding paragraph with respect to any State Party having made such a reservation.

3. Any State Party having made a reservation in accordance with the proceeding paragraph may at any time withdraw this reservation by notification to the Depositary.

Article XII

Except as provided in Article XI no reservation may be made to this Convention.

Article XIII

1. This Convention shall be open for signature in Montreal on 1 March 1991 by States participating in the International Conference on Air Law held at Montreal from 12 February to 1 March 1991. After 1 March 1991 the Convention shall be open to all States for signature at the Headquarters of the International Civil Aviation Organization in Montreal until it enters into force in accordance with paragraph 3 of this Article. Any State which does not sign this Convention may accede to it at any time.

2. This Convention shall be subject to ratification, acceptance, approval or accession by States. Instruments of ratification, acceptance, approval or accession shall be deposited with the International Civil Aviation Organization, which is hereby designated the Depositary. When depositing its instrument of ratification, acceptance, approval or accession, each State shall declare whether or not it is a producer State.

3. This Convention shall enter into force on the sixtieth day following the date of deposit of the thirty-fifth instrument of ratification, acceptance, approval or accession with the Depositary, provided that no fewer than five such States have declared pursuant to paragraph 2 of this Article that they are producer States. Should thirty-five such instruments be deposited prior to the deposit of their instruments by five producer States, this Convention shall enter into force on the sixtieth day following the date of deposit of the instrument of ratification, acceptance, approval or accession of the fifth producer State.

4. For other States, this Convention shall enter into force sixty days following the date of deposit of their instruments of ratification, acceptance, approval or accession.

5. As soon as this Convention comes into force, it shall be registered by the Depositary pursuant to Article 102 of the Charter of the United Nations and

pursuant to Article 83 of the Convention on International Civil Aviation (Chicago, 1944).

Article XIV

The Depositary shall promptly notify all signatories and States Parties of:

1. each signature of this Convention and date thereof;

2. each deposit of an instrument of ratification, acceptance, approval or accession and date thereof giving special reference to whether the State has identified itself as a producer State;

3. the date of entry into force of this Convention;

4. the date of entry into force of any amendment to this Convention or its Technical Annex;

5. any denunciation made under Article XV; and

6. any declaration made under paragraph 2 of Article XI.

Article XV

1. Any State Party may denounce this Convention by written notification to the Depositary.

2. Denunciation shall take effect one hundred and eighty days following the date on which notification is received by the Depositary.

IN WITNESS WHEREOF the undersigned Plenipotentiaries, being duly authorized thereto by their Governments, have signed this Convention.

DONE at Montreal, this first day of March, one thousand nine hundred and ninety-one, in one original, drawn up in five authentic texts in the English, French, Russian, Spanish and Arabic languages.

TECHNICAL ANNEX

PART 1: DESCRIPTION OF EXPLOSIVES

I. The explosives referred to in paragraph 1 of Article 1 of this Convention are those that:

a) are formulated with one or more high explosives which in their pure form have a vapour pressure less than 10-4 Pa at a temperature of 25C;

b) are formulated with a binder material; and

c) are, as a mixture, malleable or flexible at normal room temperature.

II. The following explosives, even though meeting the description of explosives in paragraph 1 of this Part, shall not be considered to be explosives as long as they continue to be held or used for the purposes specified below or remain incorporated as there specified, namely those explosives that:

a) are manufactured, or held, in limited quantities solely for use in duly authorized research, development or testing of new or modified explosives;

b) are manufactured, or held, in limited quantities solely for use in duly authorized training in explosives detection and/or development or testing of explosives detection equipment;

c) are manufactured, or held, in limited quantities solely for duly authorized forensic science purposes; or

d) are destined to be and are incorporated as an integral part of duly authorized military devices in the territory of the producer State within three years after the coming into force of this Convention in respect of that State. Such devices produced in this period of three years shall be deemed to be duly authorized military devices within paragraph 4 of Article IV of this Convention.

III. In this Part:

"duly authorized" in paragraph II a), b) and c) means permitted according to the laws and regulations of the State Party concerned; and

"high explosives" include but are not restricted to cycyclotetramethylenetetranitramine (HMX), pentaerythritol tetranitrate (PETN) and cyclotrimethylenetrinitramine (RDX).

PART 2: DETECTION AGENTS

A detection agent is any one of those substances set out in the following Table. Detection agents described in this Table are intended to be used to enhance the detectability of explosives by vapour detection means. In each case, the introduction of a detection agent into an explosive shall be done in such a manner as to achieve homogeneous distribution in the finished product. The minimum concentration of a detection agent in the finished product at the time of manufacture shall be as shown in the said Table.

Table

Name of detection agent	Molecular formula	Molecular weight	Minimum concentration
Ethylene glycol dinitrate (EGDN)	$C_2H_4(NO_3)_2$	152	0.2% by mass
2,3-Dimethyl-2,3-dinitrobutane (DMNB)	$C_6H_{12}(NO_2)_2$	176	0.1% by mass
para-Mononitrotoluene (p-MNT)	$C_7H_7NO_2$	137	0.5% by mass
ortho-Mononitrotoluene (o-MNT)	$C_7H_7NO_2$	137	0.5% by mass

Any explosive which, as a result of its normal formulation, contains any of the designated detection agents at or above the required minimum concentration level shall be deemed to be marked.

THE MARKING OF PLASTIC EXPLOSIVES

Parties:

Algeria[1]	Germany[2]	Nigeria
Argentina[2]	Ghana[2]	Norway[2]
Austria[2]	Greece[2]	Oman
Azerbaijan[2]	Grenada	Palau
Bahrain[2]	Guatemala[2]	Panama[2]
Barbados	Hong Kong[4]	Peru[1,2]
Belarus	Hungary[2]	Portugal
Bolivia	Iceland	Qatar[2]
Botswana[2]	India[1,2]	Romania[2]
Brazil	Japan[2]	St. Kitts & Nevis
Bulgaria[2]	Jordan[2]	Samoa[2]
Cameroon[2]	Kazakhstan[2]	Saudi Arabia[1,2]
Canada[2]	Kenya	Slovak Rep.[2]
Cape Verde	Korea	Slovenia[2]
Chile[2]	Kuwait[2]	South Africa[2]
Cuba	Kyrgyz Rep.[2]	Spain[2]
Cyprus	Latvia[2]	Sri Lanka
Czech Rep.[2]	Lebanon[2]	Sudan[2]
Denmark[2,3]	Libya	Switzerland[2]
Ecuador[2]	Liechtenstein	Tonga
Egypt[2]	Lithuania[2]	Trinidad & Tobago[2]
El Salvador[2]	Maldives[2]	Tunisia[2]
Eritrea[2]	Mali[2]	Turkey[1,2]
Estonia[2]	Malta[2]	Ukraine[2]
Finland	Mexico[2]	United Arab Emirates[2]
Former Yugoslav Republic of Macedonia[2]	Moldova	United Kingdom[2]
France[2]	Monaco[2]	United States[2]
Gambia[2]	Mongolia[2]	Uruguay
Georgia[2]	Morocco[2]	Uzbekistan[2]
	Netherlands[2]	

NOTES:

1 With reservation(s).

2 With declaration(s).

3 Not applicable to the Faroe Is.

4 CHINA is not a party to this treaty but has made it applicable to Hong Kong.

INTERNATIONAL CONVENTION FOR THE SUPPRESSION OF TERRORIST BOMBINGS

COMMENTARY

This Convention received enthusiastic support in the United States Senate after the September 11th attacks. It was originally negotiated subsequent to the 1996 Khobar Towers bombing in Saudi Arabia, and further impetus for approval by the United States was prompted by the embassy bombings in East Africa. The Convention requires criminalization of terrorist bombings directed at structures and infrastructure in a given State or extradition of the perpetrators.

As President Clinton stated when he submitted the Convention to the Senate:

> "... no country or region is exempt from the human tragedy and immense costs that result from such criminal acts (bombings) ... This Convention provides, for the first time, an international framework for cooperation among states directed toward prevention of such incidents..."

The full text of the President's Message to the Senate follows:

"LETTER OF TRANSMITTAL

THE WHITE HOUSE, *September 8, 1999.*

To the Senate of the United States:

With a view to receiving the advice and consent of the Senate to ratification, I transmit herewith the International Convention for the Suppression of Terrorist Bombings, adopted by the United Nations General Assembly on December 15, 1997, and signed on behalf of the United States of America on January 12, 1998. The report of the Department of State with respect to the Convention is also transmitted for the information of the Senate.

In recent years, we have witnessed an unprecedented and intolerable increase in acts of terrorism involving bombings in public places in various parts of the world. The United states initiated the negotiation of this convention in the aftermath of the June 1996 bombing attack on U.S. military personnel in Dhahran, Saudi Arabia, in which 17 U.S. Air Force personnel were killed as the result of a truck bombing. That attack followed other terrorist attacks including poison gas attacks in Tokyo's subways; bombing attacks by HAMAS in Tel Aviv and Jerusalem; and a bombing attack by the IRA in Manchester, England. Last year's terrorist attacks upon United States embassies in Nairobi and Dar as Salaam are recent examples of such bombings, and no country or region is exempt from the human tragedy and immense costs that result from such criminal acts. Although the penal codes of most states contain provisions proscribing these kinds of attacks, this Convention provides, for the first time, an international framework for cooperation among states directed toward prevention of such incidents and ensuing punishment of offenders, wherever found.

In essence, the Convention imposes binding legal obligations upon States Parties either to submit for prosecution or to extradite any person within their jurisdiction who commits an offense as defined in Article 2, attempts to commit such an act, participates as an accomplice, organizes or directs others to commit such an offense, or in any other way contributes to the commission of an offense by a group of persons acting with a common purpose. A State Party is subject to these obligations without regard to the place where the alleged act covered by Article 2 took place.

Article 2 of the Convention declares that any person commits any offense within the meaning of the Convention if that person unlawfully and intentionally delivers, places, discharges or detonates an explosive or other lethal device in, into or against a place of public use, a state or government facility, a public transportation system, or an infrastructure facility, with the intent (a) to cause death or serious bodily injury or (b) cause extensive destruction of such a place, facility or system, where such destruction results in or is likely to result in major economic loss. States Parties to the Convention will also be obligated to provide one another legal assistance in investigations or criminal or extradition proceedings brought in respect of the offenses set forth in Article 2.

The recommended legislation necessary to implement the Convention will be submitted to the Congress separately.

This Convention is a vitally important new element in the campaign against the scourge of international terrorism. I hope that all states will become Parties to this Convention, and that it will be applied universally. I recommend, therefore, that the Senate give early and favorable consideration to this Convention, subject to the understandings and reservation that are described in the accompanying State Department report.

WILLIAM J. CLINTON."

INTERNATIONAL CONVENTION FOR THE SUPPRESSION OF TERRORIST BOMBINGS

Adopted at New York on December 15, 1997
Entered into force 23 May 2001*

THE STATES PARTIES TO THIS CONVENTION,

HAVING IN MIND the purposes and principles of the Charter of the United Nations concerning the maintenance of international peace and security and the promotion of good-neighbourliness and friendly relations and cooperation among States,

DEEPLY CONCERNED about the worldwide escalation of acts of terrorism in all its forms and manifestations,

RECALLING the Declaration on the Occasion of the Fiftieth Anniversary of the United Nations of 24 October 1995,

RECALLING ALSO the Declaration on Measures to Eliminate International Terrorism, annexed to General Assembly resolution 49/60 of 9 December 1994, in which, *inter alia*, "the States Members of the United Nations solemnly reaffirm their unequivocal condemnation of all acts, methods and practices of terrorism as criminal and unjustifiable, wherever and by whomever committed, including those which jeopardize the friendly relations among States and peoples and threaten the territorial integrity and security of States",

NOTING that the Declaration also encouraged States "to review urgently the scope of the existing international legal provisions on the prevention, repression and elimination of terrorism in all its forms and manifestations, with the aim of ensuring that there is a comprehensive legal framework covering all aspects of the matter",

---

* Treaties and International Agreements Online, CTIA 9706.000 (Oceana Publications, Inc. <www.oceanalaw.com>.

RECALLING FURTHER General Assembly resolution 51/210 of 17 December 1996 and the Declaration to Supplement the 1994 Declaration on Measures to Eliminate International Terrorism, annexed thereto,

NOTING ALSO that terrorist attacks by means of explosives or other lethal devices have become increasingly widespread,

NOTING FURTHER that existing multilateral legal provisions do not adequately address these attacks,

BEING CONVINCED of the urgent need to enhance international cooperation between States in devising and adopting effective and practical measures for the prevention of such acts of terrorism, and for the prosecution and punishment of their perpetrators,

CONSIDERING that the occurrence of such acts is a matter of grave concern to the international community as a whole,

NOTING that the activities of military forces of States are governed by rules of international law outside the framework of this Convention and that the exclusion of certain actions from the coverage of this Convention does not condone or make lawful otherwise unlawful acts, or preclude prosecution under other laws,

HAVE AGREED as follows:

Article 1

For the purposes of this Convention:

1. "State or government facility" includes any permanent or temporary facility or conveyance that is used or occupied by representatives of a State, members of Government, the legislature or the judiciary or by officials or employees of a State or any other public authority or entity or by employees or officials of an intergovernmental organization in connection with their official duties.

2. "Infrastructure facility" means any publicly or privately owned facility providing or distributing services for the benefit of the public, such as water, sewage, energy, fuel or communications.

3. "Explosive or other lethal device" means:

(a) An explosive or incendiary weapon or device that is designed, or has the capability, to cause death, serious bodily injury or substantial material damage; or

(b) A weapon or device that is designed, or has the capability, to cause death, serious bodily injury or substantial material damage through the release, dissemination or impact of toxic chemicals, biological agents or toxins or similar substances or radiation or radioactive material.

4. "Military forces of a State" means the armed forces of a State which are organized, trained and equipped under its internal law for the primary purpose of national defence or security, and persons acting in support of those armed forces who are under their formal command, control and responsibility.

5. "Place of public use" means those parts of any building, land, street, waterway or other location that are accessible or open to members of the public, whether continuously, periodically or occasionally, and encompasses any commercial, business, cultural, historical, educational, religious, governmental, entertainment, recreational or similar place that is so accessible or open to the public.

6. "Public transportation system" means all facilities, conveyances and instrumentalities, whether publicly or privately owned, that are used in or for publicly available services for the transportation of persons or cargo.

Article 2

1. Any person commits an offence within the meaning of this Convention if that person unlawfully and intentionally delivers, places, discharges or detonates an explosive or other lethal device in, into or against a place of public use, a State or government facility, a public transportation system or an infrastructure facility:

(a) With the intent to cause death or serious bodily injury; or

(b) With the intent to cause extensive destruction of such a place, facility or system, where such destruction results in or is likely to result in major economic loss.

2. Any person also commits an offence if that person attempts to commit an offence as set forth in paragraph 1.

3. Any person also commits an offence if that person:

(a) Participates as an accomplice in an offence as set forth in paragraph 1 or 2; or

(b) Organizes or directs others to commit an offence as set forth in paragraph 1 or 2; or

(c) In any other way contributes to the commission of one or more offences as set forth in paragraph 1 or 2 by a group of persons acting with a common purpose; such contribution shall be intentional and either be made with the aim of furthering the general criminal activity or purpose of the group or be made in the knowledge of the intention of the group to commit the offence or offences concerned.

Article 3

This Convention shall not apply where the offence is committed within a single State, the alleged offender and the victims are nationals of that State, the alleged offender is found in the territory of that State and no other State has a basis under article 6, paragraph 1, or article 6, paragraph 2, of this Convention to exercise jurisdiction, except that the provisions of articles 10 to 15 shall, as appropriate, apply in those cases.

Article 4

Each State Party shall adopt such measures as may be necessary:

(a) To establish as criminal offences under its domestic law the offences set forth in article 2 of this Convention;

(b) To make those offences punishable by appropriate penalties which take into account the grave nature of those offences.

Article 5

Each State Party shall adopt such measures as may be necessary, including, where appropriate, domestic legislation, to ensure that criminal acts within the scope of this Convention, in particular where they are intended or calculated to provoke a state of terror in the general public or in a group of persons or particular persons, are under no circumstances justifiable by considerations of a political, philosophical, ideological, racial, ethnic, religious or other similar nature and are punished by penalties consistent with their grave nature.

Article 6

1. Each State Party shall take such measures as may be necessary to establish its jurisdiction over the offences set forth in article 2 when:

(a) The offence is committed in the territory of that State; or

(b) The offence is committed on board a vessel flying the flag of that State or an aircraft which is registered under the laws of that State at the time the offence is committed; or

(c) The offence is committed by a national of that State.

2. A State Party may also establish its jurisdiction over any such offence when:

(a) The offence is committed against a national of that State; or

(b) The offence is committed against a State or government facility of that State abroad, including an embassy or other diplomatic or consular premises of that State; or

(c) The offence is committed by a stateless person who has his or her habitual residence in the territory of that State; or

(d) The offence is committed in an attempt to compel that State to do or abstain from doing any act; or

(e) The offence is committed on board an aircraft which is operated by the Government of that State.

3. Upon ratifying, accepting, approving or acceding to this Convention, each State Party shall notify the Secretary-General of the United Nations of the jurisdiction it has established in accordance with paragraph 2 under its domestic law. Should any change take place, the State Party concerned shall immediately notify the Secretary-General.

4. Each State Party shall likewise take such measures as may be necessary to establish its jurisdiction over the offences set forth in article 2 in cases where the alleged offender is present in its territory and it does not extradite that person to any of the States Parties which have established their jurisdiction in accordance with paragraph 1 or 2.

5. This Convention does not exclude the exercise of any criminal jurisdiction established by a State Party in accordance with its domestic law.

Article 7

1. Upon receiving information that a person who has committed or who is alleged to have committed an offence as set forth in article 2 may be present in its territory, the State Party concerned shall take such measures as may be necessary under its domestic law to investigate the facts contained in the information.

2. Upon being satisfied that the circumstances so warrant, the State Party in whose territory the offender or alleged offender is present shall take the appropriate measures under its domestic law so as to ensure that person's presence for the purpose of prosecution or extradition.

3. Any person regarding whom the measures referred to in paragraph 2 are being taken shall be entitled to:

(a) Communicate without delay with the nearest appropriate representative of the State of which that person is a national or which is otherwise entitled to protect that person's rights or, if that person is a stateless person, the State in the territory of which that person habitually resides;

(b) Be visited by a representative of that State;

(c) Be informed of that person's rights under subparagraphs (a) and (b);

4. The rights referred to in paragraph 3 shall be exercised in conformity with the laws and regulations of the State in the territory of which the offender or alleged offender is present, subject to the provision that the said laws and regulations must enable full effect to be given to the purposes for which the rights accorded under paragraph 3 are intended.

5. The provisions of paragraphs 3 and 4 shall be without prejudice to the right of any State Party having a claim to jurisdiction in accordance with ar-

ticle 6, subparagraph 1 (c) or 2 (c), to invite the International Committee of the Red Cross to communicate with and visit the alleged offender.

6. When a State Party, pursuant to this article, has taken a person into custody, it shall immediately notify, directly or through the Secretary-General of the United Nations, the States Parties which have established jurisdiction in accordance with article 6, paragraphs 1 and 2, and, if it considers it advisable, any other interested States Parties, of the fact that such person is in custody and of the circumstances which warrant that person's detention. The State which makes the investigation contemplated in paragraph 1 shall promptly inform the said States Parties of its findings and shall indicate whether it intends to exercise jurisdiction.

Article 8

1. The State Party in the territory of which the alleged offender is present shall, in cases to which article 6 applies, if it does not extradite that person, be obliged, without exception whatsoever and whether or not the offence was committed in its territory, to submit the case without undue delay to its competent authorities for the purpose of prosecution, through proceedings in accordance with the laws of that State. Those authorities shall take their decision in the same manner as in the case of any other offence of a grave nature under the law of that State.

2. Whenever a State Party is permitted under its domestic law to extradite or otherwise surrender one of its nationals only upon the condition that the person will be returned to that State to serve the sentence imposed as a result of the trial or proceeding for which the extradition or surrender of the person was sought, and this State and the State seeking the extradition of the person agree with this option and other terms they may deem appropriate, such a conditional extradition or surrender shall be sufficient to discharge the obligation set forth in paragraph 1.

Article 9

1. The offences set forth in article 2 shall be deemed to be included as extraditable offences in any extradition treaty existing between any of the States Parties before the entry into force of this Convention. States Parties undertake to include such offences as extraditable offences in every extradition treaty to be subsequently concluded between them.

2. When a State Party which makes extradition conditional on the existence of a treaty receives a request for extradition from another State Party with which it has no extradition treaty, the requested State Party may, at its option, consider this Convention as a legal basis for extradition in respect of the offences set forth in article 2. Extradition shall be subject to the other conditions provided by the law of the requested State.

3. States Parties which do not make extradition conditional on the existence of a treaty shall recognize the offences set forth in article 2 as extraditable offences between themselves, subject to the conditions provided by the law of the requested State.

4. If necessary, the offences set forth in article 2 shall be treated, for the purposes of extradition between States Parties, as if they had been committed not only in the place in which they occurred but also in the territory of the States that have established jurisdiction in accordance with article 6, paragraphs 1 and 2.

5. The provisions of all extradition treaties and arrangements between States Parties with regard to offences set forth in article 2 shall be deemed to be modified as between State Parties to the extent that they are incompatible with this Convention.

Article 10

1. States Parties shall afford one another the greatest measure of assistance in connection with investigations or criminal or extradition proceedings brought in respect of the offences set forth in article 2, including assistance in obtaining evidence at their disposal necessary for the proceedings.

2. States Parties shall carry cut their obligations under paragraph 1 in conformity with any treaties or other arrangements on mutual legal assistance that may exist between them. In the absence of such treaties or arrangements, States Parties shall afford one another assistance in accordance with their domestic law.

Article 11

None of the offences set forth in article 2 shall be regarded, for the purposes of extradition or mutual legal assistance, as a political offence or as an offence connected with a political offence or as an offence inspired by political motives. Accordingly, a request for extradition or for mutual legal assistance based on such an offence may not be refused on the sole ground that it concerns a political offence or an offence connected with a political offence or an offence inspired by political motives.

Article 12

Nothing in this Convention shall be interpreted as imposing an obligation to extradite or to afford mutual legal assistance, if the requested State Party has substantial grounds for believing that the request for extradition for offences set forth in article 2 or for mutual legal assistance with respect to such offences has been made for the purpose of prosecuting or punishing a person on account of that person's race, religion, nationality, ethnic origin or political opinion or that compliance with the request would cause prejudice to that person's position for any of these reasons.

Article 13

1. A person who is being detained or is serving a sentence in the territory of one State Party whose presence in another State Party is requested for purposes of testimony, identification or otherwise providing assistance in obtaining evidence for the investigation or prosecution of offences under this Convention may be transferred if the following conditions are met:

(a) The person freely gives his or her informed consent; and

(b) The competent authorities of both States agree, subject to such conditions as those States may deem appropriate.

2. For the purposes of this article:

(a) The State to which the person is transferred shall have the authority and obligation to keep the person transferred in custody, unless otherwise requested or authorized by the State from which the person was transferred;

(b) The State to which the person is transferred shall without delay implement its obligation to return the person to the custody of the State from which the person was transferred as agreed beforehand, or as otherwise agreed, by the competent authorities of both States;

(c) The State to which the person is transferred shall not require the State from which the person was transferred to initiate extradition proceedings for the return of the person;

(d) The person transferred shall receive credit for service of the sentence being served in the State from which he was transferred for time spent in the custody of the State to which he was transferred.

3. Unless the State Party from which a person is to be transferred in accordance with this article so agrees, that person, whatever his or her nationality, shall not be prosecuted or detained or subjected to any other restriction of his or her personal liberty in the territory of the State to which that person is transferred in respect of acts or convictions anterior to his or her departure from the territory of the State from which such person was transferred.

Article 14

Any person who is taken into custody or regarding whom any other measures are taken or proceedings are carried out pursuant to this Convention shall be guaranteed fair treatment, including enjoyment of all rights and guarantees in conformity with the law of the State in the territory of which that person is present and applicable provisions of international law, including international law of human rights.

Article 15

States Parties shall cooperate in the prevention of the offences set forth in article 2, particularly:

(a) By taking all practicable measures, including, if necessary, adapting their domestic legislation, to prevent and counter preparations in their respective territories for the commission of those offences within or outside their territories, including measures to prohibit in their territories illegal activities of persons, groups and organizations that encourage, instigate, organize, knowingly finance or engage in the perpetration of offences as set forth in article 2;

(b) By exchanging accurate and verified information in accordance with their national law, and coordinating administrative and other measures taken as appropriate to prevent the commission of offences as set forth in article 2;

(c) Where appropriate, through research and development regarding methods of detection of explosives and other harmful substances that can cause death or bodily injury, consultations on the development of standards for marking explosives in order to identify their origin in post-blast investigations, exchange of information on preventive measures, cooperation and transfer of technology, equipment and related materials.

Article 16

The State Party where the alleged offender is prosecuted shall, in accordance with its domestic law or applicable procedures, communicate the final outcome of the proceedings to the Secretary-General of the United Nations, who shall transmit the information to the other States Parties.

Article 17

The States Parties shall carry out their obligations under this Convention in a manner consistent with the principles of sovereign equality and territorial integrity of States and that of non-intervention in the domestic affairs of other States.

Article 18

Nothing in this Convention entitles a State Party to undertake in the territory of another State Party the exercise of jurisdiction and performance of functions which are exclusively reserved for the authorities of that other State Party by its domestic law.

Article 19

1. Nothing in this Convention shall affect other rights, obligations and responsibilities of States and individuals under international law, in particular the purposes and principles of the Charter of the United Nations and international humanitarian law.

2. The activities of armed forces during an armed conflict, as those terms are understood under international humanitarian law, which are governed by that law, are not governed by this Convention, and the activities undertaken by military forces of a State in the exercise of their official duties, inasmuch as they are governed by other rules of international law, are not governed by this Convention.

Article 20

1. Any dispute between two or more States Parties concerning the interpretation or application of this Convention which cannot be settled through negotiation within a reasonable time shall, at the request of one of them, be submitted to arbitration. If, within six months from the date of the request for arbitration, the parties are unable to agree on the organization of the arbitration, any one of those parties may refer the dispute to the International Court of Justice, by application, in conformity with the Statute of the Court.

2. Each State may at the time of signature, ratification, acceptance or approval of this Convention or accession thereto declare that it does not consider itself bound by paragraph 1. The other States Parties shall not be bound by paragraph 1 with respect to any State Party which has made such a reservation.

3. Any State which has made a reservation in accordance with paragraph 2 may at any time withdraw that reservation by notification to the Secretary-General of the United Nations.

Article 21

1. This Convention shall be open for signature by all States from 12 January 1998 until 31 December 1999 at United Nations Headquarters in New York.

2. This Convention is subject to ratification, acceptance or approval. The instruments of ratification, acceptance or approval shall be deposited with the Secretary-General of the United Nations.

3. This Convention shall be open to accession by any State. The instruments of accession shall be deposited with the Secretary-General of the United Nations.

Article 22

1. This Convention shall enter into force on the thirtieth day following the date of the deposit of the twenty-second instrument of ratification, accep-

tance, approval or accession with the Secretary-General of the United Nations.

2. For each State ratifying, accepting, approving or acceding to the Convention after the deposit of the twenty-second instrument of ratification, acceptance, approval or accession, the Convention shall enter into force on the thirtieth day after deposit by such State of its instrument of ratification, acceptance, approval or accession.

Article 23

1. Any State Party may denounce this Convention by written notification to the Secretary-General of the United Nations.

2. Denunciation shall take effect one year following the date on which notification is received by the Secretary-General of the United Nations.

Article 24

The original of this Convention, of which the Arabic, Chinese, English, French, Russian and Spanish texts are equally authentic, shall be deposited with the Secretary-General of the United Nations, who shall send certified copies thereof to all States.

IN WITNESS WHEREOF, the undersigned, being duly authorized thereto by their respective Governments, have signed this Convention, opened for signature at New York on 12 January 1998.

I hereby certify that the foregoing text is a true copy of the International Convention for the Suppression of Terrorist Bombings, adopted by the General Assembly of the United Nations on 15 December 1997, the original of which is deposited with the Secretary-General of the United Nations.

For the Secretary-General
The Legal Counsel
(Under-Secretary-General for Legal Affairs)

Hans Corell

United Nations, New York
12 January 1998

THE SUPPRESSION OF TERRORIST BOMBINGS

Parties:

Albania
Algeria
Australia
Austria
Azerbaijan
Barbados
Belarus
Belize
Bolivia
Botswana
Brazil
Brunei
Bulgaria
Burma
Canada
Cape Verde
Chile
China
Costa Rica
Cote d'Ivoire
Cuba
Cyprus
Czech Rep.
Denmark
Estonia
Finland
France
Ghana
Grenada
Guatemala
Guinea
Hungary
Iceland
India
Japan
Kazakhstan
Kenya
Kyrgyz Rep.
Laos

Latvia
Lesotho
Libya
Liechtenstein
Maldives
Mali
Malta
Micronesia
Moldova
Monaco
Mongolia
Netherlands
New Zealand
Norway
Pakistan
Palau
Panama
Peru
Portugal
Russian Fed.
Rwanda
St. Kitts & Nevis
San Marino
Slovak Rep.
Spain
Sri Lanka
Sudan
Sweden
Tajikistan
Tonga
Trinidad & Tobago
Turkey
Turkmenistan
Ukraine
United Kingdom
United States
Uruguay
Uzbekistan
Yemen

LETTER OF SUBMITTAL

DEPARTMENT OF STATE
Washington, September 24, 1998.

The PRESIDENT,
The White House.

THE PRESIDENT: I have the honor to submit to you, with a view to its transmission to the Senate for advice and consent to ratification, subject to the understandings and reservation set forth below, the International Convention for the Suppression of Terrorist Bombings, adopted by the United Nations General Assembly on December 15, 1997, and signed on behalf of the United States of America on January 12, 1998 (the "Convention").

Pursuant to a proposal by the United States, the United Nations General Assembly established an *ad hoc* committee to draft an international convention for the suppression of terrorist bombings in Resolution 51/210 in December 1996. During drafting sessions in New York in February-March and September-October 1997, the *ad hoc* committee based its work on a draft prepared by the United States and several other countries and was largely able to complete a draft convention, which was then forwarded to the 52nd Session of the U.N. General Assembly for consideration in the Sixth (Legal) Committee. A Working Group of the Sixth Committee resolved the remaining issues in a manner which permitted consensus adoption of the Convention by the full Sixth Committee on November 21, 1997, and by the General Assembly itself on December 15, 1997. The United States initiated the negotiation of this convention in the aftermath of the June 1996 attack on U.S. military personnel in Dhahran, Saudi Arabia, in which nineteen persons, including seventeen U.S. servicemen, were killed as the result of a truck bombing. That attack followed other terrorist attacks in 1995-96 including poison gas attacks in Tokyo's subways; a bombing attack in Colombo, Sri Lanka; bombing attacks in Tel Aviv and Jerusalem; and a bombing attack in Manchester, England. The Convention fills an important gap in international law by expanding the legal framework for international cooperation in the investigation, prosecution and extradition of persons who engage in such bombings.

The Convention will provide a new legal basis for international cooperation in the investigation and prosecution of crimes such as the attacks on August 7, 1998, upon United States embassies in Nairobi and Dar as Salaam.

The Convention will create a regime of universal jurisdiction over the unlawful and international use of explosives and other lethal devices in, into or against various defined public places with intent to kill or cause serious bodily injury, or with intent to cause extensive destruction of the defined public place. States Parties must either submit for prosecution or extradite any person within their jurisdiction who commits an offense defined in the Convention, attempts to commit such an offense, or commits other specific ancillary offenses relating to the commission of such an offense. In creating such a legal regime, the Convention follows the precedents set by numerous terrorism conventions to which the United States is already a party, including the 1971 Convention for the Suppression of Unlawful Acts Against the Safety of Civil Aviation, the 1973 Convention on the Prevention and Punishment of Crimes Against Internationally Protected Persons, including Diplomatic Agents, the 1979 Convention Against the Taking of Hostages, and the 1988 Convention for the Suppression of Unlawful Acts Against the Safety of Maritime Navigation, with Related Protocol.

Article 1 and 2 together serve to define the offenses covered by the Convention, with Article 1 incorporating several definitions of phrases used in Article 2. Paragraph 1 of Article 2 states that any person commits an offense within the meaning of the Convention if that person unlawfully and intentionally delivers, places, discharges or detonates an explosive or other lethal device in, into or against a place of public use, a State or government facility, a public transportation system, or an infrastructure facility, with the intent to cause (a) death or serious bodily injury or (b) extensive destruction of such a place, facility or system, where such destruction results in or is likely to result in major economic loss. Paragraph 2 of Article 2 provides that any person also commits an offense if that person attempts to commit an offense as set forth in paragraph 1, and Paragraph 3 provides further that any person commits an offense if that person participates as an accomplice in an offense under paragraphs 1 or 2, organizes or directs others to commit such an offense, or in any other way contributes to the commission of one or more such offenses by a group of persons acting with a common purpose. These ancillary offenses in Paragraph 3 are more comprehensive than those included in the earlier counterterrorism conventions, and it is anticipated that they will strengthen the ability of the international community to investigate, prosecute and extradite those who conspire or otherwise contribute to the commission of offenses defined in the Convention.

Article 1 defines the four categories of locations mentioned in Article 2 where an attack gives rise to offenses under the Convention, i.e., a "place of public use," a "State or government facility," a "public transportation system," and an "infrastructure facility." These categories of locations were chosen during the negotiations and defined with a view toward criminalizing attacks in locations where attacks would be of greatest concern to the general public. In addition, Paragraph 3 of Article 1 defines "explosive or other lethal device" as including not only conventional explosive or other incendiary devices, but also toxic chemicals, biological agents or toxins or similar substances, and radiation or radioactive material. Thus, the Convention addresses not only bombings using conventional explosives such as those used in the 1996 bombing attack on U.S. servicemen in Dhahran, Saudi Arabia, and the 1998 bombings on United States embassies in East Africa, but also attacks using materials such as those employed in the 1995 attacks on the Tokyo subway system.

Article 3 makes most of the Convention's provisions inapplicable to bombing incidents that lack an international aspect. In generally limiting its scope of application to those cases involving elements from more than one State, the Convention follows the precedent set by the prior counter-terrorism conventions such as the 1971 Convention for the Suppression of Unlawful Acts Against the Safety of Civil Aviation and the 1979 Convention Against the Taking of Hostages.

Article 4 requires States Parties to make the offenses enumerated in Article 2 criminal offenses punishable by appropriate penalties that take into account their grave nature.

Article 5 requires States Parties to adopt any measures that may be necessary to ensure that criminal acts within the scope of the Convention, in particular where they are intended or calculated to create a state of terror, are not justifiable by considerations of a political, philosophical, ideological, racial, ethnic, religious or other similar nature, and are punished by penalties consistent with their grave nature.

Under Article 6, each State Party must establish its jurisdiction over the offenses set forth in Article 2 when the offenses are committed in its territory; on board a vessel flying its flag or an aircraft registered under its laws at the time the offense is committed; or where the offense was committed by a national of that State. Each State Party has discretion to establish jurisdiction over offenses set forth in Article 2 where the offense is committed against a national of that State; against a State or government facility of that State abroad, including an embassy or other diplomatic or consular premises of that State; by a stateless person who has his or her habitual residence in the territory of that State; in an attempt to compel that State to do or abstain from doing any act; or on board an aircraft which is operated by the Government of that State. Upon becoming a party to the Convention, a State must notify the United Nations Secretary General of the jurisdiction it has established under its domestic law.

Thus, under the terms of Article 6, States Parties may enact a broad array of jurisdictional bases over the offenses enumerated in Article 2. Of significant interest and value to the United States, which has many government facilities outside of U.S. territory, is the Convention's recognition of jurisdiction over attacks using explosive or other lethal devices against a State or government facility of that State abroad, including an embassy or other diplomatic or consular premises of that State. This would give the United States universally recognized jurisdiction based on this Convention, for example, to prosecute in U.S. courts the perpetrators of attacks on all U.S. Government facilities abroad, including diplomatic and consular premises, as well as to U.S. military installations such as those attacked in the 1996 Al-Khobar Towers bombing in Dhahran, Saudi Arabia. Also of significant interest and value to the United States is the provision in Article 6 providing that States Parties may criminalize conduct where the offense is committed in an attempt to compel that State to do or abstain from doing any act. This provides jurisdiction for offenses under this Convention where terrorists seek to coerce State action, even where a national or facility of that State is not the target of the attack.

In addition to the bases for jurisdiction set forth in Paragraphs 1 and 2 of Article 6, Paragraph 4 of Article 6 requires jurisdiction to be established by a State Party where the alleged offender is in its territory and is not extradited to any of the States with jurisdiction under the convention. Paragraph 5 of Article 6 makes clear that the Convention does not preclude criminal jurisdiction exercised in accordance with domestic law.

Article 7 includes certain provisions relating to offenders or alleged offenders detained for the purpose of extradition or prosecution.

In a provision of crucial importance for the Convention, Paragraph 1 of Article 8 declares that a State Party which does not extradite an alleged offender found in its territory shall "without exception whatsoever and whether or not the offense was committed on its territory" submit the case to its competent authorities for purposes of prosecution, through proceedings in accordance with the laws of that State. Those authorities are obligated to take their decision in the same manner as in the case of any other offense of a grave nature under the law of that State.

In an innovation over the prior counterterrorism conventions, the Convention includes a provision proposed by the United States in Paragraph 2 of Article 8, to the effect that the obligation in Paragraph 1 to extradite or submit for prosecution can be discharged by the temporary transfer of nationals for trial by those States Parties that could not otherwise extradite their nationals, provided both the Requesting and Requested States agree. While the United States would have preferred that the Convention include a broad universal obligation for the extradition of nationals, a number of delegations were unable to agree to such a broad provision. This provision on temporary transfer of nationals for trial is nonetheless a useful and unprecedented recognition of this practice by the international community in a binding multilateral legal instrument.

Paragraph 1 of Article 9 amends existing extradition treaties to include the offenses defined in Article 2 as extraditable offenses and provides that they shall be extraditable offenses between States which do not make extradition conditional on an extradition treaty.

Article 10 establishes general mutual legal assistance obligations between States Parties in connection with investigations or criminal or extradition proceedings brought in respect of the offenses in Article 2.

Article 11 provides that none of the offenses set forth in article 2 shall be regarded, for the purposes of extradition or mutual legal assistance, as a political offense or an offense connected with a political offense, or as an offense inspired by political motives. Accordingly, a request for extradition or mutual legal assistance may not be refused solely on such grounds. This article applies to extradition and mutual legal assistance requests involving the offenses in Article 2, and provides a useful narrowing of the political offense exception in such cases. In many modern U.S. bilateral extradition treaties there are already provisions which bar application of the political offense exception to extradition with respect to offenses under multilateral conventions to which "prosecute or extradite" obligations apply. This provision builds on this trend by making the restriction on the invocation of the political offense exception for requests based on offenses under Article 2 a matter of general application rather than dependent on the terms of individual bilateral law enforcement treaties between the Parties.

Article 12 provides that nothing in the Convention shall be interpreted as imposing an obligation to extradite or to afford mutual legal assistance if the requested State Party has substantial grounds for believing that the request for extradition for offenses set forth in Article 2 or for mutual legal assistance with respect to such offenses has been made for the purpose of prosecuting or punishing a person on account of that person's race, religion, nationality, ethnic origin or political opinion or that compliance with the request would cause prejudice to that person's position for any of these reasons. This article is similar to provisions already included in a number of U.S. bilateral extradition and mutual legal assistance treaties, as well as the 1979 International Convention Against the Taking of Hostages.

Article 13 provides and establishes various conditions for the temporary transfer to one State Party, for purposes of assistance under the Convention, of a person in custody in another State Party, provided that the person in custody in another State Party, provided that the person in question consents and the competent authorities of both States agree. This provision was proposed by the United States and is similar to provisions found in virtually all of the bilateral mutual legal assistance treaties to which the United States is a party.

Article 14 discusses the rights of persons taken into custody or regarding whom any other measures are taken or proceedings are carried out pursuant to this Convention. Article 15 states that States Parties shall cooperate in several ways in the prevention of offenses set forth in Article 2. Article 16 contains a requirement to notify the U.N. Secretary General of the final outcome of criminal proceedings relating to offenders under the Convention. Article 17 states that States Parties shall carry out their obligations under the Convention in a manner consistent with the principles of sovereign equality and territorial integrity of States and that of non-intervention in the domestic affairs of other States. Article 18 provides that nothing in the Convention entitles a State Party to undertake in the territory of another State Party the exercise of jurisdiction and performance of functions which are exclusively reserved for the authorities of that other State Party by its domestic law.

Article 19, Paragraph 1, provides that nothing in the Convention affects other rights, obligations and responsibilities of States and individuals under international law. Paragraph 2 of Article 19 contains two important exceptions from the scope of the Convention relating to activities of armed forces and military forces of a State.

Under the first exception, the Convention does not apply to the activities of "armed forces during an armed conflict," where such activities are governed by international humanitarian law. This exception is meant to exclude from the Convention's scope the activities of armed forces (which would include both armed forces of States and subnational armed forces), so long as those activities are in the course of an "armed conflict" and are governed by the law of war. Given that suspected offenders may claim the benefit of this "armed conflict" exception to avoid extradition or prosecution under the Convention, it would be useful for the United States to articulate an Understanding regarding the scope of this exception. In this respect, an appropriate source of authority would be the widely accepted provision in Paragraph 2 of Article 1 of Protocol II Additional to the Geneva Conventions of August 12, 1949, concluded at Geneva on June 10, 1977, which President Reagan transmitted to the Senate on January 29, 1987, for advice and consent to ratification. Specifically, Protocol II states that "armed conflict" does not include "internal disturbances and tensions, such as riots, isolated and sporadic acts of violence and other acts of a similar nature." Through an understanding, the United States would make clear that isolated acts of violence that include the elements of the offenses of Article 2 would be encompassed in the scope of the Convention. As a separate matter, the term "international humanitarian law" is not used by United States armed forces and could be subject to varied interpretations. It would therefore be useful for the United States to articulate in the same understanding that for purposes of this Convention this phrase has the same substantive meaning as the law of war. I therefore recommend that the following understanding to Article 19 be included in the United States instrument of ratification:

> The United States of America understands that the term "armed conflict" in Article 19 does not include internal disturbances and tensions, such as riots, isolated and sporadic acts of violence and other acts of a similar nature and that the term "international humanitarian law" has the same substantive meaning as the law of war.

The second exception in Article 19(2) exempts from the Convention's scope of application activities undertaken by military forces of a State in the exercise of their official duties. The official activities of State military forces are already comprehensively governed by other bodies of international law, such as the international instruments relating to the law of war and the international law of state responsibility. This comprehensive exclusion of official activities of State military forces from the Convention's scope was an important U.S. objective in the drafting of this Convention. While such an exclusion might be thought to be implicit in the context of the Convention, the Convention's negotiators thought it best to articulate the exclusion in light of the relatively broad nature of the conduct described in Article 2 and the fact that this conduct overlaps with common and accepted activities of State military forces. Because of the importance of this provision, I recommend that the following understanding to Article 19 be included in the United States instrument of ratification:

> The United States of America understands that, pursuant to Article 19, the Convention does not apply in any respect to the activities undertaken by military forces of States in the exercise of their official duties.

The conduct of certain civilians who act in support of official activities of State military forces are also exempted from the Convention's scope of application. The phrase "military forces of a State" is defined broadly in Paragraph 4 of Article 1 as meaning "the armed forces of a State which are organized, trained and equipped under its internal law for the primary purpose of national defense or security, and persons acting in support of those armed forces who are under their formal command, control and responsibility." In addition, because the Convention does not reach the official activities of State military forces, it similarly does not reach persons, including non-military policy-making officials of States, who might direct or organize the activities of State military forces or who might otherwise have been subject to the ancillary offenses in Article 2 if State military forces had not been excluded from the Convention's scope of application.

The Convention also provides in Article 20(1) that disputes between two or more States Parties concerning the interpretation or application of this Convention may be submitted to *ad hoc* arbitration, or, failing agreement on the organization of such arbitration, to the International Court of Justice. Article 20(1) provides that a State may make a declaration excluding this dispute-resolution obligation at the time of signature, ratification, acceptance, approval or accession. In October 1985, the United States withdrew its declaration under Article 36 of the Statute of the International Court of Justice accepting the compulsory jurisdiction of the Court. Consistent with that decision. I recommend that the following reservation to Article 20(1) be included in the United States instrument of ratification:

> Pursuant to Article 20(2) of the Convention, the United States of America declares that it does not consider itself bound by Article 20(1), but reserves the right specifically to agree to follow this or any other procedure for arbitration in a particular case.

This reservation would allow the United States to agree to an adjudication by a chamber of the Court in a particular case, if that were deemed desirable.

The Convention will enter into force on the thirtieth day following the date of deposit of the twenty-second instrument of ratification, acceptance, approval or accession. A State Party to the Convention may withdraw from the Convention on one year's notice pursuant to Article 23.

Recommended legislation necessary to implement the Convention will be submitted to the Congress.

The Department of Justice joins in recommending that this Convention be transmitted to the Senate at an early date for its advice and consent to ratification, subject to the understandings to Article 19 and reservation to Article 20(1) previously described.

Respectfully submitted,
STROBE TALBOT.

INTERNATIONAL CONVENTION FOR THE SUPPRESSION OF THE FINANCING OF TERRORISM

COMMENTARY

The necessity of reigning in international terrorist financing networks was given grim reinforcement by the events of September 11, 2001. The *International Convention for the Suppression of the Financing of Terrorism*, adopted by the U.N. General Assembly on December 9, 1999 and ratified by the U.S. on June 26, 2002, is an aggressive multilateral response to this problem.

The wording of the Convention is quite broad in stating, in Article 2, that one commits an offense "if that person by any means, directly or indirectly, unlawfully and willfully, provides or collects funds with the intention that they should be used or in the knowledge that they are to be used, in full or in part, in order to carry out . . ." certain defined terrorist acts within the Convention.

As has been seen since ratification of this Convention, broadly worded implementation legislation is being used to identify and restrict terrorist financial interests.

The full text of the President's Message to the Senate follows:

"LETTER OF TRANSMITTAL

THE WHITE HOUSE, *October 12, 2000.*

To the Senate of the United States:

With a view to receiving the advice and consent of the Senate to ratification, I transmit herewith the International Convention for the Suppression of the Financing of Terrorism, adopted by the United Nations General Assembly on December 9, 1999, and signed on behalf of the United States of America on January 10, 2000. The report of the Department of State with respect to the Convention is also transmitted for the information of the Senate.

In recent years, the United States has increasingly focused world attention on the importance of combating terrorist financing as a means of choking off the resources that fuel international terrorism. While international terrorists do not generally seek financial gain as an end, they actively solicit and raise money and other resources to attract and retain adherents and to support their presence and activities both in the United States and abroad. The present Convention is aimed at cutting off the sustenance that these groups need to operate. This Convention provides, for the first time, and obligation that States Parties criminalize such conduct and establishes an international legal framework for cooperation among States Parties directed toward prevention of such financing and ensuring the prosecution and punishment of offenders, wherever found.

Article 2 of the Convention states that any person commits an offense within the meaning of the Convention "if that person by any means, directly or indirectly, unlawfully and willfully, provides or collects funds with the intention that they should be used or in the knowledge that they are to be used, in full or in part, in order to carry out" either of two categories of terrorist acts defined in the Convention. The first category includes any act that constitutes an offense within the scope of and as defined in one of the counterterrorism treaties listed in the Annex to the Convention. The second category encompasses any other act intended to cause death or serious bodily injury to a civilian, or to any other person not taking an active part in hostilities in a situation of armed conflict, when the purpose of the act, by its nature or context, is to intimidate a population, or to compel a government or an international organization to do or to abstain from doing any act.

The Convention imposes binding legal obligations upon States Parties either to submit for prosecution or to extradite any person within their jurisdiction who commits an offense as defined in Article 2 of the Convention, attempts to commit such an act, participates as an accomplice, organizes or directs others to commit such an offense, or in any other way contributes to the commission of an offense by a group of persons acting with a common purpose. A State Party is subject to these obligations without regard to the place where the alleged act covered by Article 2 took place.

States Parties to the Convention will also be obligated to provide one another legal assistance in investigations or criminal or extradition proceedings brought in respect of the offenses set forth in Article 2.

Legislation necessary to implement the Convention will be submitted to the Congress separately.

This Convention is a critical new weapon in the campaign against the scourge of international terrorism. I hope that all countries will become Parties to this Convention at the earliest possible time. I recommend, therefore, that the Senate give early and favorable consideration to this Convention, subject to the understanding, declaration and reservation that are described in the accompanying report of the Department of State.

WILLIAM J. CLINTON"

INTERNATIONAL CONVENTION FOR THE SUPPRESSION OF THE FINANCING OF TERRORISM

Adopted at New York on December 9, 1999
Entered into force 10 April 2002*

Preamble

THE STATES PARTIES TO THIS CONVENTION,

Bearing in mind the purposes and principles of the Charter of the United Nations concerning the maintenance of international peace and security and the promotion of good-neighbourliness and friendly relations and cooperation among States,

Deeply concerned about the worldwide escalation of acts of terrorism in all its forms and manifestations,

Recalling the Declaration on the Occasion of the Fiftieth Anniversary of the United Nations, contained in General Assembly resolution 50/6 of 24 October 1995,

Recalling also all the relevant General Assembly resolutions on the matter, including resolution 49/60 of 9 December 1994 and its annex on the Declaration on Measures to Eliminate International Terrorism, in which the States Members of the United Nations solemnly reaffirmed their unequivocal condemnation of all acts, methods and practices of terrorism as criminal and unjustifiable, wherever and by whomever committed, including those which jeopardize the friendly relations among States and peoples and threaten the territorial integrity and security of States,

Noting that the Declaration on Measures to Eliminate International Terrorism also encouraged States to review urgently the scope of the existing international legal provisions on the prevention, repression and elimination

---

* Treaties and International Agreements Online, CTIA 9889.000 (Oceana Publications, Inc. <www.oceanalaw.com>.

of terrorism in all its forms and manifestations, with the aim of ensuring that there is a comprehensive legal framework covering all aspects of the matter,

Recalling General Assembly resolution 51/210 of 17 December 1996, paragraph 3, subparagraph (f), in which the Assembly called upon all States to take steps to prevent and counteract, through appropriate domestic measures, the financing of terrorists and terrorist organizations, whether such financing is direct or indirect through organizations which also have or claim to have charitable, social or cultural goals or which are also engaged in unlawful activities such as illicit arms trafficking, drug dealing and racketeering, including the exploitation of persons for purposes of funding terrorist activities, and in particular to consider, where appropriate, adopting regulatory measures to prevent and counteract movements of funds suspected to be intended for terrorist purposes without impeding in any way the freedom of legitimate capital movements and to intensify the exchange of information concerning international movements of such funds,

Recalling also General Assembly resolution 52/165 of 15 December 1997, in which the Assembly called upon States to consider, in particular, the implementation of the measures set out in paragraphs 3 (a) to (f) of its resolution 51/210 of 17 December 1996,

Recalling further General Assembly resolution 53/108 of 8 December 1998, in which the Assembly decided that the Ad Hoc Committee established by General Assembly resolution 51/210 of 17 December 1996 should elaborate a draft international convention for the suppression of terrorist financing to supplement related existing international instruments,

Considering that the financing of terrorism is a matter of grave concern to the international community as a whole,

Noting that the number and seriousness of acts of international terrorism depend on the financing that terrorists may obtain,

Noting also that existing multilateral legal instruments do not expressly address such financing,

Being convinced of the urgent need to enhance international cooperation among States in devising and adopting effective measures for the prevention of the financing of terrorism, as well as for its suppression through the prosecution and punishment of its perpetrators,

Have agreed as follows:

Article 1

For the purposes of this Convention:

1. "Funds" means assets of every kind, whether tangible or intangible, movable or immovable, however acquired, and legal documents or instruments in any form, including electronic or digital, evidencing title to, or interest in, such assets, including, but not limited, to bank credits, trav-

ellers cheques, bank cheques, bank cheques, money orders, shares, securities, bonds, drafts, letters of credit.

2. "A State or governmental facility" means any permanent or temporary facility or conveyance that is used or occupied by representatives of a State, members of Government, the legislature or the judiciary or by officials or employees of a State or any other public authority or entity or by employees or officials of an intergovernmental organization in connection with their official duties.

3. "Proceeds" means any funds derived from or obtained, directly or indirectly, through the commission of an offence set forth in article 2.

Article 2

1. Any person commits an offence within the meaning of this Convention if that person by any means, directly or indirectly, unlawfully and willfully, provides or collects funds with the intention that they should be used or in the knowledge that they are to be used, in full or in part, in order to carry out:

(a) An act which constitutes an offence within the scope of and as defined in one of the treaties listed in the annex; or

(b) Any other act intended to cause death or serious bodily injury to a civilian, or to any other person not taking an active part in the hostilities in a situation of armed conflict, when the purpose of such act, by its nature or context, is to intimidate a population, or to compel a government or an international organization to do or to abstain from doing any act.

2. (a) On depositing its instrument of ratification, acceptance, approval or accession, a State Party which is not a party to a treaty listed in the annex may declare that, in the application of this Convention to the State Party, the treaty shall be deemed not to be included in the annex referred to in paragraph 1, subparagraph (a). The declaration shall cease to have effect as soon as the treaty enters into force for the State Party, which shall notify the depositary of this fact;

(b) When a State Party ceases to be a party to a treaty listed in the annex, it may make a declaration as provided for in this article, with respect to that treaty.

3. For an act to constitute an offence set forth in paragraph 1, it shall not be necessary that the funds were actually used to carry out an offence referred to in paragraph 1, subparagraphs (a) or (b).

4. Any person also commits an offence if that person attempts to commit an offence as set forth in paragraph 1 of this article.

5. Any person also commits an offence if that person:

(a) Participates as an accomplice in an offence as set forth in paragraph 1 or 4 of this article;

(b) Organizes or directs others to commit an offence as set forth in paragraph 1 or 4 of this article;

(c) Contributes to the commission of one or more offences as set forth in paragraphs 1 or 4 of this article by a group of persons acting with a common purpose. Such contribution shall be intentional and shall either:

(i) Be made with the aim of furthering the criminal activity or criminal purpose of the group, where such activity or purpose involves the commission of an offence as set forth in paragraph 1 of this article; or

(ii) Be made in the knowledge of the intention of the group to commit an offence as set forth in paragraph 1 of this article.

Article 3

This Convention shall not apply where the offence is committed within a single State, the alleged offender is a national of that State and is present in the territory of that State and no other State has a basis under article 7, paragraph 1, or article 7, paragraph 2, to exercise jurisdiction, except that the provisions of articles 12 to 18 shall, as appropriate, apply in those cases.

Article 4

Each State Party shall adopt such measures as may be necessary:

(a) To establish as criminal offences under its domestic law the offences set forth in article 2;

(b) To make those offences punishable by appropriate penalties which take into account the grave nature of the offences.

Article 5

1. Each State Party, in accordance with its domestic legal principles, shall take the necessary measures to enable a legal entity located in its territory or organized under its laws to be held liable when a person responsible for the management or control of that legal entity has, in that capacity, committed an offence set forth in article 2. Such liability may be criminal, civil or administrative.

2. Such liability is incurred without prejudice to the criminal liability of individuals having committed the offences.

3. Each State Party shall ensure, in particular, that legal entities liable in accordance with paragraph 1 above are subject to effective, proportionate and dissuasive criminal, civil or administrative sanctions. Such sanctions may include monetary sanctions.

Article 6

Each State Party shall adopt such measures as may be necessary, including, where appropriate, domestic legislation, to ensure that criminal acts within the scope of this Convention are under no circumstances justifiable by considerations of a political, philosophical, ideological, racial, ethnic, religious or other similar nature.

Article 7

1. Each State Party shall take such measures as may be necessary to establish its jurisdiction over the offences set forth in article 2 when:

(a) The offence is committed in the territory of that State;

(b) The offence is committed on board a vessel flying the flag of that State or an aircraft registered under the laws of that State at the time the offence is committed;

(c) The offence is committed by a national of that State.

2. A State Party may also establish its jurisdiction over any such offence when:

(a) The offence was directed towards or resulted in the carrying out of an offence referred to in article 2, paragraph 1, subparagraph (a) or (b), in the territory of or against a national of that State;

(b) The offence was directed towards or resulted in the carrying out of an offence referred to in article 2, paragraph 1, subparagraph (a) or (b), against a State or government facility of that State abroad, including diplomatic or consular premises of that State;

(c) The offence was directed towards or resulted in an offence referred to in article 2, paragraph 1, subparagraph (a) or (b), committed in an attempt to compel that State to do or abstain from doing any act;

(d) The offence is committed by a stateless person who has his or her habitual, residence in the territory of that State;

(e) The offence is committed on board an aircraft which is operated by the Government of that State.

3. Upon ratifying, accepting, approving or acceding to this Convention, each State Party shall notify the Secretary-General of the United Nations of the jurisdiction it has established in accordance with paragraph 2. Should any change take place, the State Party concerned shall immediately notify the Secretary-General.

4. Each State Party shall likewise take such measures as may be necessary to establish its jurisdiction over the offences set forth in article 2 in cases where the alleged offender is present in its territory and it does not extradite that person to any of the States Parties that have established their jurisdiction in accordance with paragraphs 1 or 2.

5. When more than one State Party claims jurisdiction over the offences set forth in article 2, the relevant States Parties shall strive to coordinate their actions appropriately, in particular concerning the conditions for prosecution and the modalities for mutual legal assistance.

6. Without prejudice to the norms of general international law, this Convention does not exclude the exercise of any criminal jurisdiction established by a State Party in accordance with its domestic law.

Article 8

1. Each State Party shall take appropriate measures, in accordance with its domestic legal principles, for the identification, detection and freezing or seizure of any funds used or allocated for the purpose of committing the offences set forth in article 2 as well as the proceeds derived from such offences, for purposes of possible forfeiture.

2. Each State Party shall take appropriate measures, in accordance with its domestic legal principles, for the forfeiture of funds used or allocated for the purpose of committing the offences set forth in article 2 and the proceeds derived from such offences.

3. Each State Party concerned may give consideration to concluding agreements on the sharing with other States Parties, on a regular or case-by-case basis, of the funds derived from the forfeitures referred to in this article.

4. Each State Party shall consider establishing mechanisms whereby the funds derived from the forfeitures referred to in this article are utilized to compensate the victims of offences referred to in article 2, paragraph 1, subparagraph (a) or (b), or their families.

5. The provisions of this article shall be implemented without prejudice to the rights of third parties acting in good faith.

Article 9

1. Upon receiving information that a person who has committed or who is alleged to have committed an offence set forth in article 2 may be present in its territory, the State Party concerned shall take such measures as may be necessary under its domestic law to investigate the facts contained in the information.

2. Upon being satisfied that the circumstances so warrant, the State Party in whose territory the offender or alleged offender is present shall take the appropriate measures under its domestic law so as to ensure that person's presence for the purpose of prosecution or extradition.

3. Any person regarding whom the measures referred to in paragraph 2 are being taken shall be entitled to:

(a) Communicate without delay with the nearest appropriate representative of the State of which that person is a national or which is otherwise entitled to protect that person's rights or, if that person is a stateless person, the State in the territory of which that person habitually resides;

(b) Be visited by a representative of that State;

(c) Be informed of that person's rights under subparagraphs (a) and (b).

4. The rights referred to in paragraph 3 shall be exercised in conformity with the laws and regulations of the State in the territory of which the offender or alleged offender is present, subject to the provision that the said laws and regulations must enable full effect to be given to the purposes for which the rights accorded under paragraph 3 are intended.

5. The provisions of paragraphs 3 and 4 shall be without prejudice to the right of any State Party having a claim to jurisdiction in accordance with article 7, paragraph 1, subparagraph (b), or paragraph 2, subparagraph (b), to invite the International Committee of the Red Cross to communicate with and visit the alleged offender.

6. When a State Party, pursuant to the present article, has taken a person into custody, it shall immediately notify, directly or through the Secretary-General of the United Nations, the States Parties which have established jurisdiction in accordance with article 7, paragraph 1 or 2, and, if it considers it advisable, any other interested States Parties, of the fact that such person is in custody and of the circumstances which warrant that person's detention. The State which makes the investigation contemplated in paragraph 1 shall promptly inform the said States Parties of its findings and shall indicate whether it intends to exercise jurisdiction.

Article 10

1. The State Party in the territory of which the alleged offender is present shall, in cases to which article 7 applies, if it does not extradite that person, be obliged, without exception whatsoever and whether or not the offence was committed in its territory, to submit the case without undue delay to its competent authorities for the purpose of prosecution, through proceedings in accordance with the laws of that State. Those authorities shall take their decision in the same manner as in the case of any other offence of a grave nature under the law of that State.

2. Whenever a State Party is permitted under its domestic law to extradite or otherwise surrender one of its nationals only upon the condition that the person will be returned to that State to serve the sentence imposed as a result of the trial or proceeding for which the extradition or surrender of the person was sought, and this State and the State seeking the extradition of the person agree with this option and other terms they may deem appropriate, such a conditional extradition or surrender shall be sufficient to discharge the obligation set forth in paragraph 1.

Article 11

1. The offences set forth in article 2 shall be deemed to be included as extraditable offences in any extradition treaty existing between any of the States Parties before the entry into force of this Convention States Parties undertake to include such offences as extraditable offences in every extradition treaty to be subsequently concluded between them.

2. When a State Party which makes extradition conditional on the existence of a treaty receives a request for extradition from another State Party with which it has no extradition treaty, the requested State Party may, at its option, consider this Convention as a legal basis for extradition in respect of the offences set forth in article 2. Extradition shall be subject to the other conditions provided by the law of the requested State.

3. States Parties which do not make extradition conditional on the existence of a treaty shall recognize the offences set forth in article 2 as extraditable offences between themselves, subject to the conditions provided by the law of the requested State.

4. If necessary, the offences set forth in article 2 shall be treated, for the purposes of extradition between States Parties, as if they had been committed not only in the place in which they occurred but also in the territory of the States that have established jurisdiction in accordance with article 7, paragraphs 1 and 2.

5. The provisions of all extradition treaties and arrangements between States Parties with regard to offences set forth in article 2 shall be deemed to be modified as between States Parties to the extent that they are incompatible with this Convention.

Article 12

1. States Parties shall afford one another the greatest measure of assistance in connection with criminal investigations or criminal or extradition proceedings in respect of the offences set forth in article 2, including assistance in obtaining evidence in their possession necessary for the proceedings.

2. States Parties may not refuse a request for mutual legal assistance on the ground of bank secrecy.

3. The requesting Party shall not transmit nor use information or evidence furnished by the requested Party for investigations, prosecutions or proceedings other than those stated in the request without the prior consent of the requested Party.

4. Each State Party may give consideration to establishing mechanisms to share with other States Parties information or evidence needed to establish criminal, civil or administrative liability pursuant to article 5.

5. States Parties shall carry out their obligations under paragraphs 1 and 2 in conformity with any treaties or other arrangements on mutual legal assistance or information exchange that may exist between them. In the absence of such treaties or arrangements, States Parties shall afford one another assistance in accordance with their domestic law.

Article 13

None of the offences set forth in article 2 shall be regarded, for the purposes of extradition or mutual legal assistance, as a fiscal offence. Accordingly,

States Parties may not refuse a request for extradition or for mutual legal assistance on the sole ground that it concerns a fiscal offence.

Article 14

None of the offences set forth in article 2 shall be regarded for the purposes of extradition or mutual legal assistance as a political offence or as an offence connected with a political offence or as an offence inspired by political motives. Accordingly, a request for extradition or for mutual legal assistance based on such an offence may not be refused on the sole ground that it concerns a political offence or an offence connected with a political offence or an offence inspired by political motives.

Article 15

Nothing in this Convention shall be interpreted as imposing an obligation to extradite or to afford mutual legal assistance, if the requested State Party has substantial grounds for believing that the request for extradition for offences set forth in article 2 or for mutual legal assistance with respect to such offences has been made for the purpose of prosecuting or punishing a person on account of that person's race, religion, nationality, ethnic origin or political opinion or that compliance with the request would cause prejudice to that person's position for any of these reasons.

Article 16

1. A person who is being detained or is serving a sentence in the territory of one State Party whose presence in another State Party is requested for purposes of identification, testimony or otherwise providing assistance in obtaining evidence for the investigation or prosecution of offences set forth in article 2 may be transferred if the following conditions are met:

(a) The person freely gives his or her informed consent;

(b) The competent authorities of both States agree, subject to such conditions as those States may deem appropriate.

2. For the purposes of the present article:

(a) The State to which the person is transferred shall have the authority and obligation to keep the person transferred in custody, unless otherwise requested or authorized by the State from which the person was transferred;

(b) The State to which the person is transferred shall without delay implement its obligation to return the person to the custody of the State from which the person was transferred as agreed beforehand, or as otherwise agreed, by the competent authorities of both States;

(c) The State to which the person is transferred shall not require the State from which the person was transferred to initiate extradition proceedings for the return of the person;

(d) The person transferred shall receive credit for service of the sentence being served in the State from which he or she was transferred for time spent in the custody of the State to which he or she was transferred.

3. Unless the State Party from which a person is to be transferred in accordance with the present article so agrees, that person, whatever his or her nationality, shall not be prosecuted or detained or subjected to any other restriction of his or her personal liberty in the territory of the State to which that person is transferred in respect of acts or convictions anterior to his or her departure from the territory of the State from which such person was transferred.

Article 17

Any person who is taken into custody or regarding whom any other measures are taken or proceedings are carried out pursuant to this Convention shall be guaranteed fair treatment, including enjoyment of all rights and guarantees in conformity with the law of the State in the territory of which that person is present and applicable provisions of international law, including international human rights law.

Article 18

1. States Parties shall cooperate in the prevention of the offences set forth in article 2 by taking all practicable measures, *inter alia*, by adapting their domestic legislation, if necessary, to prevent and counter preparations in their respective territories for the commission of those offences within or outside their territories, including:

(a) Measures to prohibit in their territories illegal activities of persons and organizations that knowingly encourage, instigate, organize or engage in the commission of offences set forth in article 2;

(b) Measures requiring financial institutions and other professions involved in financial transactions to utilize the most efficient measures available for the identification of their usual or occasional customers, as well as customers in whose interest accounts are opened, and to pay special attention to unusual or suspicious transactions and report transactions suspected of stemming from a criminal activity. For this purpose, States Parties shall consider:

(i) Adopting regulations prohibiting the opening of accounts the holders or beneficiaries of which are unidentified or unidentifiable, and measures to ensure that such institutions verify the identity of the real owners of such transactions;

(ii) With respect to the identification of legal entities, requiring financial institutions, when necessary, to take measures to verify the legal existence and the structure of the customer by obtaining, either from a public register or from the customer or both, proof of incorporation, including information concerning the customer's name, legal form, address, directors and provisions regulating the power to bind the entity;

(iii) Adopting regulations imposing on financial institutions the obligation to report promptly to the competent authorities all complex, unusual large transactions and unusual patterns of transactions, which have no apparent economic or obviously lawful purpose, without fear of assuming criminal or civil liability for breach of any restriction on disclosure of information if they report their suspicions in good faith;

(iv) Requiring financial institutions to maintain, for at least five years, all necessary records on transactions, both domestic or international.

2. States Parties shall further cooperate in the prevention of offences set forth in article 2 by considering:

(a) Measures for the supervision, including, for example, the licensing, of all money-transmission agencies;

(b) Feasible measures to detect or monitor the physical cross-border transportation of cash and bearer negotiable instruments, subject to strict safeguards to ensure proper use of information and without impeding in any way the freedom of capital movements.

3. States Parties shall further cooperate in the prevention of the offences set forth in article 2 by exchanging accurate and verified information in accordance with their domestic law and coordinating administrative and other measures taken, as appropriate, to prevent the commission of offences set forth in article 2, in particular by:

(a) Establishing and maintaining channels of communication between their competent agencies and services to facilitate the secure and rapid exchange of information concerning all aspects of offences set forth in article 2;

(b) Cooperating with one another in conducting inquiries, with respect to the offences set forth in article 2, concerning:

(i) The identity, whereabouts and activities of persons in respect of whom reasonable suspicion exists that they are involved in such offences;

(ii) The movement of funds relating to the commission of such offences.

4. States Parties may exchange information through the International Criminal Police Organization (Interpol).

Article 19

The State Party where the alleged offender is prosecuted shall, in accordance with its domestic law or applicable procedures, communicate the final outcome of the proceedings to the Secretary-General of the United Nations, who shall transmit the information to the other States Parties.

Article 20

The States Parties shall carry out their obligations under this Convention in a manner consistent with the principles of sovereign equality and territorial integrity of States and that of non-intervention in the domestic affairs of other States.

Article 21

Nothing in this Convention shall affect other rights, obligations and responsibilities of States and individuals under international law, in particular the purposes of the Charter of the United Nations, international humanitarian law and other relevant conventions.

Article 22

Nothing in this Convention entitles a State Party to undertake in the territory of another State Party the exercise of jurisdiction or performance of functions which are exclusively reserved for the authorities of that other State Party by its domestic law.

Article 23

1. The annex may be amended by the addition of relevant treaties that:

   (a) Are open to the participation of all States;

   (b) Have entered into force;

   (c) Have been ratified, accepted, approved or acceded to by at least twenty-two States Parties to the present Convention.

2. After the entry into force of this Convention, any State Party may propose such an amendment. Any proposal for an amendment shall be communicated to the depositary in written form. The depositary shall notify proposals that meet the requirements of paragraph 1 to all States Parties and seek their views on whether the proposed amendment should be adopted.

3. The proposed amendment shall be deemed adopted unless one third of the States Parties object to it by a written notification not later than 180 days after its circulation.

4. The adopted amendment to the annex shall enter into force 30 days after the deposit of the twenty-second instrument of ratification, acceptance or approval of such amendment for all those States Parties having deposited such an instrument. For each State Party ratifying, accepting or approving the amendment after the deposit of the twenty-second instrument, the amendment shall enter into force on the thirtieth day after deposit by such State Party of its instrument of ratification, acceptance or approval.

Article 24

1. Any dispute between two or more States Parties concerning the interpretation or application of this Convention which cannot be settled through negotiation within a reasonable time shall, at the request of one of them, be submitted to arbitration. If, within six months from the date of the request for arbitration, the parties are unable to agree on the organization of the arbitration, any one of those parties may refer the dispute to the International Court of Justice, by application, in conformity with the Statute of the Court.

2. Each State may at the time of signature, ratification, acceptance or approval of this Convention or accession thereto declare that it does not consider itself bound by paragraph 1. The other States Parties shall not be bound by paragraph 1 with respect to any State Party which has made such a reservation.

3. Any State which has made a reservation in accordance with paragraph 2 may at any time withdraw that reservation by notification to the Secretary-General of the United Nations.

Article 25

1. This Convention shall be open for signature by all States from 10 January 2000 to 31 December 2001 at United Nations Headquarters in New York.

2. This Convention is subject to ratification, acceptance or approval. The instruments of ratification, acceptance or approval shall be deposited with the Secretary-General of the United Nations.

3. This Convention shall be open to accession by any State. The instruments of accession shall be deposited with the Secretary-General of the United Nations.

Article 26

1. This Convention shall enter into force on the thirtieth day following the date of the deposit of the twenty-second instrument of ratification, acceptance, approval or accession with the Secretary-General of the United Nations.

2. For each State ratifying accepting, approving or acceding to the Convention after the deposit of the twenty-second instrument of ratification, acceptance, approval or accession, the Convention shall enter into force on the thirtieth day after deposit by such State of its instrument of ratification, acceptance, approval or accession.

Article 27

1. Any State Party may denounce this Convention by written notification to the Secretary-General of the United Nations.

2. Denunciation shall take effect one year following the date on which notification is received by the Secretary-General of the United Nations.

Article 28

The original of this Convention, of which the Arabic, Chinese, English, French, Russian and Spanish texts are equally authentic, shall be deposited with the Secretary-General of the United Nations who shall send certified copies thereof to all States.

IN WITNESS WHEREOF, the undersigned, being duly authorized thereto by their respective Governments, have signed this Convention, opened for signature at United Nations Headquarters in New York on 10 January 2000.

Annex

1. Convention for the Suppression of Unlawful Seizure of Aircraft, done at The Hague on 16 December 1970.

2. Convention for the Suppression of Unlawful Acts against the Safety of Civil Aviation, done at Montreal on 23 September 1971.

3. Convention on the Prevention and Punishment of Crimes against Internationally Protected Persons, including Diplomatic Agents, adopted by the General Assembly of the United Nations on 14 December 1973.

4. International Convention against the Taking of Hostages, adopted by the General Assembly of the United Nations on 17 December 1979.

5. Convention on the Physical Protection of Nuclear Material, adopted at Vienna on 3 March 1980.

6. Protocol for the Suppression of Unlawful Acts of Violence at Airports Serving International Civil Aviation, supplementary to the Convention for the Suppression of Unlawful Acts against the Safety of Civil Aviation, done at Montreal on 24 February 1988.

7. Convention for the Suppression of Unlawful Acts against the Safety of Maritime Navigation, done at Rome on 10 March 1988.

8. Protocol for the Suppression of Unlawful Acts against the Safety of Fixed Platforms located on the Continental Shelf, done at Rome on 10 March 1988.

9. International Convention for the Suppression of Terrorist Bombings, adopted by the General Assembly of the United Nations on 15 December 1997.

Parties:

Afghanistan
Albania
Algeria
Andorra
Antigua and Barbuda
Argentina
Armenia
Australia
Austria
Azerbaijan
Bahamas
Bahrain
Barbados
Belarus
Belgium
Belize
Benin
Bhutan
Bolivia
Bosnia and Herzegovina
Botswana
Brazil
Brunei Darussalam
Bulgaria
Burkina Faso
Burundi
Cambodia
Canada
Cape Verde
Central African Republic
Chile
China
Colombia
Comoros
Congo
Cook Islands
Costa Rica
Côte d'Ivoire
Croatia
Cuba
Cyprus
Czech Republic
Democratic People's Republic of Korea
Democratic Republic of the Congo
Denmark[1]
Djibouti
Dominican Republic
Ecuador
Egypt
El Salvador
Equatorial Guinea
Estonia
Finland
France
Gabon
Georgia
Germany
Ghana
Greece
Grenada
Guatemala
Guinea
Guinea-Bissau
Honduras
Hungary
Iceland
India
Indonesia
Ireland
Israel
Italy
Jamaica
Japan
Jordan
Kazakhstan
Kenya
Kyrgyzstan
Latvia

Lesotho
Liberia
Libyan Arab Jamahiriya
Liechtenstein
Lithuania
Luxembourg
Madagascar
Malawi
Maldives
Mali
Malta
Marshall Islands
Mauritania
Mauritius
Mexico
Micronesia (Federated States of)
Monaco
Mongolia
Morocco
Mozambique
Myanmar
Namibia
Nauru
Netherlands[2]
New Zealand[3]
Nicaragua
Nigeria
Norway
Palau
Panama
Papua New Guinea
Paraguay
Peru
Philippines
Poland
Portugal
Republic of Korea
Republic of Moldova
Romania

Russian Federation
Rwanda
Saint Kitts and Nevis
Saint Vincent and the Grenadines
Samoa
San Marino
Saudi Arabia
Serbia and Montenegro
Seychelles
Sierra Leone
Singapore
Slovakia
Slovenia
Somalia
South Africa
Spain
Sri Lanka
Sudan
Swaziland
Sweden
Switzerland
Tajikistan
Thailand
The Former Yugoslav Republic of Macedonia
Togo
Tonga
Tunisia
Turkey
Uganda
Ukraine
United Kingdom of Great Britain and Northern Ireland
United Republic of Tanzania
United States of America
Uruguay
Uzbekistan
Venezuela
Viet Nam

THE FINANCING OF TERRORISM

NOTES

1. With a territorial exclusion with respect of the Faroe Islands and Greenland.

2. For the Kingdom in Europe.

3. With a territorial exclusion with respect to Tokelau to the effect that: "... consistent with the constitutional status of Tokelau and taking into account the commitment of the Government of New Zealand to the development of self-government for Tokelau through an act of self-determination under the Charter of the United Nations, this ratification shall not extend to Tokelau unless and until a Declaration to this effect is lodged by the Government of New Zealand with the Depositary on the basis of appropriate consultation with that territory."

DECLARATIONS

Declarations and Reservations

(Unless otherwise indicated, the declarations and reservations were made upon ratification, acceptance, approval or accession.)

Algeria

Reservation:

> Reservation of Algeria
>
> The Government of the People's Democratic Republic of Algeria does not consider itself bound by the provisions of article 24, paragraph 1, of the International Convention for the Suppression of the Financing of Terrorism.
>
> The Government of the People's Democratic Republic of Algeria declares that in order for a dispute to be submitted to arbitration or to the International Court of Justice, the agreement of all parties to the dispute shall be required in each case.

Brazil

Upon signature:

> Interpretative declarations:
>
> "Interpretative Declarations to be made by the Federal Republic of Brazil on the occasion of signing of the International Convention for the Suppression of the Financing of Terrorism:
>
> 1. As concerns Article 2 of the said Convention, three of the legal instruments listed in the Annex to the Convention have not come into force in Brazil. These are the Convention for the Suppression of Unlawful Acts against the Safety of Maritime Navigation; Protocol for the Suppression of Unlawful Acts against the Safety of Fixed Platforms Located on the Continental Shelf; and the International Convention for the Suppression of Terrorist Bombings.
>
> 2. As concerns Article 24, paragraph 2 of the said Convention, Brazil does not consider itself obligated by paragraph 1 of the said Article, given that it has not recognized the mandatory jurisdiction clause of the International Court of Justice."

Cook Islands

Declaration:

> "In accordance with the provisions of article 2, paragraph 2, subparagraph (a) of the International Convention for the Suppression of the Financing of Terrorism, the Government of the Cook Islands declares:

That in the application of this Convention, the treaties listed in the annex, referred to in article 2, paragraph 1, subparagraph (a) shall be deemed not to be included, given that the Cook Islands is not yet a party to the following Conventions:

(i) Convention on the Physical Protection of Nuclear Material, adopted at Vienna on 3 March 1980;

(ii) Protocol for the Suppression of Unlawful Acts of Violence at Airports Serving International Civil Aviation, supplementary to the Convention for the Suppression of Unlawful Acts against the Safety of Civil Aviation, done at Montreal on 24 February 1988;

(iii) Convention for the Suppression of Unlawful Acts against the Safety of Maritime Navigation, done at Rome on 10 March 1988;

(iv) Protocol for the Suppression of Unlawful Acts against the Safety of Fixed Platforms located on the Continental Shelf, done at Rome on 10 March 1988;

(v) International Convention for the Suppression of Terrorist Bombings, adopted by the General Assembly of the United Nations on 15 December 1997."

Croatia

Declaration:

"The Republic of Croatia, pursuant to Article 2 paragraph 2 of the International Convention for the Suppression of the Financing of Terrorism, declares that in the application of the Convention to the Republic of Croatia the following treaties shall be deemed not to be included in the Annex referred to in Article 2, paragraph 1, subparagraph (a) of the Convention:

1. International Convention against the Taking of Hostages, adopted by the General Assembly of the United Nations on 17 December 1979,

2. Convention for the Suppression of Unlawful Acts against the Safety of Maritime Navigation, done at Rome on 10 March 1988,

3. Protocol for the Suppression of Unlawful Acts against the Safety of Fixed Platforms located on the Continental Shelf, done at Rome on 10 March 1988,

4. International Convention for the Suppression of Terrorist Bombings, adopted by the General Assembly of the United Nations on 15 December 1997."

Cuba

Reservation:

The Republic of Cuba declares, pursuant to article 24, paragraph 2, that it does not consider itself bound by paragraph 1 of the said article, concerning the settlement of disputes arising between States Parties, inasmuch as it considers that such disputes must be settled through amicable negotiation. In consequence, it declares that it does not recognize the compulsory jurisdiction of the International Court of Justice.

Democratic People's Republic of Korea[1]

Upon signature:

Reservations:

1. The Democratic People's Republic of Korea does not consider itself bound by the provisions of article 2, paragraph 1, sub-paragraph (a) of the Convention.

2. The Democratic People's Republic of Korea does not consider itself bound by the provisions of article 14 of the Convention.

3. The Democratic People's Republic of Korea does not consider itself bound by the provisions of article 24, paragraph 1 of the Convention.

El Salvador

Declarations:

(1) Pursuant to article 2, paragraph 2 (a), the Republic of El Salvador declares that in the application of this Convention, the Convention on the Physical Protection of Nuclear Material, adopted in Vienna on 3 March 1980, shall not be considered as having been included in the annex referred to in article 2, paragraph 1 (a), since El Salvador is not currently a State party thereto;

...

(3) pursuant to article 24, paragraph 2, the Republic of El Salvador declares that it does not consider itself bound by paragraph 1 of that article, because it does not recognize the compulsory jurisdiction of the International Court of Justice; and

---

[1] With regard to the declaration made by the Government of the Democratic People's Republic of Korea upon signature, the Secretary-General received a communciation from the following State on the date indicated hereinafter:

Republic of Moldova (6 october 2003):

"The Government of the Republic of Moldova has examined the reservations made by the Government of the Democratic People's Republic of Korea upon signature of the International Convention for the Suppression of Financing of Terrorism.

The Government of the Republic of Moldova considers that the reservations with regard to article 2, paragraph 1 (a), and article 14 are incompatible with the object and purpose of the Convention, as they purport to exclude the application of core provisions of the Convention.

The Government of the Republic of Moldova recalls that, according to Article 19 (c) of the Vienna Convention on the Law of Treaties, a reservation incompatible with the object and purpose of the Convention shall not be permitted. It is in the common interest of States that treaties to which they have chosen to become parties are respected as to their object and purpose, by all parties, and that States are prepared to undertake any legislative changes necessary to comply with their obligations under the treaties.

The Government of the Republic of Moldova therefore objects to the aforesaid reservations made by the Government of the Democratic People's Republic of Korea to the International Convention for the Suppression of Financing of Terrorism.This objection shall not preclude the entry into force of the Convention between the Republic of Moldova and the Democratic People's Republic of Korea. The Convention enters into force in its entirety between the two States, without the Democratic People's Republic of Korea benefiting from its reservations."

(4) El Salvador accedes to this Convention on the understanding that such accession is without prejudice to any provisions thereof which may conflict with the principles expressed in its Constitution and domestic legal system.

Estonia

Declaration:

"[With] the following Declaration[s]:

1) pursuant to article 2, paragraph 2 of the Convention, the Republic of Estonia declares, that she does not consider itself bound by the Protocol for the Suppression of Unlawful Acts against the Safety of Fixed Platforms Located on the Continental Shelf, done at Rome, on 10 March 1988, annexed to the Convention;". . . .

France

Declarations:

Declaration pursuant to article 2, paragraph 2 (a)

In accordance with article 2, paragraph 2 (a) of this Convention, France declares that in the application of the Convention to France, the Convention of 14 December 1973 on the Prevention and Punishment of Crimes against Internationally Protected Persons, including Diplomatic Agents, shall be deemed not to be included in the annex referred to in article 2, paragraph 1, subparagraph (a), since France is not a party thereto.

Georgia

Declaration:

"In accordance with article 2.2, Georgia declares, that while applying this Convention, treaties to which Georgia is not contracting party shall not be considered as included in the annex to this Convention."

Guatemala

Declaration:

Pursuant to article 2, paragraph 2 (a) of the Convention referred to in the preceding article, the State of Guatemala, in ratifying the Convention, makes the following declaration: "In the application of this Convention, Guatemala deems the following treaties not to be included in the annex: the Convention for the Suppression of Unlawful Acts against the Safety of Maritime Navigation, signed at Rome on 10 March 1988; the Protocol for the Suppression of Unlawful Acts against the Safety of Fixed Platforms located on the Continental Shelf, done at Rome on 10 March 1988 and the International Convention for the Suppression of Terrorist Bombings, adopted by the General Assembly of the United Nations on 15 December 1997. The declaration shall cease to have effect, for each of the treaties indicated, as soon as the treaty enters into force for the State of Guatemala, which shall notify the depositary of this fact.

6 June 2002

Declaration under article 2 (2) (a):

[The Government of Guatemala notifies,]. . .pursuant to article 2, paragraph 2 of the International Convention for the Suppression of the Financing of Terrorism, that on 14 March 2002 [should read: 10 April 2002], the International Convention for the Suppression of Terrorist Bombings entered into force for the Republic of Guatemala. Accordingly, the declaration made by the Republic of Guatemala at the time of depositing its instrument of ratification that the latter Convention was deemed not to be included in the annex to the International Convention for the Suppression of the Financing of Terrorism has ceased to have effect.

THE FINANCING OF TERRORISM

Israel

"... with the following declarations:

Pursuant to Article 2, paragraph 2 (a) of the International Convention for the Suppression of the Financing of Terrorism, the Government of the State of Israel declares that in the application of the Convention the treaties to which the state of Israel is not a party shall be deemed not to be included in the Annex of the Convention.

...

Pursuant to Article 24, paragraph 2 of the Convention, the State of Israel does not consider itself bound by the provisions of Article 24, paragraph 1 of the Convention.

The Government of the State of Israel understands that the term "international humanitarian law" referred to in Article 21 of the Convention has the same substantial meaning as the term "the law of war". This body of laws does not include the provisions of the Protocols Additional to the Geneva Convention of 1977 to which the State of Israel is not a party."

Jordan

Declarations:

"1. The Government of the Hashemite Kingdom of Jordan does not consider acts of national armed struggle and fighting foreign occupation in the exercise of people's right to self-determination as terrorist acts within the context of paragraph 1(b) of article 2 of the Convention.

2. Jordan is not a party to the following treaties:

   A. Convention on the Physical Protection of Nuclear Material, adopted in Vienna on 3 March 1980.

   B. Convention for the Suppression of Unlawful Acts against the Safety of Maritime Navigation, done at Rome on 10 March 1988.

   C. Protocol for the Suppression of Unlawful Acts against the Safety of Fixed Platforms Located on the Continental Shelf, done at Rome on 10 March 1988.

   D. International Convention for the Suppression of Terrorist Bombings, adopted in New York on 15 December 1997.

Accordingly Jordan is not bound to include, in the application of the International Convention for the Suppression of the Financing of Terrorism, the offences within the scope and as defined in such Treaties."

Latvia

Declaration:

"In accordance with Article 2, paragraph 2 of the International Convention for the Suppression of the Financing of Terrorism, adopted at New York on the 9th day of December 1999, the Republic of Latvia declares that in the application of the Convention to the Republic of Latvia the following treaties shall be deemed not to be included in the annex referred to in Article 2 paragraph 1, subparagraph (a) of the Convention:

   1. International Convention against the Taking of Hostages, adopted by the General Assembly of the United Nations on 17 December 1979.

   2. Convention on the Physical Protection of Nuclear Material, adopted at Vienna on 3 March 1980.

   3. Convention for the Suppression of Unlawful Acts against the Safety of Maritime Navigation, done at Rome on 10 March 1988.

4. Protocol for the Suppression of Unlawful Acts against the Safety of Fixed Platforms located on the Continental Shelf, done at Rome on 10 March 1988. 5. International Convention for the Suppression of Terrorist Bombings, adopted by the General Assembly of the United Nations on 15 December 1997."

20 March 2003

"In accordance with Article 2, paragraph 2 of the International Convention for the Suppression of the Financing of Terrorism, adopted at New York on the 9th day of December 1999, the Republic of Latvia notifies that the following treaties have entered into force for the Republic of Latvia:

1. International Convention against the Taking of Hostages, adopted by the General Assembly of the United Nations on 17 December 1979,

2. Convention on the Physical Protection of Nuclear Material, adopted at Vienna on 3 March 1980,

3. Convention for the Suppression of Unlawful Acts against the Safety of Maritime Navigation, done at Rome on 10 March 1988,

4. Protocol for the Suppression of Unlawful Acts against the Safety of Fixed Platforms located on the Continental Shelf, done at Rome on 10 March 1988; and

5. International Convention for the Suppression of Terrorist Bombings, adopted by the General Assembly of the United Nations on 15 December 1997."

Lithuania

Reservation and declaration:

"... it is provided in paragraph 2 of Article 24 of the said Convention, the Seimas of the Republic of Lithuania declares that the Republic of Lithuania does not consider itself bound by the provisions of paragraph 1 of Article 24 of the Convention stipulating that any dispute concerning the interpretation or application of this Convention shall be referred to the International Court of Justice.

... it is provided in subparagraph a) of paragraph 2 of the said Convention, the Seimas of the Republic of Lithuania declares that in the application of this Convention to the Republic of Lithuania, the International Convention for the Suppression of Terrorist Bombings, adopted on 15 December 1997, shall be deemed not to be included in the annex referred to in subparagraph a) of paragraph 1 of Article 2 of the Convention."

Luxembourg

Declaration:

Pursuant to article 2, paragraph 2, subparagraph (a), of the Convention, Luxembourg declares that when the Convention is applied to it, the treaties listed in the annex which have not yet been ratified by Luxembourg shall be deemed not to appear in the annex.

As at the date of ratification of the Convention, the following treaties listed in the annex had been ratified by Luxembourg:

Convention for the Suppression of Unlawful Seizure of Aircraft, done at The Hague, on 16 December 1970;

Convention for the Suppression of Unlawful Acts against the Safety of Civil Aviation, done at Montreal, on 23 September 1971;

International Convention against the Taking of Hostages, adopted by the General Assembly of the United Nations, on 17 December 1979;

Convention on the Physical Protection of Nuclear Material, adopted in Vienna on 3 March 1980.

Mozambique

Declaration:

"... with the following declaration in accordance with its article 24, paragraph 2:

"The Republic of Mozambique does not consider itself bound by the provisions of article 24 paragraph 1 of the Convention.

In this connection the Republic of Mozambique states that, in the each individual case, the consent of all Parties to such a dispute is necessary for the submission of the dispute to arbitration or to the International Court of Justice."

Furthermore, the Republic of Mozambique declare that:

"The Republic of Mozambique, in accordance with its Constitution and domestic laws, may not and will not extradite Mozambique citizens.

Therefore, Mozambique citizens will be tried and sentenced in national courts".

Myanmar

Upon signature:

Reservation:

"The Government of the Union of Myanmar declares in pursuance of Article 24, paragraph (2) of the International Convention for the Suppression of the Financing of Terrorism that it does not consider itself bound by the provisions of Article 24, Paragraph (1)."

Netherlands

Declaration:

"The Kingdom of the Netherlands understands Article 10, paragraph 1, of the International Convention for the Suppression of the Financing of Terrorism to include the right of the competent judicial authorities to decide not to prosecute a person alleged to have committed such an offence, if, in the opinion of the competent judicial authorities grave considerations of procedural law indicate that effective prosecution will be impossible."

New Zealand

Declaration:

"... AND DECLARES, in accordance with Article 2, paragraph 2 (a), of the Convention, that, in the application of the Convention to New Zealand, the Convention on the Physical Protection of Nuclear Materials adopted at Vienna on [3 March 1980] shall be deemed not to be included in the annex referred to in Article 2, paragraph 1 (a), as New Zealand is not yet a party to it; ..."

Nicaragua

Declaration:

In accordance with the provisions of article 2, paragraph 2, subparagraph (a), of the International Convention for the Suppression of the Financing of Terrorism, the Government of Nicaragua declares:

That, in the application of this Convention, the treaties listed in the annex referred to in article 2, paragraph 1, subparagraph (a), shall be deemed not to be included, given that Nicaragua is not yet a party to the following conventions:

1. International Convention against the Taking of Hostages, adopted by the United Nations General Assembly on 17 December 1979.

2. Convention on the Physical Protection of Nuclear Material, adopted at Vienna on 3 March 1980.

3. Convention for the Suppression of Unlawful Acts against the Safety of Maritime Navigation, done at Rome on 10 March 1988.

4. Protocol for the Suppression of Unlawful Acts against the Safety of Fixed Platforms located on the Continental Shelf, done at Rome on 10 March 1988.

Philippines

Declaration:

"..., in ratifying the Convention, the Philippines has to declare, as it hereby declares, that in the application of the Convention the following treaties to which it is not yet a party shall be deemed not included in the annex:

(a) Protocol for the Suppression of Unlawful Acts of Violence at Airports Serving International Civil Aviation, supplementary to the Convention for the Suppression of Unlawful Acts Against the Safety of Civil Aviation;

(b) Convention for the Suppression of Unlawful Acts Against the Safety of Maritime Navigation;

(c) Protocol for the Suppression of Unlawful Acts Against the Safety of Fixed Platforms located on the Continental Shelf;

(d) International Convention for the Suppression of Terrorist Bombings.

..., this declaration shall cease to have effect upon entry into force of the said treaties with respect to the Philippines."

Republic of Moldova

Declaration and reservation:

1. Pursuant to article 2, paragraph 2 (a) of the International Convention for the Suppression of the Financing of Terrorism, the Republic of Moldova declares that in the application of the Convention the treaties the Republic of Moldova is not a party to shall be deemed not to be included in the Annex of the Convention.

2. Pursuant to article 24, paragraph 2 of the International Convention for the Suppression of the Financing of Terrorism, the Republic of Moldova declares that it does not consider itself bound by the provisions of article 24, paragraph 1 of the Convention.

Romania

Declaration:

"In accordance with Article 2, paragraph 2, subparagraph (a) of the Convention, Romania declares that, on the date of the application of this Convention to Romania, the International Convention for the Suppression of Terrorism Bombings of 15 December 1997, shall be deemed not to be included in the annex referred to in Article 2, paragraph 1, subparagraph (a)."

Russian Federation

Upon signature:

Declaration:

It is the position of the Russian Federation that the provisions of article 15 of the Convention must be applied in such a way as to ensure the inevitability of responsibility for perpetrating the crimes falling within the purview of the Convention, without prejudice to the effectiveness of international cooperation with regard to the questions of extradition and legal assistance.

Upon ratification:

Declarations:

1. ....

2. It is the position of the Russian Federation that the provisions of article 15 of the Convention must be applied in such a way as to ensure the inevitability of responsibility for perpetrating crimes falling within the purview of the Convention, without prejudice to the effectiveness of international cooperation with regard to the questions of extradition and legal assistance.

Saint Vincent and the Grenadines

Declaration and Reservation:

"In accordance with Article 2 paragraph 2 a) of the said Convention, however, the Government of Saint Vincent and the Grenadines declares that in the application of this Convention to Saint Vincent and the Grenadines the following treaties shall be deemed not to be included in the Annex referred to in its Article 2 paragraph 1(a):

1. Convention on the Physical Protection of Nuclear Material, adopted at Vienna on 3 March 1980.

2. International Convention for the Suppression of Terrorist Bombings, adopted by the General Assembly of the United Nations on 15 December 1997.

Further, in accordance with Article 24 paragraph 2 of the said Convention, the Government of Saint Vincent and the Grenadines declares that it does not consider itself bound by paragraph 1 of Article 24. The Government of Saint Vincent and the Grenadines considers that any dispute may be referred to the International Court of Justice only with the consent of all the parties to the dispute."

Singapore

Upon signature:

Reservation:

"... the Government of the Republic of Singapore makes the following reservations in relation to Article 2 and Article 24 of the 1999 International Convention for the Suppression of the Financing of Terrorism:

i) The Republic of Singapore declares, in pursuance of Article 2, paragraph 2 (a) of the Convention that in the application of this Convention, the treaty shall be deemed not to include the treaties listed in the annex of this Convention which the Republic of Singapore is not a party to.

ii) The Republic of Singapore declares, in pursuance of Article 24, paragraph 2 of the Convention that it will not be bound by the provisions of Article 24 paragraph 1 of the Convention."

Upon ratification:

"... [S]ubject to the following declarations and reservations:

Declarations and reservations:

Declarations

(1) The Republic of Singapore understands that Article 21 of the Convention clarifies that nothing in the Convention precludes the application of the law of armed conflict with regard to legitimate military objectives.

Reservations

(1) With respect to Article 2, paragraph 2 (a) of the Convention, the Republic of Singapore declares that the treaty shall be deemed not to include the treaties listed in the annex of this Convention which the Republic of Singapore is not a party to.

(2) The Republic of Singapore declares, in pursuance of Article 24, paragraph 2 of the Convention that it will not be bound by the provisions of Article 24, paragraph 1 of the Convention."

Tunisia

Reservation:

The Republic of Tunisia,

In ratifying the International Convention for the Suppression of the Financing of Terrorism adopted on 9 December 1999 by the General Assembly at its fifty-fourth session and signed by the Republic of Tunisia on 2 November 2001, declares that it does not consider itself bound by the provisions of article 24, paragraph 1, of the Convention and affirms that, in the settlement of disputes concerning the interpretation or implementation of the Convention, there shall be no recourse to arbitration or to the International Court of Justice without its prior consent.

Turkey

Declaration:

"1. The Republic of Turkey declares that the application of Paragraph 1(b) of Article (2) of the Convention does not necessarily indicate the existence of an armed conflict and the term "armed conflict", whether it is organized or not, describes a situation different from the commitment of acts that constitute the crime of terrorism within the scope of criminal law.

2. The Republic of Turkey declares its understanding that Paragraph 1(b) of Article (2) of the International Convention for the Suppression of the Financing of Terrorism, as stated in Article (21) of the said Convention, shall not prejudice the obligations of states under international law including the Charter of the United Nations, in particular the obligation of not providing financial support to terrorist and armed groups acting in the territory of other states.

3. Pursuant to Paragraph 2 of Article 24 of the International Convention for the Suppression of the Financing of Terrorism, the Republic of Turkey declares that it does not consider itself bound by the provisions of Paragraph 1 of Article (24) of the said Convention."

United States of America

Reservation:

"(a) pursuant to Article 24 (2) of the Convention, the United States of America declares that it does not consider itself bound by Article 24 (1) of the Convention; and

(b) the United States of America reserves the right specifically to agree in a particular case to follow the arbitration procedure set forth in Article 24 (1) of the Convention or any other procedure for arbitration."

Understandings:

"(1) EXCLUSION OF LEGITIMATE ACTIVITIES AGAINST LAWFUL TARGETS. The United States of America understands that nothing in the Convention precludes any State Party to the Convention from conducting any legitimate activity against any lawful target in accordance with the law of armed conflict.

(2) MEANING OF THE TERM "ARMED CONFLICT". The United States of America understands that the term "armed conflict"in Article 2 (1) (b) of the Convention does not include internal disturbances and tensions, such as riots, isolated and sporadic acts of violence, and other acts of a similar nature."

Venezuela

Reservations:

Pursuant to article 24, paragraph 2, of the International Convention for the Suppression of the Financing of Terrorism, the Bolivarian Republic of Venezuela hereby formulates an express reservation to the provisions of article 24, paragraph 1, of that Convention. Accordingly, it does not consider itself bound to resort to arbitration as a means of dispute settlement, and does not recognize the binding jurisdiction of the International Court of Justice.

Furthermore, pursuant to article 2, paragraph 2, subparagraph (a), of the International Convention for the Suppression of the Financing of Terrorism, it declares that in the application of that Convention to Venezuela, the following treaties shall be deemed not to be included in the annex referred to in article 2, paragraph 1, subparagraph (a), of that Convention until they enter into force for the Bolivarian Republic of Venezuela:

1. Convention on the Prevention and Punishment of Crimes against Internationally Protected Persons, including Diplomatic Agents, adopted by the General Assembly of the United Nations on 14 December 1973;

2. Convention on the Physical Protection of Nuclear Material, signed at Vienna on 3 March 1980;

3. Protocol on the Suppression of Unlawful Acts of Violence at Airports Serving International Civil Aviation, supplementary to the Convention for the Suppression of Unlawful Acts against the Safety of Civil Aviation, signed at Montreal on 24 February 1988;

4. Convention for the Suppression of Unlawful Acts against the Safety of Maritime Navigation, done at Rome on 10 March 1988;

5. Protocol for the Suppression of Unlawful Acts against the Safety of Fixed Platforms Located on the Continental Shelf, done at Rome on 10 March 1988;

6. International Convention for the Suppression of Terrorist Bombings, adopted by the General Assembly of the United Nations on 15 December 1997.

Viet Nam

Reservation and declaration:

"Acceding to this Convention, the Socialist Republic of Vietnam makes its reservation to paragraph 1 of Article 24 of the Convention.

The Socialist Republic of Vietnam also declares that the provisions of the Convention shall not be applied with regard to the offences set forth in the following treaties to which the Socialist Republic of Vietnam is not a party:

- International Convention against the Taking of Hostages, adopted by the General Assembly of the United Nations on 17 December 1979;

- Convention on the Physical Protection of Nuclear Material, adopted at Vienna on 3 March 1980;

- International Convention for [the] Suppression of Terrorist Bombings, adopted by the General Assembly of the United Nations on 15 December 1997."

Objections

(Unless otherwise indicated, the objections were made upon ratification, acceptance, approval or accession.)

France

4 December 2002

With regard to the reservations made by the Democratic People's Republic of Korea upon signature:

> The Government of the French Republic has examined the reservations made by the Government of the Democratic People's Republic of Korea on 12 November 2001, when it signed the International Convention on the Suppression of the Financing of Terrorism, which was opened for signature on 10 January 2000. By indicating that it does not consider itself bound by the provisions of article 2, paragraph 1, subparagraph (a), the Government of the Democratic People's Republic of Korea excludes from the definition of offences within the meaning of the Convention the financing of any act which constitutes an offence within the scope of and as defined in the treaties listed in the annex.
>
> Under article 2, paragraph 2 (a), a State Party is entitled to exclude from the definition of offences within the meaning of the Convention the financing of acts which constitute offences within the scope of and as defined in any treaty listed in the annex to which it is not party; however, it is not entitled to exclude from the definition of offences within the meaning of the Convention the financing of acts which constitute offences within the scope of and as defined in any treaty listed in the annex to which it is party. It just so happens that the Democratic People's Republic of Korea is party to some of those treaties.
>
> The Government of the French Republic lodges an objection to the reservation made by the Democratic People's Republic of Korea regarding article 2, paragraph 1 (a) of the Convention.

Netherlands

1 May 2002

With regard to the reservations made by the Democratic People's Republic of Korea upon signature:

> "The Government of the Kingdom of the Netherlands has examined the reservations made by the Government of the Democratic People's Republic of Korea regarding article 2, paragraph 1 (a), and article 14 of the International Convention for the suppression of the financing of terrorism made at the time of its signature of the said Convention.
>
> The Government of the Kingdom of the Netherlands considers that the reservations made by the Democratic People's Republic of Korea regarding article 2, paragraph 1 (a), and article 14 of the Convention are reservations incompatible with the object and purpose of the Convention.
>
> The Government of the Kingdom of the Netherlands recalls that, according to Article 19 (c) of the Vienna Convention on the law of treaties, a reservation incompatible with the object and purpose of the Convention shall not be permitted.
>
> It is in the common interest of States that treaties to which they have chosen to become party are respected, as to their object and purpose, by all parties and that States are prepared to undertake any legislative changes necessary to comply with their obligations under the treaties.
>
> The Government of the Kingdom of the Netherlands therefore objects to the aforesaid reservations made by the Government of the Democratic People's Republic of Korea to the International Convention for the suppression of the financing of terrorism.

This objection shall not preclude the entry into force of the Convention between the Kingdom of the Netherlands and the Democratic People's Republic of Korea."

21 April 2004

With regard to the declarations made by Jordan upon ratification:

". . . the Government of the Kingdom of the Netherlands has examined the Declaration relating to paragraph 1 (b) of Article 2 of the International Convention for the Suppression of the Financing of Terrorism made by the Government of Jordan at the time of its ratification of the Convention. The Government of the Kingdom of the Netherlands considers that the declaration made by Jordan is in fact a reservation that seeks to limit the scope of the Convention on a unilateral basis and which is contrary to its object and purpose, namely the suppression of the financing of terrorist acts, irrespective of where they take place or who carries them out.

The Government of the Kingdom of the Netherlands further considers the Declaration to be contrary to the terms of Article 6 of the Convention, according to which States Parties commit themselves to "adopt such measures as may be necessary, including, where appropriate, domestic legislation, to ensure that criminal acts within the scope of this Convention are under no circumstances justifiable by considerations of a political, philosophical, ideological, racial, ethnic, religious or other similar nature".

The Government of the Kingdom of the Netherlands recalls that, according to Article 19 (c) of the Vienna Convention on the Law of Treaties, a reservation incompatible with the object and purpose of the Convention shall not be permitted.

It is in the common interest of the States that treaties to which they have chosen to become party are respected, as to their object and purpose, by all parties and that States are prepared to undertake any legislative changes necessary to comply with their obligations under the treaties.

The Government of the Kingdom of the Netherlands therefore objects to the aforesaid reservation made by the Government of Jordan to the International Convention for the Suppression of the Financing of Terrorism. This objection shall not preclude the entry into force of the Convention between the Kingdom of the Netherlands and Jordan."

Norway

3 December 2002

With regard to the reservations made by the Democratic People's Republic of Korea upon signature:

"The Government of Norway has examined the reservations made by the Government of the Democratic People's Republic of Korea upon signature of the International Convention for the Suppression of the Financing of Terrorism.

It is the position of the Government of Norway that the reservations with regard to paragraph 1 (a) of Article 2 and Article 14 are incompatible with the object and purpose of the Convention, as they purport to exclude the application of core provisions of the Convention. The Government of Norway recalls that, in accordance with well-established treaty law, a reservation incompatible with the object and purpose of the Convention shall not be permitted.

The Government of Norway therefore objects to the aforesaid reservations made by the Government of the Democratic People's Republic of Korea. This objection does not preclude the entry into force, in its entirety, of the Convention between the Kingdom of Norway and the Democratic People's Republic of Korea. The Convention thus becomes operative between the Kingdom of Norway and the Democratic People's Republic of Korea without the Democratic People's Republic of Korea benefiting from these reservations."

THE FINANCING OF TERRORISM

Spain

3 Decembre 2002

With regard to the reservations made by the Democratic People's Republic of Korea upon signature:

> The Government of Spain has examined the reservations made by the Government of the Democratic People's Republic of Korea on 12 November 2001 to articles 2, paragraph 1 (a), and 14 of the International Convention for the Suppression of the Financing of Terrorism (New York, 9 December 1999).
>
> The Government of the Kingdom of Spain considers that those reservations are incompatible with the object and purpose of that Convention, since their aim is to release the People's Democratic Republic of Korea from any commitment with regard to two essential aspects of the Convention.
>
> The Government of the Kingdom of Spain observes that according to the rule of customary law embodied in article 19 (c) of the 1969 Vienna Convention on the Law of Treaties, reservations incompatible with the object and purpose of treaties are prohibited.
>
> The Government of the Kingdom of Spain therefore objects to the aforementioned reservations made by the Government of the People's Democratic Republic of Korea to the International Convention for the Suppression of Financing of Terrorism.
>
> This objection does not prevent the entry into force of the aforementioned Convention between the Kingdom of Spain and the People's Democratic Republic of Korea.

Sweden

27 November 2002

With regard to the reservations made by the Democratic People's Republic of Korea upon signature:

> "The Government of Sweden has examined the reservation made by the Democratic People's Republic of Korea at the time of its signature of the International Convention for the Suppression of the Financing of Terrorism, regarding article 2, paragraph 1, sub-paragraph (a) and article 14 of the Convention.
>
> The Government of Sweden considers those reservations made by the Democratic People's Republic of Korea incompatible with the object and purpose of the Convention.
>
> The Government of Sweden would like to recall that, according to customary international law as codified in the Vienna Convention on the Law of Treaties, a reservation incompatible with the object and purpose of a treaty shall not be permitted.
>
> It is in the common interest of States that treaties to which they have chosen to become parties are respected as to their object and purpose, by all parties, and that States are prepared to undertake any legislative changes necessary to comply with their obligations under the treaties.
>
> The Government of Sweden therefore objects to the aforesaid reservation made by the Government of the Democratic People's Republic of Korea to the International Convention for the Suppression of the Financing of Terrorism. This objection shall not preclude the entry into force of the Convention between the Democratic People's Republic of Korea and Sweden. The Convention enters into force in its entirety between the two States, without the Democratic People's Republic of Korea benefiting from its reservation."

27 January 2004

With regard to the declaration made by Israel upon ratification:

> "The Government of Sweden has examined the declaration made by Israel regarding article 21 of the International Convention for the Suppression of the Financing of Ter-

rorism, whereby Israel intends to exclude the Protocols Additionals to the Geneva Conventions from the term international humanitarian law.

The Government of Sweden recalls that the designation assigned to a statement whereby the legal effect of certain provisions of a treaty is excluded or modified does not determine its status as a reservation to the treaty. The Government of Sweden considers that the declaration made by Israel in substance constitutes a reservation.

It is the view of the Government of Sweden that the majority of the provisions of the Protocols Additional to the Geneva Conventions constitute customary international law, by which Israel is bound. In the absence of further clarification, Sweden therefore objects to the aforesaid reservation by Israel to the International Convention for the Suppression of the Financing of Terrorism.

This objection shall not preclude the entry into force of the Convention between Israel and Sweden. The Convention enters into force in its entirety between the two States, without Israel benefiting from this reservation."

United Kingdom of Great Britain and Northern Ireland

22 November 2002

With regard to the reservations made by the Democratic People's Republic of Korea upon signature:

"The signature of the Democratic People's Republic of Korea was expressed to be subject to reservations in respect of Article 2 (1) (a), Article 14 and Article 24 (1) of the Convention. The United Kingdom objects to the reservations entered by the Democratic People's Republic of Korea in respect of Article 2 (1) (a) and Article 14 of the Convention, which it considers to be incompatible with the object and purpose of the Convention."

25 February 2004

With regard to the declaration made by Jordan upon ratification:

"The Government of the United Kingdom of Great Britain and Northern Ireland have examined the Declaration relating to paragraph 1 (b) of Article 2 of the International Convention for the Suppression of the Financing of Terrorism made by the Government of Jordan at the time of its ratification of the Convention. The Government of the United Kingdom consider the declaration made by Jordan to be a reservation that seeks to limit the scope of the Convention on a unilateral basis and which is contrary to its object and purpose, namely the suppression of the financing of terrorist acts, irrespective of where they take place or who carries them out.

The Government of the United Kingdom further consider the Declaration to be contrary to the terms of Article 6 of the Convention, according to which States Parties commit themselves to "adopt such measures as may be necessary, including, where appropriate, domestic legislation, to ensure that criminal acts within the scope of this Convention are under no circumstances justifiable by considerations of a political, philosophical, ideological, racial, ethnic, religious or other similar nature".

The Government of the United Kingdom recall that, according to Article 19 (c) of the Vienna Convention on the Law of Treaties, a reservation incompatible with the object and purpose of the Convention shall not be permitted.

The Government of the United Kingdom therefore object to the aforesaid reservation made by the Government of Jordan to the International Convention for the Suppression of the Financing of Terrorism. However, this objection shall not preclude the entry into force of the Convention between the United Kingdom and Jordan."

Notifications made under article 7 (3)

(Unless otherwise indicated, the notifications were made upon ratification, acceptance, approval or accession.)

Australia

24 October 2002

"... pursuant to article 7, paragraph 3 of the Convention, ... Australia has established jurisdiction in relation to all the circumstances referred to in article 7, paragraph 2 of the Convention."

Bolivia

13 février 2002

... by virtue of the provisions of article 7, paragraph 3, of the International Convention for the Suppression of the Financing of Terrorism, the Republic of Bolivia states that it establishes its jurisdiction in accordance with its domestic law in respect of offences committed in the situations and conditions provided for under article 7, paragraph 2, of the Convention.

Chile

In accordance with article 7, paragraph 3, of the International Convention for the Suppression of the Financing of Terrorism, the Government of Chile declares that, in accordance with article 6, paragraph 8, of the Courts Organization Code of the Republic of Chile, crimes and ordinary offenses committed outside the territory of the Republic which are covered in treaties concluded with other Powers remain under Chilean jurisdiction.

Cook Islands

"... the Government of the Cook Islands makes the following notification that pursuant to article 7, paragraph 3 of the Convention, the Cook Islands establishes its jurisdiction in relation to all cases referred to in article 7, paragraph 2 of the Convention."

Croatia

"Pursuant to Article 7, paragraph 3 of the International Convention for the Suppression of the Financing of Terrorism the Republic of Croatia notifies the Secretary-General of the United Nations that it has established jurisdiction over the offence set forth in Article 2 in all the cases described in Article 7, paragraph 2 of the Convention."

Cyprus

27 December 2001

In accordance with paragraph 3 of Article 7, the Republic of Cyprus declares that by section 7.1 of the International Convention for the Suppression of the Financing of Terrorism (Ratification and other Provisions) Law No. 29 (III) of 2001, it has established jurisdiction over the offences set forth in Article 2 in all circumstances described in paragraph 2 of Article 7."

Denmark

"Pursuant to article 7, paragraph 3, of the International Convention for the Suppression of the Financing of Terrorism Denmark declares that section 6-12 of the Danish Criminal Code provide for Danish jurisdiction in respect of offences set forth in article 2 of the Convention in all the circumstances laid down in article 7, paragraph 2, of the Convention."

El Salvador

... (2) pursuant to article 7, paragraph 3, the Republic of El Salvador notifies that it has established its jurisdiction in accordance with its national laws in respect of offences committed in the situations and under the conditions provided for in article 7, paragraph 2;

Estonia

"Pursuant to article 7, paragraph 3 of the Convention, the Republic of Estonia declares that in its domestic law it shall apply the jurisdiction set forth in article 7 paragraph 2 over offences set forth in article 2."

Finland

"Pursuant to article 7, paragraph 3 of the International Convention for the Suppression of the Financing of Terrorism, the Republic of Finland establishes its jurisdiction over the offences set forth in article 2 in all the cases provided for in article 7, paragraphs 1 and 2."

France

In accordance with article 7, paragraph 3, of the Convention, France states that it has established its jurisdiction over the offences set forth in article 2 in all cases referred to in article 7, paragraphs 1 and 2.

Hungary

"The Republic of Hungary declares that it establishes its jurisdiction in all the cases provided for in Article 7, Paragraph 2 of the Convention."

Iceland

"Pursuant to article 7, paragraph 3, of the International Convention for the Suppression of the Financing of Terrorism, Iceland declares that it has established its jurisdiction over the offences set forth in article 2 of the Convention in all the cases provided for in article 7, paragraph 2, of the Convention."

Israel

Pursuant to Article 7, paragraph 3 of the Convention, the Government of the state of Israel hereby notifies the Secretary-General of the United Nations that it has established jurisdiction over the offences referred to in Article 2 in all the cases detailed in Article 7 paragraph 2.

Jordan

"Jordan decides to establish its jurisdiction over all offences described in paragraph 2 of article 7 of the Convention."

Latvia

"In accordance with Article 7, paragraph 3 of the International Convention for the Suppression of the Financing of Terrorism, adopted at New York on 9th day of December 1999, the Republic of Latvia declares that it has established jurisdiction in all cases listed in Article 7, paragraph 2."

Liechtenstein

"In accordance with article 7, paragraph 3, of the International Convention for the Suppression of the Financing of Terrorism, the Principality of Liechtenstein declares that it has established its jurisdiction over the offences set forth in article 2 of the Convention in all the cases provided for in article 7, paragraph 2, of the Convention."

THE FINANCING OF TERRORISM

Lithuania

". . . .it is provided in paragraph 3 of Article 7 of the said Convention, the Seimas of the Republic of Lithuania declares that the Republic of Lithuania shall have jurisdiction over the offences set forth in Article 2 of the Convention in all cases specified in paragraph 2 of Article 7 of the Convention."

Mexico

24 February 2003

. . . in accordance with article 7, paragraph 3, of the Convention, Mexico exercises jurisdiction over the offences defined in the Convention where:

(a) They are committed against Mexicans in the territory of another State party, provided that the accused is in Mexico and has not been tried in the country in which the offence was committed. Where it is a question of offences defined in the Convention but committed in the territory of a non-party State, the offence shall also be defined as such in the place where it was committed (art. 7, para. 2 (a));

(b) They are committed in Mexican embassies and on diplomatic or consular premises (art. 7, para. 2 (b));

(c) They are committed abroad but produce effects or are claimed to produce effects in the national territory (art. 7, para. 2 (c)).

Monaco

The Principality of Monaco reports, pursuant to article 7, paragraph 3, of the International Convention for the Suppression of the Financing of Terrorism adopted in New York on 9 December 1999, that it exercises very broad jurisdiction over the offences referred to in that Convention.

The jurisdiction of the Principality is thus established pursuant to article 7, paragraph 1, over:

(a) Offences committed in its territory: this is the case in Monaco in application of the general principle of territoriality of the law;

(b) Offences committed on board a vessel flying the Monegasque flag: this is the case in Monaco in application of article L.633-1 et seq. of the Maritime Code;

Offences committed on board an aircraft registered under Monegasque law: the Tokyo Convention of 14 September 1963, rendered enforceable in Monaco by Sovereign Order No. 7.963 of 24 April 1984, specifies that the courts and tribunals of the State of registration of the aircraft are competent to exercise jurisdiction over offences and acts committed on board it;

(c) Offences committed by a Monegasque national: the Code of Criminal Procedure states in articles 5 and 6 that any Monegasque committing abroad an act qualified as a crime or offence by the law in force in the Principality may be charged and brought to trial there.

The jurisdiction of the Principality is also established pursuant to article 7, paragraph 2 when:

(a) The offence was directed towards or resulted in the carrying out of a terrorist offence in its territory or against one of its nationals: articles 42 to 43 of the Criminal Code permit the Monegasque courts, in general terms, to punish accomplices of a perpetrator charged in Monaco with offences referred to in article 2 of the Convention;

(b) The offence was directed towards or resulted in the carrying out of a terrorist offence against a State or government facility, including diplomatic or consular premises: attacks aimed at bringing about devastation, massacres and pillage in Monegasque territory are punishable under article 65 of the Criminal Code; in addition, article 7 of the

Code of Criminal Procedure provides for the charging and trial in Monaco of foreigners who, outside the territory of the Principality, have committed a crime prejudicial to the security of the State or a crime or offence against Monegasque diplomatic or consular agents or premises;

(c) The offence was directed towards or resulted in a terrorist offence committed in an attempt to compel the State to do or abstain from doing any act: the crimes and offences in question normally correspond to one of those referred to above, directly or through complicity;

(d) The offence was committed by a stateless person who had his or her habitual residence in Monegasque territory: application of the general principle of territoriality of the law permits the charging of stateless persons having their habitual residence in Monaco;

(e) The offence was committed on board an aircraft operated by the Monegasque Government: if the Monegasque Government directly operated an aircraft or an airline, its aircraft would have to be registered in Monaco, and the Tokyo Convention of 14 September 1963 referred to above would then apply

Norway

"Declaration: In accordance with article 7, paragraph 3 of the Convention, Norway hereby declares that it has established its jurisdiction over the offences set forth in article 2, of the Convention in all cases provided for in article 7, paragraph 2, of the Convention."

Republic of Moldova

"... pursuant to article 7, paragraph 3 of the Convention for the Suppression of the Financing of Terrorism, adopted on December 9, 1999, in New York, the Republic of Moldova has established its jurisdiction over the offenses set forth in article 2 in all cases referred to in article 7, paragraph 2."

Romania

"In accordance with Article 7, paragraph 3 of the Convention, Romania declares that establishes its jurisdiction for the offences referred to in Article 2, in all cases referred to in Article 7, paragraphs 1 and 2, according with the relevant provisions of the internal law."

Russian Federation

The Russian Federation, pursuant to article 7, paragraph 3, of the Convention, declares that it establishes its jurisdiction over the acts recognized as offences under article 2 of the Convention in the cases provided for in article 7, paragraphs 1 and 2, of the Convention.

Singapore

In accordance with the provision of Article 7, paragraph 3, the Republic of Singapore gives notification that it has established jurisdiction over the offences set forth in Article 2 of the Convention in all the cases provided for in Article 7, paragraph 2 of the Convention."

Slovakia

"Pursuant to article 7, paragraph 3, of the International Convention for the Suppression of the Financing of Terrorism, the Slovak Republic declares that it shall exercise its jurisdiction as provided for under article 7, paragraph 2, subparagraphs a) to e) of the Convention."

Spain

"In accordance with the provisions of article 7, paragraph 3, the Kingdom of Spain gives notification that its courts have international jurisdiction over the offences referred to in paragraphs 1 and 2, pursuant to article 23 of the Organization of Justice Act No. 6/1985 of 1 July 1985."

THE FINANCING OF TERRORISM

Sweden

5 November 2002

"Pursuant to article 7 (3) of the International Convention for the Suppression of the Financing of Terrorism, Sweden provides the following information on Swedish criminal jurisdiction. Rules on Swedish criminal jurisdiction are laid down in Chapter 2 Section 1-5 in the Swedish Penal Code. The provisions have the following wording:

Section 1

Crimes committed in this Realm shall be adjudged in accordance with Swedish law and by a Swedish court. The same applies when it is uncertain where the crime was committed but grounds exist for assuming that it was committed within the Realm.

Section 2

Crimes committed outside the Realm shall be adjudged according to Swedish law and by a Swedish court when the crime has been committed:

1. by a Swedish citizen or an alien domiciled in Sweden,

2. by an alien not domiciled in Sweden who, after having committed the crime, has become a Swedish citizen or has acquired domicile in the Realm or who is a Danish, Finnish, Icelandic or Norwegian citizen and is present in the Realm, or

3. By any other alien who is present in the Realm, and the crime under Swedish Law can result in imprisonment for more than six months.

The first paragraph shall not apply if the act is not subject to criminal responsibility under the law of the place where it was committed or if it was committed within an area not belonging to any state and, under Swedish law, the punishment for the act cannot be more severe than a fine.

In cases mentioned in this Section, a sanction may not be imposed which is more severe than the most severe punishment provided for the crime under the law in the place where it was committed.

Section 3

Even in cases other than those listed in Section 2, crimes committed outside the Realm shall be adjudged according to Swedish law and by a Swedish court:

1. if the crime was committed on board a Swedish vessel or aircraft, or was committed in the course of duty by the officer in charge or by a member of its crew,

2. if the crime was committed by a member of the armed forces in an area in which a detachment of the armed forces was present, or if it was committed by some other person in such an area and the detachment was present for a purpose other than exercise,

3. if the crime was committed in the course of duty outside the Realm by a person employed in a foreign contingent of the Swedish armed forces,

3a. if the crime was committed in the course of duty outside the Realm by a policeman, custom officer or official employed at the coast guard, who performs boundless assignments according to an international agreement that Sweden has ratified,

4. if the crime committed was a crime against the Swedish nation, a Swedish municipal authority or other assembly, or against a Swedish public institution,

5. if the crime was committed in an area not belonging to any state and was directed against a Swedish citizen, a Swedish association or private institution, or against an alien domiciled in Sweden,

6. if the crime is hijacking, maritime or aircraft sabotage, airport sabotage, counterfeiting currency, an attempt to commit such crimes, a crime against international

THE FINANCING OF TERRORISM

law, unlawful dealings with chemical weapons, unlawful dealings with mines or false or careless statement before an international court, or

7. if the least severe punishment prescribed for the crime in Swedish law is imprisonment for four years or more.

Section 3 a

Besides the cases described in Sections 1-3, crimes shall be adjudged according to Swedish law by a Swedish court in accordance with the provisions of the Act on International Collaboration concerning Proceedings in Criminal matters.

Section 4

A crime is deemed to have been committed where the criminal act was perpetrated and also where the crime was completed or in the case of an attempt, where the intended crime would have been completed.

Section 5

Prosecution for a crime committed within the Realm on a foreign vessel or aircraft by an alien, who was the officer in charge or member of its crew or otherwise travelled in it, against another alien or a foreign interest shall not be instituted without the authority of the Government or a person designated by the Government.

Prosecution for a crime committed outside the Realm may be instituted only following the authorisation referred to in the first paragraph. However, prosecution may be instituted without such an order if the crime consists of a false or careless statement before an international court or if the crime was committed:

1. on a Swedish vessel or aircraft or by the officer in charge or some member of its crew in the course of duty,

2. by a member of the armed forces in an area in which a detachment of the armed forces was present,

3. in the course of duty outside the Realm by a person employed by a foreign contingent of the Swedish armed forces,

4. in the course of duty outside the Realm by a policeman, custom officer or official employed at the coast guard, who performs boundless assignments according to an international agreement that Sweden has ratified,

5. in Denmark, Finland, Iceland or Norway or on a vessel or aircraft in regular commerce between places situated in Sweden or one of the said states, or

6. By a Swedish, Danish, Finnish, Icelandic or Norwegian citizen against a Swedish interest."

Switzerland

Pursuant to article 7, paragraph 3, of the International Convention for the Suppression of the Financing of Terrorism, Switzerland establishes its jurisdiction over the offences set forth in article 2 in all the cases provided for in article 7, paragraph 2.

Tunisia

The Republic of Tunisia,

In ratifying the International Convention for the Suppression of the Financing of Terrorism adopted on 9 December 1999 by the General Assembly at its fifty-fourth session and signed by the Republic of Tunisia on 2 November 2001, declares that it considers itself bound by the provisions of article 7, paragraph 2, of the Convention and decides to establish its jurisdiction when:

- The offence was directed towards or resulted in the carrying out of an offence referred to in article 2, paragraph 1, subparagraph (a) or (b), in the territory of Tunisia or against one of its nationals;

- The offence was directed towards or resulted in the carrying out of an offence referred to in article 2, paragraph 1, subparagraph (a) or (b), against a Tunisian State or government facility abroad, including Tunisian diplomatic or consular facilities;

- The offence was directed towards or resulted in an offence referred to in article 2, paragraph 1, subparagraph (a) or (b), committed in an attempt to compel Tunisia to do or abstain from doing any act;

- The offence is committed by a stateless person who has his or her habitual residence in Tunisian territory;

- The offence is committed on board an aircraft operated by the Government of Tunisia.

Turkey

"... pursuant to Article 7, paragraph 3 of the International Convention for the Suppression of the Financing of Terrorism, Turkey has established its jurisdiction in accordance with its domestic law in respect of offences set forth in Article 2 in all cases referred to in Article 7, paragraph 2."

Ukraine

"Ukraine exercises its jurisdiction over the offences set forth in article 2 of the Convention in cases provided for in paragraph 2 article 7 of the Convention."

Uzbekistan

5 February 2002

"Republic of Uzbekistan establishes its jurisdiction over offences referred to in article 2 of the Convention in all cases stipulated in article 7, paragraph 2 of the Convention.".

Venezuela

By virtue of the provisions of article 7, paragraph 3, of the International Convention for the Suppression of the Financing of Terrorism, the Bolivarian Republic of Venezuela declares that it has established jurisdiction under its domestic law over offences committed in the situations and under the conditions envisaged in article 7, paragraph 2, of the Convention.

LETTER OF SUBMITTAL

DEPARTMENT OF STATE,
Washington, October 3, 2000.

The PRESIDENT,
The White House.

THE PRESIDENT: I have the honor to submit to you, with a view to its transmission to the Senate for advice and consent to ratification, subject to the understandings, declaration and reservation set forth below, the International Convention for the Suppression of the Financing of Terrorism, adopted by the United Nations General Assembly on December 9, 1999, and signed on behalf of the United States of America on January 10, 2000 (the "Convention").

Pursuant to a French-led Group of Eight ("G-8") initiative, with strong support and input from the United States, the United Nations General Assembly decided in Resolution 53/108 of a 8 December 1998 that the Ad Hoc Committee established by General Assembly Resolution 51/210 of 17 December 1996 should elaborate an international convention for the suppression of terrorist financing to supplement the existing counterterrorism conventions. Basing its work on a draft text prepared by France, the United States, and other G-8 members, the Ad Hoc Committee successfully negotiated the text during two drafting sessions in New York in March and September-October 1999, and recommended it to the Sixth (Legal) Committee for consideration. On November 18, 1999, the Sixth Committee, by consensus, recommended the draft Convention to the General Assembly for adoption. The Convention was adopted by the General Assembly, by consensus, on December 9, 1999.

The Convention fills an important gap in international law by expanding the legal framework for international cooperation in the investigation, prosecution, and extradition of persons who engage in the financing of terrorism. By filling this gap, the Convention advances a critical counterterrorism priority of the United States which was articulated in your September 21, 1998, address to the United Nations General Assembly when you called on all states to enhance their efforts to combat terrorist financing.

The Convention provides for States Parties to exercise criminal jurisdiction over the unlawful and willful provision or collection of funds with the intention that they be used or in the knowledge that they are to be used in order to carry out certain terrorist acts as defined in the Convention. In creating such a legal regime, the Convention follows the precedents set by numerous terrorism conventions to which the United States is already a party, including the 1971 Convention for the Suppression of Unlawful Acts Against the Safety of Civil Aviation, the 1973 Convention on the Prevention and Punishment of Crimes Against Internationally Protected Persons, including Diplomatic Agents, the 1979 International Convention Against the

Taking of Hostages, and the 1988 Convention for the Suppression of Unlawful Acts Against the Safety of Maritime Navigation, with Related Protocol. Like these earlier Conventions, this new Convention requires States Parties to criminalize under their domestic laws certain types of criminal offenses, and also requires parties to extradite or submit for prosecution persons accused of committing or aiding in the commission of such offenses.

Article 1 and 2 together serve to define the offenses covered by the Convention, with Article 1 incorporating several definitions of phrases used in Article 2. Article 1 includes a definition of "funds," drawn from the definition of "property" in the 1988 Convention Against Illicit Traffic in Narcotic Drugs and Psychotropic Substances, to which the United States is a party. Specifically, the definition of "funds" encompasses within its very broad scope "assets of every kind, whether tangible or intangible, movable or immovable, however acquired, and legal documents or instruments in any form, including electronic or digital, evidencing title to, or interest in, such assets. * * *" The definition was understood by all delegations to include property, and a list of illustrative examples incorporated at the end of the Article 1.1 definition further conveys its breadth.

Paragraph 1 of Article 2 states that any person commits an offense within the meaning of the Convention "if that person by any means, directly or indirectly, unlawfully and willfully, provides or collects funds with the intention that they should be used or in the knowledge that they are to be used, in full or in part, in order to carry out" either of two categories of terrorist acts. The first category includes any act which constitutes an offense within the scope of and as defined in one of the treaties listed in the annex to the Convention. The second category is any other act intended to cause death or serious bodily injury to a civilian, or to any other person not taking an active part in hostilities in a situation of armed conflict, when the purpose of such act, by its nature or context, is to intimidate a population, or to compel a government or an international organization to do or to abstain from doing any act.

With respect to the first category, the Convention annex lists nine counterterrorism conventions, ranging from the 1970 Convention for the Suppression of Unlawful Seizure of Aircraft to the 1997 International Convention for the Suppression of Terrorist Bombings ("Terrorist Bombings Convention"). The United States is a party to the first eight of the listed conventions and has signed and transmitted to the Senate for its advice and consent to ratification the Terrorist Bombings Convention (Treaty Document 106-6). Paragraph 2 of Article 2 further provides that upon depositing its instrument of ratification, acceptance, approval or accession to the Convention, a state which is not a party to one of the conventions listed in the annex may declare that in the application of the Terrorist Financing Convention to that State Party, the convention at issue shall be deemed not to be included in the annex. Article 2.2(a) further provides that this declaration ceases to have effect as soon as that state becomes a party to the relevant convention, which fact must be notified to the depository. The United States should make such a declaration with respect to the Terrorist Bombings Convention if it is not a party to that Convention at the time of the deposit of its instrument of ratification with respect to the Terrorist Financing Convention. I therefore recommend that, in the event the United States is not a party to the Terrorist Bombings Convention at the time the United States deposits its instrument of ratification of the present Convention, that the following declaration to Article 2.2 be included in the United States instrument of ratification of the Convention:

> Pursuant to Article 2.2(a) of the Convention, the United States of America declares that, in the application of this Convention to the United States, the International Convention for the Suppression of Terrorist Bombings shall be deemed not to be included in the annex referred to in paragraph 1, subparagraph (a).

In the event the United States is a party to the Terrorist Bombings Convention at the time it deposits its instrument of ratification to the Convention, such a declaration would not be deposited.

The second category of terrorist acts under Article 2.1(b) incorporates language specifically suggested by the United States. The intent, which was broadly shared by other delegations, was to define the terrorist activity meant to be addressed by the Convention in a way that excluded the legitimate actions of the military forces of states by focusing on the intentional targeting of civilians as such. In order to ensure that the Convention encompassed the financing of attacks on off-duty military personnel, as in the cases of the 1996 Al Khobar Towers bombings in Dhahran, Saudi Arabia, and the 1983 Beirut barracks bombings, the provision was expanded to also apply to attacks on "any other person not taking an active part in the hostilities in a situation of armed conflict." The qualifier requiring that the purpose of the act be to "intimidate a population, or to compel a Government" was intended and understood to eliminate mere "ordinary crime" from the scope of the Convention.

Given the importance of protecting the flexibility of the United States to conduct legitimate activities against all lawful targets and consistent with the view taken by the United States in prior counterterrorism conventions as to their nonapplicability to the activities of state military forces in the exercise of their official duties, I recommend an Understanding to make it clear that nothing in the present Convention precludes States Parties from conducting legitimate activities against all lawful targets in accordance with the law of armed conflict. Further, because suspected offenders may seek to claim the benefit of the "armed conflict" exception in Article 2.1(b) to avoid extradition or prosecution under the Convention, it would be useful for the United States to articulate an Understanding regarding the scope of this exception. In this respect, an appropriate source of authority would be the widely accepted provision in Paragraph 2 of Article 1 of Protocol II Additional to the Geneva Conventions of 12 August, 1949, concluded at Geneva on June 10, 1977, which President Reagan transmitted to the Senate on January 29, 1987, for advice and consent to ratification (Treaty Doc. 100-2). Specifically, protocol II states that "armed conflict" does not include "internal disturbances and tensions, such as riots, isolated and sporadic acts of violence and other acts of a similar nature." I therefore recommend that the following understanding be included in the United States instrument of ratification of the Convention:

> The United States of America understands that nothing in the present Convention precludes States Parties from conducting legitimate activities against all lawful targets in accordance with the law of armed conflict. The United States further understands that the term "armed conflict" in Article 2.1(b) does not include internal disturbances and tensions, such as riots, isolated and sporadic acts of violence and other acts of a similar nature.

Paragraph 3 of Article 2 provides that for an act to constitute an offense under the Convention, it shall not be necessary that the funds were actually used to carry out one of the two categories of offenses referred to in paragraph 1(a) or (b). Paragraph 4 of Article 2 provides a person also commits an offense if that person attempts to commit an offense as set forth in paragraph 1. Paragraph 5 provides further that any person commits an offense if that person participates as an accomplice in an offense under paragraphs 1 or 4, organizes or directs others to commit such an offense, or in any other way intentionally contributes to the commission of one or more such offenses by a group of persons acting with a common purpose. These ancillary offenses in paragraph 3 are more comprehensive than those included in the earlier counter-terrorism conventions to which the United States is a party, and it is anticipated that they will strengthen the ability of the international community to investigate, prosecute and extradite those who conspire or otherwise contribute to the commission of offenses defined in the Convention.

Article 3 makes most of the Convention's provisions inapplicable to acts of terrorist financing that lack an international aspect. In generally limiting its scope of application to those cases involving elements from more than one state, the Convention follows the precedent set by the prior counter-terrorism conventions to which the United States is a party such as the 1971 Convention for the Suppression of Unlawful Acts Against the Safety of Civil Aviation and the 1979 Convention Against the Taking of Hostages.

Article 4 requires States Parties to make the offenses enumerated in Article 2 criminal offenses punishable under their domestic laws by appropriate penalties that take into account their grave nature.

Article 5 provides that States Parties, in accordance with their domestic legal principles, shall take the necessary measures to enable a legal entity located in their territory or organized under their laws to be held liable when a person responsible for the management or control of that legal entity has, in that capacity, committed an offense set forth in Article 2. Such liability may be criminal, civil, or administrative and is without prejudice to the criminal liability of individuals having committed the offenses. This provision is particularly important in the context of terrorist financing where banks and other financial institutions may be intentionally misused by their senior officers to facilitate acts of terrorist financing.

Article 6 requires States Parties to adopt such measures as may be necessary to ensure that criminal acts within the scope of the Convention are not justifiable by considerations of a political, philosophical, ideological, racial, ethnic, religious or other similar nature.

Under Article 7, each State Party must establish its jurisdiction over the offenses set forth in Article 2 when the offense is committed: (1) in its territory; (2) on board a vessel flying its flag or an aircraft registered under its laws at the time the offense is committed; or (3) by a national of that State. Each State Part has discretion to establish jurisdiction over offenses set forth in Article 2 where the offense was directed towards or resulted in the carrying out of one of the two categories of terrorist acts referred to in Article 2.1(a) or (b): in the territory of that State; against national of that State; against a State or government facility of that State abroad, including diplomatic or consular premises of that State; or committed in an attempt to compel that State to do or abstain from doing any act. Each State Party also has the discretion to establish jurisdiction over offenses set forth in Article 2 where the offense is committed either by a stateless person who has his or her habitual residence in the territory of that State or on board an aircraft which is operated by the Government of that State. Upon becoming a party to the Convention, a State must notify the United Nations Secretary-General of the jurisdiction it has established under its domestic law in accordance with paragraph 2. Moreover, any changes to this jurisdiction must be immediately notified to the Secretary-General.

Thus, under the terms of Article 7, States Parties may enact a broad array of jurisdictional bases over the offenses enumerated in Article 2. Of significant interest and value to the United States, which has many government facilities outside of its territory, is the Convention's recognition of jurisdiction over the financing of terrorist attacks against a State or government facility of that State abroad, including an embassy or consular premises of that State. This would give the United States universally recognized jurisdiction based on this Convention, for example, to prosecute in U.S. courts the financiers of attacks on all U.S. Government facilities abroad, including diplomatic and consular premises such as those attacked in 1998 in Kenya and Tanzania, as well as U.S. military installations such as those attacked in the 1996 Al-Khobar Towers bombing in Dhahrden, Saudi Arabia. Also of significant interest and value to the United States is the provision in Article 7 providing that States Parties may criminalize conduct where the offense being financed is committed in an attempt to compel that State to do or abstain from doing any act. This provides jurisdiction for offenses under this Convention where terrorists seek to coerce State action, even where a national or facility of that State is not the target of the attack.

In addition to the bases for jurisdiction set forth in paragraphs 1 and 2 of Article 7, paragraph 4 of Article 7 requires jurisdiction to be established by a State Party over the offenses set forth in Article 2 where the alleged offender is present in its territory and is not extradited to any of the State Parties that have established their jurisdiction in accordance with paragraphs 1 and 2. In the event that more than one State Party claims jurisdiction over offenses set forth in Article 2, the Convention provides that they must strive to coordinate their actions appropriately. The Convention also provides that without prejudice to the norms of general international law, it does not exclude the exercise of any criminal jurisdiction established by a State Party in accordance with its domestic law.

Article 8 provides that each State Party shall take appropriate measures, in accordance with its domestic legal principles, to identify, detect and freeze, or seize any funds used or allocated for the purpose of committing the offenses set forth in Article 2, as well as the proceeds derived from such offenses, for purposes of possible forfeiture. Further, each State Party concerned may consider concluding agreements on the sharing with other States Parties, on a regular or case-by-case basis, of the funds derived from the forfeitures referred to in this Article. The Article also provides that its provisions are to be implemented without prejudice to the rights of third parties acting in good faith.

Article 9 includes certain provisions relating to offenders or alleged offenders detained for the purpose of extradition or prosecution. This article, like the Convention as a whole as well as other similar counterterrorism conventions, is not intended to create individual rights of action.

In a provision of crucial importance for the Convention, Paragraph 1 of Article 10 declares that a State Party which does not extradite an alleged offender found in its territory shall "without exception whatsoever and whether or not the offense was committed in its territory" submit the case to its competent authorities for the purpose of prosecution, through proceedings in accordance with the laws of that State. Those authorities are obligated to take their decision in the same manner as in the case of any other offense of a grave nature under the law of that State.

In an innovation over the prior counterterrorism conventions to which the United States is a party, this Convention includes a provision in paragraph 2 of Article 10 (first proposed by the United States in the Terrorist Bombings Convention) to the effect that the obligation in paragraph 1 to extradite or submit for prosecution can be discharged by the temporary transfer of nationals for trial by those States Parties that could not otherwise extradite their nationals, provided both the Requesting and Requested States agree. This provision on temporary transfer of nationals for trial is a useful recognition of this practice by the international community in a binding multilateral legal instrument.

Paragraph 1 of Article 11 amends existing extradition treaties to include the offenses defined in Article 2 as extraditable offenses and paragraph 3 provides that they shall be extraditable offenses between States Parties which do not make extradite conditional on an extradition treaty.

Article 12 establishes general mutual legal assistance obligations between States Parties in connection with investigations or criminal or extradition proceedings brought in respect of the offenses in Article 2. In an innovation over prior counterterrorism conventions, the Convention in paragraph 2 provides that States Parties may not refuse a request for mutual legal assistance on the ground of bank secrecy.

Article 13 in a related innovation over prior counterterrorism conventions provides that none of the offenses set forth in Article 2 shall be regarded, for the purposes of extradition or mutual legal assistance, as a fiscal offense and, accordingly, States Parties may not refuse a request for such assistance on the sole ground that it concerns a fiscal offense.

Article 14 provides that none of the offenses set forth in Article 2 shall be regarded, for the purposes of extradition or mutual legal assistance, as a political offense or as an offense connected with a political offense, or as an offense inspired by political motives. Accordingly, a request for extradition or mutual legal assistance may not be refused solely on such grounds. This Article provides a use-ful narrowing of the political offense exception in such cases. In many modern United States bilateral extradition treaties there are already provisions which bar application of the political offense exception to extradition with respect to offenses covered under multilateral conventions to which "prosecute or extradite" obligations apply. The 1998 Terrorist Bombings Convention was the first U.N. counterterrorism instrument to similarly limit the political offense exception. This provision builds on this trend by making the restriction on the invocation of the political offense exception for requests based on offenses under Article 2 a matter of general application rather than dependent on the terms of individual bilateral law enforcement treaties between the States Parties.

Article 15 provides that nothing in the Convention shall be interpreted as imposing an obligation to extradite or to afford mutual legal assistance if the requested State Party has substantial grounds for believing that the request for extradition for offenses set forth in Article 2 or for mutual legal assistance with respect to such offenses has been made for the purpose of prosecuting or punishing a person on account of that person's race, religion, nationality, ethnic origin or political opinion or that compliance with the request would cause prejudice to that person's position for any of these reasons. This Article is similar to provisions already included in a number of U.N. counterterrorism treaties.

Article 16 provides and establishes various conditions for the temporary transfer to one State Party, for purposes of assistance under the Convention, of a person in custody in another State Party, provided that the person in question consents and the competent authorities of both States Parties agree. This provision was also included at the suggestion of the United States in the Terrorist Bombings Convention and is similar to provisions found in virtually all of the bilateral mutual legal assistance treaties to which the United States is a party.

Article 17 discusses the rights of persons taken into custody or regarding whom any other measures are taken or proceedings are carried out pursuant to this Convention.

Article 18 states that States Parties shall cooperate in the prevention of offenses set forth in Article 2 by taking all practicable measures to prevent and counter preparations in their respective territories for the commission of those offenses within or outside their territories. The Article provides that States parties shall consider, *inter alia* a series of financial including efforts by financial institutions to identify unusual or suspicious transactions and to report transactions suspected of stemming from criminal activity.

Article 19 contains a requirement to notify the United Nations Secretary-General of the final outcome of criminal proceedings relating to alleged offenders under the Convention. Article 20 states that States Parties shall carry out their obligations under the Convention in a manner consistent with the principles of sovereign equality and territorial integrity of states and that of non intervention in the domestic affairs of other states. Article 21 provides that nothing in the Convention shall affect other rights, obligations and responsibilities of states and individuals under international law.

Article 22 provides that nothing in the Convention entitles a State Party to undertake in the territory of another State Party the exercise of jurisdiction and performance of functions which are exclusively reserved for the authorities of that other State Party by its domestic law.

Article 23 relates to the first category of offenses described in Article 2.1(a). It establishes a mechanism for expanding the scope of the Convention by adding new conventions to the Annex. The Annex may be amended by the addition of relevant treaties that: are open to participation by all States; have entered into force; and have been ratified, accepted, approved or acceded to by at least 22 States Parties to the Convention. Any State Party may propose such an amendment, and each amendment, shall be deemed adopted unless one third of the States Parties object to it in writing not later than 180 days after its circulation. Adopted amendments to the Annex shall enter into force 30 days after the deposit of the twenty-second instrument of ratification, acceptance or approval of such amendment for all those States Parties that have deposited such an instrument. Thereafter, the amendment shall enter into force for any other State Party on the thirtieth day after the deposit of its own instrument of ratification, acceptance or approval.

This mechanism ensures both that the scope of the Convention can evolve to encompass the financing of additional terrorist activity, as may be agreed by the international community, and that the scope of the present Convention is not expanded with respect to a particular State Party without that State party's explicit agreement.

Under this provision, the United States expects to deposit an instrument of acceptance of such an amendment if the treaty that is the subject of the amendment has entered into force for the United States with the advice and consent of the Senate. Otherwise, any amendment that the United States proposes to accept would be submitted to the Senate for its advice and consent.

Article 24.1 provides that disputes between two or more States Parties concerning the interpretation or application of the Convention that cannot be settled through negotiation within a reasonable time shall be submitted at the request of one of them to ad hoc arbitration, or, failing agreement on the organization of such arbitration, to the International Court of Justice. Article 24.2 provides that a State may make a declaration excluding this dispute-resolution obligation at the time of signature, ratification, acceptance, approval or accession. In October 1985, the United States withdrew its declaration under Article 36 of the Statute of the International Court of Justice accepting the compulsory jurisdiction of the Court. Consistent with that discussion, I recommend that the following reservation to Article 24.1 be included in the United States instrument of ratification:

> Pursuant to Article 24.2 of the Convention, the United States of America declares that it does not consider itself bound by Article 24.1, but reserves the right specifically to agree in a particular case to follow the arbitration procedure set forth in the Convention or any other procedure for arbitration.

This reservation would allow the United States to agree to an adjudication by a chamber of the Court in a particular case, if that were deemed desirable.

As detailed in Article 26, the Convention will enter into force on the thirtieth day following the date of deposit of the twenty-second instrument of ratification, acceptance, approval or accession. Pursuant to Article 27, a State Party to the Convention may denounce it by written notice to the United Nations Secretary-General. Denunciation will take effect one year from the date of receipt of the notification by the United States Secretary-General.

Recommended legislation necessary to implement the Convention is being prepared for separate submission to the Congress.

The Department of Justice joins in recommending that this Convention be transmitted to the Senate at an early date for its advice and consent to ratification, subject to the understanding, the declaration relating to Article 2, and the reservation to Article 24.1, previously described.

Respectfully submitted,
STROBE TALBOT

REGIONAL TERRORISM TREATIES AND CONVENTIONS

COMMENTARY

Regional agreements covering terrorism, with the exception of the OAS Convention which is the first document in this portion of the volume, are relatively recent. Five of the seven agreements were concluded in the past six years. They illustrate that international organizations are attempting to face the threat of terrorism, and to modify their views and approaches to meet what they, in a regional context, believe is needed.

The OAS *Convention to Prevent and Punish the Acts of Terrorism Taking the Forms of Crime Against Persons and Related Extortion That Are of International Significance* is not only the first in this grouping of regional agreements, it is also of interest when reflecting on the negotiations for such agreements. The Convention is essentially a document which addresses terrorist acts which it depicts as common crimes. What prompted the Convention was a series of terrorist attacks during the 1960s throughout Latin America. The ultimate product, *The Convention to Prevent and Punish the Acts of Terrorism Taking the Forms of Crimes Against Persons and Related Extortion*, entered into force on October 16, 1973. It was, at best, a watered down version of the draft which was favored by the United States which attempted to address the overall question of international terrorism. The inherent defects in the final product are described clearly by Alona E. Evans and John F. Murphy in *Legal Aspects of International Terrorism*,[1] where they point out (at page 301) that offenders might well go free based on the political exception for extradition. In summing up, the authors state:

"In sum, the convention has some potential to make a contribution toward the protection of diplomats in the hemisphere through its establishment of a system of universal criminal jurisdiction over attacks on diplomats, and of a system of *aut dedere, aut judicare,* and through its provisions for cooperation among states parties." (at page 303).

---

1   Lexington Books, Lexington, Massachusetts, 1978.

COMMENTARY

The *European Convention on the Suppression of Terrorism*, signed on January 27, 1977, followed four years later. Article 1 indicates that "none" of the following offences shall be regarded as political, listing many of the offences covered in other international agreements. Article 2 gives parties to the Convention the option to treat other offences as not being political in nature. Article 7 recognizes that a State might refuse to extradite if it has substantial grounds to believe the purpose of extradition would be to prosecute someone because of race, religion, nationality or political opinion. The convention entered into force on August 4, 1978.

In most respects the *South Asian Association for Regional Cooperation Convention on Suppression of Terrorism* mirrors the European counterpart. It incorporates offenses described in prior international agreements, and excludes them from being considered as political offenses, thus removing the obligation to extradite. In recognizing there will be instances where it should be permissible to refuse extradition, the agreement (in Article VII) states:

> "Contracting States shall not be obliged to extradite, if it appears to the requested State that by reason of the trivial nature of the case or by reason of the request for the surrender or return of a fugitive offender not being made in good faith or in the interests of justice or for any other reason it is unjust or inexpedient to surrender or return the fugitive offender."

This Article continues the practice seen in other international agreements of offering ample opportunity for a country to refuse extradition.

Eleven years later, *The Arab Convention for the Suppression of Terrorism* was concluded, taking the exceptional (for conventions) approach of setting out its definition of terrorism in Article 1(2):

> "Any act or threat of violence, whatever its motives or purposes, that occurs in the advancement of an individual or collective criminal agenda and seeking to sow panic among people, causing fear by harming them, or placing their lives, liberty or security in danger, or seeking to cause damage to the environment or to public or private installations of property or to occupying or seizing them, or seeking to jeopardize a national resources."

The approach was roundly criticized by Amnesty International which stated that the definition of terrorism is so "broad that it lends itself to wide interpretation and abuse." Amnesty International objected to many other features in the Convention, and concluded that it constituted "a serious threat to human rights."

Article 1(3) of the Convention incorporates by reference those offenses defined by other terrorism conventions. Article 2 pointedly exempts "cases of struggle by whatever means, including armed struggle, against foreign occupation and aggression for liberation and self-determination, in accordance with principles of international law," an obvious reference to the continuing conflicts in the Middle East. Article 3 describes both preventive and what it terms "suppression" measures which the Member States will undertake. It goes into far more detail than some other agreements, even spelling out "Measures for the Protection of Witnesses and Experts." The Convention's specificity allows it to be criticized for having covered either too little or too much.

It is interesting to compare the various approaches taken by these conventions and the *Treaty on Cooperation among the States Members of the Commonwealth of Independent States on Combating Terrorism*, which offers new elements. It opens with a definition of terrorism which is comprehensive and detailed, and which has some unique aspects (for example, defining "technological terrorism"). Gone are mentions of struggles against foreign occupation and for liberation and self-determination. New definitions of terrorist acts include "Threatening the life of a statesman or public figure for the purpose of putting an end to his State or other public activity or in revenge for such activity." "Technological terrorism" covers chemical, radiological, bacteriological and other methods for "undermining public safety." The Convention contains provisions for sending, and accepting, assistance from Member States when one of its Members requires such assistance. Also included are procedures rendering "special assistance" to a Member State.

As opposed to the other agreements covered in this work, *The Convention of the Organisation of the Islamic Conference on Combating International Terrorism* is unique in the emphasis it places on religious and moral rights. It begins, for example, with:

> "pursuant to the tenets of the tolerant Islamic Sharia which reject all forms of violence and terrorism, in particularly specially those based on extremism and call for protection of human rights, which provisions are paralleled by the principles and rules of international law founded on cooperation between peoples for the establishment of peace."

The Convention defines a terrorist crime as . . . "any crime executed, started or participated in to realize a terrorist objective in any of the Contracting States or against its nationals, assets or interests or facilities and nationals residing in its territory punishable by its internal law."

Following, is the almost obligatory reference to the international conventions that preceded passage of this Convention; Article 2 stipulates that "Peoples' struggle including armed struggle against foreign occupation, aggression, colonialism, and hegemony, aimed at liberation and self-determination in accordance with the principles of international law shall not be considered a terrorist crime." The statement is followed by a list of crimes which will NOT be treated as political, "even when politically motivated."

Part II of the Convention relates to actions the Parties will take for prevention of terrorism and the cooperation expected of member states.

The *OAU Convention on the Prevention and Combating of Terrorism* entered into force on December 6, 2002. The third paragraph of Article I defines a "terrorist act" as "a violation of the criminal laws of a State Party . . . " and adds the types of acts covered within the definition. The Convention then goes on to ask its Member States to pass the requisite laws and to ratify the various terrorism agreements which lay down the requirements for terrorism offenses. Once again, an exception is made to excuse actions "waged by peoples in accordance with the principles of international law for their liberation or self-determination . . . " Upon being informed that an alleged terrorist is present within a country, that country "shall take such measures as may be necessary under its national law to investigate the facts contained in the information." Regarding extradition, the Convention provides the Parties with the opportunity to register the grounds which that country will recognize as the basis for extradition. (This Convention is not reproduced in this volume; the text is available at http://untreaty.un.org/English/Terrorism/oau_e.pdf)

Shortly after the 9/11 attacks, the Organization of American States (OAS) completed negotiations on a terrorism convention. *The Inter-American Convention Against Terrorism* was formally signed on June 3, 2002 in Barbados. With virtual lightening speed (for treaty approval and consideration) it was forwarded by President Bush to the Senate for its advice and consent on November 13, 2002. Hearings on the convention were held in the Senate Foreign Relations Committee on June 17, 2004.

To its detriment, the Convention sidesteps the question of defining terrorism in an attempt to avoid the pitfall of leaving openings for many types of acts to be exempted from coverage. On the positive side there is a concerted effort to address the question of human rights while fighting international terrorism. In the provision dealing with extradition, the Convention stipulates that none of the offenses named in Article 2 shall be considered political offenses. Thus, for those offenses, a country cannot refuse to extradite based solely on the fact that it contends a political offense was committed. Article 4 reinforces the importance of preventing the funding of terrorism by implementing stringent legal and regulatory controls.

OAS CONVENTION TO PREVENT AND PUNISH THE ACTS OF TERRORISM TAKING THE FORM OF CRIMES AGAINST PERSONS AND RELATED EXTORTION THAT ARE OF INTERNATIONAL SIGNIFICANCE

Done at Washington on 2 February 1971
Entered into force on 20 October 1976*

BY THE PRESIDENT OF THE UNITED STATES OF AMERICA
A PROCLAMATION

CONSIDERING THAT:

The Convention to Prevent and Punish the Acts of Terrorism Taking the Form of Crimes Against Persons and Related Extortion That Are of International Significance was signed in behalf of the United States of America on February 2, 1971, a certified copy of which Convention, in the English, French, Portuguese, and Spanish languages, is hereto annexed;

The Senate of the United States of America by its resolution of June 12, 1972, two-thirds of the Senators present concurring therein, gave its advice and consent to ratification of the Convention;

On October 8, 1976, the President of the United States of America ratified the Convention, in pursuance of the advice and consent of the Senate;

The United States of America deposited its instrument of ratification on October 20, 1976, in accordance with the provisions of Article 11 of the Convention;

Pursuant to the provisions of Article 12 of the Convention, the Convention entered into force for the United States of America on October 20, 1976;

---

* Treaties and International Agreements Online, CTIA 8463.000 (Oceana Publications, Inc. <www.oceanalaw.com>.

OAS CONVENTION ON TERRORISM

NOW, THEREFORE, I, Gerald R. Ford, President of the United States of America, proclaim and make public the Convention, to the end that it shall be observed and fulfilled with good faith on and after October 20, 1976, by the United States of America and by the citizens of the United States of America and all other persons subject to the jurisdiction thereof.

IN TESTIMONY WHEREOF, I have signed this proclamation and caused the Seal of the United States of America to be affixed.

DONE at the city of Washington this sixteenth day of November in the year of our Lord one thousand nine hundred seventy-six and of the Independence of the United States of America the two hundred first.

By the President:
GERALD R. FORD

Secretary of State
HENRY A. KISSINGER

WHEREAS:

The defense of freedom and justice and respect for the fundamental rights of the individual that are recognized by the American Declaration of the Rights and Duties of Man and the Universal Declaration of Human Rights are primary duties of states;

The General Assembly of the Organization, in Resolution 4, of June 30, 1970, strongly condemned acts of terrorism, especially the kidnapping of persons and extortion in connection with that crime, which it declared to be serious common crimes;

Criminal acts against persons entitled to special protection under international law are occurring frequently, and those acts are of international significance because of the consequences that may flow from them for relations among states;

It is advisable to adopt general standards that will progressively develop international law as regards cooperation in the prevention and punishment of such acts; and

In the application of those standards the institution of asylum should be maintained and, likewise the principle of nonintervention should not be impaired,

THE MEMBER STATES OF THE ORGANIZATION OF AMERICAN STATES HAVE AGREED UPON THE FOLLOWING ARTICLES:

OAS CONVENTION ON TERRORISM

Article 1

The contracting states undertake to cooperate among themselves by taking all the measures that they may consider effective, under their own laws, and especially those established in this convention, to prevent and punish acts of terrorism, especially kidnapping, murder, and other assaults against the life or physical integrity of those persons to whom the state has the duty according to international law to give special protection, as well as extortion in connection with those crimes.

Article 2

For the purposes of this convention, kidnapping, murder, and other assaults against the life or personal integrity of those persons to whom the state has the duty to give special protection according to international law, as well as extortion in connection with those crimes, shall be considered common crimes of international significance, regardless of motive.

Article 3

Persons who have been charged or convicted for any of the crimes referred to in Article 2 of this convention shall be subject to extradition under the provisions of the extradition treaties in force between the parties or, in the case of states that do not make extradition dependent on the existence of a treaty, in accordance with their own laws.

In any case, it is the exclusive responsibility of the state under whose jurisdiction or protection such persons are located to determine the nature of the acts and decide whether the standards of this convention are applicable.

Article 4

Any person deprived of his freedom through the application of this convention shall enjoy the legal guarantees of due process.

Article 5

When extradition requested for one of the crimes specified in Article 2 is not in order because the person sought is a national of the requested state, or because of some other legal or constitutional impediment, that state is obliged to submit the case to its competent authorities for prosecution, as if the act had been committed in its territory. The decision of these authorities shall be communicated to the state that requested extradition. In such proceedings, the obligation established in Article 4 shall be respected.

Article 6

None of the provisions of this convention shall be interpreted so as to impair the right of asylum.

Article 7

The contracting states undertake to include the crimes referred to in Article 2 of this convention among the punishable acts giving rise to extradition in any treaty on the subject to which they agree among themselves in the future. The contracting states that do not subject extradition to the existence of a treaty with the requesting state shall consider the crimes referred to in Article 2 of this convention as crimes giving rise to extradition, according to the conditions established by the laws of the requested state.

Article 8

To cooperate in preventing and punishing the crimes contemplated in Article 2 of this convention, the contracting states accept the following obligations:

a. To take all measures within their power, and in conformity with their own laws, to prevent and impede the preparation in their respective territories of the crimes mentioned in Article 2 that are to be carried out in the territory of another contracting state.

b. To exchange information and consider effective administrative measures for the purpose of protecting the persons to whom Article 2 of this convention refers.

c. To guarantee to every person deprived of his freedom through the application of this convention every right to defend himself.

d. To endeavor to have the criminal acts contemplated in this convention included in their penal laws, if not already so included.

e. To comply most expeditiously with the requests for extradition concerning the criminal acts contemplated in this convention.

Article 9

This convention shall remain open for signature by the member states of the Organization of American States, as well as by any other state that is a member of the United Nations or any of its specialized agencies, or any state that is a party to the Statute of the International Court of Justice,[1] or any other state that may be invited by the General Assembly of the Organization of American States to sign it.

Article 10

This convention shall be ratified by the signatory states in accordance with their respective constitutional procedures.

---

1 TS 993; 59 Stat. 1055.

Article 11

The original instrument of this convention, the English, French, Portuguese, and Spanish texts of which are equally authentic, shall be deposited in the General Secretariat of the Organization of American States, which shall send certified copies to the signatory governments for purposes of ratification. The instruments of ratification shall be deposited in the General Secretariat of the Organization of American States, which shall notify the signatory governments of such deposit.

Article 12

This convention shall enter into force among the states that ratify it when they deposit their respective instruments of ratification.

Article 13

This convention shall remain in force indefinitely, but any of the contracting states may denounce it. The denunciation shall be transmitted to the General Secretariat of the Organization of American States, which shall notify the other contracting states thereof. One year following the denunciation, the convention shall cease to be in force for the denouncing state, but shall continue to be in force for the other contracting states.

STATEMENT OF PANAMA

The Delegation of Panama states for the record that nothing in this convention shall be interpreted to the effect that the right of asylum implies the right to request asylum from the United States authorities in the Panama Canal Zone, or that there is recognition of the right of the United States to grant asylum or political refuge in that part of the territory of the Republic of Panama that constitutes the Canal Zone.

IN WITNESS WHEREOF, the undersigned plenipotentiaries, having presented their full powers, which have been found to be in due and proper form, sign this convention on behalf of their respective governments, at the

OAS CONVENTION ON TERRORISM

city of Washington this second day of February of the year one thousand nine hundred seventy-one.

FOR NICARAGUA:
FOR TRINIDAD AND TOBAGO:
FOR PERU:
FOR HONDURAS:
FOR GUATEMALA:
FOR URUGUAY:
FOR BOLIVIA:
FOR ECUADOR:
FOR CHILE:
FOR BARBADOS:
FOR MEXICO:
FOR THE UNITED STATES OF AMERICA:
FOR PANAMA:
FOR COSTA RICA:
FOR BRAZIL:
FOR HAITI:
FOR PARAGUAY:
FOR THE DOMINICAN REPUBLIC:
FOR VENEZUELA:
FOR EL SALVADOR:
FOR COLOMBIA:
FOR THE ARGENTINE REPUBLIC:
FOR JAMAICA:

States which are parties:

Bolivia
Brazil
Chile[1]
Colombia
Costa Rica
Dominican Republic
Ecuador
El Salvador
Grenada
Guatemala
Honduras
Jamaica
Mexico
Nicaragua
Panama[2]
Paraguay
Peru
Trinidad & Tobago
United States
Uruguay
Venezuela

*DECLARATIONS/RESERVATIONS/DENUNCIATIONS/WITHDRAWALS

1. Chile:

(Reservation made at the time of signature)

Signature subject to ratification.

2. Panama:

(Declaration made at the time of signature)

The Delegation of Panama states for the record that nothing in this Convention shall be interpreted to the effect that the right of asylum implies the right to request asylum from the United States authorities in the Panama Canal Zone, or that there is recognition of the right of the United States to grant asylum or political refuge in that part of the territory of the Republic of Panama that constitutes the Canal Zone.

EUROPEAN CONVENTION ON THE SUPPRESSION OF TERRORISM[1]

Done at Strasbourg on 27 January 1977
Entered into force on 8 August 1978*

Authentic texts: English and French.

Registered by the Secretary-General of the Council of Europe, acting on behalf of the Parties, on 30 May 1979.

---

* Treaties and International Agreements Online, CTIA 10520.000 (Oceana Publications, Inc. <www.oceanalaw.com>.

1 Came into force on 4 August 1978, i.e., three months after the date of deposit with the Secretary-General of the Council of Europe of the third instrument of ratification, acceptance or approval, in accordance with article 11(1) and (2). Instruments of ratification, acceptance or approval were deposited as follows:

State	Date of deposit of the instrument of ratification
Austria	11 August 1977
Sweden*	15 September 1977
Germany, Federal Republic of*	3 May 1978

(With a declaration of application to Land Berlin.)

Subsequently, the Convention came into force for the following States three months after the date of deposit of their instruments of ratification, acceptance or approval with the Secretary-General of the Council of Europe, in accordance with article 11(1) and (3):

Denmark*	27 June 1978

(With effect from 28 September 1978. With a declaration of non-application to the Faroe Islands and Greenland.)

United Kingdom of Great Britain and Northern Ireland	24 July 1978

(With effect from 23 October 1978. With a declaration of application to the bailiwick of Jersey, the bailiwick of Guernsey and the Isle of Man.)

Cyprus*	26 February 1979

(With effect from 27 May 1979.)

EUROPEAN CONVENTION ON THE SUPPRESSION OF TERRORISM

THE MEMBER STATES OF THE COUNCIL OF EUROPE, SIGNATORY HERETO,

Considering that the aim of the Council of Europe is to achieve a greater unity between its members,

Aware of the growing concern caused by the increase in acts of terrorism,

Wishing to take effective measures to ensure that the perpetrators of such acts do not escape prosecution and punishment,

Convinced that extradition is a particularly effective measure for achieving this result,

HAVE AGREED as follows:

Article 1

For the purposes of extradition between Contracting States, none of the following offences shall be regarded as a political offence or as an offence connected with a political offence or as an offence inspired by political motives:

(a) An offence within the scope of the Convention for the Suppression of Unlawful Seizure of Aircraft, signed at The Hague on 16 December 1970;[2]

(b) An offence within the scope of the Convention for the Suppression of Unlawful Acts against the Safety of Civil Aviation, signed at Montreal on 23 September 1971;[3]

(c) A serious offence involving an attack against the life, physical integrity or liberty of internationally protected persons, including diplomatic agents;

(d) An offence involving kidnapping, the taking of a hostage or serious unlawful detention;

(e) An offence involving the use of a bomb, grenade, rocket, automatic firearm or letter or parcel bomb if this use endangers persons;

(f) An attempt to commit any of the foregoing offences or participation as an accomplice of a person who commits or attempts to commit such an offence.

Article 2

1. For the purposes of extradition between Contracting States, a Contracting State may decide not to regard as a political offence or as an offence connected with a political offence or as an offence inspired by political motives

---

[2] United Nations, *Treaty Series*, vol. 860, p. 105.
[3] *Ibid.*, vol. 974, p. 177.

a serious offence involving an act of violence, other than one covered by article 1, against the life, physical integrity or liberty of a person.

2. The same shall apply to a serious offence involving an act against property, other than one covered by article 1, if the act created a collective danger for persons.

3. The same shall apply to an attempt to commit any of the foregoing offences or participation as an accomplice of a person who commits or attempts to commit such an offence.

Article 3

The provisions of all extradition treaties and arrangements applicable between Contracting States, including the European Convention on Extradition,[4] are modified as between Contracting States to the extent that they are incompatible with this Convention.

Article 4

For the purposes of this Convention and to the extent that any offence mentioned in article 1 or 2 is not listed as an extraditable offence in any extradition convention or treaty existing between Contracting States, it shall be deemed to be included as such therein.

Article 5

Nothing in this Convention shall be interpreted as imposing an obligation to extradite if the requested State has substantial grounds for believing that the request for extradition for an offence mentioned in article 1 or 2 has been made for the purpose of prosecuting or punishing a person on account of his race, religion, nationality or political opinion, or that that person's position may be prejudiced for any of these reasons.

Article 6

1. Each Contracting State shall take such measures as may be necessary to establish its jurisdiction over an offence mentioned in article 1 in the case where the suspected offender is present in its territory and it does not extradite him after receiving a request for extradition from a Contracting State whose jurisdiction is based on a rule of jurisdiction existing equally in the law of the requested State.

2. This Convention does not exclude any criminal jurisdiction exercised in accordance with national law.

---

[4] United Nations, *Treaty Series*, vol. 359, p. 273; see also "Additional Protocol to the European Convention on extradition, signed at Strasbourg on 15 October 1975", *ibid.*, vol. 1161, No. A–5146.

Article 7

A Contracting State in whose territory a person suspected to have committed an offence mentioned in article 1 is found and which has received a request for extradition under the conditions mentioned in article 6, paragraph 1, shall, if it does not extradite that person, submit the case, without exception whatsoever and without undue delay, to its competent authorities for the purpose of prosecution. Those authorities shall take their decision in the same manner as in the case of any offence of a serious nature under the law of that State.

Article 8

1. Contracting States shall afford one another the widest measure of mutual assistance in criminal matters in connection with proceedings brought in respect of the offences mentioned in article 1 or 2. The law of the requested State concerning mutual assistance in criminal matters shall apply in all cases. Nevertheless this assistance may not be refused on the sole ground that it concerns a political offence or an offence connected with a political offence or an offence inspired by political motives.

2. Nothing in this Convention shall be interpreted as imposing an obligation to afford mutual assistance if the requested State has substantial grounds for believing that the request for mutual assistance in respect of an offence mentioned in article 1 or 2 has been made for the purpose of prosecuting or punishing a person on account of his race, religion, nationality or political opinion or that that person's position may be prejudiced for any of these reasons.

3. The provisions of all treaties and arrangements concerning mutual assistance in criminal matters applicable between Contracting States, including the European Convention on Mutual Assistance in Criminal Matters, are modified as between Contracting States to the extent that they are incompatible with this Convention.

Article 9

1. The European Committee on Crime Problems of the Council of Europe shall be kept informed regarding the application of this Convention.

2. It shall do whatever is needful to facilitate a friendly settlement of any difficulty which may arise out of its execution.

Article 10

1. Any dispute between Contracting States concerning the interpretation or application of this Convention, which has not been settled in the framework of article 9, paragraph 2, shall, at the request of any Party to the dispute, be referred to arbitration. Each Party shall nominate an arbitrator and the two arbitrators shall nominate a referee. If any Party has not nominated

its arbitrator within the three months following the request for arbitration, he shall be nominated at the request of the other Party by the President of the European Court of Human Rights. If the latter should be a national of one of the Parties to the dispute, this duty shall be carried out by the Vice-President of the Court or, if the Vice-President is a national of one of the Parties to the dispute, by the most senior judge of the Court not being a national of one of the Parties to the dispute. The same procedure shall be observed if the arbitrators cannot agree on the choice of referee.

2. The arbitration tribunal shall lay down its own procedure. Its decisions shall be taken by majority vote. Its award shall be final.

Article 11

This Convention shall be open to signature by the member States of the Council of Europe. It shall be subject to ratification, acceptance or approval. Instruments of ratification, acceptance or approval shall be deposited with the Secretary General of the Council of Europe.

2. The Convention shall enter into force three months after the date of the deposit of the third instrument of ratification, acceptance or approval.

3. In respect of a signatory State ratifying, accepting or approving subsequently, the Convention shall come into force three months after the date of the deposit of its instrument of ratification, acceptance or approval.

Article 12

1. Any State may, at the time of signature or when depositing its instrument of ratification, acceptance or approval, specify the territory or territories to which this Convention shall apply.

2. Any State may, when depositing its instrument of ratification, acceptance or approval or at any later date, by declaration addressed to the Secretary General of the Council of Europe, extend this Convention to any other territory or territories specified in the declaration and for whose international relations it is responsible or on whose behalf it is authorized to give undertakings.

3. Any declaration made in pursuance of the preceding paragraph may, in respect of any territory mentioned in such declaration, be withdrawn by means of a notification addressed to the Secretary General of the Council of Europe. Such withdrawal shall take effect immediately or at such later date as may be specified in the notification.

Article 13

1. Any State may, at the time of signature or when depositing its instrument of ratification, acceptance or approval, declare that it reserves the right to refuse extradition in respect of any offence mentioned in article 1 which it

considers to be a political offence, an offence connected with a political offence or an offence inspired by political motives, provided that it undertakes to take into due consideration, when evaluating the character of the offence, any particularly serious aspects of the offence, including:

(a) That it created a collective danger to the life, physical integrity or liberty of persons; or

(b) That it affected persons foreign to the motives behind it; or

(c) That cruel or vicious means have been used in the commission of the offence.

2. Any State may wholly or partly withdraw a reservation it has made in accordance with the foregoing paragraph by means of a declaration addressed to the Secretary General of the Council of Europe which shall become effective as from the date of its receipt.

3. A State which has made a reservation in accordance with paragraph 1 of this article may not claim the application of article 1 by any other State; it may, however, if its reservation is partial or conditional, claim the application of that article in so far as it has itself accepted it.

Article 14

Any Contracting State may denounce this Convention by means of a written notification addressed to the Secretary General of the Council of Europe. Any such denunciation shall take effect immediately or at such later date as may be specified in the notification.

Article 15

This Convention ceases to have effect in respect of any Contracting State which withdraws from or ceases to be a Member of the Council of Europe.

Article 16

The Secretary General of the Council of Europe shall notify the member States of the Council of:

(a) Any signature;

(b) Any deposit of an instrument of ratification, acceptance or approval;

(c) Any date of entry into force of this Convention in accordance with article 11 thereof;

(d) Any declaration or notification received in pursuance of the provisions of article 12;

(e) Any reservation made in pursuance of the provisions of article 13, paragraph 1;

(f) The withdrawal of any reservation effected in pursuance of the provisions of article 13, paragraph 2;

(g) Any notification received in pursuance of article 14 and the date on which denunciation takes effect;

(h) Any cessation of the effects of the Convention pursuant to article 15.

In witness whereof, the undersigned, being duly authorized thereto, have signed this Convention.

Done at Strasbourg, this 27th day of January 1977, in English and in French, both texts being equally authoritative, in a single copy which shall remain deposited in the archives of the Council of Europe. The Secretary General of the Council of Europe shall transmit certified copies to each of the signatory States.

For the Government of the Republic of Austria:
Willibald Pahr

For the Government of the Kingdom of Belgium:
Renaat Van Elslande

For the Government of the Republic of Cyprus:
Ioannis Christophides

For the Government of the Kingdom of Denmark:
K. B. Andersen

For the Government of the French Republic:
P. C. Taittinger[5]

For the Government of the Federal Republic of Germany:
Hans-Dietrich Genscher

For the Government of the Hellenic Republic:
Dimitri S. Bitsios

For the Government of the Icelandic Republic:
Einar Agustsson

For the Government of Ireland:

For the Government of the Italian Republic:
Gherardo Cornaggia Medici Castiglioni[6]

For the Government of the Principality of Liechtenstein:
Strasbourg, le 22 janvier 1979
Nikolaus von Liechtenstein

For the Government of the Grand Duchy of Luxembourg:
Gaston Thorn

For the Government of Malta:

---

5   With reservations.
6   With reservations.

EUROPEAN CONVENTION ON THE SUPPRESSION OF TERRORISM

For the Government of the Kingdom of the Netherlands:
 Max van der Stoel

For the Government of the Kingdom of Norway:
 Knut Frydenlund[7]

For the Government of the Portuguese Republic:
 José Medeiros Ferreira[8]

For the Government of the Kingdom of Spain:
 Strasbourg, le 27 avril 1978
  Marcelino Oreja Aguirre

For the Government of the Kingdom of Sweden:
 Karin Söder

For the Government of the Swiss Confederation:
 Pierre Graber

For the Government of the Turkish Republic:
 I. S. Çaglayangil

For the Government of the United Kingdom of Great Britain and Northern Ireland:
 Anthony Crosland

RESERVATIONS AND DECLARATIONS MADE UPON SIGNATURE

FRANCE

[Translation[9]]

In deciding to sign the European Convention on the Suppression of Terrorism today, the Government wished to demonstrate its solidarity with the other European countries in combating a danger which has created—and continues to create—a number of innocent victims and very properly arouses public feeling.

This signature is the logical consequence of the action we have been taking for several years and which has caused us on several occasions to strengthen our internal legislation and to ratify The Hague[10] and Montreal[11] Conventions on air terrorism.

It is self-evident that efficiency in this struggle must be reconciled with respect for the fundamental principles of our criminal law and of our Constitution, which states in its preamble that "anyone persecuted on account of his action for the cause of liberty has the right to asylum on the territory of the Republic".

It is also clear that such a high degree of solidarity as is provided for in the Council of Europe Convention[12] can only apply between States sharing the same ideals of freedom and democracy.

France will therefore subject the application of the Convention to certain conditions. On ratification it will make the reservations necessary to ensure that the considerations I have

---

7   With reservations.
8   With reservations.
9   Translation supplied by the Council of Europe.
10 United Nations, *Treaty Series*, vol. 860, p. 105.
11 *Ibid.*, vol. 974, p. 177.
12 *Ibid.*, vol. 87, p. 103.

just mentioned will be taken into account and that human rights will at no time be endangered.

There is a further point of very special importance to the Government: this is the success of the work of the Nine in the same field following the decisions of the European Council on 13 July 1976. We wish to avoid risks of conflict between the two texts and the Government therefore does not intend to ratify the Strasbourg Convention before the instrument which will be prepared by the Nine.

Furthermore, taking action against terrorism does not absolve us from tackling the political problem of the causes of terrorism. For in many respects the real struggle against terrorism is a struggle for a just peace which guarantees everyone's legitimate rights.

ITALY

[Translation[13]]

Italy declares that it reserves the right to refuse extradition and mutual assistance in criminal matters in respect to any offence mentioned in article 1 which it considers to be a political offence, an offence connected with a political offence or an offence inspired by political motives: in this case Italy undertakes to take into due consideration, when evaluating the character of the offence, any particularly serious aspects of the offence, including:

(a) That it created a collective danger to the life, physical integrity or liberty of persons; or

(b) That it affected persons foreign to the motives behind it; or

(c) That cruel or vicious means have been used in the commission of the offence.

NORWAY

"The Kingdom of Norway declares that it reserves the right to refuse, in conformity with the provisions laid down in article 13, paragraph 1, of the Convention, extradition in respect of any offences mentioned in article 1 if it considers it to be a political offence or connected with a political offence or inspired by political motives.

"The Kingdom of Norway does not consider itself bound by the provisions of article 8 and reserves the right to refuse requests for assistance in criminal matters in which the offence is regarded by Norwegian authorities to be a political offence or connected with a political offence or inspired by political motives."

PORTUGAL

[Translation[14]]

As requested State, Portugal will not grant extradition for offences punishable by death in the requesting State, this is, in accordance with article 11 of the European Convention on Extradition to which Portugal is not a Contracting Party.

Portugal is signing the Convention subject to the safeguard of the provisions of its constitution relating to non-extradition on political grounds.

RESERVATIONS AND DECLARATIONS—MADE UPON RATIFICATION

CYPRUS

"The Government of the Republic of Cyprus reserves the right to refuse extradition in respect of any offence mentioned in article 1 which it considers to be a political offence.

---

13 Translation supplied by the Council of Europe.
14 Translation supplied by the Council of Europe.

"(a) With respect to Article 7 of the Convention and pursuant to the Republic of Cyprus the Extension of Jurisdiction of National Courts with respect to certain Terrorist Offences Law of 1979 which has been enacted by the House of Representatives of the Republic of Cyprus on the 18th January 1979, the national courts of Cyprus can prosecute a person suspected to have committed an offence mentioned in article 1 of this Convention.

"(b) In this regard, the Government of the Republic of Cyprus wishes further to notify that its reservations and declarations made on 22nd January 1971[15] when depositing its instrument of ratification with regard to the European Convention on Extradition of 13th December 1957 are still valid."

DENMARK

"The Danish Government, in accordance with the provisions of article 13 of this Convention and subject to the undertaking contained in that article, reserves the right to refuse extradition in respect of any offence mentioned in article 1 which it considers to be a political offence."

FEDERAL REPUBLIC OF GERMANY

"With effect from the date on which the said Convention enters into force for the Federal Republic of Germany, it shall also apply to Land Berlin, subject to the rights, responsibilities and legislation of the French Republic, the United Kingdom of Great Britain and Northern Ireland and the United States of America.

"In particular, nationals of the French Republic, the United Kingdom of Great Britain and Northern Ireland or the United States of America shall not be extradited without the consent of the appropriate Sector Commandant."

SWEDEN

"The Swedish Government, in accordance with the provisions of article 13 of this Convention and subject to the undertaking contained in that article, reserves the right to refuse extradition in respect of any offence mentioned in article 1 which it considers to be a political offence."

---

15   United Nations, *Treaty Series*, vol. 789, p. 292.

EUROPEAN CONVENTION ON THE SUPPRESSION OF TERRORISM

Parties:

- Albania
- Andorra
- Armenia
- Austria
- Azerbaijan
- Belgium
- Bosnia and Herzegovina
- Bulgaria
- Croatia
- Cyprus
- Czech Republic
- Denmark
- Estonia
- Finland
- France
- Georgia
- Germany
- Greece
- Hungary
- Iceland
- Ireland
- Italy
- Latvia
- Liechtenstein
- Lithuania
- Luxembourg
- Malta
- Moldova
- Netherlands
- Norway
- Poland
- Portugal
- Romania
- Russia
- San Marino
- Serbia and Montenegro
- Slovakia
- Slovenia
- Spain
- Sweden
- Switzerland
- the former Yugoslav Republic of Macedonia
- Turkey
- Ukraine
- United Kingdom

SOUTH ASIAN ASSOCIATION (SAARC) REGIONAL CONVENTION ON SUPPRESSION OF TERRORISM

4 November 1987
Entered into force 22 August 1998*

THE MEMBER STATES OF THE SOUTH ASIAN ASSOCIATION FOR REGIONAL COOPERATION (SAARC)

MINDFUL of the principles of cooperation enshrined in the SAARC Charter;

RECALLING that at the Dhaka Summit on December 7-8, 1985, the Heads of State or Government of the Member States of the SAARC recognized the seriousness of the problem of terrorism as it affects the security and stability of the region;

ALSO RECALLING the Bangalore Summit Declaration of 17 November 1986, in which the Heads of state or Government of SAARC agreed that co-operation among SAARC States was vital if terrorism was to be prevented and eliminated from the region; unequivocally condemned all acts, methods and practices of terrorism as criminal and deplored their impact on life and property, socio-economic development, political stability, regional and international peace and cooperation, and recognized the importance of the principles laid down in UN Resolution 2625 (XXV) which among others required that each state should refrain from organizing, instigating, assisting or participating in acts of civil strife or terrorist acts in another state or acquiescing in organized activities within its territory directed towards the commission of such acts;

AWARE of the danger posed by the spread of terrorism and its harmful effect on peace, cooperation, friendship and good neighbourly relations and which could also jeopardize the sovereignty and territorial integrity of states;

---

*   Treaties and International Agreements Online, CTIA 10522.000 (Oceana Publications, Inc. <www.oceanalaw.com>.

SAARC REGIONAL CONVENTION ON SUPPRESSION OF TERRORISM

HAVE RESOLVED to take effective measures to ensure that perpetrators of terroristic acts do not escape prosecution and punishment by providing for their extradition or prosecution, and to this end,

HAVE AGREED as follows:

Article I

Subject to the overall requirements of the law of extradition, conduct constituting any of the following offences, according to the law of the Contracting State, shall be regarded as terroristic and for the purpose of extradition shall not be regarded as political offence or as an offence connected with a political offence or as an offence inspired by political motives:

a) An offence within the scope of the Convention for the Suppression of Unlawful Seizure of Aircraft, signed at the Hague on December 16, 1970;

b) An offence within the scope of the Convention for the Suppression of Unlawful acts against the safety of Civil Aviation, signed at Montreal on September 23, 1971;

c) An offence within the scope of the Convention on the Prevention and Punishment of Crimes against Internationally Protected Persons, including Diplomatic Agents, signed at New York on December 14, 1973;

d) An offence within the scope of any Convention to which SAARC Member Sates concerned are parties and which obliges the parties to prosecute or grant extradition;

e) Murder, manslaughter, assault causing bodily harm, kidnapping, hostage-taking and offences relating to firearms, weapons, explosives and dangerous substances when used as a means to perpetrate indiscriminate violence involving death or serious bodily injury to persons or serious damage to property;

f) An attempt or conspiracy to commit an offence described in sub-paragraphs (a) to (e), aiding, abetting or counseling the commission of such an offence or participating as an accomplice in the offences so described.

Article II

For the purpose of extradition between SAARC Member States, any two or more Contracting States may, by agreement, decide to include any other serious offence involving violence, which shall not be regarded as a political offence or an offence connected with a political offence or an offence inspired by political motives.

Article III

1. The provisions of all extradition treaties and arrangements applicable between Contracting States are hereby amended as between Contracting States to the extent that they are incompatible with this Convention.

2. For the purpose of this Convention and to the extent that any offence referred to in Article I or agreed to in terms of Article II is not listed as an extraditable offence in any extradition treaty existing between Contracting States, it shall be deemed to be included as such therein.

3. Contracting States undertake to include these offences as extraditable offences in any future extradition treaty to be concluded between them.

4. If a Contracting State which makes extradition conditional on the existence of a treaty receives a request for extradition from another Contracting State with which it has no extradition treaty, the requested State may, as its option, consider this Convention as the basis for extradition in respect of the offences set forth in Article I or agreed to in terms of Article II. Extradition shall be subject to the law of the requested State.

5. Contracting States, which do not make extradition conditional on the existence of a treaty, shall recognize the offences set forth in Article I or agreed to in terms of Article II as extraditable offences between themselves, subject to the law of the requested State.

Article IV

A contracting State in whose territory a person suspected of having committed an offence referred to in Article I or agreed to in terms of Article II is found and which has received a request for extradition from another Contracting State, shall, if it does not extradite that person, submit the case without exception and without delay, to its competent authorities shall take their decisions in the same manner as in the case of any offence of a serious nature under the law of the State.

Article V

For the purpose of Article IV, each Contracting State may take such measures as it deems appropriate, consistent with its national laws, subject to reciprocity, to exercise its jurisdiction in the case of an offence under Article I or agreed to in terms of Article II.

Article VI

A Contracting State in whose territory an alleged offender is found, shall, upon receiving a request for extradition from another Contracting State, take appropriate measures, subject to its national laws, so as to ensure his presence for purposes of extradition or prosecution. Such measures shall immediately be notified to the requesting State.

SAARC REGIONAL CONVENTION ON SUPPRESSION OF TERRORISM

Article VII

Contracting States shall not be obliged to extradite, if it appears to the requested State that by reason of the trivial nature of the case or by reason of the request for the surrender or return of a fugitive offender not being made in good faith or in the interests of justice or for any other reason it is unjust or inexpedient to surrender or return the fugitive offender.

Article VIII

1. Contracting States shall, subject to their national laws, afford one another the greatest measure of mutual assistance in connection with proceedings brought in respect of the offences referred to in Article I or agree to in terms of Article II, including the supply of all evidence at their disposal necessary for the proceedings.

2. Contracting States shall cooperate among themselves, to the extent permitted by their national laws, through consultations between appropriate agencies, exchange of information, intelligence and expertise and such other cooperative measures as may be appropriate, with a view to prevention terroristic activities through precautionary measures.

Article IX

1. The Convention shall be open for signature by the Member States of SAARC at the SAARC Secretariat in Kathmandu.

2. It shall be subject to ratification. Instruments of ratification shall be deposited with the Secretary-General of SAARC.

Article X

The Convention shall enter into force on the fifteenth day following the date of the deposit of the seventh Instrument of Ratification with Secretary-General of SAARC.

Article XI

The Secretary-General of SAARC shall be the depositary of this Convention and shall notify Member States of signatures to this Convention and all deposits of Instruments of Ratification. The Secretary-General shall transmit certified copies of such Instruments to each Member State. The Secretary-General shall also inform Member States of the date on which this Convention will have entered into force in accordance with Article X.

IN WITNESS WHEREOF the undersigned, being duly authorized thereto by their respective Governments have signed this Convention.

DONE at Kathmandu on this Fourth Day of November One Thousand Nine Hundred and Eighty Seven in eight Originals in the English language all texts being equally authentic.

SAARC REGIONAL CONVENTION ON SUPPRESSION OF TERRORISM

HUMAYUN RASHEED CHOUDHURY
Minister of Foreign Affairs
People's Republic of Bangladesh

DAWA TSERING
Minister of Foreign Affairs
Kingdom of Bhutan

K. NATWAR SINGH
Minister of State for External Affairs
Republic of India

FATHULLA JAMEEL
Minister of Foreign Affairs
Republic of Maldives

SHAILENDRA KUMAR UPADHYAYA
Minister for Foreign Affairs and Land Reforms
His Majesty's Government of Nepal

ZAIN NOORANI
Minister of State for Foreign Affairs
Islamic Republic of Pakistan

A.C. SHAHUL HAMEED
Minister of Foreign Affairs
Democratic Socialist Republic of Sri Lanka

ARAB CONVENTION FOR THE SUPPRESSION OF TERRORISM

Adopted by the Council of Arab Ministers of the Interior
and the Council of Arab Ministers of Justice
Signed in Cairo, 22 April 1998*

Preamble**

THE ARAB STATES SIGNATORY HERETO,

Desiring to promote mutual cooperation in the suppression of terrorist offences, which pose a threat to the security and stability of the Arab Nation and endanger its vital interests,

Being committed to the highest moral and religious principles and, in particular, to the tenets of the Islamic Sharia, as well as to the humanitarian heritage of an Arab Nation that rejects all forms of violence and terrorism and advocates the protection of human rights, with which precepts the principles of international law conform, based as they are on cooperation among peoples in the promotion of peace,

Being further committed to the Pact of the League of Arab States, the Charter of the United Nations and all the other international convents and instruments to which the Contracting States to this Convention are parties,

Affirming the right of peoples to combat foreign occupation and aggression by whatever means, including armed struggle, in order to liberate their territories and secure their right to self-determination, and independence and to do so in such a manner as to preserve the territorial integrity of each Arab country, of the foregoing being in accordance with the purposes and principles of the Charter of the United Nations and with the Organization's resolutions.

---

*   Treaties and International Agreements Online, CTIA 10519.000 (Oceana Publications, Inc. <www.oceanalaw.com>.

** Translated from the Arabic by the UN English translation service (unofficial translation).

ARAB CONVENTION FOR THE SUPPRESSION OF TERRORISM

HAVE AGREED to conclude this convention and to invite any Arab State that did not participate in its conclusion to accede hereto.

PART ONE
DEFINITIONS AND GENERAL PROVISIONS

Article 1

Each of the following terms shall be understood in the light of the definition given:

1. Contracting State

Any member State of the League of Arab States that has ratified this Convention and that has deposited its instruments of ratification with the General Secretariat of the League.

2. Terrorism

Any act or threat of violence, whatever its motives or purposes, that occurs in the advancement of an individual or collective criminal agenda and seeking to sow panic among people, causing fear by harming them, or placing their lives, liberty or security in danger, or seeking to cause damage to the environment or to public or private installations or property or to occupying or seizing them, or seeking to jeopardize a national resources.

3. Terrorist offence

Any offence or attempted offence committed in furtherance of a terrorist objective in any of the Contracting States, or against their nationals, property or interests, that is punishable by their domestic law. The offences stipulated in the following conventions, except where conventions have not been ratified by Contracting States or where offences have been excluded by their legislation, shall also be regarded as terrorist offences:

(a) The Tokyo Convention on offences and Certain Other Acts Committed on Board Aircraft, of 14 September 1963;

(b) The Hague Convention for the Suppression of Unlawful Seizure of Aircraft, of 16 December 1970;

(c) The Montreal Convention for the Suppression of Unlawful Acts against the Safety of Civil Aviation, of 23 September 1971, and the Protocol thereto of 10 May 1984;

(d) The Convention on the Prevention and Punishment of Crimes against Internationally Protected Persons, including Diplomatic Agents, of 14 December 1973;

(e) The International Convention against the Taking of Hostages, of 17 December 1979;

(f) The provisions of the United Nations Convention on the Law of the Sea, of 1982, relating to piracy on the high seas.

Article 2

(a) All cases of struggle by whatever means, including armed struggle, against foreign occupation and aggression for liberation and self-determination, in accordance with the principles of international law, shall not be regarded as an offence. This provision shall not apply to any act prejudicing the territorial integrity of any Arab State.

(b) None of the terrorist offences indicated in the preceding article shall be regarded as a political offence. In the application of this Convention, none of the following offences shall be regarded as a political offence, even if committed for political motives:

(i) Attacks on the kings, Heads of State or rulers of the contracting States or on their spouses and families;

(ii) Attacks on crown princes, vice-presidents, prime ministers or ministers in any of the Contracting States;

(iii) Attacks on persons enjoying diplomatic immunity, including ambassadors and diplomats serving in or accredited to the Contracting States;

(iv) Premeditated murder or theft accompanied by the use of force directed against individuals, the authorities or means of transport and communications;

(v) Acts of sabotage and destruction of public property and property assigned to a public service, even if owned by another Contracting State;

(vi) The manufacture, illicit trade in or possession of weapons, munitions or explosives, or other items that may be used to commit terrorist offences.

PART TWO
PRINCIPLES OF ARAB COOPERATION FOR THE SUPPRESSION OF TERRORISM

CHAPTER I
THE SECURITY FIELD

SECTION I
Measures for the prevention and suppression of terrorist offences:

Article 3

Contracting States undertake not to organize, finance or commit terrorist acts or to be accessories thereto in any manner whatsoever. In their commitment to the prevention and suppression of terrorist offence in accordance with their domestic laws and procedures, they shall endeavour:

I. Preventive measure:

(1) To prevent the use of their territories as a base for planning, organizing, executing, attempting or taking part in terrorist crime in any manner whatsoever. This includes the prevention of terrorists; infiltration into, or residence in their territories either as individuals or groups, receiving or giving refuge to them, training, arming, financing, or providing any facilitation to them;

(2) To cooperate and coordinate action among Contracting States, particularly neighbouring countries suffering from similar or common terrorist offences;

(3) To develop and strengthen systems for the detection of the movement, importation, exportation, stockpiling and use of weapons, munitions and explosives and of other means of aggression, murder and destruction as well as procedures for monitoring their passage through customs and across borders in order to prevent their transfer from one Contracting State to another or to third-party States other than for lawful purposes;

(4) To develop and strengthen systems concerned with surveillance procedures and the securing of borders and points of entry overland and by air in order to prevent illicit entry thereby;

(5) To strengthen mechanisms for the security and protection of eminent persons, vital installations and means of public transportation,

(6) To enhance the protection, security and safety of diplomatic and consular persons and missions and international and regional organizations accredited to Contracting Stages, in accordance with the relevant international agreements, which govern this subject;

(7) To reinforce security-related information activities and to coordinate them with those of each State in accordance with its information policy, with a view to exposing the objectives of terrorist groups and organizations, thwarting their schemes and demonstrating the danger they pose to security and stability;

(8) To establish, in each Contracting State, a database for the accumulation and analysis of information relating to terrorist elements, groups, movements and organizations and for the monitoring of developments with respect to the terrorist phenomenon and of successful experiences in counterterrorism, and to keep such information up to date and make it available to the competent authorities of Contracting States, within the limits established by the domestic laws and procedures of each State;

II. Measures of suppression

1. To arrest the perpetrators of terrorist offences and to prosecute them in accordance with national law or extradite them in accordance with the provision's of this Convention or of any bilateral treaty between the requesting State and the requested State;

2. To provide effective protection for those working in the criminal justice field;

3. To provide effective protection for sources of information concerning terrorist offences and for witnesses thereof;

4. To extend necessary assistance to victims of terrorism;

5. To establish effective cooperation between the relevant agencies and the public in countering terrorism by, *inter alia*, establishing appropriate guarantees and incentives to encourage the reporting of terrorist acts, the provision of information to assist in their investigation, and cooperation in the arrest of perpetrators.

SECTION II
Arab cooperation for the prevention and suppression of terrorist offences

Article 4

Contracting States shall cooperate for the prevention and suppression of terrorist offences, in accordance with the domestic laws and regulations of each State, as set forth hereunder:

I. Exchanging of information

1. Contracting States shall undertake to promote the exchange of information between and among them concerning:

(a) The activities and crimes of terrorist groups and of their leaders and members; their headquarters and training; the means and sources by which they are funded and armed; the types of weapons, munitions and explosives used by them; and other means of aggression, murder and destruction;

(b) The means of communication and propaganda used by terrorist groups, their modus operandi; the movements of their leaders and members; and the travel documents that they use.

2. Each contracting State shall undertake to notify any other Contracting State in an expeditious manner of the information it has concerning any terrorist offence that takes place in its territory and is intended to harm the interests of that State or of its nationals and to include in such notification statements concerning the circumstances surrounding the offence, those

who committed it, its victims, the losses occasioned by it and the devices and methods used in its perpetration, to the extent compatible with the requirements of the investigation and inquiry.

3. Contracting States shall undertake to cooperate with each other in the exchange of information for the suppression of terrorist offences and promptly to notify other Contracting States of all the information or data in their possession that may prevent the occurrence of terrorist offences in their territory, against their nationals or residents or against their interests.

4. Each Contracting State shall undertake to furnish any other Contracting State with any information or data in its possession that may:

(a) Assist in the arrest of a person or persons accused of committing a terrorist offence against the interests of that State or of being implicated in such an offence whether by aiding and abetting, collusion or incitement;

(b) Lead to the seizure of any weapons, munitions or explosives or any devices or funds used or intended for use to commit a terrorist offence.

5. Contracting States shall undertake to maintain the confidentiality of the information that they exchange among themselves and not to furnish it to any State that is not a Contracting State or any other party without the prior consent of the State that was the source of the information.

II. Investigations:

Contracting States shall undertake to promote cooperation among themselves and to provide assistance with respect to measures for the investigation and arrest of fugitives suspected or convicted of terrorist offences in accordance with the laws and regulations of each state.

III. Exchange of expertise:

1. Contracting States shall cooperate in the conduct and exchange of research studies for the suppression of terrorist offences and shall exchange expertise in the counterterrorism field.

2. Contracting States shall cooperate, within the limits of their resources, in providing all possible technical assistance for the formulation of programmes or the holding of joint training courses or training courses intended for one state or for a group of Contracting States, as required for the benefit of those working in counterterrorism with the aim of developing their scientific and practical abilities and enhancing their performance.

CHAPTER II
THE JUDICIAL FIELD

SECTION I
Extradition of Offenders

Article 5

Contracting States shall undertake to extradite those indicated for or convicted of terrorist offences whose extradition is requested by any of these states in accordance with the rules and conditions stipulated in this convention.

Article 6

Extradition shall not be permissible in any of the following circumstances:

(a) If the offence for which extradition is requested is regarded under the laws in force in the requested State as an offence of a political nature;

(b) If the offence for which extradition is requested relates solely to a dereliction of military duties;

(c) If the offence for which extradition is requested was committed in the territory of the requested contracting State, except where the offence has harmed the interests of the requesting State and its laws provide for the prosecution and punishment for such offences and where the requested State has not initiated any investigation or prosecution;

(d) If a final judgement having the force of *res judicata* has been rendered in respect of the offence in the requested Contracting State or in a third Contracting State;

(e) If, on delivery of the request for extradition, proceedings have been terminated or punishment has, under the law of the requesting State, lapsed because of the passage of time;

(f) If the offence was committed outside the territory of the requesting State by a person who is not a national of that State and the law of the requested State does not allow prosecution for the same category of offence when committed outside its territory by such a person;

(g) If the requesting State has granted amnesty to perpetrators of offences that include the offence in question;

(h) If the legal system of the requested State does not allow it to extradite its nationals. In this case, the requested State shall prosecute any such persons who commit in any of the other Contracting States a terrorist offence that is punishable in both States by deprivation of liberty for a period of at least one year or more. The nationality of the person whose extradition is sought shall be determined as at the date on which the offence in question was committed, and use shall be made in this regard of the investigation conducted by the requesting state.

Article 7

Should the person whose extradition is sought be under investigation, on trial or already convicted for another offence in the requested State, his concluded, the trial is completed or the sentence is imposed. The requested State may nevertheless extradite him on an interim basis for questioning or trial provided that he is returned to that State before serving the sentence imposed on him in the requesting State.

Article 8

For purposes of the extradition of offenders under this Convention, no account shall be taken of any difference there may be in the domestic legislation of Contracting States in the legal designation of the offence as a felony or a misdemeanour or in the penalty assigned to it, provided that it is punishable under the laws of both States by deprivation of liberty for a period of at least one year or more.

SECTION II
Judicial Delegation

Article 9

Each Contracting State may request any other Contracting State to undertake in its territory and on its behalf any judicial procedure relating to an action arising out of a terrorist offence and, in particular:

(a) To hear the testimony of witnesses and take depositions as evidence;

(b) To effect service of judicial documents;

(c) To execute searches and seizures;

(d) To examine and inspect evidence;

(e) To obtain relevant documents and records or certified copies thereof.

Article 10

Each of the Contracting States shall undertake to implement judicial delegations relating to terrorist offences, but such assistance may be refused in either of the two following cases:

(a) Where the request relates to an offence that is subject to investigation or prosecution in the requested State;

(b) Where granting the request might be prejudicial to the sovereignty, security or public order of the requested State.

Article 11

The request for judicial delegation shall be granted promptly in accordance with the provisions of the domestic law of the requested State. The latter may postpone the execution of the request until such time as any ongoing investigation or prosecution involving the same matter are completed or any compelling reasons for postponement cease to exist, provided that the requesting State is notified of such postponement.

Article 12

(a) A measure that is undertaken by means of a judicial delegation, in accordance with the provisions of this Conventions, shall have the same legal effect as if it had been taken by the competent authority of the requesting State

(b) The result of implementing the judicial delegation may be used only for the purpose for which the delegation is issued.

SECTION III
Judicial cooperation

Article 13

Each contracting State shall provide the other States with all possible and necessary assistance for investigations or prosecutions relating to terrorist offences.

Article 14

(a) Where one of the Contracting States has jurisdiction to prosecute a person suspected of a terrorist offence, it may request the State in which the suspect is present to take proceedings against him for that offence, subject to the agreement of that State and provided that the offence is punishable in the prosecuting State by deprivation of liberty for a period of at least one your or more. The requesting state shall, in this event, provide the requested state with all the investigation documents and evidence relating to the offence.

(b) The investigation or prosecution shall be conducted on the basis of the charge or charges made by the requesting state against the suspect, in accordance with the provisions and procedures of the law of the prosecuting state.

Article 15

The submission by the requesting state of a request for prosecution in accordance with paragraph (a) of the preceding article shall entail the suspension of the measures taken by it to pursue, investigate and prosecute the suspect whose prosecution is being requested, with the exception of those required for the purposes of the judicial cooperation and assistance, or the judicial delegation, sought by the State requested to conduct the prosecution.

Article 16

(a) The measures taken in either the requesting State or that in which the prosecution takes place shall be subject to the law of the State in which they are taken and they shall have the force accorded to them by that law.

(b) The requesting State may try or retry a person whose prosecution it has requested only if the requested State declines to prosecute him.

(c) The State requested to take proceedings shall in all cases undertake to notify the requesting State of what action it has taken with regard to the request and of the outcome of the investigation or prosecution.

Article 17

The State requested to take proceedings may take all the measures and steps established by its law with respect to the accused both before the request to take proceedings reaches it and subsequently.

Article 18

The transfer of competence for prosecution shall not prejudice the rights of the victim of the offence, who reserves the right to approach the courts of the requesting State or the prosecuting State with a view to claiming his civil-law rights as a result of the offence.

SECTION IV
Seizure of assets and proceeds derived from the offence

Article 19

(a) If it is decided to extradite the requested person, any Contracting State shall undertake to seize and hand over to the requesting State the property used and proceeds derived from or relating to the terrorist offence, whether in the possession of the person whose extradition is sought or that of a third party.

(b) Once it has been established that they relate to the terrorist offence, the items indicated in the preceding paragraph shall be surrendered even if the person to be extradited is not handed over because he has absconded or died or for any other reason.

(c) The provisions of the two preceding paragraphs shall be without prejudice to the rights of any Contracting State or of *bona fide* third parties in the property or proceeds in question.

Article 20

The State requested to hand over property and proceeds may take all the precautionary measures necessary to discharge its obligation to hand them over. It may also retain such property or proceeds on a temporary basis if they are required for pending criminal proceedings or may, for the same reason, hand them over to the requesting State on condition that they are returned.

SECTION V
Exchange of evidence

Article 21

Contracting States shall undertake to have the evidence of any terrorist offence committed in their territory against another Contracting State examined by their competent agencies, and they may seek the assistance of any other Contracting State in doing so. They shall take the necessary measures to preserve such evidence and ensure its legal validity. They alone shall examination to the State against whose interests the offence was committed, and the Contracting State or States whose assistance is sought shall not pass this information to any third party.

PART THREE
MECHANISMS FOR IMPLEMENTING COOPERATION

CHAPTER I
EXTRADITION PROCEDURES

Article 22

Requests for extradition shall be made between the competent authorities in the Contracting States directly, through their ministries of justice or the equivalent or through the diplomatic channel.

Article 23

The request for extradition shall be made in writing and shall be accompanied by the following:

(a) The original or an authenticated copy of the indictment or detention order or any other documents having the same effect and issued in accordance with the procedure laid down in the law of the requesting State;

(b) A statement of the offences for which extradition is requested, showing the time and place of their commission, their legal designation and a reference to the legal provisions applicable thereto, together with a copy of the relevant provisions;

(c) As accurate a description as possible of the person whose extradition is sought, together with any other information that may serve to establish his identity and nationality.

Article 24

1. The judicial authorities in the requesting State may apply to the requested State by any of the means of written communication for the provisional detention of the person being sought pending the presentation of the request for extradition.

2. In this case, the State from which extradition is requested may detain the person being sought on a provisional basis. If the request for extraction is not presented together with the necessary documents specified in the preceding article, the person whose extradition is being sought may not be detained for more than 30 days from the date of his arrest.

Article 25

The requesting State shall submit a request accompanied by the documents specified in article 23 of this Convention. If the requested State determines that the request is in order, its competent authorities shall grant the request in accordance with its own law and its decision shall be promptly communicated to the requesting State.

Article 36

1. In all of the cases stipulated in the two preceding articles, the period of provisional detention shall not exceed 60 days from the date of arrest.

2. During the period specified in the preceding paragraph, the possibility of provisional release is not excluded provided that the State from which extradition is requested takes any measures it considers necessary to prevent the escape of the person sought.

3. Such release shall not prevent the rearrest of the person concerned or his extradition if a request for extradition is received subsequently.

Article 27

Should the requested State consider that it requires supplementary information in order to ascertain whether the conditions stipulated in this Chapter has been met, it shall notify the requesting State accordingly and a date for the provision of such information shall be established.

Article 28

Should the requested State receive several requests for extradition from different States, either for the same offence or for different offences, it shall make its decision having regard to all the circumstances and, in particular, the possibility of subsequent extradition, the respective dates o when the requests were received, the relative seriousness of the offences and the place where the offences were committed.

CHAPTER II
PROCEDURES FOR JUDICIAL DELEGATION

Article 29

Request relating to judicial delegations shall contain the following information:

(a) The authority presenting the request;

(b) The subject of and reason for the request;

(c) An exact statement, to the extent possible, of the identity and nationality of the person concerned;

(d) A description of the offence in connection with which the request for a judicial delegation is being made, its legal designation, the penalty established for its commission, and as much information as possible on the circumstances so as to facilitate the proper functioning of the judicial delegation.

Article 30

1. The request for a judicial delegation shall be addressed by the Ministry of Justice of the requesting State to the Ministry of Justice of the requested State and shall be returned through the same channel.

2. In case of urgency, the request for a judicial delegation shall be addressed by the judicial authorities of the requesting State directly to the judicial authorities of the requested State, and a copy of the request shall be sent at the same time to the Ministry of Justice of the requested State. The request, accompanied by the documents relating to its implementation, shall be returned through the channel stipulated in the preceding paragraph.

3. The request for a judicial delegation may be sent by the judicial authorities directly to the competent authority in the requested State, and replies may be forwarded directly through this authority.

Article 31

Requests for judicial delegation and their accompanying documents must be signed and must bear the seal of the competent authority or be authenticated by it. Such documents shall be exempt from all formalities that may be required by the legislation of the requested State.

Article 32

Should an authority that receives a request for a judicial delegation not have the competence to deal with it, it shall automatically refer it to the competent authority in its State. In the event the request has been sent directly, it shall notify the requesting State in the same manner.

Article 33

Every refusal of a request for a judicial delegation must be accompanied by a statement of the grounds for such refusal.

CHAPTER III
MEASURES FOR THE PROTECTION OF WITNESSES AND EXPERTS

Article 34

If, in the estimation of a requesting State, the appearance of a witness or expert before its judicial authority is of particular importance, it shall indicate this fact in its request. The request or summons to appear shall indicate the approximate amount of the allowances and the travel and subsistence expenses and shall include an undertaking to pay them. The requested State shall invite the witness or expert to appear and shall inform the requesting State of the response.

Article 35

1. A witness or an expert who does not comply with a summons to appear shall not be subject to any penalty or coercive measure, not withstanding any contrary statement in the summons.

2. Where a witness or an expert travels to the territory of the requesting State of his own accord, he should be summoned to appear in accordance with the provisions of the domestic legislation of that State.

Article 36

1. A witness or an expert shall not be prosecuted, detained or subjected to any restrictions on his personal liberty in the territory of the requesting State in respect of any acts or convictions that preceded the person's departure from the requested State, regardless of his nationality, as long as his appearance before the judicial authorities of that State is in response to a summons.

2. No witness or expert, regardless of his nationality, who appears before the judicial authorities of a requesting State in response to a summons may be prosecuted, detained or subjected to any restriction on his personal liberty in the territory of that State in respect of any acts or convictions not specified in the summons and that preceded the person's departure from the territory of the requested State.

3. The immunity stipulated in this article shall lapse if the witness or expert sought, being free to leave, remains in the territory of the requesting State for a period of 30 consecutive days after his presence is not longer required by the judicial authorities or, having left the territory of the requesting State, has voluntarily returned.

Article 37

1. The requesting State shall take all necessary measures to protect witnesses and experts from any publicity that might endanger them, their families or their property as a result of their provision of testimony or expertise and shall, in particular, guarantee confidentiality with respect to:

(a) The date, place and means of their arrival in the requesting state;

(b) Their place of residence, their movements and the places they frequent;

(c) Their testimony and the information they provide before the competent judicial authorities.

2. The requesting State shall undertake to provide the necessary protection for the security of witnesses and experts and of members of their families that is required by their situation, the circumstances of the case in connection with which they are sought and the types of risks that can be anticipated.

Article 38

1. Where a witness or expert whose appearance, is sought by a requesting State is in custody in the requested State, he may be temporarily transferred to the location of the hearing where he is requested to provide his testimony under conditions and at times to be determined by the requested State. Such transfer may be refused if:

(a) The witness or expert in custody objects;

(b) His presence is required for criminal proceedings in the territory of the requested State;

(c) His transfer would prolong the term of his detention;

(d) There are considerations militating against his transfer.

2. The witness or expert thus transferred shall continue to be held in custody in the territory of the requesting State until such time as he is returned to the requested State unless the latter State requests that he be released.

PART FOUR
FINAL PROVISIONS

Article 39

This Convention is subject to ratification, acceptance or approval by the signatory States, and instruments of ratification, acceptance or approval shall be deposited with the General Secretariat of the League of Arab States within 30 days of the date of such ratification, acceptance or approval. The General Secretariat shall notify member States of the deposit of each such instrument and of its date.

Article 40

1. This convention shall enter into force on the thirtieth day after the date as of which instruments of ratification, acceptance or approval have been deposited by seven Arab States.

2. This Convention shall enter into force for any other Arab State only after the instrument of ratification, acceptance or approval has been deposited and 30 days have elapsed from the date of that deposit.

Article 41

No Contracting State may make any reservation that explicitly or implicitly violates the provisions of this Convention or is incompatible with its objectives.

Article 42

A contracting State may denounce this Convention only by written request addressed to the Secretary-General of the League of Arab States.

Denunciation shall take effect six months from the date the request is addressed to the Secretary-General of the League of Arab States.

The provisions of this Convention shall remain in force in respect of requests submitted before this period expires.

DONE at Cairo, this twenty-second day of April 1998, in a single copy, which shall be deposited with the General Secretariat of the League of Arab States. A certified copy shall be kept at the General Secretariat of the Council of Arab Ministers of the Interior, and certified copies shall be transmitted to each of the parties that are signatories to this Convention or that accede hereto.

In witness whereof, the Arab Ministers of the Interior and Ministers of Justice have signed this Convention on behalf of their respective states.

TREATY ON COOPERATION AMONG THE STATES MEMBERS OF THE COMMONWEALTH OF INDEPENDENT STATES IN COMBATING TERRORISM*

Done at Minsk on 4 June 1999
Entry into force 4 June 1999**

THE STATES PARTIES TO THIS TREATY, in the person of their Governments, hereinafter referred to as the Parties,

Aware of the danger posed by acts of terrorism,

Bearing in mind the instruments adopted within the United Nations and the Commonwealth of Independent States, as well as other international instruments, relating to combating the various manifestations of terrorism,

Wishing to render one another the broadest possible assistance in increasing the effectiveness of cooperation in this field,

HAVE AGREED as follows:

Article 1

For purposes of this Treaty, the terms used in it mean:

"Terrorism"—an illegal act punishable under criminal law committed for the purpose of undermining public safety, influencing decision-making by the authorities or terrorizing the population, and taking the form of:

    Violence or the threat of violence against natural or juridical persons;

    Destroying (damaging) or threatening to destroy (damage) property and other material objects so as to endanger people's lives;

---

* Translation from the Russian original provided by the United Nations Secretariat, and approved by the Executive Committee of the Commonwealth of Independent States.

** Treaties and International Agreements Online, CTIA 10846.000 (Oceana Publications, Inc. <www.oceanalaw.com>.

Causing substantial harm to property or the occurrence of other consequences dangerous to society;

Threatening the life of a statesman or public figure for the purpose of putting an end to his State or other public activity or in revenge for such activity;

Attacking a representative of a foreign State or an internationally protected staff member of an international organization, as well as the business premises or vehicles of internationally protected persons;

Other acts classified as terrorist under the national legislation of the Parties or under universally recognized international legal instruments aimed at combating terrorism;

"Technological terrorism"—the use or threat of the use of nuclear, radiological, chemical or bacteriological (biological) weapons or their components, pathogenic micro-organisms, radioactive substances or other substances harmful to human health, including the seizure, putting out of operation or destruction of nuclear, chemical or other facilities posing an increased technological and environmental danger and the utility systems of towns and other inhabited localities, if these acts are committed for the purpose of undermining public safety, terrorizing the population or influencing the decisions of the authorities in order to achieve political, mercenary or any other ends, as well as attempts to commit one of the crimes listed above for the same purposes and leading, financing or acting as the instigator, accessory or accomplice of a person who commits or attempts to commit such a crime;

"Facilities posing an increased technological and environmental danger"—enterprises, installations, plant and other facilities whose inoperability may lead to loss of human life, the impairment of human health, pollution of the environment or destabilization of the situation in a given region or a given State as a whole;

"Special anti-terrorist units"—groups of specialists formed by the Parties in accordance with their national legislation to combat acts of terrorism;

"Special items and supplies"—materials, machinery and vehicles, personal equipment for members of special anti-terrorist units including weapons and ammunition, and special items and equipment.

Article 2

The Parties shall cooperate in preventing, uncovering, halting and investigating acts of terrorism in accordance with this Treaty, their national legislation and their international obligations.

Article 3

1. Each of the Parties shall, on signing this Treaty or carrying out the domestic procedures required for its entry into force, indicate its competent authorities responsible for implementing the provisions of this Treaty.

The Parties shall immediately notify the depositary of any changes with regard to their competent authority.

2. In implementing the provisions of this Treaty, the competent authorities of the Parties shall maintain direct relations with one another.

Article 4

1. In cooperating in combating acts of terrorism, including in relation to the extradition of persons committing them, the Parties shall not regard the acts involved as other than criminal.

2. The nationality of a person accused of an act of terrorism shall be deemed to be his nationality at the time of commission of the act.

Article 5

1. The competent authorities of the Party shall, in accordance with this Treaty, other international agreements and national legislation, cooperate and assist one another by:

(a) Exchanging information;

(b) Responding to enquiries regarding the conduct of investigations;

(c) Developing and adopting agreed measures for preventing, uncovering, halting or investigating acts of terrorism, and informing one another about such measures;

(d) Adopting measures to prevent and halt preparations in their territory for the commission of acts of terrorism in the territory of another Party;

(e) Assisting in assessing the condition of the system for physical protection of facilities posing an increased technological and environmental danger, and developing and implementing measures to improve that system;

(f) Exchanging legislative texts and materials on the practice with respect to their application;

(g) Sending, by agreement between interested Parties, special anti-terrorist units to render practical assistance in halting acts of terrorism and combating their consequences;

(h) Exchanging experience on the prevention and combating of terrorist acts, including the holding of training courses, seminars, consultations and workshops;

(i) Training and further specialized training of personnel;

(j) Joint financing, by agreement between Parties, and conduct of research and development work on systems for and means of physically protecting facilities posing an increased technological and environmental danger;

(k) Implementation on a contractual basis of deliveries of special items, technology and equipment for anti-terrorist activity.

2. The procedure for sending and executing requests for extradition, for the provision of legal aid in criminal cases and for the institution of criminal proceedings shall be determined by the international agreements to which the Parties concerned are parties.

Article 6

The Parties shall, through joint consultations, jointly draw up recommendations for achieving concerted approaches to the legal regulation of issues relating to the prevention and combating of terrorist acts.

Article 7

1. Cooperation under this Treaty shall be conducted on the basis of requests by an interested Party for assistance to be rendered, or on the initiative of a Party which believes such assistance to be of interest to another Party.

2. The request for the rendering of assistance shall be made in writing. In urgent cases requests may be transmitted orally, but must be confirmed in writing not later than 72 hours thereafter, including through the use of technical text transmission facilities.

If doubt arises as to the genuineness or content of a request, additional confirmation may be requested.

Requests shall contain:

(a) The name of the competent authority requesting assistance and of the authority requested; a statement of the substance of the matter; the purpose of and justification for the request; and a description of the nature of the assistance requested;

(b) Any other information that may be useful for the proper fulfilment of the request.

3. A request for the rendering of assistance transmitted or confirmed in writing shall be signed by the head of the requesting competent authority or his deputy and shall be certified by the seal of the competent authority.

Article 8

1. The requested Party shall take all necessary measures to ensure the prompt and fullest possible fulfilment of the request.

The requesting Party shall be immediately notified of circumstances that prevent or will substantially delay the fulfilment of the request.

2. If the fulfilment of the request does not fall within the competence of the requested competent authority, it shall transmit the request to an authority of its State which is competent to fulfil it, and shall immediately so inform the requesting competent authority.

3. The requested Party shall be entitled to request additional information that is in its view needed for the proper fulfilment of the request.

4. In fulfilling a request, the legislation of the requested Party shall be applied; however, at the request of the requesting Party, its legislation may be applied if that does not contradict fundamental principles of the legislation of the requested Party or its international obligations.

5. If the requested Party considers that immediate fulfilment of the request may impede a criminal prosecution or other proceedings taking place on its territory, it may postpone fulfilment of the request or tie its fulfilment to compliance with conditions determined to be necessary following consultations with the requesting Party. If the requesting Party agrees that assistance shall be rendered to it on the proposed terms, it shall comply with those terms.

6. The requested Party shall at the request of the requesting Party take the necessary measures to ensure confidentiality of the fact that the request has been received, the content of the request and accompanying documents, and the rendering of assistance.

If it is impossible to fulfil the request without maintaining confidentiality, the requested Party shall so inform the requesting Party, which shall decide whether the request should be fulfilled under those conditions.

7. The requested Party shall inform the requesting Party as soon as possible about the results of the fulfilment of the request.

Article 9

1. The rendering of assistance under this Treaty shall be denied in whole or in part if the requested Party believes that fulfilment of the request may impair its sovereignty, security, social order or other vital interests or is in contravention of its legislation or international obligations.

2. The rendering of assistance may be denied if the act in relation to which the request was made is not a crime under the legislation of the requested Party.

3. The requesting Party shall be notified in writing of a refusal to fulfil a request in whole or in part, with an indication of the reasons for refusal listed in paragraph 1 of this Article.

Article 10

1. Each Party shall ensure confidentiality of information and documents received from another Party if they are classified as restricted or the transmitting Party considers it undesirable that they should be made public. The level of security classification of such information and documents shall be determined by the transmitting Party.

2. Results of the fulfilment of a request obtained on the basis of this Treaty may not without the consent of the Party providing them be used for purposes other than those for which they were requested and provided.

3. Transmission to a third party of information obtained by one Party on the basis of this Treaty shall require the prior consent of the Party providing the information.

Article 11

The competent authorities of the Parties shall exchange information on issues of mutual interest, including:

(a) Materials distributed in the territory of their States containing information on terrorist threats, terrorist acts in the course of preparation or committed and the identified intentions of given persons, groups of persons or organizations to commit acts of terrorism;

(b) Acts of terrorism in the course of preparation that are directed against heads of State, internationally protected persons, staff of diplomatic missions, consular institutions and international organizations of the Parties and participants in State visits and international and national political, sporting and other activities;

(c) Instances of illegal circulation of nuclear materials, chemical, bacteriological (biological) weapons or their components, highly toxic chemicals and pathogenic micro-organisms;

(d) Terrorist organizations, groups and individuals that present a threat to the State security of the Parties and the establishment of contacts between terrorist organizations, groups or individuals;

(e) Illegal armed formations employing methods of terrorist activity, their structure, members, aims and objectives;

(f) Ways, means and methods of terrorist action they have identified;

(g) Supplies and equipment that may be provided by the Parties to one another to the extent of their ability;

(h) Practice with respect to the legal and other regulatory settlement of issues related to the subject of this Treaty;

(i) Identified and presumed channels for the financing and illegal delivery to the territory of their States of weapons and other means of committing terrorist acts;

(j) Terrorist encroachments aimed at violating the sovereignty and territorial integrity of Parties;

Other issues of interest to the Parties.

Article 12

1. The Parties may, at the request or with the consent of the Party concerned, send representatives of their competent authorities, including special anti-terrorist units, to provide procedural, advisory or practical aid in accordance with this Treaty.

In such cases, the receiving Party shall notify the other Party in writing of the place and time of and procedure for crossing its State border and the nature of the problems to be dealt with, and shall promote and facilitate the necessary conditions for their effective solution, including unimpeded carriage of persons and special items and supplies and cost-free accommodation, food and use of the transport infrastructure of the receiving Party.

Any movement of a special anti-terrorist unit or of individual members of such a unit within the territory of the receiving Party shall be possible only with special permission from and under the control of the head of the competent authority of the receiving Party.

2. The procedure for the use of air, road, rail, river and maritime transport to provide aid shall be determined by the competent authorities of the Parties in agreement with the relevant ministries and departments of the receiving Party.

Article 13

1. For purposes of the effective and timely provision of aid, the Parties shall, when special anti-terrorist units cross the State border, ensure accelerated conduct of the formalities established by national legislation.

2. At the border crossing point, the commanding officer of a special anti-terrorist unit shall present the nominal role of members of the group and list of special items and supplies certified by the competent authorities of the sending Party, together with an indication of the purposes of the Unit's arrival in the territory of the receiving Party, while all members of the group shall present their national passports and documents confirming that they belong to competent authorities for combating terrorism.

3. Special items and supplies shall be exempt from customs duties and payments and must be either used during the operation for the provision of aid or removed from the territory of the receiving Party upon its conclusion.

If special circumstances make it impossible to remove the special items and supplies, the competent authorities of the sending Party shall hand them over to the competent authorities of the receiving Party.

Article 14

The decision on the procedure for conducting special measures under this Treaty shall be taken by the competent authority of the receiving Party, taking into account the views of the commanding officer of the incoming anti-terrorist unit of the other Party. If these views are not taken into account, the commanding officer shall be entitled to refuse to participate in the conduct of the special measure.

Article 15

1. The receiving Party shall refrain from any claims against a Party providing aid, including with regard to compensation for damages arising out of death, bodily injury or any other harm caused to the lives, health and property of natural persons located in the territory of the receiving Party, and also to juridical persons and the receiving Party itself, if such harm was inflicted during the performance of activities associated with the implementation of this Treaty.

2. If a participant in the special anti-terrorist unit of the sending Party inflicts harm on some person or organization while performing activities associated with the implementation of this Treaty in the territory of the receiving Party, the receiving Party shall make compensation for the harm in accordance with the provisions of national legislation which would be applied in the case of harm being inflicted by members of anti-terrorist units of the receiving Party in similar circumstances.

3. The procedure for repayment of expenses incurred by the sending Party, including expenses associated with the loss or complete or partial destruction of imported special items and supplies, shall be established by agreement between the Parties concerned.

4. If one of the Parties considers the damage caused by the actions of the special anti-terrorist unit to be disproportionate to the purposes of the operation, the differences of opinion that arise shall be settled at the bilateral level by the Parties concerned.

Article 16

For purposes of the implementation of this Treaty, the competent authorities of the Parties may where necessary hold consultations and working meetings.

Article 17

The Parties may, by mutual agreement and on the basis of separate agreements, conduct joint exercises of special anti-terrorist units and, on a reciprocal basis, organize training for representatives of another Party in their national anti-terrorist detachments.

Article 18

1. Materials, special items, technology and equipment received by the competent authorities of the Parties pursuant to this Agreement may be transferred to a third party only with the consent of and on the terms specified by the competent authority which provided such materials, special items, technology and equipment.

2. Information on the investigation methods of special anti-terrorist units and on the characteristics of special forces and of items and supplies used in providing aid under this Agreement may not be disclosed.

Article 19

The Parties concerned shall where necessary agree on the financial, organizational and technical and other conditions for the provision of assistance under this Agreement.

Article 20

1. This Treaty shall not limit the right of the Parties to conclude bilateral international agreements on issues which are the subject of this Treaty, and shall not affect the rights and obligations of Parties arising out of other international agreements to which they are parties.

2. The competent authorities of the Parties may conclude with one another agreements that regulate in more detail the procedure for implementation of this Treaty.

Article 21

Disputes arising out of the interpretation or application of this Treaty shall be resolved through consultations and negotiations between the Parties.

Article 22

This Treaty shall enter into force on the date of its signature, and for Parties whose legislation requires the completion of domestic procedures for its entry into force on the date of submission to the depositary of the relevant notification. The Parties shall notify the depositary within three months from the signature of this Treaty of the need to complete such procedures.

Article 23

This Treaty shall remain in force for five years from the date of its entry into force, and shall be automatically extended for further five-year periods unless the Parties adopt another procedure.

Each of the Parties may withdraw from this Treaty by sending written notification thereof to the depositary not less than six months prior to its withdrawal and after settling financial and other obligations that arose during the period for which this Treaty was in force.

The provisions of Article 18 of this Treaty shall continue to be applicable for a Party which withdraws from the Treaty for a further 10 years, and those of Article 10 indefinitely.

Article 24

Following the entry into force of this Treaty, it may with the consent of the Parties be acceded to by other States, including States which are not members of the Commonwealth of Independent States, by means of the transmission to the depositary of instruments of accession. Accession shall be deemed to take effect upon the expiry of 30 days from the date of receipt by the depositary of the latest notification by the Parties of consent to such accession.

Article 25

The depositary shall immediately notify the Parties of an accession to this Treaty or of the completion of domestic procedures required for its entry into force, of the date of entry into force of the Treaty and of the receipt by it of other notifications and documents.

DONE at Minsk on 4 June 1999 in one original in the Russian language. The original shall be kept in the Executive Committee of the Commonwealth of Independent States, which shall send to each State signing this Treaty a true copy thereof.

CONVENTION OF THE ORGANISATION OF THE ISLAMIC CONFERENCE ON COMBATING INTERNATIONAL TERRORISM

Adopted at Ouagadougou on 1 July 1999
Entered into force on 1 July 1999*

THE MEMBER STATES OF THE ORGANISATION OF THE ISLAMIC CONFERENCE,

Pursuant to the tenets of the tolerant Islamic Sharia which reject all forms of violence and terrorism, and in particular specially those based on extremism and call for protection of human rights, which provisions are parallelled by the principles and rules of international law founded on cooperation between peoples for the establishment of peace;

Abiding by the lofty, moral and religious principles particularly the provisions of the Islamic Sharia as well as the human heritage of the Islamic Ummah.

Adhering to the Charter of the Organisation of the Islamic Conference, its objectives and principles aimed at creating an appropriate atmosphere to strengthen cooperation and understanding among Islamic States as well as relevant OIC resolutions;

Adhering to the principles of International Law and the United Nations Charter as well as all relevant UN resolutions on procedures aimed at eliminating international terrorism, and all other conventions and international instruments to which states acceding to this Convention are parties and which call, *inter alia*, for the observance of the sovereignty, stability, territorial integrity, political independence and security of states, and non-intervention in their international affairs;

Proceeding from the rules of the Code of Conduct of the Organization of Islamic Conference for Combating International Terrorism;

---

*   Treaties and International Agreements Online, CTIA 10521.000 (Oceana Publications, Inc. <www.oceanalaw.com>.

ORGANISATION OF THE ISLAMIC CONFERENCE ON COMBATING TERRORISM

Desiring to promote cooperation among them for combating terrorist crimes that threaten the security and stability of the Islamic States and endanger their vital interests;

Being committed to combating all forms and manifestations of terrorism and eliminating its objectives and causes which target the lives and properties of people;

Confirming the legitimacy of the right of peoples to struggle against foreign occupation and colonialist and racist regimes by all means, including armed struggle to liberate their territories and attain their rights to self-determination and independence in compliance with the purposes and principles of the Charter and resolutions of the United Nations;

Believing that terrorism constitutes a gross violation of human rights, in particular the right to freedom and security, as well as an obstacle to the free functioning of institutions and socio-economic development, as it aims at destabilizing States;

Convinced that terrorism cannot be justified in any way, and that it should therefore be unambiguously condemned in all its forms and manifestations, and all its actions, means and practices, whatever its origin, causes or purposes, including direct or indirect actions of States;

Recognizing the growing links between terrorism and organized crime, including illicit trafficking in arms, narcotics, human beings and money laundering;

HAVE AGREED to conclude this Convention, calling on all Member States of the Organization of the Islamic Conference to accede to it.

PART I
Definition and General Provisions

Article 1

For the purposes of this Convention:

1. "Contracting State" or "Contracting Party" means every Member State in the Organisation of the Islamic Conference that has ratified or adhered to this Convention and deposited its instruments of ratification or adherence with the General Secretariat of the Organisation.

2. "Terrorism" means any act of violence or threat thereof notwithstanding its motives or intentions perpetrated to carry out an individual or collective criminal plan with the aim of terrorizing people or threatening to harm them or imperiling their lives, honour, freedoms, security or rights or exposing the environment or any facility or public or private property to hazards or occupying or seizing them, or endangering a national resource, or international facilities, or threatening the stability, territorial integrity, political unity or sovereignty of independent States.

3. "Terrorist Crime" means any crime executed, started or participated in to realize a terrorist objective in any of the Contracting States or against its nationals, assets or interests or foreign facilities and nationals residing in its territory punishable by its internal law.

4. Crimes stipulated in the following conventions are also considered terrorist crimes with the exception of those excluded by the legislations of Contracting States or those who have not ratified them:

a) Convention on "Offences and Other Acts Committed on Board of Aircrafts" (Tokyo, 14.9.1963).

b) Convention on "Suppression of Unlawful Seizure of Aircraft" (The Hague, 16.12.1970).

c) Convention on "Suppression of Unlawful Acts Against the Safety of Civil Aviation" signed at Montreal on 23.9.1971 and its Protocol (Montreal, 10.12.1984).

d) Convention on the "Prevention and Punishment of Crimes Against Persons Enjoying International Immunity, Including Diplomatic Agents" (New York, 14.12.1973).

e) International Convention Against the Taking of Hostages (New York, 1979).

f) The United Nations Law of the Sea Convention of 1988 and its related provisions on piracy at sea.

g) Convention on the "Physical Protection of Nuclear Material" (Vienna, 1979).

h) Protocol for the Suppression of Unlawful Acts of Violence at Airports Serving International Civil Aviation-Supplementary to the Convention for the Suppression of Unlawful Acts Against the Safety of Civil Aviation (Montreal, 1988).

i) Protocol for the Suppression of Unlawful Acts Against the Safety of Fixed Platforms on the Continental Shelf (Rome, 1988).

j) Convention for the Suppression of Unlawful Acts Against the Safety of Maritime Navigation (Rome, 1988).

k) International Convention for the Suppression of Terrorist Bombings (New York, 1997).

l) Convention on the Marking of Plastic Explosives for the purposes of Detection (Montreal, 1991)

Article 2

a. Peoples' struggle including armed struggle against foreign occupation, aggression, colonialism, and hegemony, aimed at liberation and self-determination in accordance with the principles of international law shall not be considered a terrorist crime.

b. None of the terrorist crimes mentioned in the previous article shall be considered political crimes.

c. In the implementation of the provisions of this Convention the following crimes shall not be considered political crimes even when politically motivated:

1. Aggression against kings and heads of state of Contracting States or against their spouses, their ascendants or descendants.

2. Aggression against crown princes or vice-presidents or deputy heads of government or ministers in any of the Contracting States.

3. Aggression against persons enjoying international immunity including Ambassadors and diplomats in Contracting States or in countries of accreditation.

4. Murder or robbery by force against individuals or authorities or means of transport and communications.

5. Acts of sabotage and destruction of public properties and properties geared for public services, even if belonging to another Contracting State.

6. Crimes of manufacturing, smuggling or possessing arms and ammunition or explosives or other materials prepared for committing terrorist crimes.

d. All forms of international crimes, including illegal trafficking in narcotics and human beings money laundering aimed at financing terrorist objectives shall be considered terrorist crimes.

PART II
Foundations of Islamic Cooperation for Combating Terrorism

Chapter I
In the Field of Security

Division I
Measures to Prevent and Combat Terrorist Crimes

Article 3

I. The Contracting States are committed not to execute, initiate or participate in any form in organizing or financing or committing or instigating or supporting terrorist acts whether directly or indirectly.

II. Committed to prevent and combat terrorist crimes in conformity with the provisions of this Convention and their respective domestic rules and regulations the contracting States shall see to:

(A) *Preventive Measures:*

1. Barring their territories from being used as an arena for planning, organizing, executing terrorist crimes or initiating or participating in these crimes in any form; including preventing the infiltration of terrorist elements or their gaining refuge or residence therein individually or collectively, or receiving hosting, training, arming, financing or extending any facilities to them.

2. Cooperating and coordinating with the rest of the Contracting States, particularly neighbouring countries which suffer from similar or common terrorist crimes.

3. Developing and strengthening systems relating to detecting transportation, importing, exporting stockpiling, and using of weapons, ammunition and explosives as well as other means of aggression, killing and destruction in addition to strengthening trans-border and custom controls in order to intercept their transfer from one Contracting State to another or to other States unless they are intended for specific legitimate purposes.

4. Developing and strengthening systems related to surveillance procedures, securing borders, and land, sea and air passages in order to prevent infiltration through them.

5. Strengthening systems for ensuring the safety and protection of personalities, vital installations and means of public transport.

6. Re-enforcing protection, security and safety of diplomatic and consular persons and missions; and regional and international organizations accredited in the Contracting State in accordance with the conventions and rules of international law which govern this subject.

7. Promoting security intelligence activities and coordinating them with the intelligence activities of each Contracting State pursuant to their respective intelligence policies, aimed at exposing the objectives of terrorist groups and organisations, thwarting their designs and revealing the extent of their danger to security and stability.

8. Establishing a data base by each Contracting State to collect and analyze data on terrorist elements, groups, movements and organizations and monitor developments of the phenomenon of terrorism and successful experiences in combating it. Moreover, the Contracting State shall update this information and exchange them with competent authorities in other Contracting States within the limits of the laws and regulations in every State.

(B) *Combating Measures:*

1. Arresting perpetrators of terrorists crimes and prosecuting them according to the national law or extraditing them in accordance with the

provisions of this Convention or existing Conventions between the requesting and requested States.

2. Ensuring effective protection of persons working in the field of criminal justice as well as to witnesses and investigators.

3. Ensuring effective protection of information sources and witnesses on terrorist crimes.

4. Extending necessary assistance to victims of terrorism.

5. Establishing effective cooperation between the concerned organs in the contracting States and the citizens for combating terrorism including extending appropriate guarantees and appropriate incentives to encourage informing on terrorist acts and submitting information to help uncover them and cooperating in arresting the perpetrators.

Division II
Areas of Islamic cooperation for preventing and combating terrorist crimes

Article 4

Contracting States shall cooperate among themselves to prevent and combat terrorist crimes in accordance with the respective laws and regulations of each State in the following areas:

First: Exchange of Information

1. Contracting States shall undertake to promote exchange of information among them as such regarding:

   a. Activities and crimes committed by terrorist groups, their leaders, their elements, their headquarters, training, means and sources that provide finance and weapons, types of arms, ammunition and explosives utilized as well as other ways and means to attack, kill and destroy.

   b. Means of communications and propaganda utilized by terrorist groups, how they act, movement of their leaders, their elements and their travel documents.

2. Contracting States shall expeditiously inform any other Contracting State regarding available information about any terrorist crime perpetrated in its territory aimed at undermining the interests of that State or its nationals and to state the facts surrounding the crime in terms of its circumstances, criminals involved, victims, losses, devices and methods utilized to carry out the crime, without prejudicing investigation and inquiry requisites.

3. Contracting States shall exchange information with the other Parties to combat terrorist crimes and to inform the Contracting State or other States of all available information or data that could prevent terrorist crimes within its territory or against its nationals or residents or interests.

4. The Contracting States shall provide any other Contracting State with available information or data that will:

> a. Assist in arresting those accused of committing a terrorist crime against the interests of that country or being implicated in such acts either by assistance, collusion, instigation, or financing.
>
> b. Contribute to confiscating any arms, weapons, explosives, devices or funds spent or meant to be spent to commit a terrorist crime.

5. The Contracting States undertake to respect the confidentiality of information exchanged between them and shall refrain from passing it to any non-Contracting States or other parties without prior consent of the source country.

Second: Investigation

Each Contracting State pledges to promote cooperation with other contracting states and to extend assistance in the field of investigation procedures in terms of arresting escaped suspects or those convicted for terrorist crimes in accordance with the laws and regulations of each country.

Third: Exchange of Expertise

1. Contracting States shall cooperate with each other to undertake and exchange studies and researches on combating terrorist crimes as well as exchange of expertise in this field.

2. Contracting States shall cooperate within the scope of their capabilities to provide available technical assistance for preparing programmes or holding joint training sessions with one or more Contracting State if the need arises for personnel required in the field of combating terrorism in order to improve their scientific and practical potential and upgrade their performance standards.

Fourth: Education and Information Field

The Contracting States shall cooperate in:

1. Promoting information activities and supporting the mass media in order to confront the vicious campaign against Islam, by projecting the true image of tolerance of Islam, and exposing the designs and danger of terrorist groups against the stability and security of Islamic States.

2. Including the noble human values, which proscribe the practice of terrorism in the educational curricula of Contracting States.

3. Supporting efforts aimed at keeping abreast of the age by introducing an advanced Islamic thought based on *ijtihad* by which Islam is distinguished.

Chapter II
In the Judicial Field

Section 1
Extraditing Criminals

Article 5

Contracting States shall undertake to extradite those indicted or convicted of terrorist crimes, requested for extradition by any of these countries in compliance with the rules and conditions stipulated in this Convention.

Article 6

Extradition shall not be permissible in the following cases:

1. If the Crime for which extradition is requested is deemed by the laws enforced in the requested Contracting State as one of a political nature and without prejudice to the provisions of Article 2, paragraphs 2 and 3 of this Convention for which extradition is requested.

2. If the Crime for which extradition is sought relates solely to a dereliction of military obligations.

3. If the Crime for which extradition is requested, was committed in the territory of the requested Contracting State, unless this crime has undermined the interests of the requesting Contracting State and its laws stipulate that the perpetrators of those crimes shall be prosecuted and punished providing that the requested country has not commenced investigation or trial.

4. If the Crime has been the subject of a final sentence which has the force of law in the requested Contracting State.

5. If the action at the time of the extradition request elapsed or the penalty prescribed in accordance with the law in the Contacting State requesting extradition.

6. Crimes committed outside the territory of the requesting Contracting State by a person who was not its national and the law of the requested Contracting State does not prosecute such a crime if perpetrated outside its territory by such a person.

7. If pardon was granted and included the perpetrators of these crimes in the requesting Contracting State.

8. If the legal system of the requested State does not permit extradition of its national, then it shall be obliged to prosecute whosoever commits a

terrorist crime if the act is punishable in both States by a freedom restraining sentence for a minimum period of one year or more. The nationality of the person requested for extradition shall be determined according to the date of the crime taking into account the investigation undertaken in this respect by the requesting State.

Article 7

If the person requested for extradition is under investigation or trial for another crime in the requested State, his extradition shall be postponed until the investigation is disposed of or the trial is over and the punishment implemented. In this case, the requested State shall extradite him provisionally for investigation or trial on condition that he shall be returned to it before execution of the sentence issued in the requested State.

Article 8

For the purpose of extraditing crime perpetrators according to this Convention, the domestic legislations of Contracting States shall not have any bearing as to their differences with respect to the crime being classified as a felony or misdemeanor, nor as to the penalty prescribed for it.

Section 2
Rogatory Commission

Article 9

Each Contracting State shall request from any other Contracting State to undertake in its territory rogatory action with respect to any judicial procedures concerning an action involving a terrorist crime and in particular:

1. To hear witnesses and testimonies taken as evidence.

2. To communicate legal documents.

3. To implement inquiry and detention procedures.

4. To undertake on the scene inspection and analyse evidence.

5. To obtain necessary evidence or documents or records or their certified copies.

Article 10

Each Contracting State shall implement rogatory commissions related to terrorist crimes and may reject the request for implementation with respect to the following cases:

1. If the crime for which the request is made, is the subject of a charge, investigation or trial in the country requested to implement rogatory commission.

2. If the implementation of the request prejudices the sovereignty or the security or public order of the country charged with this mission.

Article 11

The request for rogatory mission shall be implemented promptly in accordance with the provisions of the domestic laws of the requested State and which may postpone its implementation until its investigation and prosecution procedures are completed on the same subject or until the compelling reasons that called for postponement are removed. In this case the requesting State shall be informed of this postponement.

Article 12

The request for a rogatory commission related to a terrorist crime shall not be refused on the grounds of the rule of transaction confidentiality for banks and financial institutions. And in the implementation of the request the rules of the enforcing State are to be followed.

Article 13

The procedure, undertaken through rogatory commission in accordance with the provisions of this Convention, shall have the same legal effect as if it was brought before the competent authority in the State requesting rogatory commission. The results of its implementation shall only be utilized within the scope of the rogatory commission.

Section 3
Judicial Cooperation

Article 14

Each Contracting State shall extend to the other contracting parties every possible assistance as may be necessary for investigation or trial proceedings related to terrorist crimes.

Article 15

If judicial competence accrues to one of the Contracting States for the prosecution of a subject accused of a terrorist crime, this State may request the country which hosts the suspect to prosecute him for this crime subject to the host country's consent and providing the crime is punishable in that country by a freedom restraining sentence for at least one year or by a more severe sanction. In such a case the requesting State shall pass all investigation documents and evidence related to the crime to the requested State.

Investigation or trial shall be conducted on the grounds of the case or cases brought by the requesting State against the accused in accordance with the legal provisions and procedures of the country holding the trial.

Article 16

The request for trial on the basis of para (1) of the previous article, entails the suspension of procedures of prosecution, investigation and trial in the territory of the requesting State except those relating to the requisites of co-operation, assistance or rogatory commission sought by the State requested to hold the trial procedures.

Article 17

Procedures undertaken in either of the two States—the requesting State or the one where the trial is held—shall be subject to the law of the country where the procedure is executed and which shall have legal preeminence as may be stipulated in its legislation.

The requesting State shall not bring to trial or retrial the accused subject unless the requested State refuses to prosecute him.

In all cases the State requested to hold trial shall inform the requesting country of its action with respect to the request for trial and shall communicate to it the results of its investigations or trial proceedings.

Article 18

The State requested to hold trial may undertake all measures and procedures stipulated by its legislation regarding the accused both before and after the request for trial is received.

Section 4
Seized Assets and Proceeds of the Crime

Article 19

If the extradition of a subject is decided, the Contracting State shall hand over to the requesting State the assets and proceeds seized, used or related to the terrorist crime, found in the possession of the wanted subject or with a third party.

Article 20

The State requested to hand over the assets and proceeds may undertake all necessary custodial measures and procedures for the implementation of its obligation. It may also retain them provisionally if required for penal action implemented therein or hand them to the requesting State on condition that they shall be returned for the same purpose.

Section 5
Exchange of Evidence

Article 21

A Contracting State shall see to it that the evidence and effects of any terrorist crime committed on its territory against another Contracting State are examined by its competent organs and may seek assistance to that end from any other Contracting State. Moreover, it shall take every necessary step to safeguard the evidence and proof of their legal relevance. It may communicate, if requested, the result to the country whose interest were targeted by the crime. The State or States which have assisted in this case shall not pass this information to others.

PART III
Mechanism for Implementing Cooperation

Chapter I
Extradition Procedures

Article 22

The exchange of extradition requests between Contracting States shall be undertaken directly through diplomatic channels or through their Ministries of Justice or their substitute.

Article 23

A request for extradition shall be submitted in writing and shall include:

1. The original or an authenticated copy of the indictment, arrest order or any other instruments of identical weight issued in line with the conditions stipulated in the requesting State's legislation.

2. A statement of the acts for which extradition is sought specifying the dates and places, where these acts were committed and their legal implications along with reference to the legal articles under which they fall as well as a copy of these articles.

3. Description, in as much detail as possible, of the subject wanted for extradition and any other information such as to determine his identity and nationality.

Article 24

1. The judicial authorities in the requesting State may approach the requested State by any channel of written communication and seek the preventive arrest of the wanted subject pending the arrival of the extradition request.

2. In this case the requested State may effect the preventive arrest of the wanted subject. However, if the request for extradition is not submitted together with the necessary documents listed in the above article, the subject whose extradition is sought may not be detained for more than thirty days as of the day of his arrest.

Article 25

The requesting State shall send a request together with the documents listed in Article 24 of this Convention. If the requested State accepts the request as valid, its competent authorities shall implement it in accordance with its legislation and shall promptly notify the requesting State of the action undertaken.

Article 26

In all cases stipulated in the two articles above, preventive detention shall not exceed sixty days after the date of arrest.

Temporary release may be effected during the period stipulated in the previous article and the requested State shall take appropriate measures to ensure that the wanted subject does not escape.

Release shall not prevent the re-arrest of the subject and his extradition if it was requested after his release.

Article 27

If the requested State requires additional clarification to ascertain the conditions stipulated in this chapter, it shall notify the requesting State thereof and fix a date for provision of such clarifications.

Article 28

If the requested State received a number of extradition requests from various countries related to the same or diverse acts, this State shall decide upon these requests bearing in mind the circumstances and in particular the possibility of subsequent extradition, date of receiving the requests, degree of the danger of the crime and where it was committed.

Chapter II
Measures for Rogatory Commissions

Article 29

Rogatory Commission requests must specify the following:

1. The competent authority that issued the request.
2. Subject of the request and its reason.

3. The identity and nationality of the person being the subject of the rogatory commission (as may be possible).

4. Information on the crime requiring rogatory commission, its legal definition and penalty inflicted on its perpetrators along with maximum available information on its circumstances in order to ensure the efficient implementation of the rogatory commission.

Article 30

1. The request for rogatory commission shall be forwarded by the Ministry of Justice in the requesting State to the Ministry of Justice in the requested State and returned in the same way.

2. In case of expediency, the request for rogatory commission shall be directly forwarded by the judicial authorities in the requesting State to the judicial authorities in the requested State. A copy of this rogatory commission shall also be sent at the same time to the Ministry of Justice in the requested State. The rogatory commission shall be returned together with the papers concerning its implementation in the way stipulated in the previous item.

3. The request for rogatory commission may be forwarded directly from the judicial authorities to the competent authority in the requested country. Answers may be sent directly through the said authority.

Article 31

Requests for rogatory commission and accompanying documents shall be signed or stamped with the seal of a competent authority or that authorized by it. These documents shall be exempted from all formal procedures that could be required by the legislation of the requested State.

Article 32

If the authority that received the request for rogatory commission was not competent enough to deal with it, it shall automatically transfer it to the competent authority in its country. If the request is forwarded directly the answer shall reach the requesting State in the same manner.

Article 33

Any refusal for rogatory commission shall be explained.

Chapter III
Measures for Protecting Witnesses and Experts

Article 34

If the requesting State deems that the appearance of the witness or expert before its judicial authorities is of special importance, reference thereto shall be made in its request. The request or summons shall include an approximate statement in terms of compensation, travel expenses, accommodation and commitment to make these payments. The requested State shall invite the witness or expert and inform the requesting State about his/her reply.

Article 35

1. No penalty nor coercive measure may be inflicted upon the witness or expert who does not comply with the summons even if the writ provides for such a penalty.

2. If the witness or expert arrives voluntarily to the territory of the requesting State, he shall be summoned according to the provisions of the internal legislation of this State.

Article 36

1. A witness or expert may not be subjected to trial, detained or have his freedom restricted in the territory of the requesting State, for acts or court rulings that preceded his departure for the requesting State, irrespective of his nationality, as long as his appearance before the judicial authorities of the said State is based on a summons.

2. No witness or expert, whatever his nationality, appearing before the judiciary of the State in question on the basis of a summons, may be prosecuted or detained or have his freedom restricted in any way on the requesting State's territory for other acts or court decisions not mentioned in the summons and predating his departure from the State from which he is requested.

3. The immunity privileges stated in this Article shall become invalid if a witness or expert remains on the requesting State's territories for over thirty consecutive days despite his ability to return once his presence was no longer requested by the judiciary, or if he returns to the requesting State's territories after his departure.

Article 37

1. The requesting State shall undertake all necessary measures to ensure the protection of a witness or expert from publicity that could endanger him, his family or his property as a result of his testimony and in particular:

   a) To ensure confidentiality of the date and place of his arrival as well as the means involved.

   b) To ensure confidentiality of his accommodation, movements and locations where he may be found.

   c) To ensure confidentiality of the testimony and information given to the competent judicial authorities.

2. The requesting State shall provide necessary security required by the condition of the witness or expert and of his family, and circumstances of the case and types of expected risks.

Article 38

1. If the witness or expert who is summoned to the requesting State is imprisoned in the requested State, he shall be provisionally transferred to the location of the hearing at which he is to testify according to conditions and times determined by the requested State.

Transfer may be denied:

    a. If the witness or expert refuses.

    b. If his presence is necessary for undertaking criminal procedures in the territory of the requested State.

    c. If his transfer would prolong his imprisonment.

    d. If there are considerations militating against his transfer.

2. The transferred witness or expert shall remain in detention in the territory of the requesting State until he is repatriated to the requested Tate unless the latter requests his release.

PART IV
Final Provisions

Article 39

This Convention shall be ratified, or adhered to, by the Signatory States and the instruments of ratification or accession shall be deposited with the General Secretariat of the Organisation of the Islamic Conference not exceeding a period of thirty days as of the date of ratification or accession. The General Secretariat shall inform all Member States about any deposition and date of such instruments.

Article 40

1. This Convention shall enter into force thirty days after the deposit of the seventh instrument of ratification or accession at the OIC General Secretariat.

2. This Convention shall not be applicable to any other Islamic State until it deposits its instruments of ratification or accession with the General Secretariat of the Organisation of the Islamic Conference and after a period of thirty days of the date of deposition.

Article 41

It is not permissible for any Contracting State to make any reservation, explicitly or implicitly in conflict with the provisions of this Convention or deviating from its objectives.

Article 42

1. A Contracting State shall not withdraw from this Convention except by a written request to the Secretary General of the Organization of the Islamic Conference.

2. Withdrawal shall be affective six months after the date of sending the request to the Secretary General.

This Convention has been written in English, Arabic and French of equal authenticity, of one original deposited with the General Secretariat of the Organization of the Islamic Conference which shall have it registered at the United Nations Organization, in accordance with the provisions of Article 102 of its Charter. The General Secretariat shall communicate approved copies thereof to the Member States of the Organization of the Islamic Conference.

INTER-AMERICAN CONVENTION AGAINST TERRORISM

Adopted at Bridgetown on 3 June 2002*

THE STATES PARTIES TO THIS CONVENTION,

BEARING IN MIND the purposes and principles of the Charter of the Organization of American States and the Charter of the United Nations;

CONSIDERING that terrorism represents a serious threat to democratic values and to international peace and security and is a cause of profound concern to all member states;

REAFFIRMING the need to adopt effective steps in the inter-American system to prevent, punish, and eliminate terrorism through the broadest cooperation;

RECOGNIZING that the serious economic harm to states which may result from terrorist acts is one of the factors that underscore the need for cooperation and the urgency of efforts to eradicate terrorism;

REAFFIRMING the commitment of the states to prevent, combat, punish, and eliminate terrorism; and

BEARING IN MIND resolution RC.23/RES. 1/01 rev. 1 corr. 1, "Strengthening Hemispheric Cooperation to Prevent, Combat, and Eliminate Terrorism," adopted at the Twenty-third Meeting of Consultation of Ministers of Foreign Affairs.

---

* Treaties and International Agreements Online, CTIA 10221.000 (Oceana Publications, Inc. <www.oceanalaw.com>.

HAVE AGREED TO THE FOLLOWING:

Article 1
Object and purposes

The purposes of this Convention are to prevent, punish, and eliminate terrorism. To that end, the states parties agree to adopt the necessary measures and to strengthen cooperation among them, in accordance with the terms of this Convention.

Article 2
Applicable international instruments

1. For the purposes of this Convention, "offenses" means the offenses established in the international instruments listed below:

a. Convention for the Suppression of Unlawful Seizure of Aircraft, signed at The Hague on December 16, 1970.

b. Convention for the Suppression of Unlawful Acts against the Safety of Civil Aviation, signed at Montreal on September 23, 1971.

c. Convention on the Prevention and Punishment of Crimes against Internationally Protected Persons, including Diplomatic Agents, adopted by the General Assembly of the United Nations on December 14, 1973.

d. International Convention against the Taking of Hostages, adopted by the General Assembly of the United Nations on December 17, 1979.

e. Convention on the Physical Protection of Nuclear Material, signed at Vienna on March 3, 1980.

f. Protocol on the Suppression of Unlawful Acts of Violence at Airports Serving International Civil Aviation, supplementary to the Convention for the Suppression of Unlawful Acts against the Safety of Civil Aviation, signed at Montreal on February 24, 1988.

g. Convention for the Suppression of Unlawful Acts against the Safety of Maritime Navigation, done at Rome on March 10, 1988.

h. Protocol for the Suppression of Unlawful Acts against the Safety of Fixed Platforms Located on the Continental Shelf, done at Rome on March 10, 1988.

i. International Convention for the Suppression of Terrorist Bombings, adopted by the General Assembly of the United Nations on December 15, 1997.

j. International Convention for the Suppression of the Financing of Terrorism, adopted by the General Assembly of the United Nations on December 9, 1999.

2. Upon depositing its instrument of ratification to this Convention, a state party that is not a party to one or more of the international instruments

listed in paragraph 1 of this article may declare that, in application of this Convention to such state party, that particular instrument shall be deemed not to be included in that paragraph. The declaration shall cease to have effect as soon as that instrument enters into force for that state party, which shall notify the depositary of this fact.

3. When a state party ceases to be a party to one of the international instruments listed in paragraph 1 of this article, it may make a declaration, as provided in paragraph 2 of this article, with respect to that instrument.

Article 3
Domestic measures

Each state party, in accordance with the provisions of its constitution, shall endeavor to become a party to the international instruments listed in Article 2 to which it is not yet a party and to adopt the necessary measures to effectively implement such instruments, including establishing, in its domestic legislation, penalties for the offenses described therein.

Article 4
Measures to prevent, combat, and eradicate the financing of terrorism

1. Each state party, to the extent it has not already done so, shall institute a legal and regulatory regime to prevent, combat, and eradicate the financing of terrorism and for effective international cooperation with respect thereto, which shall include:

   a. A comprehensive domestic regulatory and supervisory regime for banks, other financial institutions, and other entities deemed particularly susceptible to being used for the financing of terrorist activities. This regime shall emphasize requirements for customer identification, record-keeping, and the reporting of suspicious or unusual transactions.

   b. Measures to detect and monitor movements across borders of cash, bearer negotiable instruments, and other appropriate movements of value. These measures shall be subject to safeguards to ensure proper use of information and should not impede legitimate capital movements.

   c. Measures to ensure that the competent authorities dedicated to combating the offenses established in the international instruments listed in Article 2 have the ability to cooperate and exchange information at the national and international levels within the conditions prescribed under its domestic law. To that end, each state party shall establish and maintain a financial intelligence unit to serve as a national center for the collection, analysis, and dissemination of pertinent money laundering and terrorist financing information. Each state party shall inform the Secretary General of the Organization of American States of the authority designated to be its financial intelligence unit.

2. When implementing paragraph 1 of this article, states parties shall use as guidelines the recommendations developed by specialized international and regional entities, in particular the Financial Action Task Force and, as appropriate, the Inter-American Drug Abuse Control Commission, the Caribbean Financial Action Task Force, and the South American Financial Action Task Force.

Article 5
Seizure and confiscation of funds or other assets

1. Each state party shall, in accordance with the procedures established in its domestic law, take such measures as may be necessary to provide for the identification, freezing or seizure for the purposes of possible forfeiture, and confiscation or forfeiture, of any funds or other assets constituting the proceeds of, used to facilitate, or used or intended to finance, the commission of any of the offenses established in the international instruments listed in Article 2 of this Convention.

2. The measures referred to in paragraph 1 shall apply to offenses committed both within and outside the jurisdiction of the state party.

Article 6
Predicate offenses to money laundering

1. Each state party shall take the necessary measures to ensure that its domestic penal money laundering legislation also includes as predicate offenses those offenses established in the international instruments listed in Article 2 of this Convention.

2. The money laundering predicate offenses referred to in paragraph 1 shall include those committed both within and outside the jurisdiction of the state party.

Article 7
Cooperation on border controls

1. The states parties, consistent with their respective domestic legal and administrative regimes, shall promote cooperation and the exchange of information in order to improve border and customs control measures to detect and prevent the international movement of terrorists and trafficking in arms or other materials intended to support terrorist activities.

2. In this context, they shall promote cooperation and the exchange of information to improve their controls on the issuance of travel and identity documents and to prevent their counterfeiting, forgery, or fraudulent use.

3. Such measures shall be carried out without prejudice to applicable international commitments in relation to the free movement of people and the facilitation of commerce.

Article 8
Cooperation among law enforcement authorities

The states parties shall work closely with one another, consistent with their respective domestic legal and administrative systems, to enhance the effectiveness of law enforcement action to combat the offenses established in the international instruments listed in Article 2. In this context, they shall establish and enhance, where necessary, channels of communication between their competent authorities in order to facilitate the secure and rapid exchange of information concerning all aspects of the offenses established in the international instruments listed in Article 2 of this Convention.

Article 9
Mutual legal assistance

The states parties shall afford one another the greatest measure of expeditious mutual legal assistance with respect to the prevention, investigation, and prosecution of the offenses established in the international instruments listed in Article 2 and proceedings related thereto, in accordance with applicable international agreements in force. In the absence of such agreements, states parties shall afford one another expeditious assistance in accordance with their domestic law.

Article 10
Transfer of persons in custody

1. A person who is being detained or is serving a sentence in the territory of one state party and whose presence in another state party is requested for purposes of identification, testimony, or otherwise providing assistance in obtaining evidence for the investigation or prosecution of offenses established in the international instruments listed in Article 2 may be transferred if the following conditions are met:

   a. The person freely gives his or her informed consent; and

   b. Both states agree, subject to such conditions as those states may deem appropriate.

2. For the purposes of this article:

   a. The state to which the person is transferred shall have the authority and obligation to keep the person transferred in custody, unless otherwise requested or authorized by the state from which the person was transferred.

   b. The state to which the person is transferred shall without delay implement its obligation to return the person to the custody of the state from which the person was transferred as agreed beforehand, or as otherwise agreed, by the competent authorities of both states.

c. The state to which the person is transferred shall not require the state from which the person was transferred to initiate extradition proceedings for the return of the person.

d. The person transferred shall receive, for time spent in the custody of the state to which he or she was transferred, credit toward service of the sentence being served in the state from which he or she was transferred.

3. Unless the state party from which a person is to be transferred in accordance with the present article so agrees, that person, whatever his or her nationality, shall not be prosecuted or detained or subjected to any other restriction of his or her personal liberty in the territory of the state to which that person is transferred in respect of acts or convictions prior to his or her departure from the territory of the state from which said person was transferred.

Article 11
Inapplicability of political offense exception

For the purposes of extradition or mutual legal assistance, none of the offenses established in the international instruments listed in Article 2 shall be regarded as a political offense or an offense connected with a political offense or an offense inspired by political motives. Accordingly, a request for extradition or mutual legal assistance may not be refused on the sole ground that it concerns a political offense or an offense connected with a political offense or an offense inspired by political motives.

Article 12
Denial of refugee status

Each state party shall take appropriate measures, consistent with the relevant provisions of national and international law, for the purpose of ensuring that refugee status is not granted to any person in respect of whom there are serious reasons for considering that he or she has committed an offense established in the international instruments listed in Article 2 of this Convention.

Article 13
Denial of asylum

Each state party shall take appropriate measures, consistent with the relevant provisions of national and international law, for the purpose of ensuring that asylum is not granted to any person in respect of whom there are reasonable grounds to believe that he or she has committed an offense established in the international instruments listed in Article 2 of this Convention.

Article 14
Nondiscrimination

None of the provisions of this Convention shall be interpreted as imposing an obligation to provide mutual legal assistance if the requested state party has substantial grounds for believing that the request has been made for the purpose of prosecuting or punishing a person on account of that person's race, religion, nationality, ethnic origin, or political opinion, or that compliance with the request would cause prejudice to that person's position for any of these reasons.

Article 15
Human rights

1. The measures carried out by the states parties under this Convention shall take place with full respect for the rule of law, human rights, and fundamental freedoms.

2. Nothing in this Convention shall be interpreted as affecting other rights and obligations of states and individuals under international law, in particular the Charter of the United Nations, the Charter of the Organization of American States, international humanitarian law, international human rights law, and international refugee law.

3. Any person who is taken into custody or regarding whom any other measures are taken or proceedings are carried out pursuant to this Convention shall be guaranteed fair treatment, including the enjoyment of all rights and guarantees in conformity with the law of the state in the territory of which that person is present and applicable provisions of international law.

Article 16
Training

1. The states parties shall promote technical cooperation and training programs at the national, bilateral, subregional, and regional levels and in the framework of the Organization of American States to strengthen the national institutions responsible for compliance with the obligations assumed under this Convention.

2. The states parties shall also promote, where appropriate, technical cooperation and training programs with other regional and international organizations conducting activities related to the purposes of this Convention.

Article 17
Cooperation through the Organization of American States

The states parties shall encourage the broadest cooperation within the pertinent organs of the Organization of American States, including the Inter-American Committee against Terrorism (CICTE), on matters related to the object and purposes of this Convention.

Article 18
Consultations among the parties

1. The states parties shall hold periodic meetings of consultation, as appropriate, with a view to facilitating:

   a. The full implementation of this Convention, including the consideration of issues of interest relating thereto identified by the states parties; and

   b. The exchange of information and experiences on effective means and methods to prevent, detect, investigate, and punish terrorism.

2. The Secretary General shall convene a meeting of consultation of the states parties after receiving the 10th instrument of ratification. Without prejudice to this, the states parties may hold consultations as they consider appropriate.

3. The states parties may request the pertinent organs of the Organization of American States, including CICTE, to facilitate the consultations referred to in the previous paragraphs and to provide other forms of assistance with respect to the implementation of this Convention.

Article 19
Exercise of jurisdiction

Nothing in this Convention entitles a state party to undertake in the territory of another state party the exercise of jurisdiction or performance of functions that are exclusively reserved to the authorities of that other state party by its domestic law.

Article 20
Depositary

The original instrument of this Convention, the English, French, Portuguese, and Spanish texts of which are equally authentic, shall be deposited with the General Secretariat of the Organization of American States.

Article 21
Signature and ratification

1. This Convention is open for signature by all member states of the Organization of American States.

2. This Convention is subject to ratification by the signatory states in accordance with their respective constitutional procedures. The instruments of ratification shall be deposited with the General Secretariat of the Organization of American States.

Article 22
Entry into force

1. This Convention shall enter into force on the 30th day following the date of deposit of the sixth instrument of ratification of the Convention with the General Secretariat of the Organization of American States.

2. For each state ratifying the Convention after deposit of the sixth instrument of ratification, the Convention shall enter into force on the 30th day following the deposit by such state of its instrument of ratification.

Article 23
Denunciation

1. Any state party may denounce this Convention by written notification to the Secretary General of the Organization of American States. Denunciation shall take effect one year following the date on which notification is received by the Secretary General of the Organization.

2. Such denunciation shall not affect any requests for information or assistance made during the time the Convention is in force for the denouncing state.

Parties:

- Antigua & Barbuda
- Argentina
- Bahamas
- Barbados
- Belize
- Bolivia
- Brasil
- Canada
- Chile
- Colombia
- Costa Rica
- Dominica
- Ecuador
- El Salvador
- Grenada
- Guatemala
- Guyana
- Haití
- Honduras
- Jamaica
- México
- Nicaragua
- Panamá
- Paraguay
- Perú
- República Dominicana
- San Kitts & Nevis
- Santa Lucia
- St. Vicente & Grenadines
- Suriname
- Trinidad & Tobago
- United States
- Uruguay
- Venezuela

INTER-AMERICAN CONVENTION AGAINST TERRORISM

MESSAGE FROM THE PRESIDENT OF THE UNITED STATES
TRANSMITTING
INTER-AMERICAN CONVENTION AGAINST TERRORISM
("CONVENTION")
ADOPTED AT THE THIRTY-SECOND REGULAR SESSION OF THE
GENERAL ASSEMBLY OF THE ORGANIZATION OF AMERICAN
STATES ("OAS") MEETING IN BRIDGETOWN, BARBADOS, AND
SIGNED BY THIRTY COUNTRIES, INCLUDING THE UNITED
STATES, ON JUNE 3, 2002

LETTER OF TRANSMITTAL

THE WHITE HOUSE, *November 12, 2002.*

To the Senate of the United States:

With a view to receiving the advice and consent of the Senate to ratification, I transmit herewith, the Inter-American Convention Against Terrorism, adopted at the Thirty-Second Regular Session of the OAS General Assembly meeting in Bridgetown, Barbados, on June 3, 2002, and opened for signature on that date. At that time it was signed by 30 of the 33 members attending the meeting, including the United States. It has subsequently been signed by another two member states, leaving only two states that have not yet signed. In addition, I transmit herewith, for the information of the Senate, the report of the Department of State.

The negotiation of the Interior-American Convention Against Terrorism (the "Convention") was a direct response to the terrorist attacks on the United States on September 11, 2001. At that time, the OAS was meeting in Lima, Peru, to adopt a Democratic Charter uniting all 34 democracies in the hemisphere. The OAS member states expressed their strong commitment to assist the United States in preventing such incidents from occurring again anywhere in our hemisphere. Within 10 days, the foreign ministers of the OAS member states, meeting in Washington, D.C., endorsed the idea of drafting a regional convention against terrorism. Argentina, Peru, Chile, and Mexico played particularly important roles in the development and negotiation of the Convention.

The Convention will advance important United States Government interests and enhance hemispheric security by improving regional cooperation in the fight against terrorism. The forms of enhanced cooperation include exchanges of information, exchanges of experience and training, technical cooperation, and mutual legal assistance. The convention is consistent with, and builds upon previous counterterrorism instruments and U.N. Security Council Resolution 1373, which mandates certain measures to combat terrorism.

The Convention provides for regional use of a variety of legal tools that have proven effective against terrorism and transnational organized crime in recent years. Since fighting terrorist financing has been identified as an essential part of the fight against terrorism, the Convention addresses crucial financial regulatory, as well as criminal law, aspects. Existing Federal authority is sufficient to discharge the obligations of the united States under this Convention, and therefore no implementing legislation will be required.

In particular, the Convention mandates the establishment of financial intelligence units for the collection, analysis, and dissemination of terrorist financing information and the establishment and enhancement of channels of communication between law enforcement authorities for secure and rapid exchange of information concerning all aspects of terrorist offenses; the exchange of information to improve border and customs control measures to detect and prevent movement of terrorists and terrorist-related materials; and technical cooperation and training programs.

The Convention also provides measures relating to the denial of refugee or asylum status. In addition, the Convention provides that terrorist acts may not be considered "political" offenses for which extradition or mutual legal assistance requests can be denied, and provides for other mechanisms to facilitate mutual legal assistance in criminal matters.

In sum, the Convention is in the interests of the United States and represents an important step in the fight against terrorism. I therefore recommend that the Senate give prompt and favorable consideration to the Convention, subject to the understanding that are described in the accompanying report of the Department of State, and give its advice and consent to ratification.

GEORGE W. BUSH.

INTER-AMERICAN CONVENTION AGAINST TERRORISM

LETTER OF SUBMITTAL

DEPARTMENT OF STATE,
Washington, October 7, 2002.

The PRESIDENT,
The White House.

THE PRESIDENT: I have the honor to submit to you the Inter-American Convention Against Terrorism ("Convention") adopted at the Thirty-Second Regular Session of the General Assembly of the Organization of American States ("OAS") meeting in Bridgetown, Barbados, and signed by thirty countries, including the United States, on June 3, 2002. It has been signed by two additional countries since that date. The Convention will enter into force on the thirtieth day following the date of deposit of the sixth instrument of ratification.

Introduction

The Convention reflects the rapid response of the Western Hemisphere to the September 11, 2001 attacks on the United States, as well as the outstanding solidarity among the other member states of the Hemisphere with the United States and the global coalition against terrorism.

The purpose of the Convention is to promote the prevention, punishment, and elimination of terrorism. The States Parties agree to adopt specified measures and to strengthen cooperation among themselves in furtherance of that purpose. The Convention will advance important U.S. Government interests and enhance hemispheric security by improving regional cooperation in the fight against terrorism. The forms of enhanced cooperation include exchanges of information, exchanges of experience and training, technical cooperation, and mutual legal assistance. Existing federal authority is sufficient to discharge the obligations of the United States under this Convention, and therefore no implementing legislation will be required.

Background Information

The Inter-American Convention Against Terrorism was negotiated pursuant to a mandate adopted at the Organization of American States (OAS) Foreign Ministers' meeting of consultation of September 21, 2001. The negotiations were a direct response to the attacks on the United States of September 11.

The OAS, which was meeting in Lima, Peru, on September 11, 2001, to adopt the Inter-American Democratic Charter, was the first international organization to condemn the terrorist attacks on the United States. The organization expressed its strong commitment to assist the United States in preventing such incidents from occurring again anywhere in the Hemi-

INTER-AMERICAN CONVENTION AGAINST TERRORISM

sphere. This was followed by many expressions of support from leaders of the OAS member states.

Immediately upon returning to Washington, the OAS Permanent Council began to discuss ways to demonstrate regional solidarity, to enhance cooperation in the fight against terrorism, and to take concrete steps to assist the United States. This led to the September 21 meeting of OAS Foreign Ministers, who instructed the OAS to take a number of additional measure, including drafting the Convention and revitalizing the work of the Inter-American Committee Against Terrorism (CICTE) to develop practical measures that could be implemented on an urgent basis.

Prior to the beginning of the negotiations, the UN Security Council adopted resolution 1373 (September 28, 2001), which calls upon states to "work together urgently to prevent and suppress terrorist acts, including through increased cooperation and full implementation of the relevant international conventions relating to terrorism," and "complement international cooperation by taking additional measures to prevent and suppress, in their territories through all lawful means, the financing and preparation of any acts of terrorism."

Three negotiating rounds were held, all at the OAS Headquarters in Washington: November 26–28, 2001; January 22–25, 2002; and March 18–21, 2002. Almost all of the thirty-four member states of the OAS participated in one or more of these rounds and in the inter-sessional discussions.

Essential Elements of the Convention

The Convention is designed to build upon the multilateral and bilateral instruments already in force and to which the United States is a Party by enhancing cooperation in preventing, punishing, and eradicating terrorism. It does so by elaborating for regional use a variety of legal tools that have proven effective against terrorism and transnational organized crime in recent years.

Following the model of the 1999 International Convention for the Suppression of the Financing of Terrorism, the Convention incorporates by reference the offenses set forth in ten counterterrorism instruments listed in paragraph 1 of Article 2 of the Convention. Negotiators chose this approach because of the breadth of converge already provided by these prior instruments (all crimes ordinarily recognized as terrorism-related offenses are covered, including hijackings, bombings, attacks on diplomats, and the financing of terrorism and the OAS's desire to respond rapidly to the events of September 11 and the continuing threat of terrorism in the region.

All Parties are required under the Convention to "endeavor to become a party" to the ten prior instruments (the United States is already a Party to all of the instruments). In addition to facilitating implementation of the Convention, this obligation also advances implementation of UNSCR 1373, which "calls upon" states to become Parties to these same instruments "as soon as possible." Thus, we would hope that all Parties to the Convention will have become Parties to those instruments by the time they deposit their instruments of ratification for this Convention.

However, so as not to delay a state from becoming a Party to this Convention, and in order to preserve the prerogatives of the legislative bodies in becoming Parties to the instruments listed in the Convention, the Convention provides that a state may declare that the obligations contained in the Convention do not apply to the offenses set forth in any one of the counterterrorism instruments listed in Article 2 if it is not yet a Party to that instrument or if it ceases to be a Party. This procedure provides a high degree of flexibility for states that are considering becoming Parties to this Convention, without undermining the U.S. interest in having all states become Parties to all of the other international instruments relating to terrorism.

In addition to incorporating the offenses from prior counterterrorism instruments, the Convention adopts elements from prior conventions and initiatives, in some cases expanding the scope of these elements and in other cases converting voluntary measures into legally binding ones. For example, Article 11 of the Convention prohibits Parties from denying extradition or mutual legal assistance requests on the sole ground that an offense covered by the Convention is or concerns a political offense. This provision appears in the more recent counterterrorism instruments and, by incorporating it into the Convention, its scope will be expanded to include offenses set forth in prior conventions and protocols as well.

Another example is the Convention's requirement in paragraph 1 of Article 4 that Parties institute a legal and regulatory regime to prevent, combat, and eradicate the financing of terrorism. A similar requirement can be found in UNSCR 1373, but the Convention goes further by requiring that the regime include specific elements drawn from the forty recommendations of the Financial Action Task Force on Money Laundering (FATF), an inter-governmental body whose purpose is to develop and promote policies to combat money laundering. In fulfillment of one of its requirements, the United States will notify the OAS Secretary General, upon the deposit of its instruments of ratification, the national authority designated to be its financial intelligence unit.

In addition, paragraph 2 of Article 4 of the Convention mandates that, when establishing their legal and regulatory regimes, Parties must use as "guidelines" the recommendations developed by specialized international and regional entities, in particular the FATF and, as appropriate, the Inter-American Drug Abuse Control Commission, the Caribbean Financial Action Task Force, and the South American Financial Action Task Force, which are likewise intergovernmental bodies that develop policies relating to money laundering within their respective areas. Because the recommendations of these entities can change over time, the Convention requires that Parties use the recommendations of FATF, as well as the recommendations of the other entities, as "guidelines" in implementing paragraph 1 of Article 4, rather than requiring that the Parties implement all of those recommendations in full.

Other measures incorporated into the Convention include: expanding the basis for seizure and forfeiture of funds and other assets; expansion of predicate offenses for money laundering; enhancing cooperation on border controls and among law enforcement authorities; establishment of a mechanism for transferring persons in custody for identification, testimony or other types of assistance; and denial of refugee status in cases where there are serious reasons for considering that the person has committed an offense covered by the Convention.

The Convention facilitates the implementation of many of the mandatory measures called for in UNSCR 1373 by establishing mechanisms for cooperation in the region, and by mandating that Parties take specific, concrete steps that will advance their implementation of the more general measures set forth in that resolution. Those measures include: freezing funds or assets that are used in or form the proceeds of terrorist offenses; measures relating to the denial of refugee or asylum status; affording other Parties the greatest measure of assistance in connection with criminal investigations or criminal proceedings relating to terrorist acts; and detecting and preventing the movement of terrorists and terrorist groups by effective border controls and controls on the issuance of travel and identity documents.

Article 10 establishes a procedure whereby persons in custody may be transferred to another party for the purpose of providing assistance in obtaining evidence for the investigation or prosecution of any of the listed offenses. Under this Article, the transfer would take place with the persons' consent and the agreement of the states sending and receiving the person. This provision is found in most modern U.S. mutual legal assistance treaties and in prior conventions relating to terrorism, in particular the 1997 International Convention on the Suppression of Terrorist Bombings and the 1999 International Convention on the Suppression of the Financing of Terrorism. As in those other legal instruments, it is not meant to be the exclusive means of transferring persons in custody but rather creates one possible modality for such transfers. While implicit, it may be useful in the context of the Convention to underscore this point, and I therefore recommend that the following understanding be included in the United States instrument of ratification:

The United States of America understands that, as in other treaties with such provisions, nothing in Article 10 or in this Convention precludes the involuntary transfer of persons pursuant to applicable domestic or international law.

Article 15 confirms that the Convention's implementation will take place with full respect for the rule of law, human rights, and fundamental freedoms. In addition, "international humanitarian law" is included among the other rights and obligations of states and individuals under international law that are not affected by this Convention. In this respect, the term "international humanitarian law" is used in this Convention in the same context as it is used in the 1999 International Convention on the Suppression of the Financing of Terrorism and the 1997 International Convention on the Suppression of Terrorist Bombings. This term is not used by United States armed forces and could be subject to varied interpretations.

As was the case for those two earlier instruments, it is the United States' intention, in the context of this Convention, to interpret the term consistently with our understanding of the term "law of war." To confirm the U.S. understanding on this point, I recommend that the following understanding to Article 15, paragraph 2, be included in the United States instrument of ratification:

The United States of America understands that the term "international humanitarian law" in paragraph 2 of Article 15 of the Convention has the same substantive meaning as the term "law of war."

Recent precedents exist for the conclusion of law enforcement-related treaties within the OAS framework. For example, the Inter-American Convention Against Corruption done at Caracas on March 29, 1996, was signed by the United States on June 2, 1996, and that Convention entered into force for the United States on October 29, 2000. The United States also signed the Inter-American Convention on Mutual Assistance in Criminal Matters done at Nassau on May 23, 1992, and a related Optional Protocol done at Managua on June 11, 1993, on January 10, 1995, and that Convention and its Optional Protocol entered into force for the United States on June 24, 2001.

Conclusion

Accompanying this Report is an article-by-article analysis of the Convention.

I believe that this Convention, by enhancing regional cooperation in the fight against terrorism, will enhance the security of the Western Hemisphere and the national security of the United States. I therefore recommend that the Convention be submitted to the Senate for its advice and consent to ratification subject to the understandings described herein at the earliest possible date. The Departments of Justice and Treasury join me in urging rapid ratification of the Convention.

Respectfully submitted,

COLIN L. POWELL.

Enclosure: As stated.

INTER-AMERICAN CONVENTION AGAINST TERRORISM

ARTICLE-BY-ARTICLE ANALYSIS OF THE CONVENTION TEXT
SUMMARY OF PROVISIONS

The Convention consists of a Preamble and twenty-three articles. Among the substantive articles are three articles on international cooperation against the financing of terrorism, seven articles on other types of international cooperation, three articles relating to denial of safe haven for suspected terrorists, an article on non-discrimination, and an article on protection of human rights.

Object and Purposes: Article 1 defines the purposes of the Convention as the prevention, punishment, and elimination of terrorism. The Parties commit to adopt the necessary measures and to strengthen cooperation among themselves, in accordance with the terms of the Convention.

Applicable International Instruments: The term "offenses" is used in a number of articles (Articles 4, 5, 6, 9, 10, 11, 12, and 13). Under Article 2, the term is defined to mean the offenses described in one or more of the ten international instruments relating to terrorism listed in paragraph 1 of that Article (hereinafter "listed offenses"). [FN: There are 12 UN conventions and protocols on terrorism. Following the practice adopted in the 1999 Terrorism Financing Convention, only 10 of the instruments are listed in this Convention. The 1963 Tokyo Convention on Offenses and Certain Other Acts Committed on Board Aircraft was omitted as being unnecessary in view of the more recent 1970 Hague Convention and 1971 Montreal Convention on terrorism related to aircraft. The 1991 Convention on the Marking of Plastic Explosives was omitted because it does not set forth a criminal offense.] Since it was anticipated that not all states would be Party to all ten instruments at the time of becoming Party to the Convention, Article 2 contains a mechanism for a State Party to this Convention that is not a Party to one or more of the listed international instruments to declare that the obligations contained in the Convention do not apply to the offenses set forth in any of the listed instruments if it is not yet a Party to that instrument. These provisions follow the model of the International Convention for the Suppression of Financing of Terrorism done at New York on December 9, 1999 ("Terrorism Financing Convention").

Domestic Measures: Article 3 calls upon all Parties to "endeavor" to become Parties to all ten of the instruments listed in paragraph 1 of Article 2 and to adopt the necessary measures to implement them effectively. Some delegations proposed during the negotiations to make this provision mandatory but a number of states responded that such an obligation could be read by legislatures as taking away or diminishing their involvement or prerogative in the process of becoming Parties to the ten listed instruments. A similar provision appears in paragraph 3(d) of UN Security Council Resolution 1373 (2001) ("UNSCR 1373").

Measures To Prevent, Combat, and Eradicate Financing of Terrorism: Article 4 commits each Party, to the extent that it has not already done so, to institute a legal and regulatory regime to prevent, combat, and eradicate the financing of terrorism and for effective international cooperation in that area, which includes:

- A comprehensive domestic regulatory and supervisory regime for banks and other financial institutions and other entities deemed to be susceptible to being used for the financing of terrorist activities;
- Measures to detect and monitor the movement across borders of cash, bearer negotiable instruments, and other appropriate movements of value; and
- Measures to ensure that the competent authorities have the ability to cooperate and exchange information at the national and international levels, including the establishment and maintenance of a financial intelligence unit.

These provisions are similar to provisions in the Terrorism Financing Convention and UNSCR 1373. When establishing and implementing these financial control measures, the Parties agree to use as guidelines the recommendations developed by specialized international and regional entities, in particular the Financial Action Task Force on Money Laundering (FATF) and, as appropriate, other regional entities. However, because the recommendations of these entities can change over time, the requirement is that the Parties use the recommendations of these entities as "guidelines" rather than that the Parties implement all of those recommendations in full.

Seizure and Confiscation of Funds or Other Assets; Predicate Offenses to Money Laundering: Under Article 5, each Party commits, in accordance with the procedures established in its domestic law, to take necessary measures to identify, freeze or seize, and confiscate funds or assets used or intended to be used to finance terrorist acts or the proceeds resulting from, regardless of whether the offenses were committed within or outside the jurisdiction of the State Party. This obligation extends the requirement that such funds be frozen pursuant to UNSCR 1373. Under Article 6 each Party must take the necessary measures to ensure that its domestic penal money laundering legislation includes as predicate offenses the listed offenses, regardless of whether the offenses were committed within or outside the jurisdiction of the State Party.

Cooperation on Border Controls: Article 7 requires that each Party, consistent with its respective domestic legal and administrative regimes, promote cooperation and information exchange in order to improve border and customs control measures to detect and prevent intentional movement of terrorists and trafficking in arms or other materials intended to support terrorist activities. Article 7 also obligates Parties to promote cooperation and information exchange to improve controls on issuance of travel and identity documents and to prevent counterfeiting, forgery or fraudulent use. Article 7 will facilitate implementation of paragraph 2(g) of UNSCR 1373 and takes into account the recommendations of the Subcommittee on Border Controls of the Inter-American Committee Against Terrorism (CICTE) that were adopted while the Convention was under negotiation.

Cooperation Among Law Enforcement Authorities: Under Article 8, the Parties commit to work closely with each other, consistent with their respective domestic legal and administrative systems, to enhance the effectiveness of law enforcement actions to combat the listed offenses. This Article directs Parties to establish and enhance, where necessary, channels of communication to facilitate the secure and rapid exchange of information concerning all aspects of the listed offenses.

Mutual Legal Assistance: Article 9 provides that the Parties commit to afford each other the greatest measure of expeditious mutual legal assistance with respect to the prevention, investigation, and prosecution of the listed offenses and related proceedings in accordance with existing treaties or, in the absence of a treaty, in accordance with domestic law. In terms of existing treaties, the Inter-American Convention on Mutual Assistance in Criminal Matters, done at Nassau on May 23, 1992, entered into force on April 14, 1996, and for the United States, on June 24, 2001, has only seven Parties—the United States, Canada, Ecuador, Grenada, Panama, Peru, and Venezuela. Another ten states have signed that instrument (The Bahamas, Brazil, Chile, Costa Rica, El Salvador, Mexico, Nicaragua, Paraguay, Suriname, and Uruguay).

The United States has bilateral mutual legal assistance treaties in force with sixteen OAS member states: Antigua and Barbuda, Argentina, The Bahamas, Barbados, Brazil, Canada, Dominica, Grenada, Jamaica, Mexico, Panama, St. Kitts and Nevis, St. Lucia, St. Vincent and the Grenadines, Trinidad and Tobago, and Uruguay. In the absence of a treaty, assistance would be provided pursuant to the U.S. judicial assistance statute, 28 U.S.C. 1782.

Transfer of Persons in Custody: Article 10 establishes a procedure whereby persons in custody in the territory of one Party may, with that person's consent and the agreement of both the sending and receiving states, be transferred to another for the purposes of providing assistance in obtaining evidence for the investigation or prosecution of any of the listed offenses. The Article is consistent with Article 13 of the International Convention on the Suppression of Terrorist Bombings, done at New York on December 15, 1997 ("Terrorist Bombings Convention") and Article 16 of the Terrorism Financing Convention. Although such provisions appear in most modern U.S. mutual legal assistance treaties, in the area of multilateral treaties designed to counter terrorism they are a recent innovation, and this Convention enables the mechanism to be applied among the Parties with respect to the offenses established in the eight earlier UN instruments relating to terrorism, in addition to the two most recent conventions referred to above.

INTER-AMERICAN CONVENTION AGAINST TERRORISM

As in these other legal instruments, this procedure is not meant to be the exclusive means of transferring persons in custody but rather creates one possible modality for such transfers. While implicit, it is recommended that the following understanding be included in the United States instrument of ratification:

The United States of America understands that, as in other treaties with such provisions, nothing in Article 10 or in this Convention precludes the involuntary transfer of persons pursuant to applicable domestic or international law.

Inapplicability of Political Offense Exception: Article 11 provides that the listed offenses shall not be considered political offenses or offenses connected with a political offense or offenses inspired by political motives, for purposes of extradition or mutual legal assistance. This provision is identical to Article 14 of the Terrorism Financing Convention and Article 11 of the Terrorist Bombings Convention. This provision thus requires that this principle be applied to the offenses established in the UN instruments relating to terrorism that preceded the Terrorist Bombings and Terrorism Financing Conventions.

The specific consequence of the Convention's narrowing of the political offense exception for the listed offenses will vary depending on the age of the relevant bilateral U.S. extradition treaty or mutual legal assistance treaty. Generally, under modern extradition treaties concluded by the United States, the political offense exception is already precluded for all crimes covered under "prosecute or extradite" conventions and protocols relating to terrorism to which the United States and its extradition treaty partner are Parties. Older treaties generally provide fugitives the right to claim political offense but do not expressly narrow the political offense exception by reference to the conventions and protocols relating to terrorism. As between the United States and any other Party to the Convention, the political offense provisions in these older treaties will be narrowed by virtue of Article 12, even in the absence of a provision similar to those in modern extradition treaties narrowing the political offense exception.

Denial of Refugee Status and Denial of Asylum: Article 12 and 13 facilitate implementation of paragraph 3(f) of UNSCR 1373, which calls upon all Member States to "take appropriate measures in conformity with the relevant provisions of national and international law, including international standards of human rights, before granting refugee status, for the purpose of ensuring that the asylum seeker has not planned, facilitated or participated in the commission of terrorist acts."

Article 12 requires each party to take appropriate measures, consistent with the relevant provisions of national and international law, to ensure that refugee status is not granted to any person about whom there are "serious reasons" for considering that such person has committed a listed offense.

Article 13 requires each Party, along similar lines, to ensure that asylum is not granted to any person about whom there are "reasonable grounds" to believe that such person has committed a listed offense. Article 12 tracks the specific wording of Article 1.F. of the Convention relating to the Status of Refugees, done at New York on July 28, 1951, which was incorporated by reference into the Protocol relating to the Status of Refugees, done at New York on January 31, 1967, and which entered into force for the United States on November 1, 1968. Article 1.F. states that "[t]he provisions of this Convention shall not apply to any person with respect to whom there are serious reasons for considering that: (a) he has committed a serious non-political crime against peace, a war crime, or a crime against humanity, as defined in the international instruments drawn up to make provision with respect of such crimes; (b) he has committed a serious non-political crime outside of the country of refuge prior to his admission to that country as a refugee; and (c) he has been guilty of acts contrary to the purposes and principles of the United Nations." Article 13 uses different "reasonable grounds" language because of certain differences, particularly in Latin American systems, between refugee and asylum processes.

Non-Discrimination: Article 14 states that nothing in the Convention shall be interpreted as requiring a Party to provide mutual legal assistance if the requested Party has substantial grounds to believe that the request was made for the purpose of prosecuting or punishing a person on account of that person's race, religion, nationality, ethnic origin or political opinion or that compliance with the request would cause prejudice to that person's position for any of these reasons. This language is consistent with Article 15 of the Terrorism Financing Convention and Article 12 of the Terrorist Bombings Convention.

Human Rights: Article 15 is the only article in the Convention that specifically addresses human rights matters. The Article represents a significant compromise between those states, including the United States, that believed that human rights issues were adequately addressed in other instruments and need not be mentioned in a law enforcement instrument, and those states that asserted that the history of human rights abuses in Latin America necessitated a provision addressing human rights concerns.

The first paragraph of Article 15 states that the measures carried out by the Parties under this Convention must take place with full respect for the rule of law, human rights, and fundamental freedoms.

The second paragraph of Article 15, which states that nothing in this Convention shall be interpreted as affecting other rights and obligations of states and individuals under international law, is consistent with Article 21 of the Terrorism Financing Convention and Article 19 of the Terrorist Bombings Convention. The listing of the sources of the rights and obligations is more comprehensive in the Convention than in the other two instruments at the request of many delegations that sought to have references to specific subsets of international law that they believed were relevant to the Convention. The subsets of international law that were eventually agreed to included international human rights law and international refugee law; international humanitarian law was also included, just as it was in the Terrorism Financing Convention and the Terrorist Bombing Convention.

The term "international humanitarian law" is not used by United States armed forces and can be subject to varied interpretations. It is the United States' intention, in the context of this Convention, to interpret the term consistently with its understanding of the term "law of war." To confirm the U.S. understanding on this point, it is recommended that the following understanding to this paragraph be included in the United States instrument of ratification:

> The United States of America understands that the term "international humanitarian law" in paragraph 2 of Article 15 of the Convention has the same substantive meaning as the law of war.

The third paragraph of Article 15 refers to persons taken into custody, or regarding whom other measures are taken pursuant to this Convention, and provides that they shall be guaranteed fair treatment. This language is consistent with Article 17 of the Terrorism Financing Convention and Article 14 of the Terrorist Bombings Convention.

Training: Under paragraph 1 of Article 16, the Parties commit to promote technical cooperation and training at all levels and in the framework of the OAS. The United States is already providing training and other forms of assistance to a number of countries in the region and plans to encourage and facilitate such cooperation through CICTE. However, because U.S. provision of training and assistance is subject to the availability of funds, U.S. negotiators were careful to limit the legal obligation in Article 16 to the promotion of training and assistance.

Because negotiators recognized the global nature of the terrorist threat and the global response to that threat, paragraph 2 of Article 16 directs the parties to promote, where appropriate, technical cooperation and training programs with other regional and international organizations. This provision is designed to avoid duplication of effort and to ensure that limited resources are used most effectively.

Cooperation Through the OAS: Article 17 represents a compromise between those delegations that wanted no reference to CICTE at all in the Convention and those states that wanted CICTE to be established as the follow-up mechanism for the implementation of the Convention. The United States recognized the important role that CICTE could play in the implementation of the Convention and firmly supports its work. However, the United States was not prepared to establish CICTE as the permanent implementing body for the Convention due to financial and other concerns. In order to maintain maximum flexibility during implementation, Article 17 requires only that Parties "encourage" the broadest cooperation within the pertinent OAS bodies organs, including CICTE, on matters related to the object and purpose of the Convention.

Consultation Among the Parties: Article 18 requires the parties to hold periodic meetings, as appropriate, with a view to facilitating full implementation of the Convention and the exchange of information and experiences on preventing, detecting, investigating, and punishing terrorism. It states that the OAS Secretary General shall convene a meeting of consultation after the tenth state becomes a Party to the Convention, and further states that the Parties may request the OAS, including CICTE, to facilitate the consultation and to provide other forms of assistance concerning the implementation of the Convention.

Exercise of Jurisdiction: Article 19 states that nothing in this Convention entitles a Party to undertake, in the territory of another Party, the exercise of its jurisdiction or the performance of functions that are exclusively reserved to the authorities of the other state by its domestic law. This Article is similar to Article 22 of the Terrorism Financing Convention and Article 18 of the Terrorist Bombings Convention.

Final Clauses: Articles 20–23 contain the final clauses. The OAS shall serve as depositary for the Convention. Only OAS member states may become Parties to the Convention. The Convention will enter into force on the thirtieth day following the date of deposit of the sixth instrument of ratification. A Party may denounce the convention by written notification to the Secretary General of the OAS. Denunciation would take effect one year following the date the notification is received by the Secretary General. Requests for information or assistance made while the convention is in force for that denouncing state will not be affected by the denunciation.

PROPOSED INTERNATIONAL AGREEMENTS

DRAFT INTERNATIONAL CONVENTION FOR THE SUPPRESSION OF ACTS OF NUCLEAR TERRORISM*

Background: In 1996, the UN Secretary-General (UNSG) prepared a report pursuant to UN General Assembly Resolution 50/53, in which he reviewed existing international legal instruments relating to international terrorism and concluded that there was a need to elaborate international treaties or other kinds of instruments in areas not covered by existing treaties. Among the measures the UNSG proposed was preventing the use of weapons of mass destruction (WMD) by terrorists.

The draft Convention was proposed by the Russian Federation, and considered by the Legal Committee of the UN General Assembly. UN General Assembly Resolution 51/210 of 17 December 1996 established an Ad Hoc Committee to elaborate the draft Convention.

The Russian Federation, in its explanatory note on the draft Convention, noted that the 1980 Convention on the Physical Protection of Nuclear Material had a number of substantial gaps concerning countering acts of nuclear terrorism, particularly at the stage of stopping the terrorist act and eliminating its consequences. It claimed the 1980 Convention alone was not able to eliminate the danger of nuclear terrorism in all its manifestations, and therefore, the draft Convention was aimed at combating new and dangerous manifestations of terrorism, stimulating the adoption of effective preventive measures in that sphere, and establishing a reliable international legal mechanism for cooperation at all stages of combating nuclear terrorism. The Russian Federation claimed that the draft Convention was particularly significant in that it was the first international legal instrument in the area of anti-terrorist activities that was specially designed as a "pre-emptive instrument."

---

* In the process of negotiation (as of December 2002).

DRAFT INT'L CONVENTION ON SUPPRESSION OF NUCLEAR TERRORISM

As of December 2002, the draft Convention has not yet been adopted. Two outstanding issues relating to scope remain, including lack of agreement on a definition of terrorism and use of nuclear weapons by military forces (Article 4).

Among the foremost concerns related to Article 4 is a perception among some non-nuclear weapon states (NNWS) that nuclear weapon states (NWS) might regard the draft Convention as legitimizing the possible use of nuclear weapons.

On the other hand, a number of delegations have expressed their preference to focus on the draft Comprehensive Convention on International Terrorism, since progress on the definition of terrorism would have a positive impact on the draft Nuclear Terrorism Convention.

Draft Provisions: The draft Convention defines the act of nuclear terrorism as the use or threat to use nuclear material, nuclear fuel, radioactive products or waste, or any other radioactive substances with toxic, explosive, or other dangerous properties. The definition includes the use or threat to use any nuclear installations, nuclear explosive, or radiation devices in order to kill or injure persons, damage property, or the environment or to compel persons, States, or international organizations to do or to refrain from doing any act. The unauthorized receipt through fraud, theft, or forcible seizure of any nuclear material, radioactive substances, nuclear installations, or nuclear explosive devices belonging to a State Party, or demands by the threat or use of force or by other forms of intimidation for the transfer of such material would also be regarded as acts of nuclear terrorism.

The draft Convention would apply exclusively to acts by individuals, and its scope would not include the issue of the nonproliferation of nuclear weapons or nuclear threats posed by States or intergovernmental organizations.

Compliance and Enforcement: The draft Convention would obligate the Parties to cooperate in preventing or prosecuting acts of nuclear terrorism by, for instance, adopting necessary legislative and technical measures to protect nuclear material, installations and devices, and to forestall unauthorized access to them by third parties.

The draft Convention would not affect the international law provisions on States' competence to conduct investigations on vessels that were not flying their flags or in aircraft that were not registered in their territories. States Parties would help each other in prosecuting the relevant acts and, when the prosecution is completed, any nuclear material or devices would be returned to the State Party to which they belonged. (The draft is contained in document A/AC.252/L.3.)

DRAFT INT'L CONVENTION ON SUPPRESSION OF NUCLEAR TERRORISM

Developments

2002: During the February session of the Ad Hoc Committee, informal consultations focused on the outstanding issues pertaining to the draft International Convention for the Suppression of Acts of Nuclear Terrorism. In that regard, the representative of the International Atomic Energy Agency (IAEA) briefed delegations on the Agency's measures aimed at combating acts of terrorism involving nuclear materials and other radioactive materials. In its report, the Committee recommended allocating appropriate time for the continued consideration of the outstanding issues on the nuclear terrorism Convention.

On 7 October, at its 11th meeting, the Sixth Committee established a Working Group to continue to work on the elaboration of a comprehensive convention on international terrorism, and to allocate appropriate time for the continued consideration of the outstanding issues on the nuclear terrorism Convention. At the same meeting, the Committee decided to open the Working Group to all States Members of the United Nations or members of the specialized agencies or of the IAEA.

The Working Group held two meetings on 15 and 16 October. At its first meeting on 15 October, the Working Group decided to proceed with discussions in informal consultations, which were held in two stages: the first focused on the draft comprehensive convention on international terrorism, and the second on the outstanding issues pertaining to the draft International Convention For the Suppression of Acts of Nuclear Terrorism. At the second meeting, on 16 October, the coordinator of the informal consultations presented an oral report on the results of discussions on both draft conventions. The Working Group decided to recommend to the Sixth Committee that work continue with the aim of finalizing the text of a draft comprehensive convention on international terrorism and the text of a draft international convention for the suppression of acts of nuclear terrorism, building upon the work accomplished during the meetings of the Working Group.

2001: At its February meetings, the Ad Hoc Committee delegations were unable to conduct substantive work on the draft Convention. They agreed to continue consultations to resolve outstanding issues. Some delegations favored the inclusion of provisions dealing with the dumping of radioactive waste in the draft Convention.

At the October debate on measures to eliminate international terrorism in the UNGA, views were expressed on the early completion of the draft Convention.

The meeting of the Sixth Committee Working Group was scheduled to take place from 15 to 26 October. On 18 October, the Chairman of the Ad Hoc Committee noted that work on the draft Convention had largely been completed. He noted that there remained only one outstanding issue regarding the scope of the draft Convention and that this issue required resolution at the policy level.

2000: During the Ad Hoc Committee meeting in February, the States discussed the revised text of the draft Convention prepared by the Friends of the Chair. The Australian representative, Ms. Cate Steains, reported that during the inter-sessional informal consultations, the States were unable to bridge differences concerning the scope of the draft Convention and that consultations would continue on a bilateral basis. The inter-sessional consultations as well as bilateral consultations held during the meeting revealed the existence of several important problems:

- Some delegations wanted provisions of Article 4, Par. 2 regarding the protection of nuclear installations and devices to be deleted and noted that any proposals to the contrary would be unacceptable.
- Some delegations made it clear that they did not attach high priority to the adoption of the draft Convention since much of its substance was covered by the existing conventions.
- Some delegations pointed out that the difference of opinion on the scope of the draft conventions were too fundamental to be bridged.
- Some delegations insisted that the scope of the draft Convention should be extended to cover acts of State terrorism, including acts of State armed forces.
- Some advocated the inclusion of provisions related to the dumping of radioactive waste.
- Some delegations raised the question of the legality or illegality of the possession of nuclear weapons, while others claimed that this question had no bearing on the issues before the Committee and only distracted it from substantive work.

Several delegations urged the Committee to complete the draft Convention expeditiously. The participants in the end decided to continue further inter-sessional consultations for the consideration of the Sixth Committee's Working Group in September-October.

At the September-October meetings of the Working Group and the November meeting of the Sixth Committee, it was concluded that the inter-sessional consultations had not led to successful resolution of outstanding problems and that further broader consultations might be required in the pursuit of a solution that would lead to the adoption of the draft Convention. Several speakers favored the speedy completion of work on the draft Convention as well as its adoption.

In its Resolution 55/158, the UNGA called on the Ad Hoc Committee to resolve the outstanding issues relating to the elaboration of the draft Convention. The language of the resolution suggested that the consideration of the draft Comprehensive Convention on Terrorism should take priority over the resolution of outstanding differences over the draft Convention.

1999: At the March meeting of the Ad Hoc Committee, Russia urged States to adopt the draft text as soon as possible and warned that failure to agree on the draft text would send the wrong signal to the terrorist groups. Some States supported the early agreement on the draft Convention, however a number of disagreements remained, including the scope of the draft Convention, its relationship with other international legal instruments on international terrorism, the question of armed forces and armed conflicts, and the question of the legal definition of terrorism and its relationship to anti-colonial and liberation struggles.

At the September meeting of the Sixth Committee Working Group, States agreed that broader consultations were required to find an acceptable solution to the remaining issues concerning the scope of the Convention. The Working Group was informed that while there appeared to be a willingness among delegations to continue work on the draft Convention, it was determined that the time was not opportune for the convening of informal consultations during the Working Group. The Chairman appointed Ms. Cate Steains (Australia) to act as coordinator on the issue with a view to organizing open-ended informal consultations at the appropriate time.

There were neither formal nor informal discussions on the draft Convention during the 1999 Ad Hoc Committee and Working Group meetings. Their work in 1999 was dedicated entirely to the negotiation of the Convention for the Suppression of the Financing of Terrorism.

At the November meetings of the UN Sixth Committee, some speakers favored the speedy completion of the work on the draft Convention and its adoption. Concern was expressed regarding the limited progress achieved in the resolution of the outstanding issue of the scope of its application. A point was made that, taking into consideration the risks of nuclear terrorism, the outstanding issues related to the scope of the draft Convention should be resolved as soon as possible; States were called upon to enhance efforts to overcome those remaining issues. Support was expressed for the position of the Non-Aligned Movement (NAM) members in this regard, namely that the scope of the draft Convention be expanded to include the activities of State militaries. A reference was made to the need for the treaty to encompass State terrorism as well. The view was also expressed that a distinction should be drawn between the draft Convention, as well as the issues raised by the International Court of Justice (ICJ) Advisory Opinion on Nuclear Weapons, and the use and possession of nuclear weapons by the NWS.

On 9 December, the UNGA adopted Resolution 54/100 entitled "Measures to Eliminate International Terrorism," which tasked the Ad Hoc Committee with further elaborating the draft Convention, as well as commencing consideration of a comprehensive convention dealing with international terrorism.

1998: The Ad Hoc Committee turned to the discussion of the draft Convention at its second meeting in February. Addressing the meeting, the Russian Federation said that the international community must establish effective measures to counter acts of nuclear terrorism, which could threaten global peace and security and cause irreparable damage to the environment. It said that depending on the circumstances of a criminal attack, it might fall under either the scope of the draft Convention, the 1980 Physical Protection Convention, the 1997 Terrorist Bombing Convention, a combination of them, or all of them.

During the deliberations, the substance of the draft text received general support from the States, but there was uncertainty on some specific details. States pointed out the following shortcomings of the draft Convention and concerns:

- Its definitions were too broad and, at the same time, too narrow in scope.
- Its definitions should be brought into line with the language used in established international instruments.
- The draft Convention's relationship with existing legal instruments, i.e., the 1980 Physical Protection Convention, the 1996 CTBT, and the 1997 Terrorist Bombing Convention must also be examined in order to avoid possible overlap.
- The legal gaps should not necessarily be addressed by a new instrument, rather they could be better addressed by strengthening the existing legal instruments, e.g., by drafting a protocol to the 1980 Physical Protection Convention.
- Provisions regarding jurisdiction, extradition, and legal assistance, similar to those contained in the 1997 Terrorist Bombing Convention, should be incorporated into the draft Convention.
- The Ad Hoc Committee of the UN Sixth Committee would not be the most appropriate forum for the discussion of the draft Convention since the IAEA has the most competence on the issue of nuclear material.
- The draft Convention should only deal with measures to counter terrorism and not encompass provisions on the physical protection of nuclear material.
- The scope of the draft Convention should be expanded to stress counter-terrorism and punishment.
- Special attention should be given to the problems of State terrorism.

- The draft Convention could undermine the legal use of nuclear material, therefore, the definitions should be revised to specify that the acts in question were intentional and unlawful crimes.
- The coverage of the draft Convention should be extended to the broadest possible range of radioactive material, as well as nuclear facilities, explosives, and other devices, including measures to prevent unauthorized access to such material, to protect facilities from intrusion, and to develop more effective controls against illicit trafficking.

Speaking at the meeting, the IAEA Legal Advisor said that the draft Convention's definitions of "nuclear material" should be based on definitions contained in the 1963 Vienna Convention on Civil Liability for Nuclear Damage, the 1980 Physical Protection Convention, and a Draft Safety Guide on "Preventing, Detecting and Responding to Illicit Trafficking in Radioactive Materials." Speaking on the overlap between the Draft Convention and the 1980 Convention, the IAEA representative said that the overlap regarding the crimes covered, coupled with differing jurisdictional provisions, could complicate their implementation; could lead to a Party to both instruments' choosing which instrument to apply in a given case.

After the exchange of views, States identified three main points of discussion: definitions, relationship to existing instruments covering the same subject matter, and the scope of the draft Convention. The Committee carried out a first reading of substantive elements of the draft text. Upon the closure of the February meeting of the Ad Hoc Committee, States did not reach agreement on whether to create a new Convention on nuclear terrorism or amend the 1980 Physical Protection Convention. They also disagreed on the scope of the proposed Convention. Some States proposed new articles that would safeguard the inalienable right of States to use nuclear energy for peaceful purposes and exempt the military activities of States in armed conflict or in exercise of their official duties from the scope of the draft Convention. Regarding the issue of definitions, there was a general agreement that they should focus on combating terrorist acts. A number of delegations proposed additional paragraphs to the draft Convention's preamble. According to those paragraphs, the preamble would recognize the importance of a universally agreed definition of international terrorism; recall UNGA resolutions on the importance of nuclear disarmament; emphasize the responsibility of a State for the establishment, implementation, and maintenance of a physical protection system for nuclear material, devices, and installations on its territory; stress the inherent right of all States to engage in research, production, and use of nuclear energy for peaceful purposes; and recall IAEA recommendations for physical protection of radioactive materials and facilities. Some speakers voiced concern about the difficulties that might arise if the return of stolen nuclear material was obligatory, because some States were legally precluded from returning nuclear components or products. Some delegations stressed the need to take into account the role that the IAEA could play, while others felt IAEA could have more of a limited role.

On 16 September, the UN Sixth Committee established a Working Group to follow up the work on elaborating the draft Convention carried out by the Ad Hoc Committee at its February meeting. Between 28 September and 9 October, the Working Group conducted 13 meetings, during which the Group conducted informal consultations, reviewed proposals and amendments, and produced a revised text of the draft Convention.

States noted that the revised text was generally acceptable, however disagreement on certain provisions still existed, including the scope of application (European Union), activities of armed forces in armed conflict (NAM), extradition and prosecution, inclusion of nuclear Non-Proliferation Treaty (NPT) obligations (Pakistan) in the draft Convention, the number of required ratifications (22) for the entry into force (Pakistan), and the legal definition of terrorism and its relationship to anti-colonial and liberation struggles. Group discussions reflected the need to conduct considerably more work on the provisions that are specific to nuclear terrorism.

Some States expressed hope that the UNGA would be able to adopt the draft text by the end of 1998. However, others, including those belonging to the NAM, suggested that such action on the draft Convention should be delayed pending further consultations. Some States questioned the very approach the Ad Hoc Committee and the Working Group used to fulfill their mandate to establish a comprehensive legal anti-terrorism regime. They developed separate conventions concerned with different subject matter rather than a comprehensive convention on terrorism as required to combat terrorism in all its forms and manifestations.

1997: The Ad Hoc Committee was primarily concerned with considering and adopting the text of the International Convention for the Suppression of Terrorist Bombing. On 19 November, after the UN Sixth Committee approved the draft text of this Convention, it also reaffirmed, without a vote, the mandate of the Ad Hoc Committee to continue its work on the elaboration of an International Convention For the Suppression of Nuclear Terrorism with the participation of the representatives of the IAEA.

DRAFT COMPREHENSIVE CONVENTION ON INTERNATIONAL TERRORISM*

Background: During the 1990s, the UN adopted a number of fundamental documents intended to create comprehensive international standards to deal with international terrorism. The first of these, the 1994 Declaration on Measures to Eliminate International Terrorism, annexed to UNGA Resolution 49/60 encouraged Member States to urgently review the scope of the existing international legal provisions on the prevention, repression, and elimination of terrorism with the aim of ensuring that there is a comprehensive legal framework covering all aspects of the matter. Under UN auspices, States negotiated and concluded the 1997 Terrorist Bombing Convention and the 1999 Terrorist Financing Convention. The UN Sixth (Legal) Committee and the Ad Hoc Committee established pursuant to the 1996 UNGA Resolution 52/210, are currently continuing their work to that end by negotiating the draft Comprehensive Convention on International Terrorism and the draft Convention for the Suppression of Acts of Nuclear Terrorism. The history of the negotiations of the abovementioned anti-terrorism instruments has demonstrated that although States generally agree on the importance of eradicating international terrorism, there exists important disagreements on certain issues, which so far have prevented them from taking a comprehensive approach. Such differences include:

– the legal definition of terrorism;
– the relationship between terrorism and anti-colonial and national liberation movements; and
– the activities of States' armed forces in armed conflicts and in exercise of their official duties.

---

* In the process of negotiation (as of December 2002).

DRAFT CONVENTION ON INTERNATIONAL TERRORISM

Obligations: The draft Convention obligates Parties to cooperate in the prevention and punishment of acts of terrorism. The act of terrorism, or offense, is defined[1] as a person's unlawfully and intentionally causing or threatening to cause violence by means of firearms, weapons, explosives, any lethal devices or dangerous substances, which results, or is likely to result, in death or serious bodily injury to a person, a group of persons or serious damage to property whether for public use, a State or Government facility, a public transportation system or an infrastructure facility. Acts of terrorism also include such person's attempt to commit such an offense, participate as an accomplice in the commission of such an offense, or in organizing or directing others to commit such an offense, or in contributing to the commission of such an offense. A person also commits an offense if he/she commits any of the offenses defined in the following international instruments: the 1970 Convention for the Suppression of Unlawful Seizure of Aircraft, the 1971 Convention for the Suppression of Unlawful Acts against the Safety of Civil Aviation, the 1973 Convention on the Prevention and Punishment of Crimes against Internationally Protected Persons, the 1979 International Convention against the Taking of Hostages, the 1988 Convention for the Suppression of Unlawful Acts against the Safety of Maritime Navigation, the 1988 Protocol for the Suppression of Unlawful Acts against the Safety of Fixed Platforms Located on the Continental Shelf, the 1997 International Convention for the Suppression of Terrorist Bombings, as well as any Convention, global or regional, aimed at combating terrorism.

Compliance: The draft Convention requires the Parties to establish as criminal offenses under its domestic law the aforementioned offenses, which are of such a nature as to create terror, fear, or insecurity, and to make them punishable by appropriate penalties. Such offenses shall be under no circumstances justifiable by considerations of a political, philosophical, ideological, racial, ethnic, religious, or other similar nature and are punished by penalties consistent with their grave nature.

The draft Convention obligates Parties to refrain from organizing, instigating, facilitating, financing, assisting, or participating in the commission of terrorist offenses in the territories of other States, acquiescing in, encouraging, or tolerating activities within their territories directed towards the commission of such offenses; take practical measures to ensure that their respective territories are not used for terrorist installations and training camps, or for the preparation or organization of terrorist acts intended to be committed against other States or their citizens; take appropriate measures, before granting asylum, to ensure that the asylum seeker has not engaged in terrorist activities; and cooperate in preventing and punishing terrorist acts by preventing and impeding the preparation in their respective territo-

---

[1] This definition is still under discussion.

ries of such acts by exchanging information and implementing relevant international Conventions, including the harmonization of their domestic legislation with those Conventions, and conclusion of mutual judicial assistance and extradition agreements.

The Convention requires States on whose territory a person has committed, or is alleged to have committed, a terrorist act to investigate his or her involvement in the offense and, if appropriate, take such person into custody for the purpose of prosecution or extradition. The Convention provides for the inclusion of such offenses as extraditable offenses, and in case there is no extradition treaty between the Parties, entitles them to consider the Convention as a legal basis for extradition with respect to the offenses, which are its subject matter. If a Party does not extradite the person(s), it is obliged, without exception whatsoever, to prosecute him or her.

The Parties are required to establish their jurisdiction over such offenses if they are committed in their territory, on board a vessel flying their flag or aircraft registered under their laws at the time the offense is committed, if such offenses are committed by their nationals, or if the alleged offender is present in its territory and it does not extradite that person to any of the Parties that have established their jurisdiction. The Parties also may establish their jurisdiction over such offenses if they are committed against their nationals, which are committed by a stateless person residing in their territory, or which is committed in an attempt to compel them to do or to abstain from doing any act.

Developments:

2002: During the February session of the Ad Hoc Committee, delegations made rapid progress in negotiating the majority of the 27 articles of the draft Comprehensive Convention on International Terrorism and narrowed its focus to three particularly difficult articles, which constitute the traditional controversial issues at the UN, namely the definition of terrorism and its relation to liberation movements, and possible exemptions for the activities of armed forces. The Committee discussed the report of its last session, which contains a summary of the Committee's work and organizational matters, as well as an annex detailing the amendments to the draft convention and other proposals submitted by delegations throughout the session. It also reviewed the full report of the Working Group on measures to eliminate terrorism, which covers the Group's activities over the five meetings held in 2001.

The Committee began its work by adopting its program of work and decided to proceed with discussions in informal consultations. The informal consultations commenced with discussion on Article 18 of the Comprehensive Convention and were followed by consideration of the Preamble and Article 1 on a definition of phrases in the draft Convention.

DRAFT CONVENTION ON INTERNATIONAL TERRORISM

Regarding the issue of convening a high-level conference, under the auspices of the UN, to formulate a joint organized response of the international community to terrorism in all its forms and manifestations, the delegation of Egypt informed the Ad Hoc Committee that bilateral consultations were being conducted on that issue, the results of which would be reported to the Chairman of the Committee in the meantime.

The Committee recommended establishing a Working Group to continue work on the elaboration of a Comprehensive Convention, and to allocate appropriate time for the continued consideration of the outstanding issues on the nuclear terrorism convention.

On 7 October, at its 11th meeting, the Sixth Committee established a Working Group and elected Mr. Rohan Perera (Sri Lanka) as its Chairman. At the same meeting, the Committee decided to open the Working Group to all States Members of the United Nations or members of the specialized agencies or of the International Atomic Energy Agency.

The Working Group held two meetings in October 2002. At its first meeting on 15 October, the Working Group decided to proceed with discussions in informal consultations, which were held in two stages: the first focused on the draft Comprehensive Convention, and the second on the outstanding issues pertaining to the draft International Convention for the Suppression of Acts of Nuclear Terrorism. At the second meeting, on 16 October, the Co-ordinator of the informal consultations presented an oral report on the results of discussions on both draft conventions. The Working Group decided to recommend to the Sixth Committee that work should continue with the aim of finalizing the text of a draft Comprehensive Convention on International Terrorism and the text of a draft International Convention for the Suppression of Acts of Nuclear Terrorism, building upon the work accomplished during the meetings of the Working Group.

2001: During the meeting of the Ad Hoc Committee in February, delegations discussed a revised discussion paper prepared by the Committee's Bureau and the revised draft Convention submitted by India. The States were unable to bridge differences on the matter of a high-level conference on international terrorism. While some delegations favored the soonest convening of such a conference and expressed readiness to contribute to its preparation, others expressed preference for convening the conference after the adoption of the draft Comprehensive Convention in order to use this conference to promote its universal acceptance and implementation, together with sectoral conventions in this area.

The main debate in the Ad Hoc Committee focused on the draft Comprehensive Convention. The delegations generally noted that the revised text submitted by the sponsor delegation (India) was a good basis for discussions, although the same outstanding issues remained, namely the scope of the draft Comprehensive Convention, definitions, and its relationship to other international conventions on terrorism.

Regarding the issue of definitions, some States noted that the approach that defines the conduct of a terrorist had been successfully employed in the sectoral anti-terrorism conventions. Some delegations stressed that the definition of terrorism must clearly distinguish terrorist acts from the legitimate struggle in the exercise of the right to self-determination and independence of all peoples under foreign occupation. Other delegations made the point that the legal definition of terrorism should be centered on the usual purpose of terrorism, which is to produce fear in the population or to force a Government or an international organization to take or refrain from taking some action. The view was expressed that the definition of terrorism should extend to an attempt to commit terrorist acts and that terrorist acts should not be differentiated on the basis of their scale or damage.

Some delegations believed that the definition of terrorism must necessarily cover acts of State-sponsored terrorism as well as acts of State terrorism. Others, while acknowledging that acts of State-sponsored terrorism could fall under the draft Comprehensive Convention, acts of State terrorism, i.e., acts conducted by States, fell under different legal norms, namely the UN Charter.

On the issue of scope, the delegations discussed the proposal, in which the legitimate struggle against foreign occupation, aggression, colonialism, and hegemony aimed at liberation, self-determination, and independence in accordance with international law should not be considered a terrorist crime. Proponents of this proposal (Arab countries, and other members of the Non-aligned Movement) argued that this provision should be included in the draft text, *inter alia*, in order to balance it since the revised draft text included a provision concerning the exclusion of activities of the armed forces from the scope of the draft Comprehensive Convention. Opponents of the proposal stated that while recognizing the aforementioned as a right, they objected to the notion that such a right could be exercised by whatever means, including terrorist acts, and that it would violate provisions of certain existing international conventions, namely Protocol I to the 1949 Geneva Conventions, Article 51 of which prohibits attacks on civilian populations.

As for the relationship of the draft Comprehensive Convention with the existing sectoral conventions on international terrorism, some delegations underscored the importance of preserving sectoral conventions on specific forms of terrorism and the need for a comprehensive convention to be elaborated on the basis of a holistic and comprehensive approach in terms of its content and scope. Other delegations argued that the draft Comprehensive Convention should avoid creating legal overlaps with the existing body of antiterrorism conventions and should represent an added value to the sectoral conventions by increasing their efficiency.

DRAFT CONVENTION ON INTERNATIONAL TERRORISM

Two views were expressed: (1) the "last in time" rule should be applied and, therefore, the Comprehensive Convention would supersede previous conventions to the extent that it would overlap in substance with those conventions; (2) the existing sectoral conventions would be viewed as lex specialis and would therefore remain applicable in cases where the acts in question fell within their respective purviews. The second approach prevailed in the Committee, although there was a certain degree of dissent. Those who disagreed noted that having the same acts covered by the comprehensive and respective sectoral conventions would create a disincentive for States to ratify the sectoral treaties and it would be prudent to retain primacy of the sectoral conventions. They also argued that it would not be acceptable for a Comprehensive Convention to retroactively amend sectoral conventions, as such amendments would result in inconsistencies with existing national legislation.

The events of 11 September in the United States galvanized debate on international terrorism in the UN with the hope of capitalizing on the groundswell of international solidarity emanating from recent crises to strengthen dialogue against international terrorism. On 12 September, the UNSC adopted Resolution 1368, in which it condemned the terrorist attacks against the United States, called on the international community to redouble its efforts to prevent and suppress terrorist acts by increased cooperation and full implementation of relevant international anti-terrorist conventions and Security Council resolutions, and expressed readiness to take all necessary steps to combat terrorism in all forms.

On 19 September, the UNSC called on the international community to unite in the fight against terrorism and expressed hope that the UN would be able to adopt another anti-terrorism convention in the near future.

On 28 September, the UNSC adopted Resolution 1373, which provided that States should prevent and suppress the financing of terrorism, as well as criminalize the willful provision or collection of funds for such acts, prohibit their nationals or persons or entities in their territories from making funds, financial assets, economic resources, financial or other related services available to persons who commit or attempt to commit, facilitate, or participate in the commission of terrorist acts, refrain from providing any form of support to entities or persons involved in terrorist acts; take the necessary steps to prevent the commission of terrorist acts; deny safe haven to those who finance, plan, support, or commit terrorist acts and provide safe havens; ensure that anyone who has participated in the financing, planning, preparation, or perpetration of terrorist acts or in supporting terrorist acts is brought to justice; and ensure that terrorist acts are established as serious criminal offenses in domestic laws and regulations and that the seriousness of such acts is duly reflected in sentences served.

It also called on States to intensify and accelerate the exchange of information regarding terrorist actions or movements, cooperate to prevent and suppress terrorist acts and to take action against the perpetrators of such acts, become parties to, and fully implement as soon as possible, the relevant international conventions and protocols to combat terrorism, and enhance the coordination of national, subregional, regional, and international efforts to strengthen a global response to that threat to international security. On adopting the text of the Resolution, the UNSC invoked Chapter VII of the UN Charter, which allows for the use of force. The UNSC provided for the establishment of a committee "to work on implementing the resolution's binding provisions." The UK ambassador to the UN was appointed Chairman of the Committee, with three vice-chairmen representing Colombia, Mauritius, and the Russian Federation.

On 1 October, the UN opened a debate on measures to eliminate international terrorism. Numerous participants advocated adherence to existing UN antiterrorism treaties as well as the elaboration of new legal instruments. Some delegations reiterated a proposal to convene an international conference on terrorism, emphasizing that this would be a great contribution to combating the scourge and calling on the UNGA to adopt a resolution setting in motion preparations for the event.

The delegations once again raised the question of the definition of terrorism. The Arab Group, Organization of Islamic Conference, Malaysia, Iran, and others reiterated that there should be a distinction between acts of terrorism and the legitimate struggle for self-determination, liberation, and independence. Others called for the comprehensive eradication of terrorism, "without compromise" and justification whatsoever. Pakistan noted that in order to defeat terrorism, countries should address its root causes, such as poverty, illiteracy, inequality, and injustice. As for State terrorism, some delegations, such as Iraq, called for the inclusion of this question in the comprehensive anti-terrorism instrument.

Some delegations said the situation was favorable for bridging the differences and inspired real hope that multilateral efforts to up-root the terrible growth of terrorism can make significant progress. Other delegations emphasized the need to examine all aspects of the problem, and cautioned against "looking at the trees where a forest existed," with priority to be given to achieving a comprehensive solution to the problem. A number of delegations favored strengthening the existing instruments.

The UNSC, as well as numerous delegations, urged States to forge agreement on a Comprehensive Convention against international terrorism that would provide for the level of cooperation and coordination recognized as essential for effective action by Member States to combat terrorism.

The debates demonstrated that although the need to combat international terrorism was recognized by all States, the usual problems and disagreements remained. Closing the five-day debate in the UNGA on measures to eliminate international terrorism, the UNGA President urged Member

DRAFT CONVENTION ON INTERNATIONAL TERRORISM

States to accelerate the work of the UNGA with a view to early conclusion of the pending conventions on international terrorism in order to enhance the capacity of the international community to combat terrorism and requested the UN Sixth Committee to expedite its work and submit its report to the General Assembly as early as possible, preferably by 15 November.

The Sixth Committee's Working Group meeting took place from 15-26 October, where delegates reached agreement on most of the articles. During this period, the Working Group held five meetings and continued its work on the elaboration of a draft comprehensive convention on international terrorism on the basis of the text submitted by India. Through these meetings, the Working Group considered draft articles and those articles were subsequently reviewed in informal consultations. Following the informal consultations and written proposals by delegations, the Chairman of the Working Group prepared the texts for the revised articles. While the final text of the draft international convention has been extensively debated, the question of the scope of its application remained to be resolved again. The Chairman of the Working Group, in that regard, called upon the delegations to bring the negotiation of the instrument to a successful conclusion at the current session of the Working Group.

At its first meeting, the Chairman of the Working group appointed Mr. Richard Rowe from Australia as the new coordinator for the draft Convention. The Chairman also brought the issue of convening a high-level conference under the auspices of the UN on measures to eliminate international terrorism to the attention of the delegations. At its fifth meeting held on 26 October, the report of the Working Group was considered and adopted by the Working group.

2000: During the February session of the Ad Hoc Committee, delegations generally spoke in favor of a sectoral approach in the work of the Committee, i.e., a step-by-step approach in adopting conventions concerning the specific types of terrorist acts and related activities, although they noted that the work of the Committee would be incomplete without addressing the question of a Comprehensive Convention on international terrorism. India announced that it revised the text of the draft Convention (A/C.6/55/1) and circulated it among the delegations for comments. Some support was expressed for the elaboration of a Comprehensive Convention that should focus on subject matters that had not been addressed by the previous conventions.

Delegations highlighted the importance of international cooperation in combating international terrorism and noted that such cooperation should be based upon international law and the UN Charter and should focus on concrete, effective, and practical measures.

Some delegations expressed support for a high-level conference on terrorism to formulate a joint organized response of the international community to international terrorism in all its forms and manifestations. The delegations proposed that such a conference should serve to facilitate consensus among States on measures to combat terrorism, elaborate a legal definition of terrorism, focus on concrete measures to strengthen the existing framework of international cooperation, provide an opportunity to fill in any existing gaps in the legal framework in combating terrorism, enhance the implementation of relevant international instruments, and promote cooperation among the law enforcement authorities. Others said such a conference would just be an exercise in rhetoric and distract States from conducting practical work.

At the September-October meetings of the Sixth Committee's Working Group, and the November meeting of the UN Sixth Committee the States continued the discussion over a high-level conference on international terrorism and a Comprehensive Convention to combat international terrorism. Most of the delegations supported the idea of convening such a conference, but in order for it to be successful, the objectives and modalities of the conference should be carefully delineated. It was concluded that further consultations were required on the question of the conference. On the issue of the draft Convention, India introduced its revised text of the proposed draft Convention, on the basis of which the Working Group commenced it deliberations, both in formal and informal formats. Based on the discussions, India revised the text once again.

A number of delegations drew the Committee's attention to specific instances of State-sponsored terrorism. Several speakers also noted that globalization had given rise to new forms of terrorism, such as cyber-terrorism. States were urged to refrain from granting asylum to terrorists and not to allow their territories to be used as safe havens for terrorists. It was also underscored that measures aimed at combating terrorism should be conducted in conformity with the principles of the Charter of the United Nations and relevant norms and rules of international law, in particular international human rights and humanitarian law.

States expressed general support for the continuation of elaboration of the draft Convention. However, as during the previous meetings, there were problems that prevented the delegations from achieving consensus, namely problems related to the scope and definition of offenses, the relationship of the draft Convention with the existing conventions and the need for, and the content of, the annexes to the draft Convention. Some delegations stressed that the future convention should complement and complete existing counter-terrorism conventions, primarily by filling gaps, rather than replacing, duplicating, or undercutting them. Others were of the view that the instrument should be comprehensive in scope, containing a definition of terrorism, making a clear distinction between terrorist acts and the legitimate struggle of peoples for national liberation from colonial and other forms of alien domination and foreign occupation, as well as covering all aspects of the problem of terrorism, including State terrorism and the activities of armed forces. However, there were concerns that such an approach was contrary to international law and existing UN resolutions. It was further suggested that the proposed draft Convention should cover terrorist attacks against private as well as public facilities.

In its Resolution 55/158 of 12 December, the UNGA extended the mandate of the Ad Hoc Group to elaborate a Comprehensive Convention on international terrorism in 2001 and authorize it to keep on the Committee's agenda the question of convening a high-level conference under the UN auspices to formulate a joint organized response to international terrorism in all its forms and manifestations. The language of the resolution suggested that the consideration of the draft comprehensive Convention should be prioritized over the resolution of outstanding differences over the draft Convention for the Suppression of Acts of Nuclear Terrorism.

1999: In June, the participants of the first Summit of the Heads of State and Government of Latin America and the Caribbean and the European Union, held in Rio de Janeiro, adopted a set of Priorities for Action, among which they committed themselves to intensify international cooperation to combat terrorism, based on the principles established in the UN framework, to advance the signing and ratification of the UN conventions and protocols, and to strengthen the international legal framework on the subject, supporting the elaboration of instruments to fight terrorism.

In July, the Heads of State and Government of the Member States of the Organization of African Unity adopted the Algiers Declaration, which called for effective and efficient international cooperation to combat terrorism through a speedy conclusion of a Global International Convention for the Prevention and Control of Terrorism in all its forms and the convening of an International Summit Conference under the auspices of the UN to consider this phenomenon and the means to combat it.

In October, the Foreign Ministers of the Commonwealth of Independent States (CIS) issued a statement, which called for "compliance with international conventions against terrorism and the continuation of work to strengthen the international legal system for combating terrorism."

In October, UNSC Resolution 1269 called upon all States, *inter alia*, to prevent and suppress terrorist acts; prevent and suppress preparation and financing of any acts of terrorism; deny those who plan, finance, or commit terrorist acts safe havens by ensuring their apprehension and prosecution or extradition; and exchange information and cooperate on administrative and judicial matters in order to prevent the commission of terrorist acts.

During the November meetings of the UN Sixth Committee, support was also expressed for the elaboration of a Comprehensive Convention on international terrorism, and for the text prepared by India, which was viewed as an adequate basis for such work. It was proposed by some that the Comprehensive Convention consider the question of a legal definition of terrorism. A point was made, however, that the draft text proposed by India contained many controversial issues and that the necessity and feasibility of elaborating such a convention should be studied carefully. The view was also expressed that the proposed instrument should avoid broad definitional questions and focus rather on its scope. Some speakers reiterated their position regarding the need to distinguish between terrorism and the legitimate struggle by national liberation movements for self-determination and independence, and called for the formulation of a universal legal definition of terrorism. At the same time, it was pointed out that reaching agreement on such a definition was difficult and that the United Nations had been more successful when focusing on treaties that criminalized specific manifestations of terrorism. Support was expressed for the convening of a high level conference in 2000 under the auspices of the United Nations to formulate a joint response to terrorism.

On 9 December, the UNGA adopted Resolution 54/110, entitled "Measures to Eliminate International Terrorism," in which it empowered the Ad Hoc Committee to address means of further developing a comprehensive legal framework of conventions dealing with international terrorism and begin consideration with a view to elaborate a Comprehensive Convention on international terrorism.

1998: India submitted a draft Convention on the Suppression of Terrorism, (A/C.6/51/6) which it circulated among the States during the 1998 Session of the UNGA.

WORKING DOCUMENT SUBMITTED BY INDIA ON THE DRAFT COMPREHENSIVE CONVENTION ON INTERNATIONAL TERRORISM*

THE STATES PARTIES TO THIS CONVENTION,

Recalling the existing international conventions relating to various aspects of the problem of international terrorism, in particular the Convention on Offences and Certain Acts Committed on Board Aircraft, signed at Tokyo on 14 September 1963; the Convention for the Suppression of Unlawful Seizure of Aircraft, signed at The Hague on 16 December, 1970; the Convention for the Suppression of Unlawful Acts against the Safety of Civil Aviation, signed at Montreal on 23 September, 1971; the Convention on the Prevention and Punishment of Crimes against Internationally Protected Persons, including Diplomatic Agents, adopted by the General Assembly of the United Nations on 14 December, 1973, the International Convention against the Taking of Hostages, adopted by the General Assembly of the United Nations on 17 December, 1979; the Convention on the Physical Protection of Nuclear Material, signed at Vienna on 3 March, 1980; the Protocol for the Suppression of Unlawful Acts of Violence at Airports Serving International Civil Aviation, supplementary to the Convention for the Suppression of Unlawful Acts against the Safety of Civil Aviation, signed at Montreal on 24 February, 1988; the Convention for the Suppression of Unlawful Acts against the Safety of Maritime Navigation, done at Rome on 10 March, 1988; the Protocol for the Suppression of Unlawful Acts against the Safety of Fixed Platforms Located on the Continental Shelf, done at Rome on 10 March, 1988; the Convention on the Marking of Plastic Explosives for the Purpose of Detection, signed at Montreal on 1 March, 1991;

---

* Submitted on 28 August 2000.

the International Convention for the Suppression of Terrorist Bombings, adopted by the General Assembly of the United Nations on 15 December, 1997; the International Convention for the Suppression of the Financing of Terrorism, adopted by the General Assembly of the United Nations on 9 December, 1999,

Recalling also General Assembly resolution 49/60 of 9 December, 1994 and the Declaration on Measures to Eliminate International Terrorism annexed thereto,

Recalling further General Assembly resolution 51/20 of 17 December, 1996 and the Declaration of supplement the 1994 declaration on measures to Eliminate International Terrorism annexed thereto,

Deeply concerned about the worldwide escalation of acts of terrorism in all its forms, which endanger or take innocent lives, jeopardize fundamental freedoms and seriously impair the dignity of human beings,

Reaffirming their unequivocal condemnation of all acts, methods and practices of terrorism as criminal and unjustifiable, wherever and by whomever committed, including those which jeopardize friendly relations among states and people and threaten the territorial integrity and security of States,

Recognizing that acts, methods and practices of terrorism constitute a grave violation of the purposes and principles of the United Nations, which may pose a threat to international peace and security, jeopardize friendly relations among States, hinder international cooperation and aim at the undermining of human rights, fundamental freedoms and the democratic basis of society,

Recognizing also that the financing, planning and inciting of terrorist acts are also contrary to the purposes and principles of the United Nations, and that it is the duty of the States Parties to bring to justice those who have participated in such terrorist acts,

Convinced that the suppression of acts of international terrorism, including those which are committed or supported by States, directly or indirectly, is an essential element in the maintenance of international peace and security and the sovereignty and territorial integrity of States,

Realizing the need for a comprehensive convention on international terrorism,

Have resolved to take effective measure to prevent acts of terrorism and to ensure that perpetrators of terrorist acts do not escape prosecution and punishment by providing for their extradition or prosecution, and to that end HAVE AGREED AS FOLLOWS:

Article 1

For the purpose of this Convention:

1. "State or government facility" includes any permanent or temporary facility or conveyance that is used or occupied by representatives of a

State, members of government, the legislature or the judiciary or by officials or employees of a State or any other public authority or entity or by employees or officials of an intergovernmental organization in connection with their official duties.

2. " Military forces of a State" means the armed forces of a State which are organized, trained and equipped under its internal law for the primary purpose of national defence or security, and persons acting in support of those armed forces who are under their formal command, control and responsibility.

3. "Infrastructure facility" means any publicly or privately owned facility providing or distributing services for the benefit of the public, such as water, sewerage, energy, fuel or communications, and banking services, telecommunications and information networks.

4. "Place of public use" means those parts of any building, land, street, waterway or other location that are accessible or open to members of the public, whether continuously, periodically or occasionally, and encompasses any commercial, business, cultural, historical, educational, religious, governmental, entertainment, recreational or similar place that is so accessible or open to the public.

5. "Public Transportation Systems" means all facilities, conveyances and instrumentalities, whether publicly or privately on, that are used in or for publicly available services for transportation of persons or cargo.

Article 2:

1. Any person commits an offence within the meaning of this Convention if that person, by any means, unlawfully and intentionally, does an Act intended to cause:

(a) Death or serious bodily injury to any person; or

(b) Serious damage to a State or government facility, a public transportation system, communication system or infrastructure facility with the intent to cause extensive destruction of such a place, facility or system, or where such destruction results or is likely to result in major economic loss; when the purpose of such act, by its nature or contacts, is to intimidate a population, or to compel a government or an international organization to do or abstain from doing any act.

2. Any person also commits an offense if that person attempts to commit an offense or participate as an accomplice in an offence as set forth in paragraph 1.

3. Any person also commits an offense if that person:

(a) Organizes, directs or instigate others to commit an offense as set forth in paragraphs 1 or 2; or

(b) aids, abets, facilitates or counsels the commission of such an offense; or

(c) In any other way contributes the commission of one or more offenses referred in paragraphs 1, 2 or 3 (a) by a group of persons acting with a common purpose; such contribution shall be intentional and either be met with the aim of furthering the general criminal activity or purpose of the group or be met in the knowledge of the intention of the group to commit the offence or offences concerned.

Article 3:

This Convention shall not apply where the offence is committed within a single State, the alleged offender is a national of that State and is present in the territory of that State and no other state has a basis under article 6, paragraph 1, or article 6, paragraph 2, to exercise jurisdiction except that the provision of articles 10 to 22 shall, as appropriate, apply in those cases.

Article 4:

Each State Party shall adopt such measures as may be necessary;

(a) To establish as criminal offences under its domestic law. The offences set forth in article 2;

(b) To make those offences punishable by appropriate penalties which take into account the grave nature of those offences.

Article 5:

Each State Party shall adopt such measures as may be necessary, including, where appropriate, domestic legislation, to ensure that criminal acts within the scope of this Convention are under no circumstances justifiable by considerations of a political, philosophical, ideological, racial, ethnic, religious or other similar nature.

Article 6:

1. Each State Party shall take such measure as may be necessary to establish its jurisdiction over the offences referred to in article 2 in the following cases:

(a) When the offence is committed in the territory in that State or on board a ship or aircraft registered in that State;

(b) When the alleged offender is a national of that State or is a person who has his or her habitual residence in its territory;

(c) When the offence is committed wholly or partially outside its territory, if the effect of the conduct or intended effects constitute or result, within its territory in the commission of an offence referred to in article 2.

2. A State may also establish its jurisdiction over any such offence when its committed:

(a) By a stateless person whose habitual is in that State; or

(b) With respect to a national of that State; or

(c) Against a State or government facility of that state abroad, including an embassy or other diplomatic or consular premises of that state or

(d) In an attempt to compel that state to do or abstain from doing any act; or

(e) On board a ship or aircraft which is operated by the government of that state.

3. Each state Party shall take such measures as may be necessary to establish its jurisdiction over the offences referred to in article 2 in cases where the alleged offender is present in its territory and where it does not extradite such person to any of these States Parties that have established their jurisdiction in accordance with paragraphs 1 or 2

4. When more than one State Party claims jurisdiction over the offences set forth in article 2 the relevant State Parties shall strive to coordinate their actions appropriately, in particular concerning the conditions for prosecution and the modalities for mutual legal assistance.

5. This Convention does not exclude any criminal jurisdiction exercised in accordance with national law.

Article 7:

States Parties shall take appropriate measures, before granting asylum, for the purpose of ensuring that asylum is not granted to any person in respect of whom there are reasonable grounds indicating his involvement in any offence referred to in article 2.

Article 8:

State Parties shall cooperate in the prevention of the offences set forth in article 2, particularly:

(a) By taking all practicable measures, including, if necessary, adapting their domestic legislation, to prevent and counter preparation in their respective territories for the commission, by whom so ever and in whatever manner, of those offences within or outside their territories, including:

i. Measures to prohibit in their territories the establishment and operation of installations and training for the commission, within or outside their territories, of offences referred to in article 2; and

ii. Measures to prohibit the illegal activities of the persons, groups and organizations that encourage, instigate, organize, knowingly finance or engage in the commission, within or outside their territories, offences referred to in article 2;

(b) By exchanging accurate and verified information in accordance with their national law, and coordinating administrative and other measures taken as appropriate to prevent the commission of offences as referred to in article 2.

Article 9:

1. Each State Party, in accordance with its domestic legal principles, shall take the necessary measures to enable a legal entity located in its territory or organized under its laws to be held liable when a person responsible for the management or control of that legal entity has, in that capacity committed an offence referred to in article 2. Such liability may be criminal civil or administrative.

2. Such liability is incurred without prejudice to the criminal liability of individuals having committed the offences.

3. Each State Party shall ensure in particular, that legal entities liable in accordance with paragraph 1 above are subject to effective, proportionate and dissuasive criminal, civil or administrative sanctions. Such sanctions may include monetary sanctions.

Article 10:

1. Upon receiving information that a person who has committed or who is alleged to have committed an offence referred to in article 2 may be present in its territory, the state party concern shall take such measures as may be necessary under its domestic law to investigate the facts contained in the information.

2. Upon being satisfied that the circumstances so warrant, the state party in whose territory the offender or alleged offender is present shall take the appropriate measures under its domestic law so as to ensure that person's presence for the purpose of prosecution or extradition.

3. Any person regarding whom the measures refer to in paragraph 2 are being taken shall be entitled to:

(a) communicate without delay with the nearest appropriate representative of the state of which that person is a national or which is otherwise entitled to protect that person's right or, if that person is a stateless person the state in the territory of which that person habitually resides;

(b) Be visited by a representative of that State;

(c) Be informed of that person's rights under subparagraphs (a) and (b).

4. The rights referred to in paragraph 3 shall be exercised in conformity with the laws and regulations of the State in the territory of which the of-

fender or the alleged offender is present subject to the provision that the said laws and regulations much enable full effect to be given to the purposes for which the rights accorded under paragraph 3 are intended.

5. The provisions of paragraphs 3 and 4 shall be without the prejudice to the right of any State Party having acclaimed to jurisdiction in accordance with article 6, paragraphs 1 (b), or 2(b), to invite the International Committee of the Red Cross to communicate with and visit the alleged offender.

6. When a State Party, pursuant to the present article, has taken a person into custody, it shall immediately notify, directly or through the Secretary-General of the United Nations, the States Parties which have established jurisdiction in accordance with article 6, paragraph 1 or 2, and if it considers it advisable, any other interested States Parties, of the fact that such person is in custody and of the circumstances which warrant that person's detention. The State which makes the investigation contemplated in paragraph 1 shall promptly inform the said States Parties of its findings and shall indicate whether it intends to exercise jurisdiction.

Article 11:

1. The State Party in whose territory the alleged offender is found shall, if it does not extradite the person, be obliged, without exception whose so ever and whether or not the offence was committed in its territory, to submit the case to its competent authorities for the purpose of prosecution through proceedings in accordance with law of the state. Those authorities shall take their decision in the same manner as in the case of any ordinary offence of a grave nature under the law of that state.

2. Whenever the State party is permitted under its domestic law to extradite or otherwise surrender one of its nationals only upon the condition that the person will be returned to that state to serve the sentence imposed as a result of the trial or proceeding for which the extradition or surrender of the person was sought and that State and the State seeking the extradition of the person agree with this option and other terms they may deem appropriate, such a conditional extradition or surrender shall be sufficient to discharge the obligation set forth in paragraph 1.

Article 12:

Any person who is taken into custody or regarding whom any other measures are taken or proceedings are carried out pursuant to this Convention shall be guaranteed fair treatment, including enjoyment of all rights and guarantees in conformity with law of the state in the territory of which that person is present and applicable provisions of international law, including international human rights law.

Article 13:

1. State Parties shall afford one another the greatest measure of assistance in connection with investigations or criminal or extradition proceedings brought in respect of the offences set forth in article 2, including assistance in obtaining evidence at their disposal necessary for the proceedings.

2. State Parties shall carryout their obligations under paragraph 1 in conformity with any treaties or other arrangements on mutual legal assistance that may exist between them. In the absence of such treaties or arrangements. States Parties shall afford one another assistance in accordance with their domestic law.

3. State Parties which are not bound by a bilateral treaty or arrangement of mutual legal assistance may, at their discretion, apply the procedure set out in Annex II.

Article 14:

None of the offences referred to in article 2 and the acts which constitute an offence within the scope of and as defined in one of the treaties listed in Annex I shall be regarded, for the purposes of extradition or mutual legal assistance, as a political offence or as an offence connected with a political offence or as an offence inspired by political motives. Accordingly, a request for extradition or for mutual legal assistance based on such an offence may not be refused on the sole ground that it concerns a political offence or an offence connected with a political offence or an offence inspired by political motives.

Article 15:

Nothing in this Convention shall be interpreted as imposing an obligation to extradite or to afford mutual legal assistance, if the requested State Party has substantial grounds for believing that the request for extradition for offences set forth in article 2 or for mutual legal assistance with respect to such offences has been made for the purpose of prosecuting or punishing a person on account of that person's race, religion, nationality, ethnic origin or political opinion or that compliance with the request would cause prejudice to that person's position for any of these reasons.

Article 16:

A person who is being detained or is serving a sentence in the territory of one State Party whose presence in another State Party is requested for purposes of identification, testimony or otherwise providing assistance in obtaining evidence for the investigation or prosecution of offences under the Convention may be transferred if the following conditions are met:

   (a) The person freely gives his or her informed consent, and

(b) The competent authorities of both States Parties agree, subject to such conditions as those States Parties may deem appropriate.

2. For the purposes of this article:

(a) The State to which the person is transferred shall have the authority and obligation to keep the person transferred in custody, unless otherwise requested or authorized by the State from which the person was transferred;

(b) The State to which the person is transferred shall without delay implement its obligations to return the person to the custody of the State from which the person was transferred as agreed beforehand, or as otherwise agreed, by the competent authorities of both States;

(c) The State to which the person is transferred shall not require the State from which the person was transferred to initiate extradition proceedings for the return of the person;

(d) The person transferred shall receive credit for service of the sentence being served in the State from which he was transferred for the time spent in the custody of the State to which he was transferred.,

3. Unless the State party from which a person is to be transferred in accordance with this article so agrees, that person, whatever his or her nationality, shall not be prosecuted or detained or subjected to any other restriction of his or her personal liberty in the territory of the State to which that person is transferred in respect of acts or convictions anterior to his or her departure form the territory of the State from which such person was transferred.

Article 17:

1. The offences referred to in article 2 shall be deemed to be included as extraditable offences in any extradition treaty existing between any of the States Parties before the entry into force of this Convention. States parties undertake to include such offences as extraditable offences in every extradition treaty to be subsequently concluded between them

2. When a State Party which makes extradition conditional or the existence of a treaty receives a request from another State party with which it has no extradition treaty, the requested State may, at it option, consider this Convention as a legal basis for extradition in respect of the offences set forth in article 2. Extradition shall be subject to the other conditions provided by the law of the requested State.

3. State Parties which do not make extradition conditional on the existence of a treaty shall recognize the offences referred to in article 2 as extraditable offences between themselves, subject to the conditions provided for by the law of the requested State.

4. If necessary, the offences set forth in article 2 shall be treated, for the purposes of extradition between State Parties, as if they had committed not only in the place in which they occurred but also in the territory of the States that have established jurisdiction in accordance with article 6, paragraphs 1 and 2.

5. The provisions of all extradition treaties and arrangements between States Parties with regard to offences set forth in article 2 shall be deemed to be modified as between States parties to the extent that they are incomparable with this Convention.

6. State Parties which, pursuant to paragraph 2 of this article, have agreed to consider this Convention as a legal basis for extradition in respect of the offences set forth in article 2 may consider utilizing the procedures set out in Annex III.

Article 18:

1. Nothing in this Convention shall affect other rights, obligations and responsibilities of States and individuals under international laws, in particular the purposes and principles of the Charter of the United Nations and international humanitarian law.

2. The activities of armed forces during an armed conflict, as those terms are understood under international law, which are governed by that law, are not governed by this Convention, and the activities undertaken by the military forces of a State in the exercise of their official duties, in as much as they are governed by other rules of international law, are not governed by this Convention.

Article 19:

The State party where the alleged offender is prosecuted shall, in accordance with its domestic law or applicable procedures, communicate the final outcome of the proceedings to the Secretary-General of United Nations, who shall transmit the information to the other State Parties.

Article 20:

The states shall carry out their obligations under the Convention in a manner consistent with the principles of sovereign equality and territorial integrity of States and that of non-intervention in the domestic affairs of other states.

Article 21:

Nothing in this Convention shall affect other rights, obligations and responsibilities of States and individuals under international law, in particular the purposes of the Charter of United Nations, international humanitarian law and other relevant conventions;

Article 22:

Nothing in this Convention entitles a State party to undertake in the territory of another State Party the exercise of jurisdiction or performance of function which are exclusively reserved for the authorities of that other State Party by the domestic law.

Article 23:

1. Any dispute between two or more State Parties concerning the interpretations or application of his Convention which cannot be settled through negotiation within a reasonable time shall, at the request of one of them, be submitted to arbitration. If, within six months from the date of the request for arbitration, the parties are unable to agree on the organization of the arbitration, any one of those parties may refer the dispute to the International Court of Justice, by application, in conformity with the Statute of the Court.

2. Each State may at the time of signature, ratification, acceptance or approval of this Convention or accession thereto declare that it does not consider itself bound by paragraph 1. The other State Parties shall not be bound by paragraph 1 with respect to any State party which has made such a reservation.

3. Any State which made a reservation in accordance with paragraph 2 may at any time withdraw that reservation by notification of the Secretary-General of the United Nations.

Article 24:

1. This Convention is open for signature by all States from _____ to _____ at United Nations Headquarters in New York.

2. This Convention is subject to ratification, acceptance or approval. The instruments of ratification, acceptance or approval shall be deposited with the Secretary-General of the United Nations.

3. This Convention shall be open to accession by any State. The instruments of accession shall be deposited with Secretary-General of the United Nations.

Article 25:

1. This Convention shall enter into force thirty days after twenty-two instruments of ratification, acceptance, approval or accession have been deposited with the Secretary-General of the United Nations.

2. For each State ratifying, accepting, approving or acceding to the Convention after the deposit of the twenty-second instrument of ratification, acceptance, approval or accession, the Convention shall enter into force on the thirtieth day after the deposit by such State of its instruments of ratification, acceptance, approval or accession.

Article 26:

1. A State may denounce this Convention by written notification to the Secretary-General of the United Nations.

2. Denunciation shall take effect one year following the date on which notification is received by the Secretary-General of the United Nations.

Article 27:

The original of this Convention, of which the Arabic, Chinese, English, French, Russian and Spanish texts are equally authentic, shall be deposited with the Secretary-General of the United Nations, who shall send certified copies thereof to all States.

In WITNESS WHEREOF, the undersigned, being duly authorized thereto by their respective Governments, have signed this Convention, opened for signature at United Nations Headquarter in New York on _____ 2000.

Annex I:
Exclusion of political offence

1. Convention on offences and Certain Acts Committed on Board Aircraft, signed at Tokyo on 14 September 1963.

2. Convention for the Suppression of Unlawful Seizure of Aircraft, signed at the Hague on 16 December 1970.

3. Convention for the suppression of Unlawful Acts against the Safety of Civil Aviation, signed at Montreal on 23 September 1971.

4. Convention on the Prevention and Punishment of Crimes against International Protected Persons, including Diplomatic Agents, adopted by the General Assembly of the United Nations on 14 December 1973.

5. International Convention against the Taking of Hostages, adopted by the General Assembly of the United Nations on 17 December 1979.

6. Convention on the Physical Protection of Nuclear Material, signed at Vienna on 3 March, 1980.

7. Protocol for the Suppression of Unlawful Acts of Violence at Airports serving International Civil Aviation, supplementary to the Convention for the Suppression of Unlawful Acts against the Safety of Civil Aviation, signed at Montreal on 24 February, 1988.

8. Convention for the suppression of Unlawful Acts against the safety of Maritime Navigation, done at Rome on 10 March, 1988.

9. Protocol for the Suppression of Unlawful Acts against the Safety of Fixed Platforms Located on Continental Shelf, done at Rome on 10 March, 1988

10. Convention on the Marking of Plastic Explosives for the Purpose of Detection, signed at Montreal on 1 March, 1991.

11. International Convention for the Suppression of Terrorist bombings, adopted by the General Assembly of the United Nations on 15 December, 1997.

12. International Convention for the Suppression for the Financing Of the Terrorism, adopted by the General Assembly of the United Nations on 9 December, 1999.

Annex II
Procedure for mutual legal assistance:

1. State Parties shall afford one another pursuant to this Annex the widest measure of mutual legal assistance in investigations, prosecutions and judicial proceedings in relation to criminal offences established in accordance with article 3.

2. Mutual legal assistance to be afforded in accordance with this Annex may be requested for any of the following purposes:

(a) Taking evidence or statements from persons;

(b) Effecting service of judicial documents;

(c) Executing searches and seizures;

(d) Examining objects and sites;

(e) Providing information and evidentiary items;

(f) Providing originals or certified copies of relevant documents and records including bank, financial, corporate or business records;

(g) Identifying or tracing proceeds, property, instrumentalities or other things for evidentiary purposes.

3. State Parties may afford one another any other forms of mutual legal assistance allowed by the domestic or the requested party.

4. Upon request, State Parties shall facilitate or encourage to the extent consistent with the domestic law and practice, the presence or availability of persons, including persons in custody, who consent to assist in investigation or participate in proceedings.

5. A State shall not decline to render mutual legal assistance under this annex on the ground of bank secrecy.

6. The provisions of this annex shall not affect the obligations under any other treaty, bilateral or multilateral, which governs or will govern in whole or in part mutual legal assistance in criminal matters.

7. The State Party may apply, at their discretion, paragraphs 8 to 19 of this annex to requests made pursuant to this annex if they are not otherwise bound by any treaty of mutual legal assistance. If the state parties are bound by such a treaty, the corresponding provisions of that treaty shall ap-

ply unless the state parties agree to apply paragraphs 8 to 19 of this annex in lieu thereof.

8. States Party shall designate an authority or, when necessary authorities, which shall have the responsibility the power to execute requests for mutual legal assistance or to transmit them to the competent authorities for execution. The authority or authorities designated for this purpose shall be notified to the Secretary-General of the United Nations. Transmission of requests for mutual legal assistance and any communications related their to shall be effected between the authorities designated by the State parties; this requirement shall be without prejudice to the right of a State to require that such requests and communications be addressed to it through the diplomatic channel and in urgent circumstances, where the States agree, through channels of the International Criminal Police Organization – Interpol, if possible.

9. Requests shall be made in writing in a language acceptable to the requested State. The language or languages acceptable to each State shall be notified to the Secretary-General of United Nations. In urgent circumstances, and where agreed by the States Parties, requests may be made orally, but shall be confirmed in writing forthwith.

10. A request for mutual legal assistance shall contain:

> a. The identity of the authority making the request;
>
> b. The subject matter and nature of the investigation, prosecution or proceedings, to which the request relates; and the name and the functions of the authority, conducting such investigations, prosecution or proceeding;
>
> c. A summary of the relevant facts, except in respect of requests for the purpose of service of judicial documents.
>
> d. A description of the assistance sought and details of any particular procedure the requesting party wishes to be followed;
>
> e. Where possible, the identity, location and nationality of any person concerned;
>
> f. The purpose for which the evidence, information or action is sought.

11. The requested state may request additional information when it appears necessary for the execution of the request in accordance with its domestic law or when it facilitate such execution.

12. A request shall be executed in accordance with the domestic law of the requested state and; to the extent not contrary to the domestic law of the requested State and where possible, in accordance with procedures specified in the request.

13. The requesting state shall not transmit or use information or evidence furnished by the requested state for investigations, prosecutions or proceedings other than those stated in the request without the prior consent of the requested state.

14. The requesting state may require that the requested state keep confidential the fact and substance of the request except to the extent necessary to execute the request. If the requested state cannot comply with the requirement of confidentiality, it shall promptly inform the requesting state.

15. Mutual legal assistance may be refused:

a. If the request is not made in conformity with provisions of this annex;

b. If the requested state considers that execution of the request is likely to prejudice its sovereignty, security, public order or other essential interest;

c. If the authorities of the requested state would be prohibited by its domestic laws from carrying out the action requested with regard to any similar offence, had it been subject to investigation, prosecution, or proceedings under their own jurisdiction;

d. If it would be contrary to the legal systems of the requested state relating to mutual legal assistance for the request to be granted.

16. Any assistance under this annex may not be refused on the sole ground that it concerns political offence or an offence connected with a political offence or an offence inspired by political motives.

17. Reasons shall be given for any refusal of mutual legal assistance.

18. The requested state may postpone mutual legal assistance on the ground that it interferes with an ongoing investigation, prosecution or proceeding. In such a case, the requested state shall consult with the requesting state to determine if the assistance can still be given subject to such terms and conditions as the requested deems necessary.

19. A witness, expert or other person who consents to give evidence in a proceeding or to assist in an investigation, prosecution or judicial proceeding in the territory of the requesting state shall not be prosecuted, detained, punished or subjected to any other restriction of his or her personal liberty in that territory in respect of acts, omissions or convictions prior to his departure from the territory of the requested state. Such safe conduct shall cease when the witness, expert or other person having had, for a period of fifteen consecutive days, or for any period agreed upon by the states parties from the date on which he or she has been officially informed that his or her presence is no longer required by the judicial authorities and opportunity of living, has nevertheless remain voluntarily in the territory or, having left it, has returned of his or her own free will.

20. The ordinary costs of executing a request shall be borne by the requested state, unless otherwise agreed by the states concerned. If expenses of a substantial or extraordinary nature are or will be required to fulfill the request, the state parties shall consult to determine the terms and conditions under which the requests will be executed as well as the manner in which the costs shall be borne.

21. The state parties shall consider, as may be necessary, the possibility of concluding bilateral or multilateral agreements or arrangements that would server the purpose of give practical effect to or enhance the provisions of this annex.

Annex III:
Extradition Procedure:

1. The offences referred to article 2 shall be deemed to be included as extraditable offences in any extradition treaty existing between State Parties. The State Parties undertake to include such offences as extraditable offences in every extradition to be concluded between them

2. The State Parties that do not make extradition conditional on the existence of a treaty shall recognize the offences referred to in article 2 as extraditable offences between themselves subject to the conditions provided by the law of the requested state.

3. The offences referred to in article 2 shall be treated, for the purpose of extradition between States Parties, as if they had been committed not only in the place in which they occurred but also in the territories of the requested State Parties.

4. The State Parties may, at their discretion, apply paragraphs 5 to 18 of this Annex to requests for extradition in respect of offences referred to in article 2 if they are not bound by a treaty of extradition. If these states are bound by such a treaty, the corresponding provisions of that treaty shall apply unless the states agree to apply paragraphs 5 to 18 of this annex in lieu thereof.

5. States Parties shall designate an authority, or when necessary, authorities, which shall have the responsibility and power to execute requests for extradition or to transmit them to the competent authorities for execution. The authority or the authorities designated for this purpose shall be notified to the Secretary-General of the United Nations. Transmission of requests for extradition and any communication related thereto shall be effected between the authorities designated by the state parties; this requirement shall be without prejudice to the right of a State to require that such requests and communications be addressed to it through diplomatic channels and, in urgent circumstances, where the State Parties agree, through channels of the International Criminal Police Organization – Interpol, if possible.

6. Requests shall be made in writing in a language acceptable to the requested state. In urgent circumstances and where agreed by the state parties, requests may be made orally, but shall be confirmed in writing forthwith.

7. A request for extradition shall contain:

a. The identity of the authority making the request;

b. As accurate a description as possible of the person sought, together with any other information which would help to establish the identity, location and nationality of the person concerned.

c. A summary of the facts of the offence for which extradition is requested; and

d. The text, if any, of the law defining that offence and prescribing the maximum punishment for that offence.

8. If the request relates to a person already convicted and sentenced, it shall also be accompanied by:

a. A certificate of the conviction and sentence; and

b. A statement that the person is not entitled to question the conviction and sentence and showing how much of the sentence has not been carried out.

9. If the requested state considers that the evidence produced or information supplied is not sufficient in order to enable a decision to be taken as to the request, additional evidence or information shall be submitted within such time as the requested state may require.

10. A request shall be executed in accordance with domestic law of the quested state and, to the extent not contrary to the domestic law of the quested state and where possible, in accordance with the procedures specified in the request.

11. The requesting state shall not transmit or use information or evidence furnished by the requested state for investigations, prosecutions or proceedings other than those stated in the request without the prior consent of the requested state.

12. Any person who is returned to the territory of the requesting state under this Convention shall not be dealt with in the territory of the requesting state for or in respect of any offence committed before he was returned to that territory other than the offence in respect of which he was returned, any lesser offence disclosed by the facts proved for the purpose of securing his return other than an offence in relation to which an order for his return could not lawfully be made, or any other offence in respect of which the requested state may consent to his being dealt with.

13. The provisions of paragraph 12 of this annex shall not apply to offences committed after the return of a person under this annex or matters arising in relation to such offences, or when the person having had the opportunity to leave the territory of the requesting state has not done so within sixty days of his final discharge, or has returned to that territory after having left it.

14. If extradition of the same person, whether for the same offence or for different offences, is requested by two States Parties, or by a state and a third state with which the requested state has an extradition arrangement, the requested state shall determine to which state the person shall be extradited.

15. When a request for extradition is granted, the requested state shall, upon request and as far as its law allows, hand over to the requesting state articles, which may serve as proof for evidence of the offence. If the article in question are liable to seizure or confiscation in the territory of the requested state, the latter may, in connection with pending proceedings, temporarily retain them or hand them over on condition that they are returned. This provision shall not prejudice the rights of the requested state of any person other than the persons sought. When these rights exist, the articles shall on request to be returned to the requested state without charge as soon as possible after the end of the proceedings.

16. Reasons shall be given for any refusal of extradition.

17. If criminal proceedings against the person sought are instituted in the territory of the requested state, or the person is lawfully detained in consequence of criminal proceedings, the decision whether or not to extradite the person may be postponed until the criminal proceedings have been completed or he or she is no longer detained.

18. The ordinary costs of executing a request shall be borne by the requested state, unless otherwise agreed by the state parties concerned. If expenses of a substantial or extraordinary nature are or will be required to fulfill the request, the State Parties shall consult to determine the terms and conditions under which the requests will be executed as well as the manner in which the costs shall be borne.

19. The State Parties shall consider, as may be necessary, the possibility of concluding bilateral or multilateral agreements or arrangements that would serve the purposes of, give practical effect to, or enhance the provisions of this Annex.

APPENDICES

STATUS OF INTERNATIONAL CONVENTIONS PERTAINING TO INTERNATIONAL TERRORISM[1]

Extract from the Report of the Secretary-General on Measures to Eliminate International Terrorism (Doc. A/58/116), as Updated on 31 December 2003

Currently, there are 21 global or regional treaties pertaining to the subject of international terrorism. Each instrument listed below is represented by the letter shown on the left, which is featured in the tables that follow to reflect the status of that instrument:

A. Convention on Offences and Certain Other Acts Committed on Board Aircraft, signed at Tokyo on 14 September 1963 (entered into force on 4 December 1969): status as at 30 November 2003;[2]

B. Convention for the Suppression of Unlawful Seizure of Aircraft, signed at The Hague on 16 December 1970 (entered into force on 14 October 1971): status as at 30 November 2003;[2]

C. Convention for the Suppression of Unlawful Acts against the Safety of Civil Aviation, signed at Montreal on 23 September 1971 (entered into force on 26 January 1973): status as at 30 November 2003;[2]

D. Convention on the Prevention and Punishment of Crimes against Internationally Protected Persons, including Diplomatic Agents, adopted by the General Assembly of the United Nations on 14 December 1973 (entered into force on 20 February 1977): status as at 31 December 2003;[3]

E. International Convention against the Taking of Hostages, adopted by the General Assembly of the United Nations on 17 December 1979 (entered into force on 3 June 1983): status as at 31 December 2003;[3]

F. Convention on the Physical Protection of Nuclear Material, signed at Vienna on 3 March 1980 (entered into force on 8 February 1987): status as at 30 November 2003;[4]

G. Protocol for the Suppression of Unlawful Acts of Violence at Airports Serving International Civil Aviation, supplementary to the Convention for the Suppression of Unlawful Acts against the Safety of Civil Aviation, signed at Montreal on 24 February 1988 (entered into force on 6 August 1989): status as at 30 November 2003;[2]

H. Convention for the Suppression of Unlawful Acts against the Safety of Maritime Navigation, done at Rome on 10 March 1988 (entered into force on 1 March 1992): status as at 30 November 2003;[5]

I. Protocol for the Suppression of Unlawful Acts against the Safety of Fixed Platforms Located on the Continental Shelf, done at Rome on 10 March 1988 (entered into force on 1 March 1992): status as at 30 November 2003;[5]

J. Convention on the Marking of Plastic Explosives for the Purpose of Detection, signed at Montreal on 1 March 1991 (entered into force on 21 June 1998): status as at 30 November 2003;[2]

K. International Convention for the Suppression of Terrorist Bombings, adopted by the General Assembly of the United Nations on 15 December 1997 (entered into force on 23 May 2001): status as at 31 December 2003;[3]

L. International Convention for the Suppression of the Financing of Terrorism, adopted by the General Assembly of the United Nations on 9 December 1999 (entered into force on 10 April 2002): status as at 31 December 2003;[3]

M. Arab Convention on the Suppression of Terrorism, signed at a meeting held at the General Secretariat of the League of Arab States in Cairo on 22 April 1998 (entered into force on 7 May 1999): status as at 16 June 2003;

N. Convention of the Organization of the Islamic Conference on Combating International Terrorism, adopted at Ouagadougou on 1 July 1999; status as at 30 June 2003;

O. European Convention on the Suppression of Terrorism, concluded at Strasbourg on 27 January 1977 (entered into force on 4 August 1978): status as at 30 November 2003;[6]

P. OAS Convention to Prevent and Punish Acts of Terrorism Taking the Form of Crimes against Persons and Related Extortion that are of International Significance, concluded at Washington, D.C., on 2 February 1971 (entered into force on 16 October 1973): status as at 30 November 2003;[7]

Q. OAU Convention on the Prevention and Combating of Terrorism, adopted at Algiers on 14 July 1999 (entered into force on 6 December 2002): status as at 15 May 2003;

STATUS OF INTERNATIONAL CONVENTIONS ON INTERNATIONAL TERRORISM

R. SAARC Regional Convention on Suppression of Terrorism, signed at Kathmandu on 4 November 1987 (entered into force on 22 August 1988): all seven States members of SAARC (Bangladesh, Bhutan, India, Maldives, Nepal, Pakistan and Sri Lanka) are parties to the Convention;

S. Treaty on Cooperation among States Members of the Commonwealth of Independent States in Combating Terrorism, done at Minsk on 4 June 1999: status as at 19 June 2003;

T. Inter-American Convention against Terrorism, adopted at Bridgetown on 3 June 2002: status as at 30 November 2003;[7]

U. Protocol Amending the European Convention on the Suppression of Terrorism, adopted at Strasbourg, on 15 May 2003: status as at 30 November 2003.[6]

Notes:

1. Updated information on individual conventions may be found at http://untreaty.un.org/English/Terrorism.asp. Additional information on these conventions is available at http://untreaty.un.org/ENGLISH/bible/englishinternetbible/bible.asp and http://untreaty.un.org/ English/Teventen.asp.

2. www.icao.int/cgi/goto_leb.pl?icao/en/le/treaty.htm.

3. www.un.org/law.

4. www.iaea.org/worldatom/Documents/Legal

5. www.imo.org.

6. www.legal.coe.int.

7. www.oas.org/.

STATUS OF INTERNATIONAL CONVENTIONS ON INTERNATIONAL TERRORISM

Table 1
Total participation in international conventions pertaining to international terrorism

Signature																				
A	B	C	D	E	F	G	H	I	J	K	L	M	N	O	P	Q	R	S	T	U
40	76	59	25	39	45[a]	68	41	39	51	58	132	22[b]	6	45	19	41[c]	-	8	33	38
Ratification, accession or succession																				
A	B	C	D	E	F	G	H	I	J	K	L	M	N	O	P	Q	R	S	T	U
176	177	179	144	136	96[a]	138	95	87	98	115	107	16[b]	8[b]	41	15	22[c]	7	5	6	1

a Includes the European Atomic Energy Community, which is not listed in table 2.
b Includes the Palestinian Authority.
c Includes the Saharawi Arab Democratic Republic.

STATUS OF INTERNATIONAL CONVENTIONS ON INTERNATIONAL TERRORISM

Table 2
Status of participation in international conventions pertaining to international terrorism

State	A	B	C	D	E	F	G	H	I	J	K	L	M	N	O	P	Q	R	S	T	U
Afghanistan		B								J											
Albania																					U
Algeria											K	L	M	N	O		Q				
Andorra												L									U
Angola															O		Q				
Antigua and Barbuda																				T	
Argentina		B	C			F	G	H	I	J	K	L									
Armenia												L							S		U
Australia		B	C	D		F						L									
Austria		B	C		E	F	G	H		J	K	L			O						U
Azerbaijan																					
Bahamas								H	I			L			O				S	T	
Bahrain												L	M								
Bangladesh																					
Barbados	A	B	C									L								T	
Belarus		B	C	D			G	H	I	J	K	L			O						
Belgium	A	B	C		E	F	G	H	I	J	K	L									
Belize										J		L								T	
Benin		B										L					Q				

STATUS OF INTERNATIONAL CONVENTIONS ON INTERNATIONAL TERRORISM

State	A	B	C	D	E	F	G	H	I	J	K	L	M	N	O	P	Q	R	S	T	U
Bhutan												L									
Bolivia					E					J		L				P				T	
Bosnia and Herzegovina												L			O						
Botswana			C									L									
Brazil	A	B	C			F	G	H	I	J	K	L					Q			T	
Brunei Darussalam								H	I												
Bulgaria		B	C	D		F	G	H	I	J		L			O						
Burkina Faso	A													N			Q				
Burundi		B	C								K	L					Q				
Cambodia		B										L									
Cameroon							G										Q				
Canada	A	B	C	D	E	F	G	H	I	J	K	L								T	
Cape Verde												L									
Central African Republic												L					Q				
Chad		B	C																		
Chile		B			E		G	H	I	J		L				P	Q			T	
China							G	H	I			L									
Colombia	A	B								J		L				P				T	
Comoros											K	L	M				Q				

408   INTERNATIONAL TERRORISM AGREEMENTS

STATUS OF INTERNATIONAL CONVENTIONS ON INTERNATIONAL TERRORISM

State	Signature																				
	A	B	C	D	E	F	G	H	I	J	K	L	M	N	O	P	Q	R	S	T	U
Congo (Republic of the)	A		C				G					L					Q				
Cook Islands																					
Costa Rica		B	C				G	H	I		K	L				P				T	
Côte d'Ivoire							G			J	K	L					Q				
Croatia												L			O						U
Cuba												L									
Cyprus			C								K	L			O						U
Czech Republic											K	L			O						
Democratic People's Republic of Korea							G					L									
Democratic Republic of the Congo					E		G					L					Q				
Denmark	A	B	C	D		F	G	H	I	J	K	L	M		O						
Djibouti												L									
Dominica																					
Dominican Republic		B	C		E	F		H				L				P	Q			T	
Ecuador	A	B		D				H		J		L	M			P				T	
Egypt			C		E		G	H		J	K	L		N			Q				

DOCUMENTS AND COMMENTARY 409

STATUS OF INTERNATIONAL CONVENTIONS ON INTERNATIONAL TERRORISM

State	Signature																				
	A	B	C	D	E	F	G	H	I	J	K	L	M	N	O	P	Q	R	S	T	U
El Salvador		B			E											P				T	
Equatorial Guinea		B															Q				
Eritrea																					
Estonia											K	L			O		Q				U
Ethiopia		B	C				G														
Fiji		B	C														Q				
Finland	A	B		D	E	F	G	H		J	K	L			O						U
France	A	B				F	G	H	I	J	K	L			O						U
Gabon		B	C		E		G			J		L									
Gambia		B																			
Georgia												L			O		Q				U
Germany	A	B	C	D	E	F	G			J	K	L			O		Q				U
Ghana		B					G			J		L									
Greece	A	B	C		E	F	G	H	I	J	K	L			O		Q				U
Grenada					E	F													S	T	
Guatemala	A	B	C	D	E							L				P				T	
Guinea										J		L					Q				
Guinea-Bissau										J		L					Q				
Guyana																				T	
Haiti			C		E	F														T	
Holy See	A																				

STATUS OF INTERNATIONAL CONVENTIONS ON INTERNATIONAL TERRORISM

State	Signature																				
	A	B	C	D	E	F	G	H	I	J	K	L	M	N	O	P	Q	R	S	T	U
Honduras					E					J		L				P				T	
Hungary		B	C	D		F	G	H			K	L			O						U
Iceland				D			G				K	L			O						U
India		B	C								K	L									
Indonesia	A	B				F	G					L									
Iran (Islamic Republic of)		B																			
Iraq		B			E			H	I		K		M								U
Ireland	A					F	G				K	L			O						
Israel	A	B	C		E	F	G	H	I	J	K	L									
Italy	A	B	C	D	E	F	G	H	I		K	L			O						U
Jamaica	A	B	C		E	G					L				P						
Japan	A	B			E						K	L									
Jordan		B	C				G	H	I	J		L	M								
Kazakhstan												L							S		
Kenya																	Q				
Kiribati																					
Kuwait		B					G			J		L	M								
Kyrgyzstan																			S		
Lao People's Democratic Republic		B	C																		
Latvia												L			O						

STATUS OF INTERNATIONAL CONVENTIONS ON INTERNATIONAL TERRORISM

State	A	B	C	D	E	F	G	H	I	J	K	L	M	N	O	P	Q	R	S	T	U
Lebanon							G			J			M								
Lesotho					E							L					Q				
Liberia	A				E		G	H	I												
Libyan Arab Jamahiriya												L	M				Q				
Liechtenstein		B				F						L			O						U
Lithuania											K				O						
Luxembourg		B	C		E	F	G				K	L			O		Q				U
Madagascar	A									J	K	L									
Malawi							G														
Malaysia		B					G														
Maldives																					
Mali										J		L					Q				
Malta							G					L			O						
Marshall Islands												L									
Mauritania													M								
Mauritius					E		G			J		L									
Mexico	A	B	C				G			J		L				P	Q			T	
Micronesia (Federated States of)												L									
Monaco											K	L									

STATUS OF INTERNATIONAL CONVENTIONS ON INTERNATIONAL TERRORISM

State	A	B	C	D	E	F	G	H	I	J	K	L	M	N	O	P	Q	R	S	T	U
Mongolia		B	C	D		F						L									
Morocco						F	G	H	I			L	M								
Mozambique												L					Q				
Myanmar												L									
Namibia												L					Q				
Nauru																					
Nepal											K										
Netherlands	A	B	C	D	E	F	G	H	I	J	K	L			O						U
New Zealand		B	C		E		G	H	I			L									
Nicaragua			C	D						J		L				P				T	
Niger	A	B	C			F	G														
Nigeria	A																				
Niue																					
Norway	A	B		D	E	F	G	H	I	J	K	L			O		Q				U
Oman							G			J			M	N							
Pakistan	A	B																			
Palau																					
Panama	A	B	C		E	F					K	L				P				T	
Papua New Guinea																					
Paraguay		B	C	D						J		L				P				T	
Peru							G					L				P				T	

STATUS OF INTERNATIONAL CONVENTIONS ON INTERNATIONAL TERRORISM

State	A	B	C	D	E	F	G	H	I	J	K	L	M	N	O	P	Q	R	S	T	U
Philippines	A	B	C		E	F	G	H	I		K	L									
Poland		B	C	D		F	G	H	I		K	L			O						U
Portugal	A	B	C		E	F	G				K	L			O						U
Qatar													M								
Republic of Korea	A					F	G			J		L									
Republic of Moldova												L			O				S		U
Romania		B	C	D		F	G				K	L			O						
Russian Federation		B	C	D		F	G	H	I		K	L			O				S		U
Rwanda		B	C	D								L					Q				
Saint Kitts and Nevis												L								T	
Saint Lucia																				T	
Saint Vincent and the Grenadines							G					L								T	
Samoa												L									
San Marino												L			O						U
Sao Tome and Principe																					
Saudi Arabia	A						G	H	I			L	M	N							
Senegal	A	B	C		E		G			J							Q				

STATUS OF INTERNATIONAL CONVENTIONS ON INTERNATIONAL TERRORISM

State	Signature																				
	A	B	C	D	E	F	G	H	I	J	K	L	M	N	O	P	Q	R	S	T	U
Serbia and Montenegro						F						L			O						U
Seychelles																					
Sierra Leone		B						H	I			L									
Singapore		B	C									L		N			Q				
Slovakia											K	L			O						
Slovenia											K	L			O						U
Solomon Islands																					
Somalia												L	M								
South Africa		B	C			F					K	L					Q				
Spain	A	B	C			F	G	H	I	J	K	L			O						U
Sri Lanka							G				K	L									
Sudan											K	L	M				Q				
Suriname					E															T	
Swaziland																	Q				
Sweden	A	B		D	E		G	H	I		K	L			O						U
Switzerland	A	B	C		E	F	G			J		L			O						U
Syrian Arab Republic													M								
Tajikistan												L							S		
Thailand		B										L									

STATUS OF INTERNATIONAL CONVENTIONS ON INTERNATIONAL TERRORISM

State	A	B	C	D	E	F	G	H	I	J	K	L	M	N	O	P	Q	R	S	T	U
													Signature								
The former Yugoslav Republic of Macedonia											K	L			O						U
Togo					E		G			J		L					Q				
Tonga																					
Trinidad and Tobago		B	C													P					
Tunisia				D																	
Turkey		B	C			F	G	H	I	J	K	L	M	N	O		Q				U
Turkmenistan											K										
Tuvalu																					
Uganda					E		G	H			K	L									
Ukraine		B	C	D			G		I	J		L	M		O		Q				U
United Arab Emirates							G														
United Kingdom of Great Britain and Northern Ireland	A	B	C	D	E	F	G	H	I	J	K	L			O						U
United Republic of Tanzania																	Q				

STATUS OF INTERNATIONAL CONVENTIONS ON INTERNATIONAL TERRORISM

State	Signature																				
	A	B	C	D	E	F	G	H	I	J	K	L	M	N	O	P	Q	R	S	T	U
United States of America	A	B	C	D	E	F	G	H	I	J	K	L				P				T	
Uruguay											K	L				P				T	
Uzbekistan											K	L									
Vanuatu																					
Venezuela	A	B	C				G				K	L				P				T	
Viet Nam																					
Yemen			C										M								
Zambia																					
Zimbabwe																					

DOCUMENTS AND COMMENTARY

STATUS OF INTERNATIONAL CONVENTIONS ON INTERNATIONAL TERRORISM

State	Ratification, accession or succession																			
	A	B	C	D	E	F	G	H	I	J	K	L	M	N	O	P	Q	R	S	T	U
Afghanistan	A	B	C	D	E	F		H	I	J	K	L									
Albania	A	B	C	D	E	F	G	H	I		K	L			O						
Algeria	A	B	C	D	E	F	G	H		J	K	L	M				Q				
Andorra																					
Angola	A	B	C																		
Antigua and Barbuda	A	B	C	D	E	F						L					Q				
Argentina	A	B	C	D	E	F	G	H		J	K										
Armenia	A		C	D		F	G												S		
Australia	A	B	C	D	E	F	G	H	I		K	L									
Austria	A	B	C	D	E	F	G	H	I	J	K	L			O						
Azerbaijan		B	C	D	E		G			J	K										
Bahamas	A	B	C	D	E																
Bahrain	A	B	C				G			J			M	N							
Bangladesh	A	B	C															R			
Barbados	A	B	C	D	E		G	H	I	J	K	L									
Belarus	A	B	C	D	E	F	G	H	I	J	K										
Belgium	A	B	C		E	F	G								O						
Belize	A	B	C	D	E		G				K	L									
Benin	A	B		D	E						K										
Bhutan	A	B	C	D	E													R			

STATUS OF INTERNATIONAL CONVENTIONS ON INTERNATIONAL TERRORISM

State	A	B	C	D	E	F	G	H	I	J	K	L	M	N	O	P	Q	R	S	T	U
Bolivia	A	B	C	D	E	F	G	H	I	J	K	L				P					
Bosnia and Herzegovina	A	B	C	D	E	F	G	H	I		K	L			O						
Botswana	A	B	C	D	E	F	G	H	I			L									
Brazil	A	B	C	D	E	F	G	H	I	J	K					P					
Brunei Darussalam	A	B	C	D	E		G				K	L									
Bulgaria	A	B	C	D	E	F	G	H	I	J	K	L			O						
Burkina Faso	A	B	C	D	E		G				K	L									
Burundi	A	B	C	D																	
Cambodia	A	B	C				G														
Cameroon	A	B	C	D	E		G	H	I	J											
Canada	A	B	C	D	E	F	G	H	I	J	K	L								T	
Cape Verde	A	B	C	D	E	F	G	H	I	J	K	L					Q				
Central African Republic	A	B	C				G														
Chad	A	B	C	D	E		G														
Chile	A	B	C	D	E	F	G	H	I	J	K	L									
China	A	B	C	D	E	F	G	H	I		K										
Colombia	A	B	C	D		F										P					
Comoros	A	B	C	D	E						K	L					Q				
Congo (Republic of the)	A	B	C																		

STATUS OF INTERNATIONAL CONVENTIONS ON INTERNATIONAL TERRORISM

State	\multicolumn{21}{c}{Ratification, accession or succession}
	A	B	C	D	E	F	G	H	I	J	K	L	M	N	O	P	Q	R	S	T	U
Cook Islands																					
Costa Rica	A	B	C	D	E	F	G	H	I		K	L				P					
Côte d'Ivoire	A	B	C	D	E		G				K	L									
Croatia	A	B	C	D	E	F	G					L			O						
Cuba	A	B	C	D	E	F	G	H	I	J	K	L									
Cyprus	A	B	C	D	E	F	G	H	I	J	K	L			O						
Czech Republic	A	B	C	D	E	F	G			J	K				O						
Democratic People's Republic of Korea	A	B	C	D	E		G														
Democratic Republic of the Congo	A	B	C	D																	
Denmark	A	B	C	D	E	F	G	H	I	J	K	L			O						
Djibouti	A	B	C										M								
Dominica					E			H													
Dominican Republic	A	B	C	D												P					
Ecuador	A	B	C	D	E	F	G	H	I	J		L									
Egypt	A	B	C	D	E		G	H	I	J			M	N			Q				
El Salvador	A	B	C	D	E		G	H	I	J	K	L				P				T	
Equatorial Guinea	A	B	C	D	E	F					K	L					Q				

STATUS OF INTERNATIONAL CONVENTIONS ON INTERNATIONAL TERRORISM

State								Ratification, accession or succession												
	A	B	C	D	E	F	G	H	I	J	K	L	M	N	O	P	Q	R	S	T	U
Eritrea										J							Q				
Estonia	A	B	C	D	E	F	G	H		J	K	L			O						
Ethiopia	A	B	C	D	E		G				K						Q				
Fiji	A	B	C				G														
Finland	A	B	C	D	E	F	G	H	I	J	K	L			O						
France	A	B	C	D	E	F	G	H	I	J	K	L			O						
Gabon	A	B	C	D			G														
Gambia	A	B	C				G	H		J											
Georgia	A	B	C				G			J		L			O						
Germany	A	B	C	D	E	F	G	H	I	J	K				O						
Ghana	A	B	C	D	E	F	G	H	I	J	K	L					Q				
Greece	A	B	C	D	E	F	G	H	I	J	K				O						
Grenada	A	B	C	D	E	F	G	H	I	J	K	L				P					
Guatemala	A	B	C	D	E	F	G			J	K	L				P					
Guinea	A	B	C				G				K	L									
Guinea-Bissau		B	C																		
Guyana	A	B	C				G	H	I												
Haiti	A	B	C	D	E																
Holy See																					
Honduras	A	B	C	D	E			H		J	K	L									
Hungary	A	B	C	D	E	F	G	H	I	J	K				O						
Iceland	A	B	C	D	E	F	G	H	I	J	K	L			O						

STATUS OF INTERNATIONAL CONVENTIONS ON INTERNATIONAL TERRORISM

State	A	B	C	D	E	F	G	H	I	J	K	L	M	N	O	P	Q	R	S	T	U
India	A	B	C	D	E	F	G	H	I		K	L						R			
Indonesia	A	B	C			F															
Iran (Islamic Republic of)	A	B	C	D			G														
Iraq	A	B	C	D			G														
Ireland	A	B	C			F	G			J					O						
Israel	A	B	C	D		F	G				K	L									
Italy	A	B	C	D	E	F	G	H	I			L			O						
Jamaica	A	B	C	D																	
Japan	A	B	C	D	E	F	G	H	I	J	K	L									
Jordan	A	B	C	D	E		G			J		L	M								
Kazakhstan	A	B	C	D	E		G				K	L									
Kenya	A	B	C	D	E	F	G	H	I	J	K	L					Q		S			
Kiribati																					
Kuwait	A	B	C	D	E		G	H	I	J	K										
Kyrgyzstan	A	B	C	D	E		G			J	K	L									
Lao People's Democratic Republic	A	B	C	D	E	F	G														
Latvia	A	B	C	D	E	F	G	H	I	J	K	L			O				S		
Lebanon	A	B	C	D	E	F	G	H	I	J	K	L	M								
Lesotho	A	B	C		E						K	L					Q				
Liberia	A	B	C	D	E		G	H	I		K	L									

STATUS OF INTERNATIONAL CONVENTIONS ON INTERNATIONAL TERRORISM

State	Ratification, accession or succession																			
	A	B	C	D	E	F	G	H	I	J	K	L	M	N	O	P	Q	R	S	T	U
Libyan Arab Jamahiriya	A	B	C	D	E	F	G	H	I			L	M				Q				
Liechtenstein	A	B	C	D	E	F	G	H	I	J	K	L			O						
Lithuania	A	B	C	D	E	F	G	H	I	J		L			O						
Luxembourg	A	B	C		E	F	G			J		L			O						
Madagascar	A	B	C	D	E		G				K	L									
Malawi	A	B	C	D	E						K	L									
Malaysia	A	B	C	D							K										
Maldives	A	B	C	D			G			J	K	L						R			
Mali	A	B	C	D	E	F	G	H	I	J	K	L		N			Q				
Malta	A	B	C	D	E	F	G	H	I		K	L			O						
Marshall Islands	A	B	C	D	E	F	G	H	I	J	K	L									
Mauritania	A	B	C	D	E	F	G				K	L									
Mauritius	A	B	C	D	E		G				K										
Mexico	A	B	C	D	E	F	G	H	I	J	K	L				P	Q				
Micronesia (Federated States of)			C				G	H			K	L									
Monaco	A	B	C	D	E	F	G	H	I	J	K	L									
Mongolia	A	B	C	D	E	F	G	H	I	J	K	L									
Morocco	A	B	C	D		F	G	H	I	J	K	L	M							T	
Mozambique	A	B	C	D	E	F	G	H	I		K	L					Q				

DOCUMENTS AND COMMENTARY

STATUS OF INTERNATIONAL CONVENTIONS ON INTERNATIONAL TERRORISM

State	Ratification, accession or succession																				
	A	B	C	D	E	F	G	H	I	J	K	L	M	N	O	P	Q	R	S	T	U
Myanmar	A	B	C				G	H			K										
Namibia						F															
Nauru	A	B	C																		
Nepal	A	B	C	D	E																
Netherlands	A	B	C	D	E	F	G	H	I	J	K	L			O			R			
New Zealand	A	B	C	D	E		G	H	I			L									
Nicaragua	A	B	C	D	E		G				K	L				P				T	
Niger	A	B	C	D																	
Nigeria	A	B	C				G			J		L									
Niue																					
Norway	A	B	C	D	E	F	G	H	I	J	K	L			O						U
Oman	A	B	C	D	E	F	G	H	I				M	N							
Pakistan	A	B	C	D	E	F	G	H	I		K							R			
Palau	A	B	C	D	E		G	H	I	J		L									
Panama	A	B	C	D	E	F	G	H	I	J	K	L				P					
Papua New Guinea	A	B	C	D	E		G				K	L									
Paraguay	A	B	C	D	E	F	G														
Peru	A	B	C	D	E	F	G	H	I	J	K	L				P				T	
Philippines	A	B	C	D	E	F															
Poland	A	B	C	D	E	F		H	I			L			O						
Portugal	A	B	C	D	E	F	G	H	I	J	K	L			O						

STATUS OF INTERNATIONAL CONVENTIONS ON INTERNATIONAL TERRORISM

State	Ratification, accession or succession																				
	A	B	C	D	E	F	G	H	I	J	K	L	M	N	O	P	Q	R	S	T	U
Qatar	A	B	C	D				H	I	J											
Republic of Korea	A	B	C	D	E	F	G	H	I	J											
Republic of Moldova	A	B	C	D	E	F	G			J	K	L			O				S		
Romania	A	B	C	D	E	F	G	H	I	J		L			O						
Russian Federation	A	B	C	D	E	F	G	H	I		K	L			O						
Rwanda	A	B	C	D	E		G				K	L					Q				
Saint Kitts and Nevis					E			H		J		L									
Saint Lucia	A	B	C				G														
Saint Vincent and the Grenadines	A	B	C	D	E		G	H	I			L									
Samoa	A	B	C				G			J		L									
San Marino											K				O						
Sao Tome and Principe													M	N							
Saudi Arabia	A	B	C		E		G			J											
Senegal	A	B	C		E		G				K						Q				
Serbia and Montenegro	A	B	C	D	E	F	G				K	L			O						
Seychelles	A	B	C	D	E	F		H	I	J	K										

STATUS OF INTERNATIONAL CONVENTIONS ON INTERNATIONAL TERRORISM

State	\multicolumn{21}{c}{Ratification, accession or succession}																				
	A	B	C	D	E	F	G	H	I	J	K	L	M	N	O	P	Q	R	S	T	U
Sierra Leone	A	B	C	D	E						K	L									
Singapore	A	B	C				G			J		L									
Slovakia	A	B	C	D	E	F	G	H	I	J	K	L			O						
Slovenia	A	B	C	D	E	F	G	H	I	J	K				O						
Solomon Islands	A		C																		
Somalia																					
South Africa	A	B	C	D	E		G	H	I	J	K	L					Q				
Spain	A	B	C	D	E	F	G	H	I	J	K	L			O						
Sri Lanka	A	B	C	D	E		G	H	I	J	K	L						R			
Sudan	A	B	C	D	E	F	G	H	I	J	K	L	M	N							
Suriname	A	B	C		E		G			J											
Swaziland	A	B	C	D	E	F	G	H	I	J	K	L									
Sweden	A	B	C	D	E	F	G	H	I	J	K	L			O						
Switzerland	A	B	C	D	E	F	G	H	I	J	K	L			O						
Syrian Arab Republic	A	B	C	D	E		G	H	I				M								
Tajikistan	A	B	C		D	E		F	G				K						S		
Thailand	A	B	C				G														
The former Yugoslav Republic of Macedonia	A	B	C	D	E	F	G			J											

STATUS OF INTERNATIONAL CONVENTIONS ON INTERNATIONAL TERRORISM

State	A	B	C	D	E	F	G	H	I	J	K	L	M	N	O	P	Q	R	S	T	U
										Ratification, accession or succession											
Togo	A	B	C	D	E		G	H	I	J	K	L					Q				
Tonga	A	B	C	D	E	F	G	H	I	J	K	L									
Trinidad and Tobago	A	B	C	D	E	F	G	H	I	J	K										
Tunisia	A	B	C	D	E	F	G	H	I	J		L	M	N			Q				
Turkey	A	B	C	D	E	F	G	H	I	J	K	L			O						
Turkmenistan	A	B	C	D	E		G	H	I		K										
Tuvalu																					
Uganda	A	B	C	D	E	F	G	H	I	J	K	L									
Ukraine	A	B	C	D	E	F	G	H	I	J	K	L			O						
United Arab Emirates	A	B	C	D	E	F	G		I	J			M								
United Kingdom of Great Britain and Northern Ireland	A	B	C	D	E	F	G	H	I	J	K				O						
United Republic of Tanzania	A	B	C		E		G	H	I	J		L					Q				
United States of America	A	B	C	D	E	F	G	H	I	J	K	L				P					
Uruguay	A	B	C	D	E	F	G	H	I	J	K	L				P					
Uzbekistan	A	B	C	D	E	F	G	H	I	J	K	L									
Vanuatu	A	B	C					H	I												

STATUS OF INTERNATIONAL CONVENTIONS ON INTERNATIONAL TERRORISM

State	Ratification, accession or succession																				
	A	B	C	D	E	F	G	H	I	J	K	L	M	N	O	P	Q	R	S	T	U
Venezuela	A	B	C		E						K	L				P					
Viet Nam	A	B	C	D			G	H	I			L									
Yemen	A	B	C	D	E			H	I		K		M								
Zambia	A	B	C							J											
Zimbabwe	A	B	C																		

428 INTERNATIONAL TERRORISM AGREEMENTS

SIGNIFICANT TERRORIST INCIDENTS 1961-2003:

A BRIEF CHRONOLOGY*

First U.S. Aircraft Hijacked, May 1, 1961: Puerto Rican born Antuilo Ramierez Ortiz forced at gunpoint a National Airlines plane to fly to Havana, Cuba, where he was given asylum. Ambassador to Guatemala Assassinated, August 28, 1968: U.S. Ambassador to Guatemala John Gordon Mein was murdered by a rebel faction when gunmen forced his official car off the road in Guatemala City and raked the vehicle with gunfire.

Ambassador to Japan Attacked, July 30, 1969: U.S. Ambassador to Japan A.H. Meyer was attacked by a knife-wielding Japanese citizen.

Ambassador to Brazil Kidnapped, September 3, 1969: U.S. Ambassador to Brazil Charles Burke Elbrick was kidnapped by the Marxist revolutionary group MR-8.

Attack on the Munich Airport, February 10, 1970: Three terrorists attacked El Al passengers in a bus at the Munich Airport with guns and grenades. One passenger was killed and 11 were injured. All three terrorists were captured by airport police. The Action Organization for the Liberation of Palestine and the Popular Democratic Front for the Liberation of Palestine claimed responsibility for the attack.

U.S. Agency for International Development Adviser Kidnapped, July 31, 1970: In Montevideo, Uruguay, the Tupamaros terrorist group kidnapped AID Police adviser Dan Mitrione; his body was found on August 10.

"Bloody Friday," July 21, 1972: An Irish Republican Army (IRA) bomb attacks killed eleven people and injure 130 in Belfast, Northern Ireland. Ten days later, three IRA car bomb attacks in the village of Claudy left six dead.

---

* U.S. State Department, Office of the Historian Bureau of Public Affairs; http://www.state.gov/r/pa/ho/pubs/fs/5902.htm.

SIGNIFICANT TERRORIST INCIDENTS 1961-2003

Munich Olympic Massacre, September 5, 1972: Eight Palestinian "Black September" terrorists seized eleven Israeli athletes in the Olympic Village in Munich, West Germany. In a bungled rescue attempt by West German authorities, nine of the hostages and five terrorists were killed.

Ambassador to Sudan Assassinated, March 2, 1973: U.S. Ambassador to Sudan Cleo A. Noel and other diplomats were assassinated at the Saudi Arabian Embassy in Khartoum by members of the Black September organization.

Consul General in Mexico Kidnapped, May 4, 1973: U.S. Consul General in Guadalajara Terrence Leonhardy was kidnapped by members of the People's Revolutionary Armed Forces.

Attack and Hijacking at the Rome Airport, December 17, 1973: Five terrorists pulled weapons from their luggage in the terminal lounge at the Rome airport, killing two persons. They then attacked a Pan American 707 bound for Beirut and Tehran, destroying it with incendiary grenades and killing 29 persons, including 4 senior Moroccan officials and 14 American employees of ARAMCO. They then herded 5 Italian hostages into a Lufthansa airliner and killed an Italian customs agent as he tried to escape, after which they forced the pilot to fly to Beirut. After Lebanese authorities refused to let the plane land, it landed in Athens, where the terrorists demanded the release of 2 Arab terrorists. In order to make Greek authorities comply with their demands, the terrorists killed a hostage and threw his body onto the tarmac. The plane then flew to Damascus, where it stopped for two hours to obtain fuel and food. It then flew to Kuwait, where the terrorists released their hostages in return for passage to an unknown destination. The Palestine Liberation Organization disavowed the attack, and no group claimed responsibility for it.

Ambassador to Cyprus Assassinated, August 19, 1974: U.S. Ambassador to Cyprus Rodger P. Davies and his Greek Cypriot secretary were shot and killed by snipers during a demonstration outside the U.S. Embassy in Nicosia.

Domestic Terrorism, January 27-29, 1975: Puerto Rican nationalists bombed a Wall Street bar, killing four and injuring 60; two days later, the Weather Underground claims responsibility for an explosion in a bathroom at the U.S. Department of State in Washington.

Entebbe Hostage Crisis, June 27, 1976: Members of the Baader-Meinhof Group and the Popular Front for the Liberation of Palestine (PFLP) seized an Air France airliner and its 258 passengers. They forced the plane to land in Uganda. On July 3 Israeli commandos successfully rescued the passengers.

Assassination of Former Chilean Diplomat, September 21, 1976: Exiled Chilean Foreign Minister Orlando Letelier was killed by a car-bomb in Washington.

SIGNIFICANT TERRORIST INCIDENTS 1961-2003

Kidnapping of Italian Prime Minister, March 16, 1978: Premier Aldo Moro was seized by the Red Brigade and assassinated 55 days later.

Ambassador to Afghanistan Assassinated, February 14, 1979: Four Afghans kidnapped U.S. Ambassador Adolph Dubs in Kabul and demanded the release of various "religious figures." Dubs was killed, along with four alleged terrorists, when Afghan police stormed the hotel room where he was being held.

Iran Hostage Crisis, November 4, 1979: After President Carter agreed to admit the Shah of Iran into the US, Iranian radicals seized the U.S. Embassy in Tehran and took 66 American diplomats hostage. Thirteen hostages were soon released, but the remaining 53 were held until their release on January 20, 1981.

Grand Mosque Seizure, November 20, 1979: 200 Islamic terrorists seized the Grand Mosque in Mecca, Saudi Arabia, taking hundreds of pilgrims hostage. Saudi and French security forces retook the shrine after an intense battle in which some 250 people were killed and 600 wounded.

U.S. Installation Bombing, August 31, 1981: The Red Army exploded a bomb at the U.S. Air Force Base at Ramstein, West Germany.

Assassination of Egyptian President, October 6, 1981: Soldiers who were secretly members of the Takfir Wal-Hajira sect attacked and killed Egyptian President Anwar Sadat during a troop review.

Murder of Missionaries, December 4, 1981: Three American nuns and one lay missionary were found murdered outside San Salvador, El Salvador. They were killed by members of the National Guard, and the killers are currently in prison.

Assassination of Lebanese Prime Minister, September 14, 1982: Premier Bashir Gemayel was assassinated by a car bomb parked outside his party's Beirut headquarters.

1983

Colombian Hostage-taking, April 8, 1983: A U.S. citizen was seized by the Revolutionary Armed Forces of Colombia (FARC) and held for ransom.

Bombing of U.S. Embassy in Beirut, April 18, 1983: Sixty-three people, including the CIA's Middle East director, were killed and 120 were injured in a 400-pound suicide truck-bomb attack on the U.S. Embassy in Beirut, Lebanon. The Islamic Jihad claimed responsibility.

Naval Officer Assassinated in El Salvador, May 25, 1983: A U.S. Navy officer was assassinated by the Farabundo Marti National Liberation Front.

North Korean Hit Squad, October 9, 1983: North Korean agents blew up a delegation from South Korea in Rangoon, Burma, killing 21 persons and injuring 48.

SIGNIFICANT TERRORIST INCIDENTS 1961-2003

Bombing of Marine Barracks, Beirut, October 23, 1983: Simultaneous suicide truck-bomb attacks were made on American and French compounds in Beirut, Lebanon. A 12,000-pound bomb destroyed the U.S. compound, killing 242 Americans, while 58 French troops were killed when a 400-pound device destroyed a French base. Islamic Jihad claimed responsibility.

Naval Officer Assassinated in Greece, November 15, 1983: A U.S. Navy officer was shot by the November 17 terrorist group in Athens, Greece, while his car was stopped at a traffic light.

1984

Kidnapping of Embassy Official, March 16, 1984: The Islamic Jihad kidnapped and later murdered Political Officer William Buckley in Beirut, Lebanon. Other U.S. citizens not connected to the U.S. government were seized over a succeeding two-year period.

Restaurant Bombing in Spain, April 12, 1984: Eighteen U.S. servicemen were killed and 83 people were injured in a bomb attack on a restaurant near a U.S. Air Force Base in Torrejon, Spain.

Temple Seizure, June 5, 1984: Sikh terrorists seized the Golden Temple in Amritsar, India. One hundred people died when Indian security forces retook the Sikh holy shrine.

Assassination of Indian Prime Minister, October 31, 1984: Premier Indira Gandhi was shot to death by members of her security force.

1985

Kidnapping of U.S. Officials in Mexico, February 7, 1985: Under the orders of narcotrafficker Rafael Caro Quintero, Drug Enforcement Administration agent Enrique Camarena Salazar and his pilot were kidnapped, tortured and executed.

TWA Hijacking, June 14, 1985: A Trans-World Airlines flight was hijacked en route to Rome from Athens by two Lebanese Hizballah terrorists and forced to fly to Beirut. The eight crew members and 145 passengers were held for seventeen days, during which one American hostage, a U.S. Navy sailor, was murdered. After being flown twice to Algiers, the aircraft was returned to Beirut after Israel released 435 Lebanese and Palestinian prisoners.

Attack on a Restaurant in El Salvador, June 19, 1985: Members of the FMLN (Farabundo Marti National Liberation Front) fired on a restaurant in the Zona Rosa district of San Salvador, killing four Marine Security Guards assigned to the U.S. Embassy and nine Salvadorean civilians.

Air India Bombing, June 23, 1985: A bomb destroyed an Air India Boeing 747 over the Atlantic, killing all 329 people aboard. Both Sikh and Kashmiri terrorists were blamed for the attack. Two cargo handlers were killed at Tokyo airport, Japan, when another Sikh bomb exploded in an Air Canada aircraft en route to India.

Soviet Diplomats Kidnapped, September 30, 1985: In Beirut, Lebanon, Sunni terrorists kidnapped four Soviet diplomats. One was killed but three were later released.

Achille Lauro Hijacking, October 7, 1985: Four Palestinian Liberation Front terrorists seized the Italian cruise liner in the eastern Mediterranean Sea, taking more than 700 hostages. One U.S. passenger was murdered before the Egyptian government offered the terrorists safe haven in return for the hostages' freedom.

Egyptian Airliner Hijacking, November 23, 1985: An EgyptAir airplane bound from Athens to Malta and carrying several U.S. citizens was hijacked by the Abu Nidal Group.

Airport Attacks in Rome and Vienna, December 27, 1985: Four gunmen belonging to the Abu Nidal Organization attacked the El Al and Trans World Airlines ticket counters at Rome's Leonardo da Vinci Airport with grenades and automatic rifles. Thirteen persons were killed and 75 were wounded before Italian police and Israeli security guards killed three of the gunmen and captured the fourth. Three more Abu Nidal gunmen attacked the El Al ticket counter at Vienna's Schwechat Airport, killing three persons and wounding 30. Austrian police killed one of the gunmen and captured the others.

1986

Aircraft Bombing in Greece, March 30, 1986: A Palestinian splinter group detonated a bomb as TWA Flight 840 approached Athens airport, killing four U.S. citizens.

Berlin Discothèque Bombing, April 5, 1986: Two U.S. soldiers were killed and 79 American servicemen were injured in a Libyan bomb attack on a nightclub in West Berlin, West Germany. In retaliation U.S. military jets bombed targets in and around Tripoli and Benghazi.

Kimpo Airport Bombing, September 14, 1986: North Korean agents detonated an explosive device at Seoul's Kimpo airport, killing 5 persons and injuring 29 others.

1987

Bus Attack, April 24, 1987: Sixteen U.S. servicemen riding in a Greek Air Force bus near Athens were injured in an apparent bombing attack, carried out by the revolutionary organization known as November 17.

SIGNIFICANT TERRORIST INCIDENTS 1961-2003

Downing of Airliner, November 29, 1987: North Korean agents planted a bomb aboard Korean Air Lines Flight 858, which subsequently crashed into the Indian Ocean.

Servicemen's Bar Attack, December 26, 1987: Catalan separatists bombed a Barcelona bar frequented by U.S. servicemen, resulting in the death of one U.S. citizen.

1988

Kidnapping of William Higgins, February 17, 1988: U.S. Marine Corps Lieutenant Colonel W. Higgins was kidnapped and murdered by the Iranian-backed Hizballah group while serving with the United Nations Truce Supervisory Organization (UNTSO) in southern Lebanon.

Naples USO Attack, April 14, 1988: The Organization of Jihad Brigades exploded a car-bomb outside a USO Club in Naples, Italy, killing one U.S. sailor.

Attack on U.S. Diplomat in Greece, June 28, 1988: The Defense Attaché of the U.S. Embassy in Greece was killed when a car-bomb was detonated outside his home in Athens.

Pan Am 103 Bombing, December 21, 1988: Pan American Airlines Flight 103 was blown up over Lockerbie, Scotland, by a bomb believed to have been placed on the aircraft by Libyan terrorists in Frankfurt, West Germany. All 259 people on board were killed.

1989

Assassination of U.S. Army Officer, April 21, 1989: The New People's Army (NPA) assassinated Colonel James Rowe in Manila. The NPA also assassinated two U.S. government defense contractors in September.

Bombing of UTA Flight 772, September 19, 1989: A bomb explosion destroyed UTA Flight 772 over the Sahara Desert in southern Niger during a flight from Brazzaville to Paris. All 170 persons aboard were killed. Six Libyans were later found guilty in absentia and sentenced to life imprisonment.

Assassination of German Bank Chairman, November 30, 1989: The Red Army Faction assassinated Deutsche Bank Chairman Alfred Herrhausen in Frankfurt.

1990

U.S. Embassy Bombed in Peru, January 15, 1990: The Tupac Amaru Revolutionary Movement bombed the U.S. Embassy in Lima, Peru.

U.S. Soldiers Assassinated in the Philippines, May 13, 1990: The New People's Army (NPA) killed two U.S. Air Force personnel near Clark Air Force Base in the Philippines.

SIGNIFICANT TERRORIST INCIDENTS 1961-2003

1991

Attempted Iraqi Attacks on U.S. Posts, January 18-19, 1991: Iraqi agents planted bombs at the U.S. Ambassador to Indonesia's home residence and at the USIS library in Manila.

Sniper Attack on the U.S. Embassy in Bonn, February 13, 1991: Three Red Army Faction members fired automatic rifles from across the Rhine River at the U.S. Embassy Chancery. No one was hurt.

Assassination of former Indian Prime Minister, May 21, 1991: A female member of the LTTE (Liberation Tigers of Tamil Eelam) killed herself, Prime Minister Rajiv Gandhi, and 16 others by detonating an explosive vest after presenting a garland of flowers to the former Prime Minister during an election rally in the Indian state of Tamil Nadu.

1992

Kidnapping of U.S. Businessmen in the Philippines, January 17-21, 1992: A senior official of the corporation Philippine Geothermal was kidnapped in Manila by the Red Scorpion Group, and two U.S. businessmen were seized independently by the National Liberation Army and by Revolutionary Armed Forces of Colombia (FARC).

Bombing of the Israeli Embassy in Argentina, March 17, 1992: Hizballah claimed responsibility for a blast that leveled the Israeli Embassy in Buenos Aires, Argentina, causing the deaths of 29 and wounding 242.

1993

Kidnappings of U.S. Citizens in Colombia, January 31, 1993: Revolutionary Armed Forces of Colombia (FARC) terrorists kidnapped three U.S. missionaries.

World Trade Center Bombing, February 26, 1993: The World Trade Center in New York City was badly damaged when a car bomb planted by Islamic terrorists exploded in an underground garage. The bomb left 6 people dead and 1,000 injured. The men carrying out the attack were followers of Umar Abd al-Rahman, an Egyptian cleric who preached in the New York City area.

Attempted Assassination of President Bush by Iraqi Agents, April 14, 1993: The Iraqi intelligence service attempted to assassinate former U.S. President George Bush during a visit to Kuwait. In retaliation, the U.S. launched a cruise missile attack 2 months later on the Iraqi capital Baghdad.

1994

Hebron Massacre, February 25, 1994: Jewish right-wing extremist and U.S. citizen Baruch Goldstein machine-gunned Moslem worshippers at a mosque in West Bank town of Hebron, killing 29 and wounding about 150.

SIGNIFICANT TERRORIST INCIDENTS 1961-2003

FARC Hostage-taking, September 23, 1994: FARC rebels kidnapped U.S. citizen Thomas Hargrove in Colombia.

Air France Hijacking, December 24, 1994: Members of the Armed Islamic Group seized an Air France Flight to Algeria. The four terrorists were killed during a rescue effort.

1995

Attack on U.S. Diplomats in Pakistan, March 8, 1995: Two unidentified gunmen killed two U.S. diplomats and wounded a third in Karachi, Pakistan.

Tokyo Subway Station Attack, March 20, 1995: Twelve persons were killed and 5,700 were injured in a Sarin nerve gas attack on a crowded subway station in the center of Tokyo, Japan. A similar attack occurred nearly simultaneously in the Yokohama subway system. The Aum Shinri-kyo cult was blamed for the attacks.

Bombing of the Federal Building in Oklahoma City, April 19, 1995: Right-wing extremists Timothy McVeigh and Terry Nichols destroyed the Federal Building in Oklahoma City with a massive truck bomb that killed 166 and injured hundreds more in what was up to then the largest terrorist attack on American soil.

Kashmiri Hostage-taking, July 4, 1995: In India six foreigners, including two U.S. citizens, were taken hostage by Al-Faran, a Kashmiri separatist group. One non-U.S. hostage was later found beheaded.

Jerusalem Bus Attack, August 21, 1995: HAMAS claimed responsibility for the detonation of a bomb that killed 6 and injured over 100 persons, including several U.S. citizens.

Attack on U.S. Embassy in Moscow, September 13, 1995: A rocket-propelled grenade was fired through the window of the U.S. Embassy in Moscow, ostensibly in retaliation for U.S. strikes on Serb positions in Bosnia.

Saudi Military Installation Attack, November 13, 1995: The Islamic Movement of Change planted a bomb in a Riyadh military compound that killed one U.S. citizen, several foreign national employees of the U.S. government, and over 40 others.

Egyptian Embassy Attack, November 19, 1995: A suicide bomber drove a vehicle into the Egyptian Embassy compound in Islamabad, Pakistan, killing at least 16 and injuring 60 persons. Three militant Islamic groups claimed responsibility.

1996

Papuan Hostage Abduction, January 8, 1996: In Indonesia, 200 Free Papua Movement (OPM) guerrillas abducted 26 individuals in the Lorenta nature preserve, Irian Jaya Province. Indonesian Special Forces members rescued the remaining nine hostages on May 15.

Kidnapping in Colombia, January 19, 1996: Revolutionary Armed Forces of Colombia (FARC) guerrillas kidnapped a US citizen and demanded a $1 million ransom. The hostage was released on May 22.

Tamil Tigers Attack, January 31, 1996: Members of the Liberation Tigers of Tamil Eelam (LTTE) rammed an explosives-laden truck into the Central Bank in the heart of downtown Colombo, Sri Lanka, killing 90 civilians and injuring more than 1,400 others, including 2 US citizens.

IRA Bombing, February 9, 1996: An Irish Republican Army (IRA) bomb detonated in London, killing 2 persons and wounding more than 100 others, including 2 U.S. citizens.

Athens Embassy Attack, February 15, 1996: Unidentified assailants fired a rocket at the U.S. Embassy compound in Athens, causing minor damage to three diplomatic vehicles and some surrounding buildings. Circumstances of the attack suggested it was an operation carried out by the 17 November group.

ELN Kidnapping, February 16, 1996: Six alleged National Liberation Army (ELN) guerrillas kidnapped a U.S. citizen in Colombia. After 9 months, the hostage was released.

HAMAS Bus Attack, February 26, 1996: In Jerusalem, a suicide bomber blew up a bus, killing 26 persons, including three U.S. citizens, and injuring some 80 persons, including three other US citizens.

Dizengoff Center Bombing, March 4, 1996: HAMAS and the Palestine Islamic Jihad (PIJ) both claimed responsibility for a bombing outside of Tel Aviv's largest shopping mall that killed 20 persons and injured 75 others, including 2 U.S. citizens.

West Bank Attack, May 13, 1996: Arab gunmen opened fire on a bus and a group of Yeshiva students near the Bet El settlement, killing a dual U.S./Israeli citizen and wounding three Israelis. No one claimed responsibility for the attack, but HAMAS was suspected.

AID Worker Abduction, May 31, 1996: A gang of former Contra guerrillas kidnapped a U.S. employee of the Agency for International Development (AID) who was assisting with election preparations in rural northern Nicaragua. She was released unharmed the next day after members of the international commission overseeing the preparations intervened.

Zekharya Attack, June 9, 1996: Unidentified gunmen opened fire on a car near Zekharya, killing a dual U.S./Israeli citizen and an Israeli. The Popular Front for the Liberation of Palestine (PFLP) was suspected.

Manchester Truck Bombing, June 15, 1996: An IRA truck bomb detonated at a Manchester shopping center, wounding 206 persons, including two German tourists, and caused extensive property damage.

Khobar Towers Bombing, June 25, 1996: A fuel truck carrying a bomb exploded outside the US military's Khobar Towers housing facility in Dhahran, killing 19 U.S. military personnel and wounding 515 persons, including 240 U.S. personnel. Several groups claimed responsibility for the attack.

ETA Bombing, July 20, 1996: A bomb exploded at Tarragona International Airport in Reus, Spain, wounding 35 persons, including British and Irish tourists. The Basque Fatherland and Liberty (ETA) organization was suspected.

Bombing of Archbishop of Oran, August 1, 1996: A bomb exploded at the home of the French Archbishop of Oran, killing him and his chauffeur. The attack occurred after the Archbishop's meeting with the French Foreign Minister. The Algerian Armed Islamic Group (GIA) is suspected.

Sudanese Rebel Kidnapping, August 17, 1996: Sudan People's Liberation Army (SPLA) rebels kidnapped six missionaries in Mapourdit, including a U.S. citizen, an Italian, three Australians, and a Sudanese. The SPLA released the hostages 11 days later.

PUK Kidnapping, September 13, 1996: In Iraq, Patriotic Union of Kurdistan (PUK) militants kidnapped four French workers for Pharmaciens Sans Frontieres, a Canadian United Nations High Commissioner for Refugees (UNHCR) official, and two Iraqis.

Assassination of South Korean Consul, October 1, 1996: In Vladivostok, Russia, assailants attacked and killed a South Korean consul near his home. No one claimed responsibility, but South Korean authorities believed that the attack was carried out by professionals and that the assailants were North Koreans. North Korean officials denied the country's involvement in the attack.

Red Cross Worker Kidnappings, November 1, 1996: In Sudan a breakaway group from the Sudanese People's Liberation Army (SPLA) kidnapped three International Committee of the Red Cross (ICRC) workers, including a U.S. citizen, an Australian, and a Kenyan. On 9 December the rebels released the hostages in exchange for ICRC supplies and a health survey for their camp.

Paris Subway Explosion, December 3, 1996: A bomb exploded aboard a Paris subway train as it arrived at the Port Royal station, killing two French nationals, a Moroccan, and a Canadian, and injuring 86 persons. Among those injured were one U.S. citizen and a Canadian. No one claimed responsibility for the attack, but Algerian extremists are suspected.

Abduction of US. Citizen by FARC, December 11, 1996: Five armed men claiming to be members of the Revolutionary Armed Forces of Colombia

(FARC) kidnapped and later killed a U.S. geologist at a methane gas exploration site in La Guajira Department.

Tupac Amaru Seizure of Diplomats, December 17, 1996: Twenty-three members of the Tupac Amaru Revolutionary Movement (MRTA) took several hundred people hostage at a party given at the Japanese Ambassador's residence in Lima, Peru. Among the hostages were several US officials, foreign ambassadors and other diplomats, Peruvian Government officials, and Japanese businessmen. The group demanded the release of all MRTA members in prison and safe passage for them and the hostage takers. The terrorists released most of the hostages in December but held 81 Peruvians and Japanese citizens for several months.

1997

Egyptian Letter Bombs, January 2-13, 1997: A series of letter bombs with Alexandria, Egypt, postmarks were discovered at Al-Hayat newspaper bureaus in Washington, New York City, London, and Riyadh, Saudi Arabia. Three similar devices, also postmarked in Egypt, were found at a prison facility in Leavenworth, Kansas. Bomb disposal experts defused all the devices, but one detonated at the Al-Hayat office in London, injuring two security guards and causing minor damage.

Tajik Hostage Abductions, February 4-17, 1997: Near Komsomolabad, Tajikistan, a paramilitary group led by Bakhrom Sodirov abducted four United Nations (UN) military observers. The victims included two Swiss, one Austrian, one Ukrainian, and their Tajik interpreter. The kidnappers demanded safe passage for their supporters from Afghanistan to Tajikistan. In four separate incidents occurring between Dushanbe and Garm, Bakhrom Sodirov and his group kidnapped two International Committee for the Red Cross members, four Russian journalists and their Tajik driver, four UNHCR members, and the Tajik Security Minister, Saidamir Zukhurov.

Venezuelan Abduction, February 14, 1997: Six armed Colombian guerrillas kidnapped a US oil engineer and his Venezuelan pilot in Apure, Venezuela. The kidnappers released the Venezuelan pilot on 22 February. According to authorities, the FARC is responsible for the kidnapping.

Empire State Building Sniper Attack, February 23, 1997: A Palestinian gunman opened fire on tourists at an observation deck atop the Empire State Building in New York City, killing a Danish national and wounding visitors from the United States, Argentina, Switzerland, and France before turning the gun on himself. A handwritten note carried by the gunman claimed this was a punishment attack against the "enemies of Palestine."

ELN Kidnapping, February 24, 1997: National Liberation Army (ELN) guerrillas kidnapped a U.S. citizen employed by a Las Vegas gold corporation who was scouting a gold mining operation in Colombia. The ELN demanded a ransom of $2.5 million.

SIGNIFICANT TERRORIST INCIDENTS 1961-2003

FARC Kidnapping, March 7, 1997: FARC guerrillas kidnapped a U.S. mining employee and his Colombian colleague who were searching for gold in Colombia. On November 16, the rebels released the two hostages after receiving a $50,000 ransom.

Hotel Nacional Bombing, July 12, 1997: A bomb exploded at the Hotel Nacional in Havana, injuring three persons and causing minor damage. A previously unknown group calling itself the Military Liberation Union claimed responsibility.

Israeli Shopping Mall Bombing, September 4, 1997: Three suicide bombers of HAMAS detonated bombs in the Ben Yehuda shopping mall in Jerusalem, killing eight persons, including the bombers, and wounding nearly 200 others. A dual U.S./Israeli citizen was among the dead, and 7 U.S. citizens were wounded.

OAS Abductions, October 23, 1997: In Colombia ELN rebels kidnapped two foreign members of the Organization of American States (OAS) and a Colombian human rights official at a roadblock. The ELN claimed that the kidnapping was intended "to show the international community that the elections in Colombia are a farce."

Yemeni Kidnappings, October 30, 1997: Al-Sha'if tribesmen kidnapped a U.S. businessman near Sanaa. The tribesmen sought the release of two fellow tribesmen who were arrested on smuggling charges and several public works projects they claim the government promised them. They released the hostage on November 27.

Murder of U.S. Businessmen in Pakistan, November 12, 1997: Two unidentified gunmen shot to death four U.S. auditors from Union Texas Petroleum Corporation and their Pakistani driver after they drove away from the Sheraton Hotel in Karachi. The Islami Inqilabi Council, or Islamic Revolutionary Council, claimed responsibility in a call to the U.S. Consulate in Karachi. In a letter to Pakistani newspapers, the Aimal Khufia Action Committee also claimed responsibility.

Tourist Killings in Egypt, November 17, 1997: Al-Gama'at al-Islamiyya (IG) gunmen shot and killed 58 tourists and four Egyptians and wounded 26 others at the Hatshepsut Temple in the Valley of the Kings near Luxor. Thirty-four Swiss, eight Japanese, five Germans, four Britons, one French, one Colombian, a dual Bulgarian/British citizen, and four unidentified persons were among the dead. Twelve Swiss, two Japanese, two Germans, one French, and nine Egyptians were among the wounded.

1998

UN Observer Abductions, February 19, 1998: Armed supporters of late Georgian president Zviad Gamsakhurdia abducted four UN military observers from Sweden, Uruguay, and the Czech Republic.

SIGNIFICANT TERRORIST INCIDENTS 1961-2003

FARC Abduction, March 21-23, 1998: FARC rebels kidnapped a US citizen in Sabaneta, Colombia. FARC members also killed three persons, wounded 14, and kidnapped at least 27 others at a roadblock near Bogota. Four U.S. citizens and one Italian were among those kidnapped, as well as the acting president of the National Electoral Council (CNE) and his wife.

Somali Hostage-takings, April 15, 1998: Somali militiamen abducted nine Red Cross and Red Crescent workers at an airstrip north of Mogadishu. The hostages included a U.S. citizen, a German, a Belgian, a French, a Norwegian, two Swiss, and one Somali. The gunmen were members of a sub-clan loyal to Ali Mahdi Mohammed, who controlled the northern section of the capital.

IRA Bombing, Banbridge, August 1, 1998: A 500-pound car bomb planted by the Real IRA exploded outside a shoe store in Banbridge, North Ireland, injuring 35 persons and damaging at least 200 homes.

U.S. Embassy Bombings in East Africa, August 7, 1998: A bomb exploded at the rear entrance of the U.S. Embassy in Nairobi, Kenya, killing 12 U.S. citizens, 32 Foreign Service Nationals (FSNs), and 247 Kenyan citizens. Approximately 5,000 Kenyans, 6 U.S. citizens, and 13 FSNs were injured. The U.S. Embassy building sustained extensive structural damage. Almost simultaneously, a bomb detonated outside the U.S. Embassy in Dar es Salaam, Tanzania, killing 7 FSNs and 3 Tanzanian citizens, and injuring 1 U.S. citizen and 76 Tanzanians. The explosion caused major structural damage to the U.S. Embassy facility. The U.S. Government held Usama Bin Laden responsible.

IRA Bombing, Omagh, August 15, 1998: A 500-pound car bomb planted by the Real IRA exploded outside a local courthouse in the central shopping district of Omagh, Northern Ireland, killing 29 persons and injuring over 330.

Colombian Pipeline Bombing, October 18, 1998: A National Liberation Army (ELN) planted bomb exploded on the Ocensa pipeline in Antioquia Department, killing approximately 71 persons and injuring at least 100 others. The pipeline is jointly owned by the Colombia State Oil Company Ecopetrol and a consortium including U.S., French, British, and Canadian companies.

Armed Kidnapping in Colombia, November 15, 1998: Armed assailants followed a U.S. businessman and his family home in Cundinamarca Department and kidnapped his 11-year-old son after stealing money, jewelry, one automobile, and two cell phones. The kidnappers demanded $1 million in ransom. On January 21, 1999, the kidnappers released the boy.

1999

Angolan Aircraft Downing, January 2, 1999: A UN plane carrying one U.S. citizen, four Angolans, two Philippine nationals and one Namibian was shot down, according to a UN official. No deaths or injuries were reported. Angolan authorities blamed the attack on National Union for the Total Independence of Angola (UNITA) rebels. UNITA officials denied shooting down the plane.

Ugandan Rebel Attack, February 14, 1999: A pipe bomb exploded inside a bar, killing five persons and injuring 35 others. One Ethiopian and four Ugandan nationals died in the blast, and one U.S. citizen working for USAID, two Swiss nationals, one Pakistani, one Ethiopian, and 27 Ugandans were injured. Ugandan authorities blamed the attack on the Allied Democratic Forces (ADF).

Greek Embassy Seizure, February 16, 1999: Kurdish protesters stormed and occupied the Greek Embassy in Vienna, taking the Greek Ambassador and six other persons hostage. Several hours later the protesters released the hostages and left the Embassy. The attack followed the Turkish Government's announcement of the successful capture of the Kurdistan Workers' Party (PKK) leader Abdullah Ocalan. Kurds also occupied Kenyan, Israeli, and other Greek diplomatic facilities in France, Holland, Switzerland, Britain, and Germany over the following days.

FARC Kidnappings, February 25, 1999: FARC kidnapped three U.S. citizens working for the Hawaii-based Pacific Cultural Conservancy International. On March 4, the bodies of the three victims were found in Venezuela.

Hutu Abductions, March 1, 1999: 150 armed Hutu rebels attacked three tourist camps in Uganda, killed four Ugandans, and abducted three U.S. citizens, six Britons, three New Zealanders, two Danish citizens, one Australian, and one Canadian national. Two of the U.S. citizens and six of the other hostages were subsequently killed by their abductors.

ELN Hostage-taking, March 23, 1999: Armed guerrillas kidnapped a U.S. citizen in Boyaca, Colombia. The National Liberation Army (ELN) claimed responsibility and demanded $400,000 ransom. On 20 July, ELN rebels released the hostage unharmed following a ransom payment of $48,000.

ELN Hostage-taking, May 30, 1999: In Cali, Colombia, armed ELN militants attacked a church in the neighborhood of Ciudad Jardin, kidnapping 160 persons, including six U.S. citizens and one French national. The rebels released approximately 80 persons, including three U.S. citizens, later that day.

Shell Platform Bombing, June 27, 1999: In Port Harcourt, Nigeria, armed youths stormed a Shell oil platform, kidnapping one U.S. citizen, one Nigerian national, and one Australian citizen, and causing undetermined damage. A group calling itself "Enough is Enough in the Niger River" claimed responsibility. Further seizures of oil facilities followed.

AFRC Kidnappings, August 4, 1999: An Armed Forces Revolutionary Council (AFRC) faction kidnapped 33 UN representatives near Occra Hills, Sierra Leone. The hostages included one U.S. citizen, five British soldiers,

SIGNIFICANT TERRORIST INCIDENTS 1961-2003

one Canadian citizen, one representative from Ghana, one military officer from Russia, one officer from Kyrgystan, one officer from Zambia, one officer from Malaysia, a local Bishop, two UN officials, two local journalists, and 16 Sierra Leonean nationals.

Burmese Embassy Seizure, October 1, 1999: Burmese dissidents seized the Burmese Embassy in Bangkok, Thailand, taking 89 persons hostage, including one U.S. citizen.

PLA Kidnapping, December 23, 1999: Colombian People's Liberation Army (PLA) forces kidnapped a U.S. citizen in an unsuccessful ransoming effort.

Indian Airlines Airbus Hijacking, December 24, 1999: Five militants hijacked a flight bound from Katmandu to New Delhi carrying 189 people. The plane and its passengers were released unharmed on December 31.

2000

Car bombing in Spain, January 27, 2000: Police officials reported unidentified individuals set fire to a Citroen car dealership in Iturreta, causing extensive damage to the building and destroying 12 vehicles. The attack bore the hallmark of the Basque Fatherland and Liberty (ETA).

RUF Attacks on U.N. Mission Personnel, May 1, 2000: On 1 May in Makeni, Sierra Leone, Revolutionary United Front (RUF) militants kidnapped at least 20 members of the United Nations Assistance Mission in Sierra Leone (UNAMSIL) and surrounded and opened fire on a UNAMSIL facility, according to press reports. The militants killed five UN soldiers in the attack. RUF militants kidnapped 300 UNAMSIL peacekeepers throughout the country, according to press reports. On 15 May in Foya, Liberia, the kidnappers released 139 hostages. On 28 May, on the Liberia and Sierra Leone border, armed militants released unharmed the last of the UN peacekeepers. In Freetown, according to press reports, armed militants ambushed two military vehicles carrying four journalists. A Spaniard and one U.S. citizen were killed in a May 25 car bombing in Freetown for which the RUF was probably responsible. Suspected RUF rebels also kidnapped 21 Indian UN peacekeepers in Freetown on June 6. Additional attacks by RUF on foreign personnel followed.

Diplomatic Assassination in Greece, June 8, 2000: In Athens, Greece, two unidentified gunmen killed British Defense Attaché Stephen Saunders in an ambush. The Revolutionary Organization 17 November claimed responsibility.

ELN Kidnapping, June 27, 2000: In Bogota, Colombia, ELN militants kidnapped a 5-year-old U.S. citizen and his Colombian mother, demanding an undisclosed ransom.

Kidnappings in Kyrgyzstan, August 12, 2000: In the Kara-Su Valley, the Islamic Movement of Uzbekistan took four U.S. citizens hostage. The Americans escaped on August 12.

Church Bombing in Tajikistan, October 1, 2000: Unidentified militants detonated two bombs in a Christian church in Dushanbe, killing seven persons and injuring 70 others. The church was founded by a Korean-born U.S. citizen, and most of those killed and wounded were Korean. No one claimed responsibility.

Helicopter Hijacking, October 12, 2000: In Sucumbios Province, Ecuador, a group of armed kidnappers led by former members of defunct Colombian terrorist organization the Popular Liberation Army (EPL), took hostage 10 employees of Spanish energy consortium REPSOL. Those kidnapped included five U.S. citizens, one Argentine, one Chilean, one New Zealander, and two French pilots who escaped four days later. On January 30, 2001, the kidnappers murdered American hostage Ronald Sander. The remaining hostages were released on February 23 following the payment of $13 million in ransom by the oil companies.

Attack on U.S.S. Cole, October 12, 2000: In Aden, Yemen, a small dingy carrying explosives rammed the destroyer U.S.S. Cole, killing 17 sailors and injuring 39 others. Supporters of Usama Bin Laden were suspected.

Manila Bombing, December 30, 2000: A bomb exploded in a plaza across the street from the U.S. Embassy in Manila, injuring nine persons. The Moro Islamic Liberation Front was likely responsible.

2001

Srinagar Airport Attack and Assassination Attempt, January 17, 2001: In India, six members of the Lashkar-e-Tayyba militant group were killed when they attempted to seize a local airport. Members of Hizbul Mujaheddin fired two rifle grenades at Farooq Abdullah, Chief Minister for Jammu and Kashmir. Two persons were wounded in the unsuccessful assassination attempt.

BBC Studios Bombing, March 4, 2001: A car bomb exploded at midnight outside of the British Broadcasting Corporation's main production studios in London. One person was injured. British authorities suspected the Real IRA had planted the bomb.

Suicide Bombing in Israel, March 4, 2001: A suicide bomb attack in Netanya killed 3 persons and wounded 65. HAMAS later claimed responsibility.

ETA Bombing, March 9, 2001: Two policemen were killed by the explosion of a car bomb in Hernani, Spain.

Airliner Hijacking in Istanbul, March 15, 2001: Three Chechens hijacked a Russian airliner during a flight from Istanbul to Moscow and forced it to fly to Medina, Saudi Arabia. The plane carried 162 passengers and a crew of 12. After a 22-hour siege during which more than 40 passengers were released, Saudi security forces stormed the plane, killing a hijacker, a passenger, and a flight attendant.

Bus Stop Bombing, April 22, 2001: A member of HAMAS detonated a bomb he was carrying near a bus stop in Kfar Siva, Israel, killing one person and injuring 60.

Philippines Hostage Incident, May 27, 2001: Muslim Abu Sayyaf guerrillas seized 13 tourists and 3 staff members at a resort on Palawan Island and took their captives to Basilan Island. The captives included three U.S. citizens: Guellermo Sobero and missionaries Martin and Gracia Burnham. Philippine troops fought a series of battles with the guerrillas between June 1 and June 3 during which 9 hostages escaped and two were found dead. The guerrillas took additional hostages when they seized the hospital in the town of Lamitan. On June 12, Abu Sayyaf spokesman Abu Sabaya claimed that Sobero had been killed and beheaded; his body was found in October. The Burnhams remained in captivity until June 2002.

Tel-Aviv Nightclub Bombing, June 1, 2001: HAMAS claimed responsibility for the suicide bombing of a popular Israeli nightclub that caused over 140 casualties.

HAMAS Restaurant Bombing, August 9, 2001: A HAMAS-planted bomb detonated in a Jerusalem pizza restaurant, killing 15 people and wounding more than 90. The Israeli response included occupation of Orient House, the Palestine Liberation Organization's political headquarters in East Jerusalem.

Suicide Bombing in Israel, September 9, 2001: The first suicide bombing carried out by an Israeli Arab killed 3 persons in Nahariya. HAMAS claimed responsibility.

Death of "the Lion of the Panjshir", September 9, 2001: Two suicide bombers fatally wounded Ahmed Shah Massoud, a leader of Afghanistan's Northern Alliance, which had opposed both the Soviet occupation and the post-Soviet Taliban government. The bombers posed as journalists and were apparently linked to al-Qaida. The Northern Alliance did not confirm Massoud's death until September 15.

Terrorist Attacks on U.S. Homeland, September 11, 2001: Two hijacked airliners crashed into the twin towers of the World Trade Center. Soon thereafter, the Pentagon was struck by a third hijacked plane. A fourth hijacked plane, suspected to be bound for a high-profile target in Washington, crashed into a field in southern Pennsylvania. The attacks killed 3,025 U.S. citizens and other nationals. President Bush and Cabinet officials indicated that Usama Bin Laden was the prime suspect and that they considered the United States in a state of war with international terrorism. In the aftermath of the attacks, the United States formed the Global Coalition Against Terrorism.

Attack on the Jammu and Kashmir Legislature, October 1, 2001: After a suicide car bomber forced the gate of the state legislature in Srinagar, two gunmen entered the building and held off police for seven hours before being killed. Forty persons died in the incident. Jaish-e-Muhammad claimed responsibility.

Anthrax Attacks, October-November 2001: On October 7 the U.S. Centers for Disease Control and Prevention (CDC) reported that investigators had detected evidence that the deadly anthrax bacterium was present in the building where a Florida man who died of anthrax on October 5 had worked. Discovery of a second anthrax case triggered a major investigation by the Federal Bureau of Investigation (FBI). The two anthrax cases were the first to appear in the United States in 25 years. Anthrax subsequently appeared in mail received by television networks in New York and by the offices in Washington of Senate Majority Leader Tom Daschle and other members of Congress. Attorney General John Ashcroft said in a briefing on October 16, "When people send anthrax through the mail to hurt people and invoke terror, it's a terrorist act."

Assassination of an Israeli Cabinet Minister, October 17, 2001: A Palestinian gunman assassinated Israeli Minister of Tourism Rehavam Zeevi in the Jerusalem hotel where he was staying. The Popular Front for the Liberation of Palestine (PFLP) claimed to have avenged the death of PFLP Mustafa Zubari.

Attack on a Church in Pakistan, October 28, 2001: Six masked gunmen shot up a church in Bahawalpur, Pakistan, killing 15 Pakistani Christians. No group claimed responsibility, although various militant Muslim groups were suspected.

Suicide Bombings in Jerusalem, December 1, 2001: Two suicide bombers attacked a Jerusalem shopping mall, killing 10 persons and wounding 170.

Suicide Bombing in Haifa, December 2, 2001: A suicide bomb attack aboard a bus in Haifa, Israel, killed 15 persons and wounded 40. HAMAS claimed responsibility for both this attack and those on December 1 to avenge the death of a HAMAS member at the hands of Israeli forces a week earlier.

Attack on the Indian Parliament, December 13, 2001: Five gunmen attacked the Indian Parliament in New Delhi shortly after it had adjourned. Before security forces killed them, the attackers killed 6 security personnel and a gardener. Indian officials blamed Lashkar-e-Tayyiba and demanded that Pakistan crack down on it and on other Muslim separatist groups in Kashmir.

2002

Ambush on the West Bank, January 15, 2002: Palestinian militants fired on a vehicle in Beit Sahur, killing one passenger and wounding the other. The dead passenger claimed U.S. and Israeli citizenship. The al-Aqsa Martyrs' Battalion claimed responsibility.

Shooting Incident in Israel, January 17, 2002: A Palestinian gunman killed 6 persons and wounded 25 in Hadera, Israel, before being killed by Israeli police. The al-Aqsa Martyrs' Brigades claimed responsibility as revenge for Israel's killing of a leading member of the group.

Drive-By Shooting at a U.S. Consulate, January 22, 2002: Armed militants on motorcycles fired on the U.S. Consulate in Calcutta, India, killing 5 Indian security personnel and wounding 13 others. The Harakat ul-Jihad-I-Islami and the Asif Raza Commandoes claimed responsibility. Indian police later killed two suspects, one of whom confessed to belonging to Lashkar-e-Tayyiba as he died.

Bomb Explosion in Kashmir, January 22, 2002: A bomb exploded in a crowded retail district in Jammu, Kashmir, killing one person and injuring nine. No group claimed responsibility.

Kidnapping of Daniel Pearl, January 23, 2002: Armed militants kidnapped Wall Street Journal reporter Daniel Pearl in Karachi, Pakistan. Pakistani authorities received a videotape on February 20 depicting Pearl's murder. His grave was found near Karachi on May 16. Pakistani authorities arrested four suspects. Ringleader Ahmad Omar Saeed Sheikh claimed to have organized Pearl's kidnapping to protest Pakistan's subservience to the United States, and had belonged to Jaish-e-Muhammad, an Islamic separatist group in Kashmir. All four suspects were convicted on July 15. Saeed Sheikh was sentenced to death, the others to life imprisonment.

Suicide Bombing in Jerusalem, January 27, 2002: A suicide bomb attack in Jerusalem killed one other person and wounded 100. The incident was the first suicide bombing made by a Palestinian woman.

Suicide Bombing in the West Bank, February 16, 2002: A suicide bombing in an outdoor food court in Karmei Shomron killed 4 persons and wounded 27. Two of the dead and two of the wounded were U.S. citizens. The Popular Front for the Liberation of Palestine (PFLP) claimed responsibility.

Suicide Bombing in the West Bank, March 7, 2002: A suicide bombing in a supermarket in the settlement of Ariel wounded 10 persons, one of whom was a U.S. citizen. The PFLP claimed responsibility.

Suicide Bombing in Jerusalem, March 9, 2002: A suicide bombing in a Jerusalem restaurant killed 11 persons and wounded 52, one of whom was a U.S. citizen. The al-Aqsa Martyrs' Brigades claimed responsibility.

Drive-By Shooting in Colombia, March 14, 2002: Gunmen on motorcycles shot and killed two U.S. citizens who had come to Cali, Colombia, to negotiate the release of their father, who was a captive of the FARC. No group claimed responsibility.

Grenade Attack on a Church in Pakistan, March 17, 2002: Militants threw grenades into the Protestant International Church in Islamabad, Pakistan, during a service attended by diplomatic and local personnel. Five persons,

SIGNIFICANT TERRORIST INCIDENTS 1961-2003

two of them U.S. citizens, were killed and 46 were wounded. The dead Americans were State Department employee Barbara Green and her daughter Kristen Wormsley. Thirteen U.S. citizens were among the wounded. The Lashkar-e-Tayyiba group was suspected.

Car Bomb Explosion in Peru, March 20, 2002: A car bomb exploded at a shopping center near the U.S. Embassy in Lima, Peru. Nine persons were killed and 32 wounded. The dead included two police officers and a teenager. Peruvian authorities suspected either the Shining Path rebels or the Tupac Amaru Revolutionary Movement. The attack occurred 3 days before President George W. Bush visited Peru.

Suicide Bombing in Jerusalem, March 21, 2002: A suicide bombing in Jerusalem killed 3 persons and wounded 86 more, including 2 U.S. citizens. The Palestinian Islamic Jihad claimed responsibility.

Suicide Bombing in Israel, March 27, 2002: A suicide bombing in a noted restaurant in Netanya, Israel, killed 22 persons and wounded 140. One of the dead was a U.S. citizen. The Islamic Resistance Movement (HAMAS) claimed responsibility.

Temple Bombing in Kashmir, March 30, 2002: A bomb explosion at a Hindu temple in Jammu, Kashmir, killed 10 persons. The Islamic Front claimed responsibility.

Suicide Bombing in the West Bank, March 31, 2002: A suicide bombing near an ambulance station in Efrat wounded four persons, including a U.S. citizen. The al-Aqsa Martyrs' Brigades claimed responsibility.

Armed attack on Kashmir, April 10, 2002: Armed militants attacked a residence in Gando, Kashmir, killing five persons and wounding four. No group claimed responsibility.

Synagogue Bombing in Tunisia, April 11, 2002: A suicide bomber detonated a truck loaded with propane gas outside a historic synagogue in Djerba, Tunisia. The 16 dead included 11 Germans, one French citizen, and three Tunisians. Twenty-six German tourists were injured. The Islamic Army for the Liberation of the Holy Sites claimed responsibility.

Suicide Bombing in Jerusalem, April 12, 2002: A female suicide bomber killed 6 persons in Jerusalem and wounded 90 others. The al-Aqsa Martyrs' Brigades claimed responsibility.

Car Bombing in Pakistan, May 8, 2002: A car bomb exploded near a Pakistani navy shuttle bus in Karachi, killing 12 persons and wounding 19. Eleven of the dead and 11 of the wounded were French nationals. Al-Qaida was suspected of the attack.

Parade Bombing in Russia, May 9, 2002: A remotely-controlled bomb exploded near a May Day parade in Kaspiisk, Dagestan, killing 42 persons

SIGNIFICANT TERRORIST INCIDENTS 1961-2003

and wounding 150. Fourteen of the dead and 50 of the wounded were soldiers. Islamists linked to al-Qaida were suspected.

Attack on a Bus in India, May 14, 2002: Militants fired on a passenger bus in Kaluchak, Jammu, killing 7 persons. They then entered a military housing complex and killed 3 soldiers and 7 military dependents before they were killed. The al-Mansooran and Jamiat ul-Mujahedin claimed responsibility.

Bomb Attacks in Kashmir, May 17, 2002: A bomb explosion near a civil secretariat area in Srinagar, Kashmir, wounded 6 persons. In Jammu, a bomb exploded at a fire services headquarters, killing two and wounding 16. No group claimed responsibility for either attack.

Hostage Rescue Attempt in the Philippines, June 7, 2002: Philippine Army troops attacked Abu Sayyaf terrorists on Mindanao Island in an attempt to rescue U.S. citizen Martin Burnham and his wife Gracia, who had been kidnapped more than a year ago. Burnham was killed but his wife, though wounded, was freed. A Filipino hostage was killed, as were four of the guerrillas. Seven soldiers were wounded.

Car Bombing in Pakistan, June 14, 2002: A car bomb exploded near the U.S. Consulate and the Marriott Hotel in Karachi, Pakistan. Eleven persons were killed and 51 were sounded, including one U.S. and one Japanese citizen. Al Qaida and al-Qanin were suspected.

Suicide Bombing in Jerusalem, June 19, 2002: A suicide bombing at a bus stop in Jerusalem killed 6 persons and wounded 43, including 2 U.S. citizens. The al-Aqsa Martyrs' Brigades claimed responsibility.

Suicide Bombing in Tel Aviv, July 17, 2002: Two suicide bombers attacked the old bus station in Tel Aviv, Israel, killing 5 persons and wounding 38. The dead included one Romanian and two Chinese; another Romanian was wounded. The Islamic Jihad claimed responsibility.

Bombing at the Hebrew University, July 31, 2002: A bomb hidden in a bag in the Frank Sinatra International Student Center of Jerusalem's Hebrew University killed 9 persons and wounded 87. The dead included 5 U.S. citizens and 4 Israelis. The wounded included 4 U.S. citizens, 2 Japanese, and 3 South Koreans. The Islamic Resistance Movement (HAMAS) claimed responsibility.

Suicide Bombing in Israel, August 4, 2002: A suicide bomb attack on a bus in Safed, Israel, killed 9 persons and wounded 50. Two of the dead were Philippine citizens; many of the wounded were soldiers returning from leave. HAMAS claimed responsibility.

Attack on a School in Pakistan, August 5, 2002: Gunmen attacked a Christian school attended by children of missionaries from around the world. Six persons (two security guards, a cook, a carpenter, a receptionist, and a private citizen) were killed and a Philippine citizen was wounded. A group called al-Intigami al-Pakistani claimed responsibility.

SIGNIFICANT TERRORIST INCIDENTS 1961-2003

Attack on Pilgrims in Kashmir, August 6, 2002: Armed militants attacked a group of Hindu pilgrims with guns and grenades in Pahalgam, Kashmir. Nine persons were killed and 32 were wounded. The Lashkar-e-Tayyiba claimed responsibility.

Assassination in Kashmir, September 11, 2002: Gunmen killed Kashmir's Law Minister Mushtaq Ahmed Lone and six security guards in Tikipora. Lashkar-e-Tayyiga, Jamiat ul-Mujahedin, and Hizb ul-Mujahedin all claimed responsibility. Other militants attacked the residence of the Minister of Tourism with grenades, injuring four persons. No group claimed responsibility.

Ambush on the West Bank, September 18, 2002: Gunmen ambushed a vehicle on a road near Yahad, killing an Israeli and wounding a Romanian worker. The al-Aqsa Martyrs' Brigades claimed responsibility.

Suicide Bomb Attack in Israel, September 19, 2002: A suicide bomb attack on a bus in Tel Aviv killed 6 persons and wounded 52. One of the dead was a British subject. HAMAS claimed responsibility.

Attack on a French Tanker, October 6, 2002: An explosive-laden boat rammed the French oil tanker Limburg, which was anchored about 5 miles off al-Dhabbah, Yemen. One person was killed and 4 were wounded. Al-Qaida was suspected.

Car Bomb Explosion in Bali, October 12, 2002: A car bomb exploded outside the Sari Club Discotheque in Denpasar, Bali, Indonesia, killing 202 persons and wounding 300 more. Most of the casualties, including 88 of the dead, were Australian tourists. Seven Americans were among the dead. Al-Qaida claimed responsibility. Two suspects were later arrested and convicted. Iman Samudra, who had trained in Afghanistan with al-Qaeda and was suspected of belonging to Jemaah Islamiya, was sentenced to death on September 10, 2003.

Chechen Rebels Seize a Moscow Theater, October 23-26, 2002: Fifty Chechen rebels led by Movsar Barayev seized the Palace of Culture Theater in Moscow, Russia, to demand an end to the war in Chechnya. They seized more than 800 hostages from 13 countries and threatened to blow up the theater. During a three-day siege, they killed a Russian policeman and five Russian hostages. On October 26, Russian Special Forces pumped an anesthetic gas through the ventilation system and then stormed the theater. All of the rebels were killed, but 94 hostages (including one American) also died, many from the effects of the gas. A group led by Chechen warlord Shamil Basayev claimed responsibility.

Assassination of an AID Official, October 28, 2002: Gunmen in Amman assassinated Laurence Foley, Executive Officer of the U.S. Agency for International Development Mission in Jordan. The Honest People of Jordan claimed responsibility.

SIGNIFICANT TERRORIST INCIDENTS 1961-2003

Suicide Bombing in Jerusalem, November 21, 2002: A suicide bomb attack on a bus on Mexico Street in Jerusalem killed 11 persons and wounded 50 more. One of the dead was a Romanian. HAMAS claimed responsibility.

Attack on Temples in Kashmir, November 24, 2002: Armed militants attacked the Reghunath and Shiv temples in Jammu, Kashmir, killing 13 persons and wounding 50. The Lashkare-e-Tayyiba claimed responsibility.

Attacks on Israeli Tourists in Kenya, November 28, 2002: A three-person suicide car bomb attack on the Paradise Hotel in Mombasa, Kenya, killed 15 persons and wounded 40. Three of the dead and 18 of the wounded were Israeli tourists; the others were Kenyans. Near Mombasa's airport, two SA-7 shoulder-fired missiles were fired as an Arkia Airlines Boeing 757 that was carrying 261 passengers back to Israel. Both missiles missed. Al-Qaida, the Government of Universal Palestine in Exile, and the Army of Palestine claimed responsibility for both attacks. Al-Ittihad al-Islami was also suspected of involvement.

Attack on a Bus in the Philippines, December 26, 2002: Armed militants ambushed a bus carrying Filipino workers employed by the Canadian Toronto Ventures Inc. Pacific mining company in Zamboanga del Norte. Thirteen persons were killed and 10 wounded. Philippine authorities suspected the Moro Islamic Liberation Front (MILF), which had been extorting money from Toronto Ventures. The Catholic charity Caritas-Philippines said that Toronto Ventures had harassed tribesmen who opposed mining on their ancestral lands.

Bombing of a Government Building in Chechnya, December 27, 2002: A suicide bomb attack involving two explosives-laden trucks destroyed the offices of the pro-Russian Chechen government in Grozny. The attack killed over 80 people and wounded 210. According to a Chechen website run by the Kavkaz Center, Chechen warlord Shamil Basayev claimed responsibility.

2003

Suicide Bombings in Tel Aviv, January 5, 2003: Two suicide bomb attacks killed 22 and wounded at least 100 persons in Tel Aviv, Israel. Six of the victims were foreign workers. The Al-Aqsa Martyrs' Brigades claimed responsibility.

Night Club Bombing in Colombia, February 7, 2003: A car bomb exploded outside a night club in Bogota, Colombia, killing 32 persons and wounding 160. No group claimed responsibility, but Colombian officials suspected the Colombian Revolutionary Armed Forces (FARC) of committing the worst terrorist attack in the country in a decade.

Assasination of a Kurdish Leader, February 8, 2003: Members of Ansar al-Islam assassinated Kurdish legislator Shawkat Haji Mushir and captured two other Kurdish officials in Qamash Tapa in northern Iraq. Suicide **Bombing in Haifa, March 5, 2003**: A suicide bombing aboard a bus in Haifa, Israel, killed 15 persons and wounded at least 40. One of the dead claimed U.S. as well as Israeli citizenship. The bomber's affiliation was not immediately known.

Suicide Bombing in Netanya, March 30, 2003: A suicide bombing in a cafe in Netanya, Israel, wounded 38 persons. Only the bomber was killed. Islamic Jihad claimed responsibility and called the attack a "gift" to the people of Iraq.

Unsuccessful Hostage Rescue Attempt in Colombia, May 5, 2003: The FARC killed 10 hostages when Colombian special forces tried to rescue them from a jungle hideout near Urrao, in Colombia's Antioquia State. The dead included Governor Guillermo Gavira and former Defense Minister Gilberto Echeverri Mejia, who had been kidnapped in April 2002.

Truck Bomb Attacks in Saudi Arabia, May 12, 2003: Suicide bombers attacked three residential compounds for foreign workers in Riyadh, Saudi Arabia. The 34 dead included 9 attackers, 7 other Saudis, 9 U.S. citizens, and one citizen each from the United Kingdom, Ireland, and the Philippines. Another American died on June 1. It was the first major attack on U.S. targets in Saudi Arabia since the end of the war in Iraq. Saudi authorities arrested 11 al-Qaida suspects on May 28.

Truck Bombing in Chechnya, May 12, 2003: A truck bomb explosion demolished a government compound in Znamenskoye, Chechnya, killing 54 persons. Russian authorities blamed followers of a Saudi-born Islamist named Abu Walid. President Vladimir Putin said that he suspected that there was an al-Qaida connection.

Attempted Assassination in Chechnya, May 12, 2003: Two female suicide bombers attacked Chechen Administrator Mufti Akhmed Kadyrov during a religious festival in Iliskhan Yurt. Kadyrov escaped injury, but 14 other persons were killed and 43 were wounded. Chechen rebel leader Shamil Basayev claimed responsibility.

Suicide Bomb Attacks in Morocco, May 16, 2003: A team of 12 suicide bombers attacked five targets in Casablanca, Morocco, killing 43 persons and wounding 100. The targets were a Spanish restaurant, a Jewish community, a Jewish cemetery, a hotel, and the Belgian Consulate. The Moroccan Government blamed the Islamist al-Assirat al-Moustaquim (The Righteous Path), but foreign commentators suspected an al-Qaida connection.

Suicide Bomb Attack in Jerusalem, May 18, 2003: A suicide bomb attack on a bus in Jerusalem's French Hill district killed 7 persons and wounded 20. The bomber was disguised as a religious Jew. HAMAS claimed responsibility.

Suicide Bombing in Afula, May 19, 2003: A suicide bomb attack by a female Palestinian student killed 3 persons and wounded 52 at a shopping mall in

Afula, Israel. Both Islamic Jihad and the al-Aqsa Martyrs' Brigades claimed responsibility.

Suicide Bombing in Jerusalem, June 11, 2003: A suicide bombing aboard a bus in Jerusalem killed 16 persons and wounded at least 70, one of whom died later. HAMAS claimed responsibility, calling it revenge for an Israeli helicopter attack on HAMAS leader Abdelaziz al-Rantisi in Gaza City the day before.

Truck Bombing in Northern Ossetia, August 1, 2003: A suicide truck bomb attack destroyed a Russian military hospital in Mozdok, North Ossetia and killed 50 persons. Russian authorities attributed the attack to followers of Chechen rebel leader Shamil Basayev.

Hotel Bombing in Indonesia, August 5, 2003: A car bomb exploded outside the Marriott Hotel in Jakarta, Indonesia, killing 10 persons and wounding 150. One of the dead was a Dutch citizen. The wounded included an American, a Canadian, an Australian, and two Chinese. Indonesian authorities suspected the Jemaah Islamiah, which had carried out the October 12, 2002 bombing in Bali.

Bombing of the Jordanian Embassy in Baghdad, August 7, 2003: A car bomb exploded outside the Jordanian Embassy in Baghdad, Iraq, killing 19 persons and wounding 65. Most of the victims were apparently Iraqis, including 5 police officers. No group claimed responsibility.

Suicide Bombings in Israel and the West Bank, August 12, 2003: The first suicide bombings since the June 29 Israeli-Palestinian truce took place. The first, in a supermarket at Rosh Haayin, Israel, killed one person and wounded 14. The second, at a bus stop near the Ariel settlement in the West Bank, killed one person and wounded 3. The al-Aqsa Martyrs' Brigades claimed responsibility for the first; HAMAS claimed responsibility for the second.

Bombing of the UN Headquarters in Baghdad, August 19, 2003: A truck loaded with surplus Iraqi ordnance exploded outside the United Nations Headquarters in Baghdad's Canal Hotel. A hospital across the street was also heavily damaged. The 23 dead included UN Special Representative Sergio Viera de Mello. More than 100 persons were wounded. It was not clear whether the bomber was a Baath Party loyalist or a foreign Islamic militant. An al-Qaeda branch called the Brigades of the Martyr Abu Hafz al-Masri later claimed responsibility.

Suicide Bombing in Jerusalem, August 19, 2003: A suicide bombing aboard a bus in Jerusalem killed 20 persons and injured at least 100, one of whom died later. Five of the dead were American citizens. HAMAS and Islamic Jihad claimed responsibility, although HAMAS leader al-Rantisi said that his organization remained committed to the truce while reserving the right to respond to Israeli military actions.

SIGNIFICANT TERRORIST INCIDENTS 1961-2003

Car Bomb Kills Shi'ite Leader in Najaf, August 29, 2003: A car bomb explosion outside the Shrine of the Imam Ali in Najaf, Iraq killed at least 81 persons and wounded at least 140. The dead included the Ayatollah Mohammed Bakir al-Hakim, one of four leading Shi'ite clerics in Iraq. Al-Hakim had been the leader of the Supreme Council for the Islamic Revolution in Iraq (SCIRI) since its establishment in 1982, and SCIRI had recently agreed to work with the U.S.-sponsored Iraqi Governing Council. It was not known whether the perpetrators were Baath Party loyalists, rival Shi'ites, or foreign Islamists.

Suicide Bombings in Israel, September 9, 2003: Two suicide bombings took place in Israel. The first, at a bus stop near the Tsrifin army base southeast of Tel Aviv, killed 7 soldiers and wounded 14 soldiers and a civilian. The second, at a café in Jerusalem's German Colony neighborhood, killed 6 persons and wounded 40. HAMAS did not claim responsibility until the next day, although a spokesman called the first attack "a response to Israeli aggression."

Assassination of an Iraqi Governing Council Member, September 20, 2003: Gunmen shot and seriously wounded Akila Hashimi, one of three female members of the Iraqi Governing Council, near her home in Baghdad. She died September 25.

A Second Attack on the UN Headquarters in Baghdad, September 22, 2003: A suicide car bomb attack on the UN Headquarters in Baghdad killed a security guard and wounded 19 other persons.

Suicide Bombing in Israel, October 4, 2003: A Palestinian woman made a suicide bomb attack on a restaurant in Haifa, killing 19 persons and wounding at least 55. Islamic Jihad claimed responsibility for the attack. The next day, Israel bombed a terrorist training camp in Syria.

Attacks in Iraq, October 9, 2003: Gunmen assassinated a Spanish military attaché in Baghdad. A suicide car bomb attack on an Iraqi police station killed 8 persons and wounded 40.

Car Bombings in Baghdad, October 12, 2003: Two suicide car bombs exploded outside the Baghdad Hotel, which housed U.S. officials. Six persons were killed and 32 wounded. Iraqi and U.S. security personnel apparently kept the cars from actually reaching the hotel.

Bomb Attack on U.S. Diplomats in the Gaza Strip, October 15, 2003: A remote-controlled bomb exploded under a car in a U.S. diplomatic convoy passing through the northern Gaza Strip. Three security guards, all employees of DynCorp, were killed. A fourth was wounded. The diplomats were on their way to interview Palestinian candidates for Fulbright scholarships to study in the United States. Palestinian President Arafat and Prime Minister Qurei condemned the attack, while the major Palestinian militant groups denied responsibility. The next day, Palestinian security forces arrested several suspects, some of whom belonged to the Popular Resistance Committees.

Rocket Attack on the al-Rashid Hotel in Baghdad, October 26, 2003: Iraqis using an improvised rocket launcher bombarded the al-Rashid Hotel in Baghdad, killing one U.S. Army officer and wounding 17 persons. The wounded included 4 U.S. military personnel and seven American civilians. Deputy Secretary of Defense Paul D. Wolfowitz, who was staying at the hotel, was not injured. After visiting the wounded, he said, "They're not going to scare us away; we're not giving up on this job."

Assassination of a Deputy Mayor in Baghdad, October 26, 2003: Two gunmen believed to be Baath Party loyalists assassinated Faris Abdul Razaq al-Assam, one of three deputy mayors of Baghdad. U.S. officials did not announce al-Assam's death until October 28.

Wave of Car Bombings in Baghdad, October 27, 2003: A series of suicide car bombings in Baghdad killed at least 35 persons and wounded at least 230. Four attacks were directed at Iraqi police stations, the fifth and most destructive was directed at the International Committee of the Red Cross headquarters, where at least 12 persons were killed. A sixth attack failed when a car bomb failed to explode and the bomber was wounded and captured by Iraqi police. U.S. and Iraqi officials suspected that foreign terrorists were involved; the unsuccessful bomber said he was a Syrian national and carried a Syrian passport. After a meeting with Administrator L. Paul Bremer, President Bush said, "The more successful we are on the ground, the more these killers will react."

Suicide Bombing in Riyadh, November 8, 2003: In Riyadh, a suicide car bombing took place in the Muhaya residential compound, which was occupied mainly by nationals of other Arab countries. Seventeen persons were killed and 122 were wounded. The latter included 4 Americans. The next day, Deputy Secretary of State Armitage said al-Qaeda was probably responsible.

Truck Bombing in Nasiriyah, November 12, 2003: A suicide truck bomb destroyed the headquarters of the Italian military police in Nasiriyah, Iraq, killing 18 Italians and 11 Iraqis and wounding at least 100 persons.

Synagogue Bombings in Istanbul, November 15, 2003: Two suicide truck bombs exploded outside the Neve Shalom and Beth Israel synagogues in Istanbul, killing 25 persons and wounding at least 300 more. The initial claim of responsibility came from a Turkish militant group, the Great Eastern Islamic Raiders' Front, but Turkish authorities suspected an al-Qaeda connection. The next day, the London-based newspaper al-Quds al-Arabi received an e-mail in which an al-Qaeda branch called the Brigades of the Martyr Abu Hafz al-Masri claimed responsibility for the Istanbul synagogue bombings.

SIGNIFICANT TERRORIST INCIDENTS 1961-2003

Grenade Attacks in Bogota, November 15, 2003: Grenade attacks on two bars frequented by Americans in Bogota killed one person and wounded 72, including 4 Americans. Colombian authorities suspected FARC (the Revolutionary Armed Forces of Colombia). The U.S. Embassy suspected that the attacks had targeted Americans and warned against visiting commercial centers and places of entertainment.

More Suicide Truck Bombings in Istanbul, November 20, 2003: Two more suicide truck bombings devastated the British HSBC Bank and the British Consulate General in Istanbul, killing 27 persons and wounding at least 450. The dead included Consul General Roger Short. U.S., British, and Turkish officials suspected that al-Qaeda had struck again. The U.S. Consulate in Istanbul was closed, and the Embassy in Ankara advised American citizens in Istanbul to stay home.

Car Bombing in Kirkuk, November 20, 2003: A suicide car bombing in Kirkuk killed 5 persons. The target appeared to be the headquarters of the Patriotic Union of Kurdistan. PUK officials suspected the Ansar al-Islam group, which was said to have sheltered fugitive Taliban and al-Qaeda members after the U.S. campaign in Afghanistan.

Attacks on Other Coalition Personnel in Iraq, November 29-30, 2003: Iraqi insurgents stepped up attacks on nationals of other members of the Coalition. On November 29, an ambush in Mahmudiyah killed 7 out of a party of 8 Spanish intelligence officers. Iraqi insurgents also killed two Japanese diplomats near Tikrit. On November 30, another ambush near Tikrit killed two South Korean electrical workers and wounded two more. A Colombian employee of Kellogg Brown & Root was killed and two were wounded in an ambush near Balad.

Train Bombing in Southern Russia, December 5, 2003: A suicide bomb attack killed 42 persons and wounded 150 aboard a Russian commuter train in the south Russian town of Yessentuki. Russian officials suspected Chechen rebels; President Putin said the attack was meant to disrupt legislative elections. Chechen rebel leader Aslan Maskhadov denied any involvement.

Suicide Bombing in Moscow, December 9, 2003: A female suicide bomber killed 5 other persons and wounded 14 outside Moscow's National Hotel. She was said to be looking for the State Duma.

Suicide Car Bombings in Iraq, December 15, 2003: Two days after the capture of Saddam Hussein, there were two suicide car bomb attacks on Iraqi police stations. One at Husainiyah killed 8 persons and wounded 20. The other, at Ameriyah, wounded 7 Iraqi police. Guards repelled a second vehicle.

SIGNIFICANT TERRORIST INCIDENTS 1961-2003

Office Bombing in Baghdad, December 19, 2003: A bomb destroyed the Baghdad office of the Supreme Council of the Islamic Revolution in Iraq, killing a woman and wounding at least 7 other persons.

Suicide Car Bombing in Irbil, December 24, 2003: A suicide car bomb attack on the Kurdish Interior Ministry in Irbil, Iraq, killed 5 persons and wounded 101.

Attempted Assassination in Rawalpindi, December 25, 2003: Two suicide truck bombers killed 14 persons as President Musharraf's motorcade passed through Rawalpindi, Pakistan. An earlier attempt on December 14 caused no casualties. Pakistani officials suspected Afghan and Kashmiri militants. On January 6, 2004, Pakistani authorities announced the arrest of 6 suspects who were said to be members of Jaish-e-Muhammad.

Suicide Bombing in Israel, December 25, 2003: A Palestinian suicide bomber killed 4 persons at a bus stop near Petah Tikva, Israel. The Popular Front for the Liberation of Palestine claimed responsibility for the attack in retaliation for Israeli military operations in Nablus that had begun two days earlier.

Restaurant Bombing in Baghdad, December 31, 2003: A car bomb explosion outside Baghdad's Nabil Restaurant killed 8 persons and wounded 35. The wounded included 3 Los Angeles Times reporters and 3 local employees.

This document, based entirely on public sources, was prepared for background information and reference purposes. It is not intended to be a complete or comprehensive account of all terrorist incidents during these years, and it is not an official expression of U.S. policy. Please email questions or commentsto History@State.gov.

Office of the Historian
Bureau of Public Affairs
U.S. Department of State
March 2004